Ascending India and Its State Capacity

Ascending India *and* Its State Capacity

Extraction, Violence, and Legitimacy

SUMIT GANGULY & WILLIAM R. THOMPSON

Yale UNIVERSITY PRESS/NEW HAVEN & LONDON

Copyright © 2017 by Sumit Ganguly and William R. Thompson
All rights reserved.
This book may not be reproduced, in whole or in part, including illustrations, in any form (beyond that copying permitted by Sections 107 and 108 of the U.S. Copyright Law and except by reviewers for the public press), without written permission from the publishers.

Yale University Press books may be purchased in quantity for educational, business, or promotional use. For information, please e-mail sales.press@yale.edu (U.S. office) or sales@yaleup.co.uk (U.K. office).

Set in Minion type by Newgen North America.
Printed in the United States of America.

Library of Congress Control Number: 2016943627
ISBN: 978-0-300-21592-2 (hardcover : alk. paper)

A catalogue record for this book is available from the British Library.

This paper meets the requirements of ANSI/NISO Z39.48-1992 (Permanence of Paper).

10 9 8 7 6 5 4 3 2 1

For our mothers, Nandini Ganguly and Jacquelyn Thompson

Contents

Acknowledgments ix

ONE The Indian State's Capacity to Get Things Done 1

TWO Ascending Major Powers 24

STATE CAPACITY

THREE Conceptualizing and Measuring State Strength 53

FOUR Extraction and Legitimacy 75

FIVE Violence Monopoly 96

STATE-CAPACITY COROLLARIES

ECONOMIC

SIX The Economy 127

SEVEN Infrastructure 157

EIGHT Inequality 182

POLITICAL

NINE Democratic Institutions   200

TEN Grand Strategy   229

ELEVEN Defense and Security Policies   251

SUMMARY AND CONCLUSION

TWELVE Ascending India—Its State-Capacity Problems and Prospects   271

Notes   287
Index   329

Acknowledgments

We gratefully acknowledge the financial assistance of the Smith Richardson Foundation in support of the writing of this book. Brandon Miliate and Nicolas Blarel, graduate students in the Department of Political Science at Indiana University, Bloomington, helped with the final logistics of this book manuscript, and we wish to thank them for their efforts. We are also indebted to Jaya Chatterjee and Ann-Marie Imbornoni at Yale University Press and freelancers Kate Davis and Fred Kameny for their assistance in getting this book into print.

O · N · E

The Indian State's Capacity to Get Things Done

Long impoverished, India is on the rise in economic and military terms. Its gross domestic product is expanding faster than population growth, and India is becoming one of the world's largest economies. Defense and foreign policies tend to expand in response to capability improvements. Indian foreign policy and military concerns, long centered on South Asia, have grown to encompass a much wider proportion of Indo-Pacific Asia.[1] Indian ambitions have also expanded: a popular question is whether or when India will ascend to the world's power elite and be accorded great power status.

Part of this great power discourse has to do with whether India has the appropriate prerequisites for great power status. Is its economy sufficiently large and sophisticated enough to pay for elite status? Is the Indian state strong enough to mobilize resources and make policies, as other great powers do? Do Indian armed forces have sufficient power-projection capabilities to support great power behavior? We understand why these questions are raised but we think they are misplaced. Historically, states have ascended to elite or great power status without satisfying minimal thresholds of attributes thought to differentiate the powerful from the less powerful. Once they gain greater military-political status, they either improve their capabilities or they stumble along with various weaknesses more or less intact. We assume that status-mobility processes have not changed all that much. India will either be promoted to the great power ranks or not, but it will not be determined by India first attaining some elite membership attributes.

We will certainly address this great power ascent issue, but it is not the principal part of the book's motivation. Foremost, we are intrigued by the Indian state itself. Political scientists tend to focus on failed, weak, and strong states. Little attention is given to the "in-betweeners"—the states that are neither completely weak nor entirely strong. We utilize the great power theme only as an initial "hook" to look more closely at the Indian state. In particular, we want to use the opportunity to focus more precisely on what state capacity is about conceptually and empirically. Many discussions of state capacity either remain stuck at the conceptual level or skip it altogether and dwell solely on its measurement. Our preference is to start with a conceptual delimitation of state capacity (in our case, relying on K. J. Holsti's analysis highlighting extraction, violence monopoly, and legitimacy; see chapters 3–5) and show how these multiple facets can be measured and compared with other states in the Indian context.

We claim no crystal ball about whether Indian economic growth will continue. We do not know to what extent India's external and internal security will deteriorate. Nor do we know how India's military capability expansion programs will fare. Obviously, we cannot even forecast whether or when India might ascend to great power status. But we do think that there are other, additional problems that could hobble India's ability to get things done at home and abroad. We think India's state capacity is just such a liability. Moreover, it is not just another liability. State capacity or the political capability to do things as a state is critical to continued economic growth, the development of military capabilities to project power and influence abroad, and the ability to maintain some semblance of political order at home. Without enough state capacity, all of these other goals may become unattainable.

Yet any attempt at assessing state capacity in India must necessarily take into account the markedly divergent capacities of the Indian state. There is little question, as many boosters of India's rise have argued, that the Indian state has evinced considerable ability to tackle diverse challenges since its emergence from the collapse of the British Indian Empire. It has, for the most part, successfully fended off external challenges to its territorial integrity; it has worn down a series of secessionist insurgencies and has managed to cope with the many fissiparous tendencies of ethnic, class, and religious cleavages that some analysts thought would rend the country apart in the 1960s. Nor has it quite been overcome with the Malthusian nightmare that some had so confidently predicted that it would confront.[2] And yet state capacity remains paradoxical in India. India does not possess a weak state, but neither does it have a strong state. Its state capacity falls in between the conventional weak-strong continuum. As a consequence, the Indian state manifests both strengths and weaknesses, sometimes simultaneously, sometimes intermittently.

For example, on January 31, 2012, the Indian Ministry of Defense (MoD) finally announced a clear-cut winner in the bidding war for the purchase of 126 medium multi-role combat aircraft (MMRCA) for the Indian Air Force (IAF). The winner was the French-made Rafale fighter jet. After years of deliberation and trials, the Ministry of Defense, based upon the evaluation and trials of the Indian Air Force, had short-listed the Dassault Rafale and the European consortium (composed of the Franco-German EADS, the United Kingdom's BAE Systems, and Italy's Finmeccanica) Typhoon. In the end, the decision was made apparently on the basis of cost and the preference of IAF pilots. The total cost of the order was expected to run between US$15 and $20 billion.[3] According to a prominent U.S. defense analyst, the technical process of vetting the various competitors and then short-listing the two European fighters had been nothing less than thorough, extensive, and exhaustive.[4]

The selection process, from start to finish, lasted five years. Though slow and cumbersome, the process—unlike a number of major defense purchases, which had been tainted with accusations of graft and corruption—from a procedural standpoint was entirely aboveboard and professionally conducted.[5]

On the same day that the Indian MoD announced this decision to make this extremely costly weapons system, it was also reported that after sixty-four years of independence from British colonial rule, India's population on an average received a mere 4.4 years of schooling. The same report underscored that the ratio of primary school teachers to students in India was three times that of the People's Republic of China (PRC).[6]

These two accounts bookend the paradox of the Indian state. India has the capacity, however cumbrous, to carry through a major defense acquisition subjecting it to the most demanding technical evaluation along with rigorous fiscal scrutiny. Yet it has failed dramatically to extend the benefits of primary education to the vast majority of its population. This is hardly surprising given that India until the 1990s had disproportionately emphasized tertiary over primary education. Even with a renewed emphasis on primary education, an important study comparing the PRC and India revealed that as recently as 2004, teacher absenteeism was as high as 25 percent.[7]

Undoubtedly, the India of today is a far cry from the poverty-stricken, militarily weak, socially fractured, and diplomatically isolated country of the Cold War. Nevertheless, unless its leadership can tackle problems ranging from corruption to bureaucratic stagnation to political dysfunction, its hope for a solid global standing and great power status in the twenty-first century will remain just a hope. State capacity is about getting things done, and there are a plethora of things to get done in India, whether or not elite status in world politics is in the offing.

Even so, state capacity does not function in a vacuum. It functions in a political-economic environment that is either supportive or not—or perhaps some variegated mixture of both help and hindrance. The environment in which states operate is also shaped by what states do or do not do. Thus we also need to explore the state's economic landscape and selected aspects of its political institutional framework. Throughout our inquiry we ask whether Indian state capacity, economic foundation, and institutional bases are likely to support or hinder great power behavior. But this type of question is not our most central concern. As noted, it is more a vehicle for examining the complexities of state-making in an in-between power—albeit one with some potential for ascent.

Our Plan of Attack

Although highly developed state capacities have not been the hallmarks of earlier ascending great powers, great powers, once designated as such, have tended to develop more state capacity—at least until or unless being defeated conclusively in major power warfare. To support these assertions, chapter 2 examines the ascent of states conventionally accorded great power status in the past century and a half (Italy, Germany, the United States, Japan). We view this chapter as laying a foundation for the topics that follow. Toward that end, we sketch a framework for interpreting the rise of India and especially its state capacity.

Chapters 3–5 focus on measuring state capacity utilizing a conceptualization developed by K. J. Holsti.[8] Holsti's focus on state capacity or strength encompasses three factors: extraction, violence monopoly, and legitimacy. We develop indicators for each of these subconcepts in order to show where India falls on the state-capacity spectrum. The answer is roughly in the middle of the array of all states in the international system, although its individual state-making subcomponents actually vary from low to moderately high. Its fiscal extraction capability is relatively weak but improving, albeit slowly. Its monopoly of violence has yet to occur. Multiple separatist and other types of conflicts are underway and have been underway since the advent of independence. At the same time, these conflicts tend to be waged on the peripheries of the Indian state, where "boundary" tensions might be most expected (defining who should be considered in and outside the state). Yet that does not mean that peripheralization of internal war is guaranteed for the future. On legitimacy, the Indian state does surprisingly well, given the scope of the problems with which it has to contend and the imperfect outcomes achieved to date. Overall, nevertheless, the Indian state does not compare well to the other BRIC states (Brazil, Russia, China)—presumably its most likely competitors for greater status in the international system.

In chapters 6–11, we shift gears somewhat and review ancillary problems that both limit and reflect moderate state capacity. The focus of chapter 6—the economy—provides a critical foundation for or potential roadblock to expanding state capacity. Chapter 7 looks at infrastructural problems that underpin or hamper economic growth and improved quality of life. Chapter 8 examines the state of income inequality in India. The next three chapters return the focus to political issues. Chapter 9 looks at political institutions and democracy. Moving up in international politics requires a strategy and new military hardware. Thus, chapter 10 looks at changes in India's grand strategy over time and weaknesses associated with its future plans. Chapter 11 examines defense policies and movements toward acquiring capabilities that will permit India to project its influence over longer distances than has hitherto been the case. In all six of these "corollary" chapters, the emphasis is placed on problems that need addressing, while, at the same time, we need to recognize where appropriate gains have been made since 1947. Even so, these topics configure the landscape in which state capacity operates (see fig. 1.1) and, as such, they demonstrate various ways in which state capacity is manifested and constrained.[9]

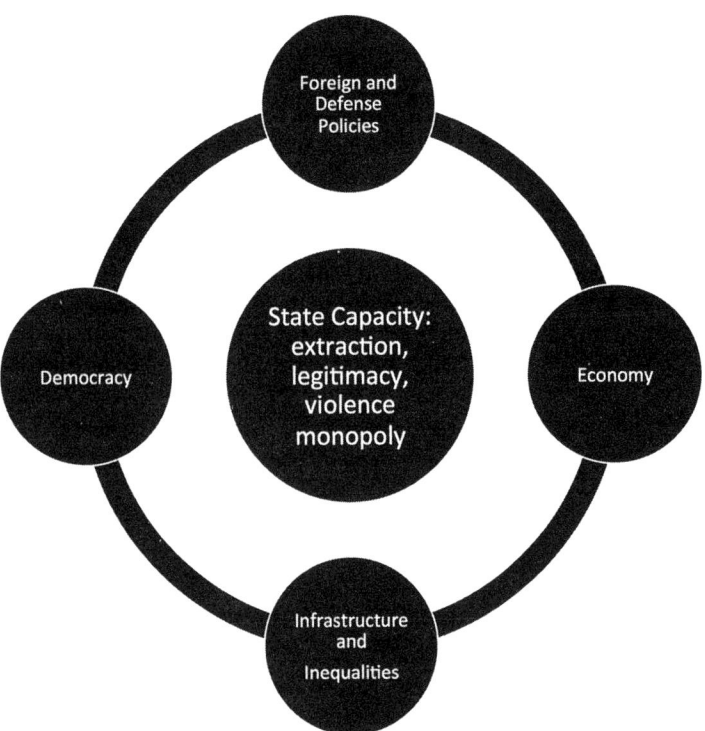

Figure 1.1. State Capacity and Selected Aspects of Its Immediate Environment

In chapter 12, we try to make sense of the eleven chapters that have preceded it. Again, we reiterate that India does not have to possess some minimal state capacity to become a great power. Whether or not India is elevated to great power status, the weaknesses of its current state capacity will definitely hamper India's effectiveness at home and abroad. Nor can we exclude the possibility that the combination of the great problems India faces and the less-than-great capacity it possesses to do something about those problems will discourage other states from bestowing higher political status on India.

Before we tackle our various foci, however, some preliminary issues need addressing. Observers speculate about India's ambitions for greater status. Is there concrete evidence that Indian decision-makers actually entertain such notions? Putting aside this question, why pick on India? Is it a good case for analysis? Obviously, we think it is, but why is it a good case? Surely, others have written on the Indian state. What do we hope to contribute with a new study?

Ascending India

Barely a decade ago, the National Intelligence Council's *Global Trends 2020* report highlighted the imminent rise of India, outlining its likely impact on a host of international regimes ranging from climate change to trade. More recently, during his maiden visit to the country in November 2010, U.S. President Barack Obama said, "India is not just a rising power; India has already risen."[10] Indeed, in a subsequent statement that left many of his Indian interlocutors almost breathless, he even proffered qualified American support for India's entry as a permanent member of a reformed and expanded United Nations Security Council. Two years later, then defense secretary Leon Panetta called India a "linchpin" in the U.S. "pivot" to Asia, while former secretary of state Hillary Clinton described the U.S.-India tie as a "critical bilateral relationship."[11] Neither the NIC report, President Obama's affirmation, nor the cabinet minister's praise was out of step with conventional wisdom. For over a decade, India had been one of the four so-called BRIC nations, destined to play increasingly major roles in the global economy. Spokesmen from both past governments and the current regime in New

Delhi have expressed India's interest in achieving great power status. For example, in a speech given at Harvard University in 2003, Yashwant Sinha, then the minister for External Affairs in the National Democratic Alliance, made a spirited case for a recognition of India's great power status.[12] A year later, the Bharatiya Janata Party (BJP) made great power status by 2020 a campaign pledge.[13] In 2006, Charlie Rose, in a televised interview, asked the former prime minister, Manmohan Singh, point-blank whether India wanted to be a great power. Singh's reply was yes.[14] More recently at a speech given at the annual Shangri-La Dialogue of the International Institute of Strategic Studies held in Singapore in 2015, the Indian foreign secretary, Dr. Subrahmanyam Jaishankar, referred to India as a "leading power."[15]

Another obtrusive indicator of great power aspirations is the emerging blue-water navy designed for deployment in the Indian Ocean and perhaps beyond to the Pacific. The two hallmark icons of blue-water navies and power projection in the post-1945 era are aircraft carriers and nuclear ballistic missile submarines. India is working toward a two-carrier battle-group formation and has authorized the building of a number of SLBM (sea-launched ballistic missile) submarines for deployment in the latter portion of the 2020s.[16] India also has a rather ambitious space program with steadily expanding range that parallels the development of ballistic missiles.

There can be little doubt that Indian decision-makers have great power ambitions and that they are working on improving their military capabilities at sea, in the air, and on land. Prime Minister Narendra Modi, accordingly, increased Indian military spending by 12 percent in his first year in office.[17] A veto power in the United Nations has long been an Indian goal.[18] The parameters of Indian foreign policy are also shifting beyond the immediate region to the "extended neighborhood" (Middle East and Southeast Asia).[19] These changes have hardly gone unnoticed by observers.[20]

Certainly, there has been reason for such optimism. Indian economic growth suddenly seemed impressive and inevitable. Until the recent global economic downturn, the Indian economy was the second fastest growing in the world, reaching a rate of 9.8 percent in October 2009. Poverty dropped 5 percentage points between 2004 and 2009, according to the widely accepted Indian National Sample Survey.[21] Meanwhile, Indian firms have been going global. In 2006, Indian steel magnate Lakshmi Mittal purchased the French company Arcelor, creating the world's largest mining and steel firm. In 2008, the Indian conglomerate Tata purchased the iconic British Jaguar and Land Rover brands from Ford. And, despite some uncertainty now hovering over India's investment climate, key global firms continue to bet on India. In late June, Coca-Cola, which had left India in the early 1970s, decided to invest $5 billion by 2020.[22] Similarly, Swedish furniture retailer Ikea announced that it would invest almost $2 billion in the next few years.[23]

On foreign policy, India has shown growing global aspirations—and capabilities. It is the fifth largest player in the reconstruction of war-ravaged Afghanistan, and its reach extends well beyond its neighborhood. At the 2012 G-20 summit in Los Cabos, Mexico, former prime minister Manmohan Singh had pledged $20 billion to an endowment designed to shore up the International Monetary Fund's lending capacity. Toward the end of 2013, India launched a mission to Mars, which embedded India within a small group of states with ambitious space programs.[24]

Unfortunately, the fascination with India's growing economic clout and foreign-policy overtures has glossed over its institutional limitations, the many quirks of its political culture, and the significant economic and social challenges it faces. To cite but one example, at least 30 percent of Indian agricultural produce spoils because the country has failed to develop a viable supply chain.[25] Foreign investors could alleviate, if not solve, that problem. But thanks to the intransigence of a small number of political parties and organized interest groups, India has refused to open its markets to outsiders. Until India can meet basic challenges like this, its greatness will remain a matter of rhetoric, not fact.

The rise of India, nonetheless, is predicated on various strong assumptions that may prove to be unwarranted. Even if great power status is attained, it may prove to be a hollowed-out triumph, given various liabilities linked to the assumptions. One of these assumptions is that economic growth will be both inevitable and continuously positive. But what if economic growth is not inevitable? When India began to liberalize its economy after the 1991 financial crisis, many analysts concluded that the country was on a glide path to growth.[26] The sheer size of India's market, its wealth of entrepreneurial talent, and its functioning legal system all seemed to herald economic success. Sadly, these sunny assessments overlooked key hurdles. Despite the spurt in economic growth, significant segments of India's slothful bureaucratic apparatus, as well as an entire generation of politicians, remained either hostile or unconvinced of the utility and significance of the reforms. Furthermore, even as India liberalized its economy, it did not move with dispatch to create new institutions that could adequately monitor and set transparent rules for a more open market. The resistance to reforms from segments of India's bureaucracy, the failure to create new institutions, plus a new propensity for populist programs using new revenue sources have conspired to produce disastrous consequences for both the economy and the polity.

For the bureaucrats, the reforms signaled an end to what eminent Indian economist Raj Krishna had sardonically referred to as the "license-permit-quota raj"—a labyrinthine set of regulations, rules, and restrictions over which they had exercised considerable discretion. With the advent of these reforms, they lost their ability to extract rents from hapless businessmen and -women and industrialists. Not surprisingly, in an attempt to protect their entrenched interests, they sought to stall the implementation of new rules at every turn.

Many Indian politicians remained wedded to an anachronistic model of state-led growth. Powerful groups with vested interests in the existing economic order—from well-subsidized farmers to well-entrenched industrial labor unions—opposed reform. And the rise of coalition politics, with all their uncertainties, threatened coherent government action. These factors have now come together to create a perfect storm for India.

In the last quarter of 2012, India's economy grew at a mere 5.3 percent—its worst performance in nearly a decade. Some Indian policy-makers have attributed this downturn to the European fiscal crisis and the global economic slowdown.[27] Growth rates in 2013 and 2014 improved somewhat, with the economy clocking in at 6.9 percent and 7.2 percent respectively.[28] Despite the uptick in the economy, several indigenous problems continue to dog it.[29] Indian politicians of all ideologies have supported unsustainable spending in an effort to placate the country's increasing politically mobilized population. Farmers in significant parts of India pay little or nothing for electricity, but officials refuse to challenge their subsidies. Politicians fret about raising gasoline prices for fear that the middle class will revolt. And to avoid student unrest, they have allowed the university system to reach a breaking point, because the fee structure cannot meet even a fraction of operating costs.

The United Progressive Alliance regime did pass legislation designed to assure access to a minimal caloric intake for every Indian citizen. The goal of this proposed legislation is laudable, but a number of prominent economists have warned that the government simply cannot afford it. Nevertheless, because of the program's political popularity, the regime remained committed to implementing it, even though the fiscal deficit already stands at nearly 5 percent of the country's gross domestic product. The exigencies of winning elections mean that populism is likely to trump fiscal prudence with disastrous economic consequences. The result of all this electoral pandering has been a fiscal deficit of about 6 percent of gross domestic product in 2012. Matters, however, did improve with the advent of a new BJP-led government in 2014. It managed, in part because of a more favorable global economic environment (and especially significantly lower oil prices), to bring the deficit down to 4 percent.[30]

Nevertheless, a host of challenges remain. India's leadership has also failed to reform the country's behemoth public sector. For example, the state-owned Air India requires routine infusions of cash, but the government refuses to privatize the company lest it anger organized labor. On the flip side, entrepreneurs are hobbled by antiquated legal regimes and idiosyncratic rule-making. Outdated land-acquisition laws, which still need updating, have stopped a range of industrial projects, and quirky policy shifts have undermined growing fields like telecommunications.[31]

What's more, some analysts are now arguing that the absence of transparent regulatory and legal frameworks has opened new vistas of corruption.[32] Indeed, the lack of a clearly defined legal regime led to an ad hoc auction of the 2G spectrum in 2008. The flawed auction may have cost the treasury as much as $40 billion, according to an independent government watchdog.[33] Another scandal has emerged which suggests that in 2004 state-owned coal seams were sold at well-below-market prices.[34] Unsurprisingly, the specter of legal uncertainty combined with rampant corruption has had a chilling effect on foreign investment. All this makes India's future economic growth seem far from assured.

The fond hope of some Indian political commentators was that the 2014 national elections would put an end to much of the policy paralysis that has currently gripped the political system. Yet such hopes may be little more than mere wistfulness. The problems that the country now confronts are the result of years, if not decades, of institutional slackness and neglect, dubious political choices, and flawed policies. Fixing them will require more than a changing of the guard. But now that the guard has changed, we will see to what extent the accumulated problems can or will be tackled. The first year of the Modi regime has only reinforced the idea that something more than a changing of the guard will be needed to make headway on multiple fronts.

The postreform generation of politicians was pleased with increased revenues that ensued from greater growth and productivity. However, they showed scant regard for fiscal rectitude, as large segments of the population, which were hitherto economically disenfranchised, sought improved living standards in a booming economy. To ensure continued political support, the political class resorted to a host of populist schemes without the slightest regard for their financial soundness. These included the creation of guaranteed work schemes for individuals below the poverty line. In principle, such an assurance of work was a desirable public policy goal. However, without mechanisms in place to ensure that this system actually benefited the targeted population, its actual implementation became yet another source of corruption and a drain on the exchequer.

A second assumption is that some proportion of the hypothesized expanding economic surplus will be devoted to upgrading Indian military capabilities to the level expected of a great power. But what if the expansion of Indian military-projection capabilities does not appear to be forthcoming anytime soon? Even if some gains in Indian economic growth and military capability are likely, will that suffice to promote India into the great power ranks?

At the end of the Cold War, India found itself mostly at the margins of the global order. Such an outcome was virtually foreordained. Its strategy of economic growth had yielded poor results: growth had been anemic and poverty reduction limited.[35] In the realm of foreign policy, its uneven commitment to the doctrine of nonalignment had failed to elicit significant support in any part of the world. Since the mid-1990s, however, it has enjoyed much attention in the international arena.

Confronted with the abrupt collapse of the Soviet Union, the principal source of its weaponry and a guarantor of its security since 1971, India's foreign policy also underwent significant changes.[36] It abandoned what the Indian political scientist Ramesh Thakur had aptly characterized as its "bunker mentality."[37] Furthermore, it steadily, if reluctantly, came to terms with the emergence of the United States as the sole surviving superpower and sought to alter a long-frosty relationship. Simultaneously, it turned its attention toward the vibrant economies of Southeast Asia ending a period of extended neglect.[38] Finally, for all practical purposes, its grand strategy, nonalignment, ceased to have much meaning in the absence of the U.S.-Soviet competition.[39]

In May 1998, the country finally put an end to its policy of nuclear ambiguity and crossed the Rubicon to become a nuclear power.[40] Initially, India faced much global opprobrium as a consequence of the nuclear tests.[41] However, deft and sustained Indian diplomacy led to a gradual erosion of the sanctions regime that had been imposed on the country in the wake of the tests. With sustained economic growth, an incipient but overt nuclear weapons program and the adoption of a more pragmatic foreign policy, India acquired a newfound status in the global order.

Establishing a nuclear missile program is one way to attain some degree of reach beyond the boundaries of the state. But they constitute only one military capability arena. Conventional air and naval capabilities must also be upgraded if India is to move beyond the status of a heavyweight in South Asian or regional affairs. There is little question, moreover, that India is now dramatically expanding its naval reach and airlift capabilities.[42] And contrary to popular belief, these expansive plans are not a significant financial burden, because, according to recent

World Bank estimates, India's military expenditures are less than 3 percent of its GDP.[43] Even with slower economic growth over the next few years, India should be able to arm itself more than adequately.

The problem, however, lies in its cumbersome, slothful, and, until recently, corruption-ridden weapons-acquisition process. Ironically, the effort to clean up this process has resulted in complex bureaucratic and legal procedures, further slowing what was already a glacial pace. For example, the decision to replace India's aging fighters with new multirole combat aircraft has been ongoing for the better part of a decade, even though the new plane has already been chosen. The extraordinary complexity and sluggishness of the process do not bode well for India's ability to swiftly acquire and deploy the military capabilities it will need if it hopes to project power throughout the region.

Nor have indigenous efforts to build up military capabilities been successful. For example, faced with the increasing obsolescence of its MiG-21 fleet, India finally began work on a light combat aircraft in 1990 after much deliberation. The first prototype flew in 2001, but it was ten years before the initial steps to raise a single squadron for the Indian Air Force finally went into effect. What's more, the aircraft's engine is American, its radar systems were built with Israeli assistance, and some of its munitions are of Russian origin. If India really wants to be a regional military power, it will have to either strengthen its indigenous efforts or radically streamline its foreign military-acquisition process.

Still, in early August 2013, one of the country's recently retrofitted Soviet-era Kilo-class submarines blew up and sank off a naval base in Mumbai, emphasizing India's military vulnerability at a time when China's navy is making steady inroads into the Indian Ocean. Days before the tragedy at the naval base, a carefully negotiated ceasefire along the Line of Control (the de facto international border) in the disputed state of Jammu and Kashmir was breached, resulting in the deaths of five Indian soldiers. Subsequent clashes suggest that the ceasefire is at best intermittent.

From time to time there have been minor thaws in India-Pakistan relations, but the two countries remain far apart on the critical question that has bedeviled their relations since independence: the disputed status of the state of Jammu and Kashmir. That rivalry will only intensify as the United States and the NATO-led International Security Assistance Force withdraw from Afghanistan. The Pakistani military establishment's obsession with "strategic depth" against India has not abated, nor has its commitment to install a pliant regime in Afghanistan post-2014. India's political leadership, which has made significant economic, strategic, and diplomatic investments in Afghanistan, is equally unlikely to cede ground for fear that a neo-Taliban regime will emerge.

Consequently, relations are likely to cool markedly in the near future. And a return to the periodic crises that dogged India-Pakistan relations in the 1980s and 1990s will be distracting and expensive. India's military mobilization against Pakistan in the wake of the December 2001 terrorist attack on the Indian Parliament cost the country approximately $1 billion. Until tensions abate, India will have to remain vigilant along its western border, increase its military spending, and focus its diplomatic energies on keeping the peace. It will remain tied to its neighbor, and its aspirations to transcend regional politics will remain unfulfilled.

Not only does India now face renewed external threats at sea and on land, but it is also witnessing a resurgence of ethnic and religious strife in critical parts of the country. In August 2013, riots swept through Kishtwar, a town in Jammu in the southern part of the contested state. Such communal violence apart, a Maoist insurgency has become endemic to significant parts of the country. Earlier in 2013, notably in June and July, the insurgents struck at will against police and paramilitary posts in the states of Jharkhand and Chhattisgarh.

After the defeat of the BJP in 2004, many secular Indian intellectuals had celebrated. They genuinely believed that the dark shadow of ethnic nationalism was receding and that the country could renew its civic and plural traditions. Such optimism, while understandable, was premature.

The Hindu right, which was ascendant in the 1990s, has yet to abandon its supremacist ideology, and its membership is holding steady. Narendra Modi, a highly divisive figure known for his anti-Muslim sentiments, became prime minister in 2014. What's more, small numbers of Muslims have also become increasingly radicalized—by the intransigence of the Hindu right and the siren call of Islamism from the Middle

East. Some of these radicals have links to global and Pakistan-based Islamist organizations, and some have even been connected to acts of violence on Indian soil. Unfortunately, beyond sounding the tocsin about the dangers of domestic militancy, India's policy-makers have not taken serious steps to stem its rise. Their inaction in the face of this very real danger, in turn, feeds the BJP's charge that the secular political parties in India are guilty of pandering to minority extremism.

Obviously, the long-term consequences of this kind of religious and ethnic conflict could be extremely toxic. Continued and persistent outbreaks of Hindu-Muslim violence will have a chilling effect on foreign investment; they will sap the energies of India's political leadership, and they will damage India's global image as a secular, democratic state.

The Indian Case

Our book touches on a variety of social-political and economic processes. Our main contribution is targeted in two areas: (1) improving our information base on an ascending India, and (2) expanding our understanding of state-making in India in particular—not only for its own intrinsic value but also as a representative of a state that is neither strong nor weak. Most of the work on the Indian state is descriptive. Our project focuses on India but does so from a perspective informed and influenced by other analyses of state-making.[44] At the same time, we are attempting to move beyond the current literature on state-making by focusing on a relatively new case and simultaneously examining multiple dimensions of state capacity empirically.

As noted, circumstances appear to be propelling India toward major power status. In the past two hundred years, however, only five other states (Italy, Germany, Japan, the United States, and China) have made this transition. Three of the five subsequently lost their elite status in combat, thereby underlining the destabilizing nature of these passages to and from the ranks of the world system's elite states. There are, of course, various idiosyncratic factors associated with the ascent of major powers. Italy, the weakest of all the great powers, encountered significant problems in first liberating and then unifying its multiple provinces and was usually forced to rely on other major powers to assert its preferences in international politics. Germany fared much better on the unification front but became ensnared in successive major power confrontations that it was likely to lose. Japan's rise to prominence was characterized by a persistent elite belief in the need for control of Asian space to relieve its industrial resource inadequacies. Seeking control of this space or at least access to it brought Japan into serial conflict with first China, then Russia, and then Britain and the United States. By comparison, the United States enjoyed the distinctive advantages of developing in a home region characterized by little in the way of substantial competition once Britain gave up on its efforts to contain U.S. expansion in the Americas. The contrasts are vivid between the U.S. experience and the reemergence of Chinese major power, marked by resistance to Japanese occupation, intensive internal warfare, and almost immediate confrontation with the world's leading power over Korea, Taiwan, and Vietnam.

Our goal is not to retell these complex stories. Rather, we are interested in the role of the state in managing the problems that are generated by these turbulent environments. The argument is not that the state of the state is the only important factor in success or failure in world (and domestic) politics, but it must be counted as one of the more significant factors. At the same time, we lack an elaborated conceptual basis for evaluating the state of the state and its transformation over time. Most studies have focused more on the weak and strong end points of the state-capacity continuum. But how does one move a state from weakness toward greater strength?

India is an especially good case to analyze. It has very good prospects to be the next great power to emerge. Yet its state has always been considered to be problematic. Moreover, it has been argued that third-world states are unlikely petri dishes for the emergence of strong states. Strong states elsewhere have tended to be the product of participation in intense, increasingly total warfare. This type of experience, so far, has been denied to third-world states. They tend to fight internal wars at home and limited wars, if at all, with neighbors. Neither type of war leads to a perceived need for an acutely mobilized population and resources for survival. As a consequence, limited warfare experience, something not unknown to India, leaves less trace than might otherwise be expected in terms of state revenue extraction, state control over order within its boundaries, and the identification of the population with its state. To the extent that India's relatively underdeveloped state persists, it cannot help but handicap its emergence and performance as a great power.

But theory and conceptualization are subject to empirical assessment. We conceptualize and measure the three main components of state strength (extraction capacity, monopoly of violence, and citizen identification/legitimacy) in the Indian context. How does India compare to other states in general, to other BRICs, and to earlier emerging great powers? Are these components unchanging or is there evidence to suggest movement toward greater state strength? Whatever the answer, what might we expect in terms of the implications for Indian democracy or foreign policy? State strength, of course, has implications for many different areas of policy, which we will touch on selectively (e.g., creating infrastructure for economic development or addressing inequalities and illiteracy).

While we do not argue that observers have ignored the state of the Indian state totally, most projections of Indian ascent are focused on the sheer size of India's population and economy. Similarly, the main blockages to Indian success include such undeniable problems as poverty, inequality, and inadequate infrastructure. Yet it is unlikely that these problems will be addressed, let alone resolved, by demographic and economic change alone. State coordination in tackling policy problems will be critical. Our question is whether the Indian state is likely to be up to the task. If not, the handicaps and policy problems are likely to persist well into the future. They should also influence how Indian foreign policy responds to problems in its external environment.

Earlier Works on Rising India

India's sudden rise has generated a spate of literature that suggests that the country may well be on a pathway toward great power status in the twenty-first century. Indeed, this enthusiasm about India's sudden rise stands in marked contrast to the lugubrious prognoses of India's likely trajectory in the 1970s, when the noted Swedish Nobel Prize–winning economist Gunnar Myrdal despaired about India's ability to tackle its innumerable socioeconomic problems and referred to it as a "soft state."[45] The term acquired greater popularity after *The Washington Post*'s India correspondent Bernard Nossiter made it the title of a particularly gloomy book on India.[46]

More recently, a kindred literature suggests that despite myriad social, political, and even economic bottlenecks, India is increasingly a country that one must reckon with. Interestingly enough, much of the journalistic literature that provides vivid accounts of India's abrupt and dramatic rise nevertheless asserts qualified claims. It suggests that while India's transformation has indeed been dramatic and unexpected, it still faces multiple pitfalls and its growth and development could still falter. While the role of the state is central to many of these problems, too often it is left implicit.

The tone, substance and argument of Edward Luce's *In Spite of the Gods: The Strange Rise of Modern India* exemplifies this cautiously optimistic perspective.[47] Luce is acutely aware of India's multiple challenges. Despite these hurdles, Luce contends that a number of key political choices have unleashed specific social forces that could well prevent the country from slipping back to a state of torpor. He also argues that the skill with which India can handle its fractious relationship with the People's Republic of China (PRC), in tandem with its burgeoning relationship with the United States, will have a significant impact on its future in the global order.

As might be expected of any journalistic account, the work does not provide a systematic analysis or assessment of the quality or efficacy of India's political institutions and policy choices. Consequently, Luce seeks to illustrate India's prospects and limits through the use of a limited handful of social, political, and economic indicators and a series of telling anecdotes.

A much less compelling portrait of India emerges from Giridharadas's *India Calling: An Intimate Portrait of a Nation's Remaking*. The principal drawback of this account is that it is mostly descriptive and has the quality of a travelogue. It is replete with accounts of profound social and cultural changes that are underway in the country. However, there is little effort to make a judgment on the significance of the transformations that are underway and the sustainability thereof.[48]

The most recent entrant into this arena is Simon Denyer's *Rogue Elephant: Harnessing the Power of India's Unruly Democracy*. The book, composed of a series of compelling vignettes, highlights some of the promises as well as the pitfalls of India's chaotic democracy. Despite the gripping quality of the book, its central thesis is unexceptional: India has to overcome a vast legacy of flawed economic choices, and that it may be able to do so is thanks to an emergent middle class with greater expectations, a range of social activists, and the sheer forces of technological change.[49]

Some of the policy-oriented literature, while more attentive to the role of institutions and policy choices, is also not bereft of limitations. Not surprisingly, this literature too has been generated in response to India's unexpected ability to shed many of the policies that had hobbled its growth and limited its international standing. One of the most prominent examples thereof is Stephen P. Cohen's book, *India: Emergent Power*.[50] The work of a noted American academic, it primarily focuses on the quality of India's foreign and security policy-making institutions and their assets and limitations. While Cohen expresses optimism about India's rise, he also underscores that the country faces a number of institutional shortcomings and pathologies that could hobble it from its current trajectory. Though his discussion is sound and displays a firm grasp of the intricacies of policy-making in India, any discussion of India's domestic institutional capabilities is largely tangential.

At least one quasi-academic work merits some discussion. This is Dietmar Rothermund's book, *India: The Rise of an Asian Giant*.[51] Rothermund, a noted German historian of modern India, has produced a work that is both comprehensive and accessible. However, it suffers from two important limitations. The work does not reflect any original scholarship. Instead it is a deft work of synthesis drawing on a wide sweep of secondary sources. Ironically, in its attempt to be all encompassing it also suffers from a degree of superficiality. The breadth of coverage prevents it from exploring any of the issues that it discusses, ranging from India's agricultural policies to its quest for nuclear weapons in any depth.

India: The Emerging Giant, the work of an important economist, Arvind Panagariya, also deserves some discussion.[52] This is perhaps the most comprehensive and topical account of India's economic performance to date. Panagariya provides sufficient historical perspective, explains how India embarked upon its present path of rapid growth, and then assesses a number of issue areas that the country needs to address to sustain its growth. He also discusses the need for continued reforms and suggests possible policy options. These are the obvious strengths to this work. However, the work does not really deal with questions of institutional competence and efficacy. Nor for that matter does it deal with questions of social cleavages, political stability, or political order. Consequently, the limitations of this book are rather obvious.

Finally, the work of a political scientist, Amrita Narlikar, which compares the rise of three emergent global powers—India, China and Brazil—is also worthy of mention. Her focus is different from the vast majority of the other works surveyed here. Instead of devoting the bulk of her attention to the attributes and features that might make India a global power, she chooses instead to devote her attention to the negotiating behavior of new powers in the global order. Two critical assumptions undergird her work. At one level, she argues that the negotiating behaviors of new powers differ from those of more established states. The second assumption that undergirds her analysis is that an understanding of the negotiating strategies of these powers is especially critical when there is much uncertainty about their intentions. She concludes, based on the available evidence, that India's negotiating strategy, even in the wake of its increased economic prowess, does not indicate a willingness to accommodate itself to the expectations of a series of extant global regimes. She concludes that such a strategy may eventually backfire on India as powerful states that uphold existing institutional arrangements may tire of India's unwillingness to undertake burden-sharing commensurate with its expanding capabilities.[53]

Narlikar's contribution comes closest to addressing questions pertaining to the likelihood of India's rise. However, her discussion is mostly focused on India's external behavior and not on its domestic assets, capabilities, and shortcomings.

As this brief survey shows, there is an important lacuna in the existing literature. For all the useful and invaluable features of these various works, it is apparent that none of them provide a systematic evaluation of the capacity of India's institutions to maintain domestic political order, cope with the challenges of sustaining economic growth and reducing poverty, guaranteeing its national security, and enabling the country to play a substantial role in global politics.

It is precisely this lacuna that this book seeks to address. To that end it seeks to assess the robustness and efficacy of India's political institutions (and economic landscape) to cope with a range of challenges the country faces. Of course, even if the great power aspirations were completely off the board, the challenges remain to be resolved in some fashion. In making the assessment we will draw on a wide corpus of literature on state-making. The assessment will also make explicit comparisons with a number of other states that successfully managed to make a transition from regional to great power status.

Despite the wave of upbeat analyses, few, if any, have undertaken a careful assessment of the country's institutional capabilities to harness its material resources and to bear appropriate international burdens, which a more elite status would necessarily entail. A focus on state capacity is desirable because it can provide critical clues about how a polity could harness vital sinews of power or fail to do so. At a more scholarly level, this book will also try to develop a more robust basis for assessing the concept of state capacity, one that in its current form remains underdeveloped.

But what is state capacity, and where does it fit within a trajectory of rising power or ascendance in world politics? Chapters 2–5 take on these questions. First, we look at the relatively recent history of states ascending to great power status. Emphasis is placed on the absence of firm qualifying criteria for elite status in world politics. States become great powers because other powerful states accord them increased status. Why they do that cannot always be predicted. It depends on a constellation of material assets, local ambitions, and contingent factors. As a consequence, pinning down just when a state became a great power can be a somewhat arbitrary exercise.

One thing that will become more clear in the next chapter is that new great powers do not have to possess extensive state capacity. If they survive, they are likely to improve their state capacity, because it is difficult to perform great power roles without some development in this area. Be that as it may, the conceptualization of state capacity remains to be pinned down. It is a term that means many things to different observers, and that is unfortunate. We cannot make much analytical progress if basic concepts mean so many different things. Accordingly, we devote three chapters (3, 4, and 5) to examining the implications of an existing definition of "state capacity"—one that we think deserves centrality in our discourse on what state capacity entails. We explore the implications of Holsti's conceptualization by looking at the relative presence or absence of extraction, legitimacy, and the monopoly of state violence—the main emphases of K. J. Holsti's conceptualization of state strength—in the emergence of recent great powers and in contemporary India and some of its BRIC competitors.

T · W · O

Ascending Major Powers

We live in an era of structural change. The global system leader's position has declined relative to what it once was. States that were once impoverished are climbing their way up the economic income ladder. One or two of them are large enough, it would appear, to eventually challenge the world's lead economy position. But such a challenge is not likely in the immediate future. It will require a great deal more economic development, for one thing. China and India still possess low-income economies, and they need to continue moving toward high-income economies. Not many countries have been successful in this type of transition. Stalling in the middle-income level may be just as probable as ascending ultimately to the top of the system. Along the way, however, a variety of facilitative and constraining factors will be likely to make some difference. Leading candidates for contributing to successful ascents, for instance, are political leadership and state strength.

There is also an intermediate prize for ascending states—great power status. It is not necessary to be the strongest state in the entire system to achieve most goals state decision-makers might have. The great power title recognizes elite status in a global hierarchy, which only a few states can attain. It is not so much the title that is so important but the acknowledgment that a state is near the top of the pecking order and therefore entitled to the perks that go along with the status. The most important perk may be a seat at the table at which significant decisions are made about global policies and rules. Veto power in the UN Security Council comes close to capturing this type of influence, but it is only one institutional manifestation of great power in the international system.

Great power status has a distinctive history. It is not simply an honorific title that is bandied about or asserted from time to time. Students of international relations do not agree on the prerequisites for this status, but there is some rough agreement on which states have held the rank and when. Table 2.1 outlines the codification of comings and goings in great power status as specified by Jack S. Levy. Mirroring the Eurocentric bias of international relations scholars, the great power elite circle began with five powers stretching from England in northwestern Europe to the Ottoman Empire in southeastern Europe. No states entered the elite column in the sixteenth or eighteenth centuries. Two new powers (the Netherlands and Sweden) ascended in the early seventeenth century, but both were gone a century later. In the eighteenth century,

Table 2.1. Levy's Great Power Schedule

Century	Great power	Non–great power
Late 15th	France, England, Austria, Spain, Ottoman Empire	
Early 17th	Netherlands (1609), Sweden (1617)	
Late 17th		Ottoman Empire (1699)
Early 18th	Russia (1721), Prussia (1740)	Netherlands (1713), Sweden (1721)
Early 19th		Spain (1808)
Mid- to late 19th	Italy (1861), United States (1898)	
Early 20th	Japan (1905)	
Mid-20th	China (1949)	

Source: Jack S. Levy, War in the Modern Great Power System, 1495–1975 *(Lexington: University Press of Kentucky, 1983).*

the new recruits (Russia and Prussia) proved to have more staying power. Italy and the United States were anointed as great powers in the second half of the nineteenth century, while Japan and China achieved their ranks in the first half of the twentieth century.

Just how many of these states have survived as great powers into the twenty-first century is debatable. Levy prefers to view the European great powers as surviving into the post-1945 era, but an argument could be made just as easily that the great power status of Britain, France, Germany (as the heir to Prussia), and Italy—as well as Japan, did not survive the Second World War. Most of the other elite states lost their status in earlier wars, leaving only China, Russia, and the United States. Yet China's entry around the time of the Korean War is arguable, and Russia's continued great power status after the demise of the Soviet Union is also contestable. No one argues that these states do not have claims to elite status; it is more a matter of their claims possessing various weaknesses that render their elite status less than open-and-shut cases.

That great power status emerged in the European region is awkward in a global context. When the great powers were confined to home bases in Europe, it was easier to mix powers possessing decidedly regional capabilities (such as Austria and Sweden) with powers that had extraregional capabilities (such as the Netherlands and England/Britain). The main question was which states mattered most in Europe. Once the reference point expanded beyond Europe, it became less clear just what the criteria for club membership were.

Putting aside the equally nebulous criteria used in earlier centuries, a look at the more recent entrants (post-1850) and their capability attributes (population, military size, and energy consumption as a proxy for economic/technological wealth and development) underlines the fuzziness of the status prerequisites that might have been considered important at the time of ascension to great power status.[1] Figure 2.1 shows proportional scores for great power population size at the time of attainment of status.[2] In Figure 2.1, it is possible to say that the population size of the new great powers had been increasing prior to their elevation in rank. In two cases, Italy and Germany, the population increases reflected the integration of a number of smaller states around the Pied-

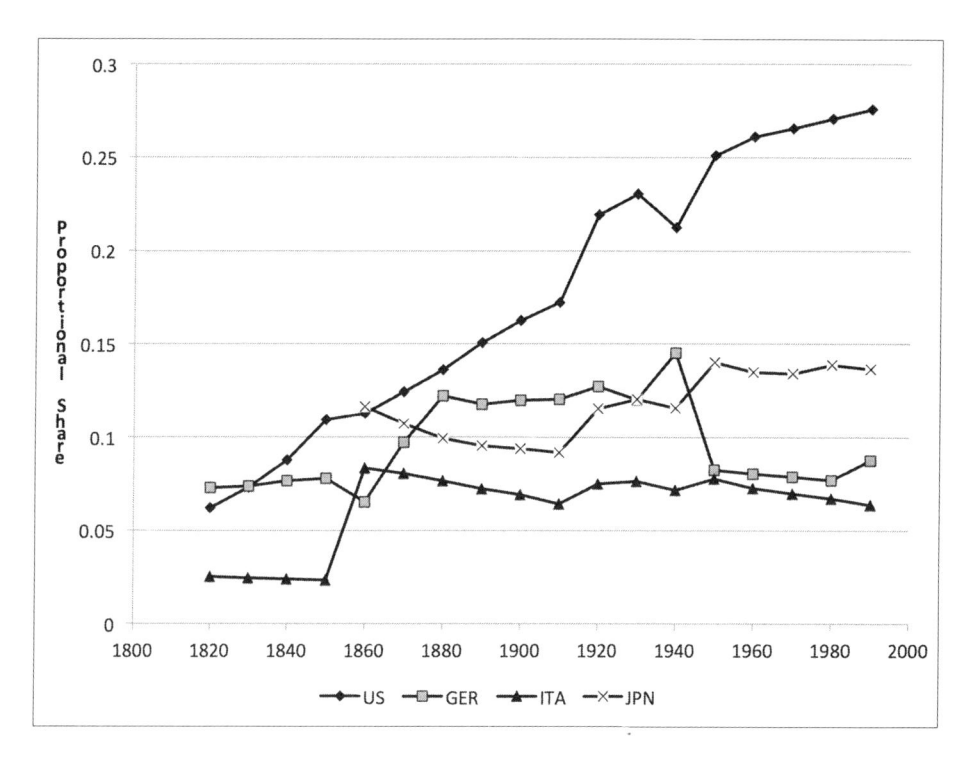

Fig. 2.1. Proportional Share of Population

mont and Prussian cores. In the U.S. case, it was more a matter of European immigration, local birth rates, and the territorial expansion of the former thirteen colonies. Nonetheless, there is no discernible threshold criterion. Italy was promoted with less than 10 percent, Germany with less than 15 percent, and the United States with less than 20 percent. The relative size of the Japanese population was actually declining prior to 1905 and only expanded afterward. China's huge population size (not shown in fig. 2.1) guaranteed it a large share of the great power pool, but that had been the case for decades, if not centuries, prior to 1949.

The story is not made any clearer by examining the number of military personnel. Italy, Germany, and the United States all demonstrate increases in military personnel as they were moving into the great power club (fig. 2.2) but, again, there is no threshold pattern. Italy, the United States, and Japan were in the vicinity of 5 percent, while Germany was

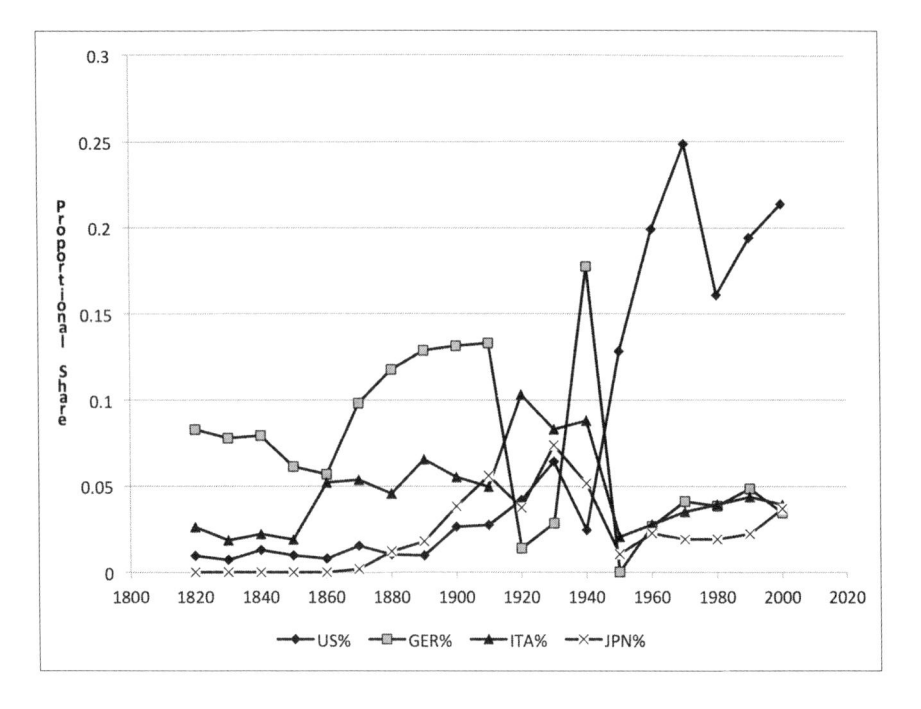

Fig. 2.2. Proportional Share of Military Personnel

well above that threshold. All three states record much more impressive expansion of their military forces subsequently in World Wars I and II. This outcome could be viewed in two ways. Either substantial changes in relative military force were only to come later, or great power status acknowledged early their ability to expand in a period of intensive combat. Actually, both statements are probably correct, but if great power status is based on perceived potential, we will have problems ascertaining how much potential was considered necessary.

A third take on minimal criteria for great power looks at energy consumption per capita as a proxy for economic/technological prowess. Figure 2.3 underscores Italy's lack of a claim to much in the way of industrialization prior to 1861. Germany and the United States had much better claims. Germany had a proportional score close to 15 percent, but the U.S. claim was much stronger (close to 35 percent) by 1898. Japan's position at ascension to great power status was little better than Italy's. China's industrialization really only commenced after it had attained its

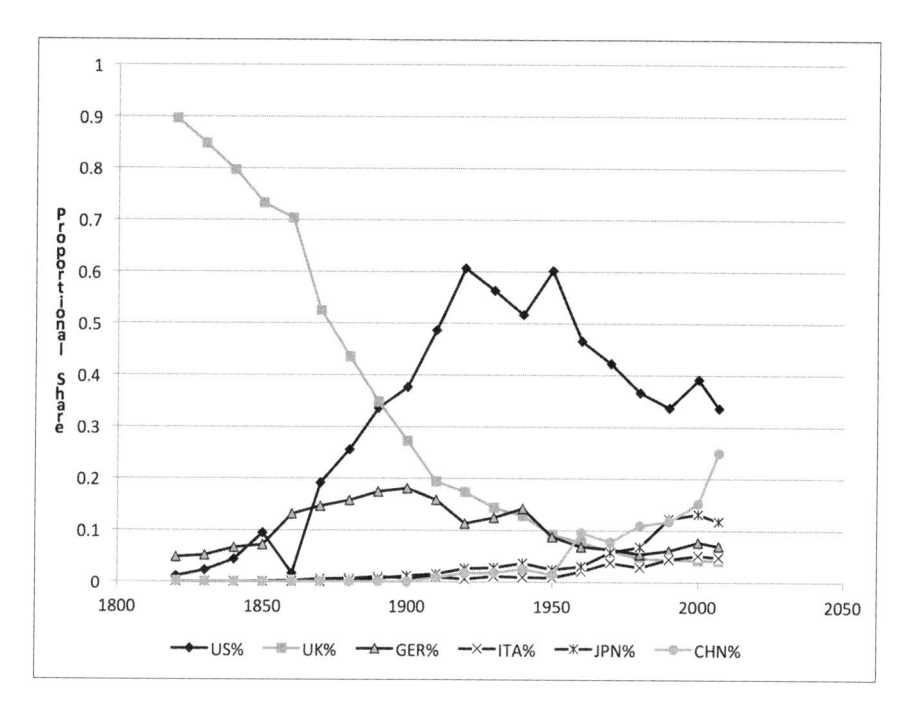

Fig. 2.3. Proportional Share of Energy Consumption per Capita

promotion after World War II and the end of its long-running civil war.[3] Once again, if there is a pattern here, it is not readily discernible.

Population size, the size of the armed forces, and industrialization are all linked in some way to elite status in the international system. Yet looking at the entry points of immediate past great powers, one would be hard-pressed to say how these indicators of capability might be linked to status attainment. It seems more accurate to say that elevation to the great power club is not predicated on satisfying specific minimal criteria pertaining to possessing above-average capabilities. Not shown in the figures are the battlefield demonstrations, which do seem closely linked to the timing of rank promotion. Italy needed considerable help in military matters, but Germany had defeated both Austria-Hungary and France, the United States defeated Spain, Japan had defeated China and Russia, and China had defended its borders against the perceived threat of U.S. invasion. But even here the pattern is muddled. Victory is not required. Nor did all of the great powers-to-be have to defeat other great powers. Some did and some did not. We are forced to conclude that elevation to great power status requires some capabilities, but it is difficult to capture precisely how much of anything is required. That would suggest, perhaps not surprisingly, that the process is highly subjective. Other great powers decide who is in their club and who is not, based no doubt on varying criteria.[4] Sometimes it is a matter of convenience, as in the persistent weakness of the Italian claim. Sometimes it is a matter of demonstrated capabilities that are hard to deny—as in the Japanese claim. In contrast, the U.S. promotion in 1898 had to be more about its growing economic power and potential to fill out the military expectations associated with great power status. Defeating Spain was not in itself a great feat, although it did require marshaling forces in the Caribbean and Manila Bay.

Just as we have no concrete criteria for elevation to great power status, we also have little in the way of theories that explain how it comes about. An exception is Zakaria's analysis of the rise of the United States.[5] Zakaria's argument can be summarized very easily. He argues that there are two leading candidates, both variations on types of realism. Defensive realism contends that "nations expand their political interests when they become increasingly insecure."[6] However, Zakaria rejects this argument because he finds little correlation between periods of insecurity and expansion of interests. He favors the other candidate that is associated with classical realism: "nations expand their political interests abroad when their relative power increases."[7] We have already seen some support for this argument in the data sketched in figures 2.1 through 2.3, even if it was not clear how much relative power increase was needed.

Still, as a theory, the argument that relative power increase drives expanded external activities is missing causal mechanisms linking power and behavior. Zakaria provides a useful hint when he quotes Choucri and North in support of the classical realist argument: "Despite proclamations of nonintervention or even genuinely peaceful intentions, a growing state tends to expand its activities and interests outward—colliding with the spheres of influence of other states—and find itself embroiled in international conflicts, crises and wars. . . . The more a state grows, and thus the greater its capabilities, the more likely it is to follow such a tendency."[8]

We can use a slightly modified version of Choucri and North's lateral-pressure theory to fill in the missing causal mechanisms.

1. Actors are motivated by needs for energy resources to sustain life and by psychologically generated wants, desires, and aspirations related to energy acquisition.
2. In order to satisfy needs, wants, and desires, actors make demands upon themselves, their environment, and other actors.
3. The larger the number of people in a community, organization, or society, the greater will be the volume of needs, wants, and demands.
4. The more advanced the level of technology, the greater will be the amount and the wider the range of resources required and thought to be needed.
5. Demands combine with capabilities to yield actions, but actions will be constrained by the availability of appropriate capabilities and/or resources.
6. To satisfy demands, actors tend to use domestic resources first. If local resources are absent or as local resources diminish or become too expensive, actors will attempt to expand their external activities—lateral pressure (for example, trade, diplomatic representation, military basing, and/or territorial expansion).
7. To satisfy demands, actors may need to improve underdeveloped capabilities. The likelihood of capability development, in turn, is a function of available resources, the volume of demands, and the intensity of crises that accelerate the need for capability development.
8. Actors who persuade others that they possess capabilities that are sufficiently superior in these activities tend to be treated as elite powers or "great powers," albeit subject to some lag for late developers.

These eight theoretical statements translate into the argument that population size and technological development increase demands for resources. Depending on the amount of resources available at home and the capabilities to acquire resources, variable levels of activities away from the home base can be anticipated. Choucri and North were more interested in what happened after multiple actors began increasing their external activities and colliding with one another in the process of doing so. For our own purposes, we do not need to follow the process that far. Great powers are states with different types of capability—bulk size, technological development, or some combination of the two—and that are motivated to become more active in external affairs. If they impress elite decision-makers of other states sufficiently that they have the appropriate qualifications, they can eventually be expected to join the elite circles. It also helps if existing elites view the promotion(s) as advantageous in some way for their own purposes.[9] Figure 2.4 summarizes this theoretical argument about the attainment of great power status.

Figure 2.4 highlights how population and technological development leads to demands that are mediated by capabilities and national endowments before getting to international activity. Population concentrations and national endowments tend to be subject to luck-of-the-draw distributions. It is possible to encourage population increases, and it is equally possible to exploit endowments more or less well. But it is difficult to create large populations overnight. They grow over decades and centuries. National endowments are even less susceptible to creation. At best, states can try to take a neighbor's endowments if they face deficits at home. It worked for Prussia in 1741 when it seized Silesia from Austria. France failed to hold on to the Saarland's coal, and Iraq was even less successful in acquiring Kuwait's petroleum in 1991. Increas-

Population size ↘
                    Demands → | Capabilities ↓↑ Domestic Resources | → External Activity Expansion → Subjective Attainment Great Power Status
Technological ↗
Development

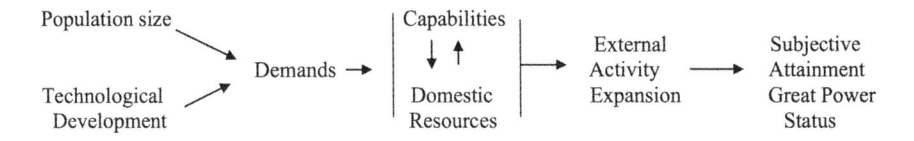

Fig. 2.4. Attaining Great Power Status

ingly, it has become difficult to conquer one's way to a better national-resource endowment. On the other hand, the nature of technological progress has reduced some of the dependency on raw materials.

Technological development is different. It is susceptible to creation and facilitation, much more so at least than population size and national endowment. Contrary to how economic processes are often portrayed, economic growth and technological development are never autonomous processes. They do not take place without assistance. Facilitative political leadership and state institutions are necessary to construct conducive contexts for ascent. Decisions have to be made on which development paths to pursue. Infrastructure must be constructed. Obstacles such as low education levels, inequality, and health and sanitation levels must be reduced. Conflicts among rich, poor, and marginalized groups must be managed. The inflow of investment and resources from abroad must be encouraged. The potential for increased conflict with neighbors and established major powers must also be managed, lest these potential diversions become constraints on further economic development.

Choucri and North envision population size and technology as two different inputs into the demands for resources and expansion. The way history has worked, we think that may have been true in earlier centuries. In the twenty-first century, it is increasingly clear that it will be the interaction between population size and technology that matters most. A large population with an underdeveloped economy could once be militarily competitive. Eighteenth-century Russia is a good example. A large population with an underdeveloped economy can probably no longer be competitive in either the military or the economic sense.

It was also possible once for states with small populations but very strong technology to be competitive. Seventeenth-century Netherlands illustrates this point. But that no longer is the case. Small states with state-of-the-art technology can currently occupy lucrative niches in the world economy, but they are less likely to be fully competitive with the strongest military powers. The history of successive great powers has been one of periodic eclipses, with bigger, stronger powers emerging and overshadowing some of the older elite states that were consequently forced to drop out of international competition.[10]

Ascent Dynamics

Yet there is definitely a missing link in figure 2.4. Greater international activity, clearly, does not lead automatically to the attainment of great power status. Other factors intervene at this stage. Table 2.2 charts a brief auxiliary theory of what happens in this missing link on the ascent path to great power status.[11] Successful ascent is most likely when domestic and international environments are favorable. What does that mean? If we reduce the factors that are most important to influences that either promote ascent (stimuli) or hold ascent back (constraints), favorable environments can be described as low on constraints and strong on stimuli. Constraints can be political or economic. Depending on the era, great power status implies some ability to pay for competitive military forces. In the nineteenth and twentieth centuries the capability that was most critical was industrialization. States did not have to be fully industrialized to qualify as great powers, but they needed to be moving toward industrialization to pay for their competitive elite status. Problems in achieving industrialization, therefore, amounted to a major category of domestic economic constraint.

Possible domestic political constraints are multiple in number. For our purposes, they can be reduced to factors that limit the ability of the state to mobilize resources and support for national and international activities. One can have ample resources but no ability or interest to do anything with them. In such a case, an attempt to acquire great power status is less probable. Institutional weaknesses and societal fragmentation are most likely to lead to political constraints on expanded activity. If the preferences of important domestic groups cancel each other out

Table 2.2. The Conditions for Great Power Ascents

	International constraints	International stimuli
Domestic constraints	Ascent unlikely	Ascent handicapped or delayed
Domestic stimuli	Successful ascent less likely	Successful ascent likely

or paralyze concerted actions, or if the political institutions are simply not up to the task, the political constraints are apt to be fairly critical.

The last crop of new great powers (Italy, Germany, the United States, and Japan) all emerged with considerable political and economic constraints that needed to be overcome in some fashion. Italy was the most constrained and, as a consequence, the "least of the great powers."[12] Once the most innovative and affluent part of Europe, as the medieval era gave way to the early modern, Italy was increasingly marginalized by shifting trade routes in the fifteenth and sixteenth centuries, which reduced significantly its former middleman role in east-west trade. Once an autonomous subsystem in which the major cities competed with one another in Mediterranean and European trade, Italy after 1494 was penetrated by, and subordinated to, the Franco-Spanish rivalry, which became the central conflict axis in western Europe through the mid-seventeenth century.

One of the partial legacies of Spanish control over much of the Italian "boot" was a persistent cleavage between northern and southern Italy. Northern Italy possessed major cities and an agrarian base not unlike France. Southern Italy was more like Latin America, with large estates and a peasantry with limited literacy. Since neither the north nor the south was well endowed with the type of resources that would encourage industrialization, it was not possible for a manufacturing north to exploit the south as a source of raw materials. Instead, southern Italy has served to function as a major constraint on Italian economic growth. Only the advent of electrification in the north enabled Italian economic growth to begin catching up with its European neighbors.

Politically, both north and south were fragmented in the nineteenth century. Several wars, led by Piedmont in the north with external assistance, were required to begin bringing the pieces back together in a semblance of a unified state. While Piedmont served as the integrative core power, it was not an especially strong one and, on its own, could not be expected to defeat its Austrian rival for control of northern Italy. French and, later, German support was required to keep Italy in the European game. Coercive adventures in East (Ethiopia) and North Africa (Libya) were all predicated on the inability of Italy to compete with European great powers in the home region. The continuation of international expansion, if it were to occur, might only be contemplated outside Europe.

Piedmont complemented its own geopolitical weaknesses by bestowing a weak monarchy on the new Italian state. In turn, the weak monarchy attempted unsuccessfully to compete occasionally with a legislature that reflected only too well the persistent regional fragmentation of Italy. Poorly institutionalized political parties could do little to fill the void prior to the post–World War I era. The gradual expansion of an initially very limited enfranchisement only made Italian politics more difficult to steer. Post–World War I fascism may have made Italy look stronger in some respects, but it would be more accurate to say that Italy never overcame its political-economic constraints during its tenure as a nominal great power.

Germany replaced Prussia, which had once been the weakest great power prior to the promotion of Italy. Prussia's weaknesses had been due primarily to small size, limited resources, and bad location. Germany's constraints were much different. By expanding to encompass all of the German states (minus Austria, which had contested control of greater Germany), Germany inherited two cleavages that had not characterized Prussia. An east-west axis distinguished a conservative, grain-growing, Junker-controlled Prussia from a more urbanized, increasingly industrialized and liberal west. A north-south axis separated Protestants from Catholics. While Prussia did constitute a strong integrative core power, it no longer controlled directly the new state's industrialized economic core. But Prussia did supply a strong monarchy that initially controlled Germany's legislature through an adroit chancellor (Bismarck). With Bismarck's dismissal in 1890, monarchical control over German politics and its parliament proved to be less predictable. Initially at least, political coordination was made somewhat more difficult by a federal system in which taxes were raised primarily by the constituent states and not the federal center.

Although Germany resembled Italy in terms of its fragmentation at the outset, Germany had more resources with which to work and stronger leadership. Its size and technological successes vaulted Germany to be the lead economy in Europe and a possible successor to Britain at the global level. In the end, none of that proved all that beneficial to Germany, but in the short run its economic prowess, in conjunction with the region's lead army, did help overcome problems associated with domestic cleavages and political leadership. The economic and military capabilities also clearly reinforced Germany's claim to great power status.

If Italy and Germany began their great power tenures as fragmented states, the United States emerged in the late nineteenth century as a state once so divided that a full-fledged Civil War had been waged to determine which half would predominate. The North was industrializing while the South was dedicated to an agrarian plantation economy, at one time fueled by slave labor. The North won the Civil War, occupied the South, but ultimately backed away from radically changing the South's political economy other than abolishing the slavery institution.

Decision-makers also backed away from retaining the strong and well-armed state created to win the Civil War. But divided as it was, the United States benefited from relatively well developed political institutions in its party/legislature and judicial systems that, in tandem, proved sufficient to create a national economy demanded by industrialization prior to the emergence of a powerful chief executive or even much centralization in the U.S. federal system in the twentieth century.

In this respect, it is important to highlight that a conventionally strong state was not necessary to facilitate the development of a strong state. It was not just the creation of a national market unhindered by subnational boundaries and regulations that was critical. As Skowronek notes, labor organizations, nationally oriented corporations, and trusts/oligopolies emerged in the second half of the nineteenth century.[13] Labor and business clashed violently. Different types of business interests clashed. New technology appeared that required both facilitation and regulation. Conflicts were inevitable. In order to maintain some semblance of order in the economy, governmental adjustments were required. In the U.S. case, a series of Republican Party leaders were given credit for both creating a powerful state to win the 1861–1865 Civil War and allowing it to atrophy through the 1870s. Afterward, the same party struggled to manipulate congressional hearings, carefully screened Supreme Court justice appointments, and contributed to the development of an independent central state bureaucracy. The driving factor was the urge to be reelected, and the basic strategy was to advance Northern industrial interests at the expense of Southern economic preferences and needs. It did not require a conspiracy—only an environment that consistently rewarded adherence to persistent goals given pressing political-economic problems, rational politicians seeking reelection, and a number of decades of political combat in which not all of the battles were won or winnable. As Skowronek puts it, crisis, conflict and increasing complexity combined to lead to governmental expansion in the late nineteenth century.[14] The process did not end then, of course. More crises, continuing conflict, and greater complexity followed—as did more governmental expansion.

Placing explanatory emphasis on the three "c's" (crisis, conflict, and complexity) does not guarantee a concrete outcome. Presumably, the combination could lead to political chaos (another "c") or simply political paralysis. In the American case, however, it did not, although presumably considerable trial and error was involved.

Lockwood also attributes a trial-and-error approach to the Japanese experience.[15] No explicit planning was involved. As industrialization and a national economy emerged, the governmental response was incremental and sufficiently flexible to recognize and correct its errors eventually. It is also described as "energetic" in taking steps to improve transportation and communications, to establish new industries, and to modernize the army and navy.[16] Moreover, industrialization altered the political-economic environment fundamentally. A traditional and quite narrow elite was gradually broadened, while at the same time the state's resources for dealing with problems were expanded. It also helped that agrarian workers were largely politically passive through World War I.

But industrialization also changed foreign-policy stakes and goals. A major economic constraint for Japan was the relative absence of industrial raw materials at home but readily available in Manchuria and Southeast Asia. Satisfying the prerequisites for fueling industrialization encouraged some groups to insist on an imperial presence in Asia. It was not the only strategy conceivable, but as industrialization progressed, the attractiveness of a coercive solution to its economic problems became more acute and stimulated more aggressive action on the part of Japanese state agents, interest groups, and decision-makers.

Domestic political stimuli, thus, tend to work just the opposite of the restraining effects of constraints. Expanding economic wealth, technological complexity, and increased interest in trade lead to interests in increased international activity. So too do political leadership and strong institutions that can coordinate domestic activities in order to participate more effectively in international activities.

Internationally, perhaps the greatest constraint is a highly hierarchical distribution of power and resources. The ascent of new great powers is less likely when power is highly concentrated in the international system (unless the new great powers have recently won their "spurs" in battle).[17] More probable are great powers emerging in periods of power deconcentration. Of course, this observation tends toward the tautological because the emergence of new great power candidates is one of the more important ingredients for periods of power deconcentration. Still, less hierarchy in the international system should not only encourage great power candidates to make bids for greater status, it should also signify less capability on the part of the defenders of the systemic status quo to resist the new bids.

Similarly, the most prominent types of international stimuli to increased activity are perceived threats to national security and opportunities to improve national position. Sometimes it is difficult to tell one from the other. Italy expanded in Ethiopia and Libya because it could not take on Austria-Hungary to regain territories that were deemed belonging to Italy or France in Tunisia. Germany sought its place "in the sun," which led to naval and colonial expansion. The United States had long resisted expanding into the Caribbean but leaped at the opportunity to take Cuba and the Philippines away from Spain. Japan fought both China and Russia separately in its initial plans to predominate in Korea and Manchuria.

India and Great Power Status

While the consensus on how economies acquire greater complexity and affluence is less developed than it should be, we know even less about how political leadership and state institutions facilitate and constrain upward mobility in the international system. Our appreciation for political leadership tends to be anecdotal. Our understanding of states is most focused on the strong and weak ends of the continuum. We know that some states have considerable capacity and that others have very little. It is not necessary to choose between examining political leadership and state strength, but it is probably not prudent to do both at the same time. Of the two, state strength seems to have more potential for generalization, and it is on this question that the next chapter will focus.

Our theoretical material on state-making distinguishes readily between "strong" and "weak" states. But what about the in-between states —those that are neither strong nor weak? India is such a state and therefore provides a good anchor point for this examination. Beginning with a new metric for comparing state capacity, which combines indicators on extraction capability, weapons monopoly, and citizen identification, India can be shown to fall roughly in the middle of the pack of some 130 states for which data are available. That may not be a disadvantageous position for a fairly new state, but India has clear aspirations to join the great power ranks. Can a medium-capacity state reasonably anticipate ascension to global elite status? Historically, the answer would appear to lie in the affirmative, but not without caveats. That is, weaknesses at home tend to hobble both continued economic ascent and foreign-policy activities abroad. Elite rank may be acquired, but we can assume that its activation will be handicapped in various ways.

A useful place to continue where we left off with explaining state expansion to great power status is with Nayar and Paul's list of ten elements that are deemed essential for newly claiming major power status.[18] They specify four "hard power" resources (military, economic, technological/knowledge, and demographic), which overlap with the sources of increased demand in figure 2.4, and six "soft power" resources (norms, international institutional leadership, culture, state capacity, strategy/diplomacy, and national leadership), which flesh out what are summarized as capabilities in figure 2.4. It is a good list but it is only a list. Clearly, all ten items are not equally important. Listing state capacity as a soft power resource is even a bit curious. Moreover, how the elements are connected is left unspecified.

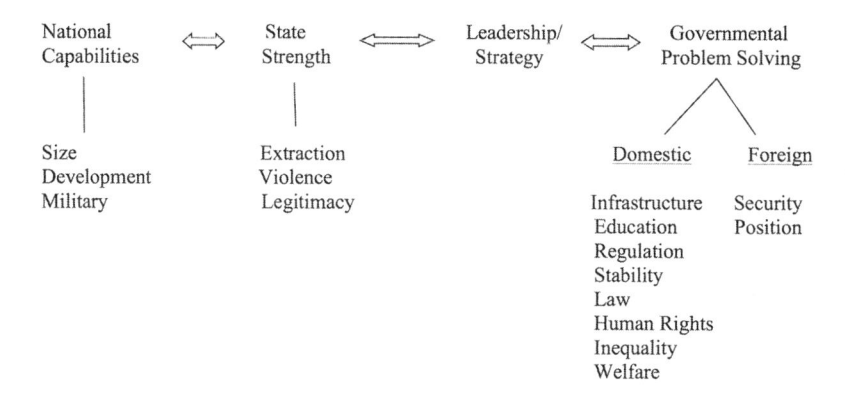

```
National          State            Leadership/      Governmental
Capabilities  ⟷   Strength   ⟷    Strategy    ⟷    Problem Solving
    |                |                              /        \
Size             Extraction                     Domestic    Foreign
Development      Violence
Military         Legitimacy                     Infrastructure  Security
                                                Education       Position
                                                Regulation
                                                Stability
                                                Law
                                                Human Rights
                                                Inequality
                                                Welfare
```

Fig. 2.5. State Strength and the Ascent Problem

The list is easily reconfigured into the model sketched in figure 2.5. National capabilities frame the potential for great powerhood, as we have implied before. A credible military force; a large, developed, and thriving economy; a large, skilled, and expanding population; and a competitive technological base are all vital to establishing claims to elite status in world politics. Just how much military force, what size economy and population, and what type of technology vary by century. Yet some mixture of formidable capability base is critical. Aspiring elite powers either have to possess this foundation or they have to acquire it as quickly as possible to sustain their status.

Unlike in Nayar and Paul, "state capacity" is conceptualized in figure 2.5 as "state strength," and while it certainly possesses soft attributes, it also has a claim to a "hard power" resource status on par with the national capabilities set. State strength, in conjunction with national leadership and strategy, translates resources into governmental problem solving. State strength is often equated with capacity, as in the extraction of tax and manpower resources for national projects, but there is more involved. A case will be made in this analysis for interpreting state strength as a combination of extraction, violence, and legitimacy. No claim is made that aspiring elite powers must have strong states to qualify as major powers. However, the possession of a less-than-strong state will be a serious liability in the quest for higher status. As in the case of the resource foundation, a handicapped state structure can be overcome to some extent by strenuous and clever leadership. Ultimately, though, the constraints of weaknesses—whether they are located in the resource foundation and/or the state, can be expected to impede both the ascent toward greater status and its maintenance once achieved—as we argued earlier (see table 2.2). Capabilities are less likely to be translated into influence abroad. Governmental problems at home are less likely to be resolved.

We will be focusing on the Indian state in the chapters that follow. But why exactly is India in the running for ascent into the great power ranks now? After all, in terms of its capability foundation, it has been a large state since its independence in 1947. A case could have been made for giving it a permanent seat on the UN Security Council from the outset but was not. In its home region, it has been unquestionably the preeminent state, albeit not without intermittent challenges from Pakistan. India's accession to the nuclear power ranks is relatively recent, but not that recent.

Perhaps the main reason for ongoing discussions about India's future status is its BRIC categorization. Brazil, Russia, India, and China have been anointed as the four economies most likely to become the largest in the world.[19] In this respect, they could surpass the current largest economy, the United States, not only in absolute size but also in terms of economic development. As shown in figure 2.6, there is an income-technological trajectory by which less developed (low income or low gross domestic product per capita) can move up the income ladder toward the peak position at the pinnacle of the system. At the peak, the most developed economy in the world economy operates at the technological frontier, innovating new ways of producing and transporting commodities.

There is no reason to assume that the system's lead economy position will be monopolized permanently by one state forever. On the contrary, some turnover is probable. While there are definitely advantages to possessing the lead economy, the leadership in economic innovation can prove to be disadvantageous. Leading can result in complacency and a reluctance to experiment with new ways of doing things when the old ways have worked so well. Each generation of new technology de-

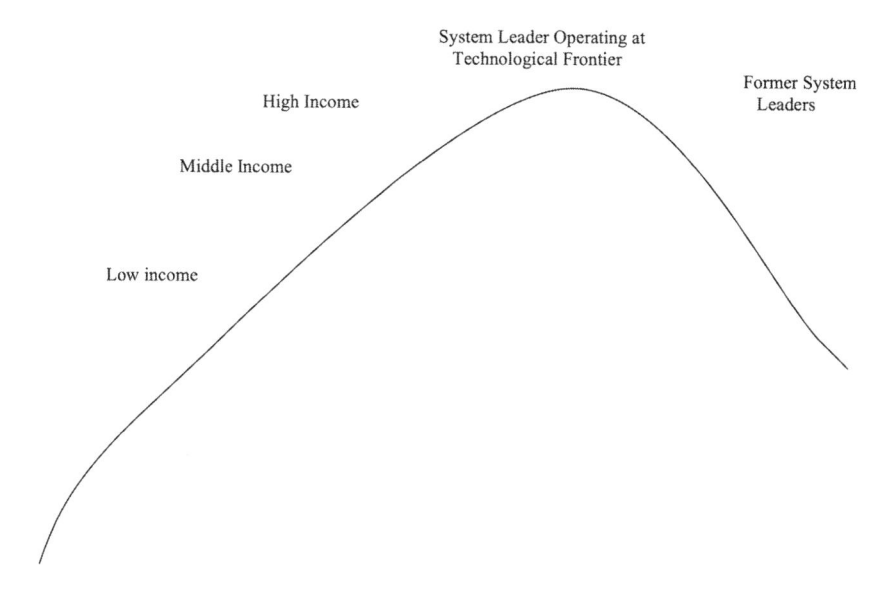

Fig. 2.6. The Income-Technology Trajectory

pends on resources that may be readily available in some places but not in others. An advantaged economy in one era may be disadvantaged in another. Smaller leaders may ultimately be eclipsed by economies that are simply larger and better endowed.

Historically, there has been turnover in the identity of the world's lead economy. The United States supplanted Britain. Britain had earlier supplanted the Netherlands. It is possible to trace this process back even farther but the point remains that lead economies come and go. Perhaps it is now approaching time for an even larger economy to supplant the U.S. lead. But there are two assumptions associated with BRIC discussions. One is that the world's largest economies will also become the world's highest income economies. This possibility is by no means guaranteed. China, for instance, has been the world's largest economy before. So has India—as shown in figure 2.7.[20] That status did not automatically confer technological leadership in the world economy.[21] Absolute size is not a prerequisite to technological leadership and may even be detrimental.[22] Thus, any or all of the BRICs could become the world economy's largest without moving all the way up the development trajectory shown in figure 2.6.

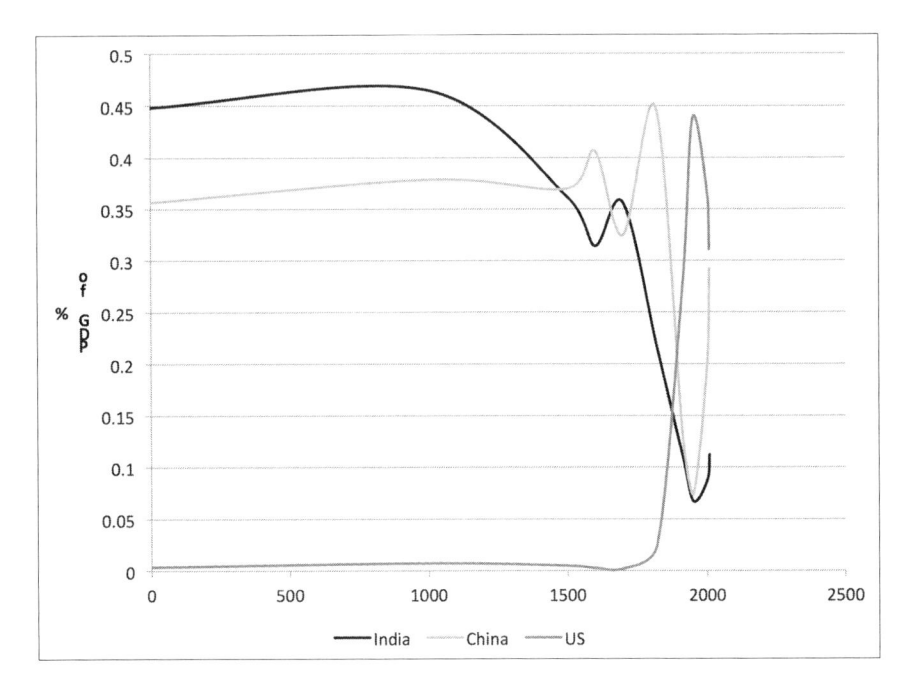

Fig. 2.7. Historical GDP Shares

In this context, there is a significant problem known as the "middle-income trap." Low-income economies can move toward middle-income status, replacing less productive, agrarian labor with industrial productivity and copying technology already developed. There comes a point, however, at which this development strategy no longer works. The gains from replacing agrarian productivity have been realized. Standard technologies have been duplicated. The next step up the ladder requires developing the ability to create new technologies and to implement them as quickly as they are being developed elsewhere—as opposed to simply borrowing from the existing technological inventory. Succeeding at making this step up is by no means straightforward or perhaps even likely for all four BRICs. Hence, movement up the income ladder can be stalled at various points.

Figure 2.8 charts numbers for national gross domestic product per capita over time for the four BRICs. Exactly where the dividing line is between high and middle income is somewhat arbitrary and, of course,

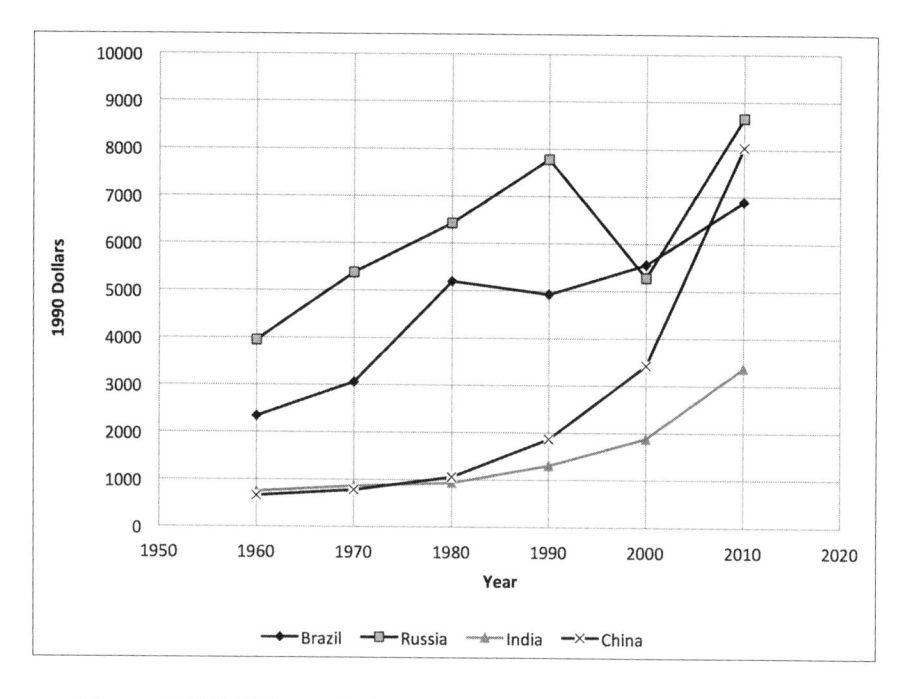

Fig. 2.8. BRIC GDP per Capita, 1960–2010 *Note: Gross domestic product per capita is expressed in 1990 International Geary-Khamis dollars based on information reported in Angus Maddison, http://www.ggdc.net/maddison/maddison-project/home.htm, accessed. February 24, 2016, and the group continuing to update the Maddison data set. See J. Bolt and J. L. van Zanden, "Collaborative Research on Historical National Accounts,"* Economic History Review *67, 3: 627–651, and at www.ggdc .net/maddison/maddison-project/home.htm, accessed February 24, 2016.*

changes from decade to decade. For figure 2.8, a very minimalist threshold might be viewed as ranging approximately from US$3,000 (in 1960) to $7,623 (in 2010).[23] Russia had earlier managed to break into the high-income group but only barely and encountered major problems in staying there. More recently, Russian income has rebounded but primarily by selling raw materials—a strategy that cannot be sustained in the long term. Brazil has hovered in the vicinity of the threshold without breaking through as yet—a good illustration of the middle-income trap. China and India started very definitively from low-income levels. China has passed the 25 percent threshold; India has some way to go.

If the Russian economy continues to have difficulties staying in the high-income category, however marginally, one would expect it to have continuing and mounting problems in maintaining its major power military arsenal, largely inherited from its superpower days. Should Brazil not be able to break out of the middle-income category in the near future, its claims to major power status will be seriously jeopardized. Faltering Chinese growth would deflate or at least slow widespread expectations about China becoming the world's lead economy. Steady progress toward escaping the middle-income trap will be needed by India to at least buttress its own claims to major power status. Economic wealth is not destiny in world politics, but the international system seems to be moving toward development and technological complexity being primary prerequisites for maintaining, if not acquiring, elite status.[24]

Table 2.3 helps clarify this potential problem. At the low-income level, policy needs to be focused on creating a setting in which domestic production can be expanded successfully either through home consumption, exports, or, more likely, some combination. Yet the low wages and related cost competitiveness of low-income economies is unlikely to remain constant. Economic growth implies higher wages and some decline in cost competitiveness. Private and public policy foci need to shift to meeting increased and different kinds of demand at home, as well as to developing new products and markets abroad. The demands for stronger institutions to support these activities shift. For middle-income countries to continue growing, there is a greater emphasis on fostering greater skills and innovation through higher education and qualitative improvements in governance for more-complex societies.

Homi Kharas, in particular, argues that political leadership may be the most critical factor in evading the inability to move beyond the middle-income level.[25] Government needs to encourage economic growth over the multigenerational long term. Ascent in the income trajectory is unlikely to be continuous or extremely rapid. There will be setbacks, slowdowns, and crises, as well as various costs in terms of social disruptions and increased political conflict. All of this requires management, both in the short term and long term. It also requires constructing an institutional context in which continued economic growth can take place.

Table 2.3. Low- and Middle-Income Policy Strategies

Income status	Public and private policy strategies
Low	Expand domestic production capabilities; save and/or borrow to build infrastructure, cities, and education networks; marshal societal resources and deploy effectively; work to avoid the low-income trap
Middle	Encourage and facilitate expanded demand from growing middle class for commodities characterized by higher quality and diversity; develop new processes, products, and markets to expand exports in response to higher wages and declining cost competitiveness; improve institutions for property rights, capital markets, competition; address growing income distribution disparities that might stifle the expansion of economic demand; work to avoid the middle-income trap

Sources: Based on Homi Kharas, "Realizing the Asian Century: Mega-challenges and Risks," in Asia 2050: Realizing the Asian Century, *ed. Harinder S. Kohli, Ashok Sharma, and Anil Sood (New Delhi: Sage, 2011), 52–53.*

The second assumption has to do with the political-military status that may come with increased economic/technological status. If the BRICs substantially improve their economic status, does it necessarily follow that they will also become major powers in international politics? There are three problems here. One is that two of the BRICs (Russia and China) are already considered major powers. Their elite status did not depend on possessing the largest or fastest growing economies in the world economy. Russia has been a major power since at least the early eighteenth century. For a time, it seemed to challenge the U.S. lead during the Cold War before collapsing temporarily and is only now slowly reemerging as an elite state. For a long time, China was sufficiently powerful to remain outside the Western-centric international system but was drawn in eventually and subordinated in the nineteenth century. It was able to throw off its subordination to some extent after World War II and fight the United States to a draw in Korea.

If two of the BRICs are already major powers, the linkage between BRIC status and acquiring great power status is murky. The fact that Germany and Japan, two other states with very successful economies after 1945, have yet to attain great power status makes the connection between economic success and military-political status all the more hazy. Finally, the third problem with this BRIC–great power assumption is that in the past great power status has had to be earned on the battlefield. New great powers did not necessarily have to win or fight major power opponents, although both characteristics would help, but they did have to demonstrate significant military-political capability—with or without an equivalent economic capability foundation. BRIC commentators appear to believe that the rites of passage for great powers have been altered. Perhaps they have, but if they have, it remains unclear to what extent that is the case and/or what new minimal criteria might be requisite.

All of this discussion only means that we need to exercise caution in assuming that BRIC status necessarily means high-income economies operating at the system's technological frontier and/or achieving automatic great power status soon. These things may come in time or they may not. Some of the things may come about while others do not. However, there are some expectations that seem more probable. One is that whatever processes are likely to unfold, it is unlikely that they will unfold without help. By this we mean that economic growth processes are neither autonomous nor sufficient to create great powers. As depicted in figures 2.7 and 2.8, various factors intervene in the translation of capability and status in world politics. Leaders and their strategies make some difference, but so does the state through which each operates. Strong leaders, on occasion, can work miracles with weak states for a while. Yet they cannot be expected to provide sufficient governance on the basis of their charisma and personality alone. There are clear limitations on what can be done without the institutional support of a reasonably well functioning state. Roads and ports do not get built. Students are not educated adequately. Poverty and inequalities foster rebellion and separatism. Ethnic tensions go unmanaged. Rampant corruption erodes faith in the political system. Bureaucratic inertia stifles the prospects for positive changes. Foreign investors look elsewhere for safer bets to make money. Vested interests from older regimes are not defeated politically so that new ways of doing things can at least be attempted.

This chapter has reviewed patterns associated with great power ascents in previous centuries. Theories to account for ascent, successful and otherwise, have been outlined. Still, the precise criteria for attaining great power status remain hazy. Size matters. Technological development certainly helps, just as it may provide expanded motivation for international activities. What is clear from a survey of previous ascents is that strong states are not a prerequisite for achieving elite status in world politics. Yet the absence of this institutional capacity may constitute a major domestic constraint. Continued economic growth and resource mobilization hinge on effective state interventions. Problems with state capacity, therefore, should be expected to hinder the rise of states to great power status. Similarly, once higher status has been achieved, problems with state capacity should be expected to get in the way of operationalizing an elite position in world politics.

But we need something more than the ambiguities of "state capacity" to explore further this issue of state strengths and weaknesses. Moreover, we need something more than the familiar labels of strong, weak, and failed states. Most states fit none of these labels. They fall in between the continuum end points of strong and failed states. Although a large number of states may appear to be relatively weak, they more often reflect mixed bags of moderate strengths and blatant weaknesses. Their capacities are neither omnipotent nor entirely missing. They are instead middling. To elaborate this conceptualization of state capacity, it is necessary to first contemplate what states do. We do this by relying on K. J. Holsti's concept of state strength in the next three chapters, which focus on extraction, violence monopoly, and legitimacy.[26] But we take the argument one step further by also measuring these components of state strength—in order to better identify where specific states fall on the state-capacity continuum.

State Capacity

T·H·R·E·E

Conceptualizing and Measuring State Strength

We are relatively familiar with the minimum expectations for armed forces, economic/technological, and demographic requirements for major power status.[1] State strength has received far less attention in this respect. In other respects, we have developed an expansive literature on strong, weak, and failed states. Yet many, if not most, states are something in between the strong and weak end points of the continuum, and we do not know much about them or their respective capacities. At the same time, there are also substantial disagreements about which states are strong and which ones are weak. One of the problems here is that some states are essentially weak in some ways but have constructed strong coercive apparatuses. Are police states full-fledged strong states or something less? What about states with ample resources for state activities that are contingent on the exploitation of natural resources? Are they strong or weak, or something in between? Then there are states that have some potential for escaping the weak-state trap. The BRICs, for instance, are experiencing rapid economic growth, their bureaucratic infrastructures are becoming more complex, and the tasks taken on by states are requiring the expansion of state activities. Must state development be stymied by the absence of total warfare? Or is it possible that new dynamics for creating strong states will emerge in the twenty-first century?

For all of these reasons, we need to learn more about state-making in the "in between" of the conceptual continuum of strong versus weak/failed states. India, we will argue, is an excellent candidate for study because in many respects its current state falls more or less in the middle if we array a large number of states on relatively precise operationalizations of strong/weak states. It is not a police state, but it is definitely one of the leading BRICs. Moreover, it has some potential for becoming a great power in the international system, and it is already predominant in the South Asian region. Presumably, the exercise of greater power in world politics will require further state development. How likely is it in the Indian case? For that matter, how much has postindependent Indian state development progressed to date? What are its prospects for further state development?

To pursue the question of Indian state-building further requires an immediate turn to greater precision in what is meant by state strength. Too often, arguments conflate what states are able to achieve with coercive power with the power of the organization that at least nominally supervises the achievements. But military strength should not be confused with organizational strength. It is possible to have a great deal of one without much of the other. In this context, we subscribe to K. J. Holsti's definition of state strength: "It is ... the capacity of the state to command loyalty—the right to rule—to extract the resources necessary to rule and provide services, to maintain that essential element of sovereignty, a monopoly over the legitimate use of force within defined territorial limits, and to operate within the context of a consensus-based political community."[2]

Holsti's definition confuses the issue just a bit by arranging the order of the definition's components in the way that he does. "Command loyalty," "the right to rule," and "operate within the context of a consensus-based political community" all refer to legitimacy. Do citizens think that their governments possess authority—that is, are they the appropriate political decision-makers for their society, and just how appropriate are they? "To extract the resources necessary to rule and provide services" is customarily abbreviated as resource-extraction capability and is invariably a standard component in state strength assessments. Finally, "to maintain that essential element of sovereignty, a monopoly over the legitimate use of force within defined territorial limits" is another frequently invoked component of state strength. Does the state control the use of force, or must it contend with private armies and regional warlords that operate without state sanction?

Although Holsti views the political consensus about the state's authority to be the most important feature, the components are interactive. Resource extraction is critical for state functioning at home and abroad. If taxes cannot be raised, armed forces cannot be maintained to provide security. Nor can other governmental services be provided. Implicit in the extraction-services exchange is that it works best when it is viewed as an exchange, with citizens voluntarily surrendering an appropriate amount of resources to pay for desired services. If the mass of the population view themselves as oppressed subjects, not citizens or full-fledged members of the community, the resource surrendering is apt to be less voluntary. Something similar occurs if the state demands too many resources or provides too few services. States must also monopolize the legitimate use of force within the state's boundaries. States that cannot guarantee some minimal level of internal security are unlikely to be viewed as worthy recipients of either taxes or legitimacy.

If these criteria are the main ingredients for state strength, we need to develop indexes encompassing measures of (1) resource extraction, (2) legitimacy, and (3) armed-force, or violence, monopoly.

Still, there is one element that is missing. It is possible for governments to stay in power, monopolize armed force, and extract resources without a great deal of legitimacy. Taylor refers to this as the police state problem. Most arguments about state strength focus on what Western observers regard as good governance (for example, legitimacy) but relatively strong states can be constructed on the basis of brute force. Taylor's table 3.1 differentiates among "civil" states, which emphasize the qualitative dimension of governance; "police" states, which survive by constructing regimes that stress coercive capacity to demand compliance; and "weak" states, which do poorly in both spheres. Taylor's criticism of the qualitative bias of most state strength seems well taken, but all it means is that we need to expand the resource-extraction/state-capacity dimension to include coercive extraction.

Table 3.1. Taylor's State Capacity and Quality

	State quality	
State capacity	Low	High
High	Police states	Civil states
Low	Weak states	

Source: Based on Brian D. Taylor, State Building in Putin's Russia: Policing and Coercion after Communism *(Cambridge: Cambridge University Press, 2011), 20.*

Measurement

Measuring anything in politics, let alone state strength, is never straightforward. However, others have tried their hands at it and we can learn something from their efforts. By and large, state strength measurements usually arise in analyses of civil war and in studies discussing failed states. Fortunately, for our purposes, Hendrix has already reviewed the measurement of "state capacity" in the civil-war literature.[3] Table 3.2 summarizes what he found. Multiple indicators have been used to capture three different emphases on state capacity or strength: military, bureaucratic/administrative, and political institution quality and coherence.

Military capacity refers to the standard Weberian focus on the state's monopoly of the use of legitimate force within the state's boundaries. As noted in table 3.2, this dimension has been operationalized most often in terms of the size of the state's military—expressed either in terms of personnel or expenditures. Bureaucratic/administrative capacity stresses the ability of the state to monitor problems and to address them in a way that is considered to be fair and unbiased. This type of capacity/strength has been measured in a variety of ways, ranging from surveys of bureaucratic quality to tax extraction capabilities. Hendrix's third capacity type is political institution quality and coherence. Here, the measurement emphasis has usually been placed on assuming that regimes that are neither consolidated autocracies nor democracies are likely to be less coherent and to be characterized by poor-quality institutions.

Hendrix's three types of state capacity are not identical to Holsti's three conceptual emphases (legitimacy, resource extraction, violence monopoly), but they clearly overlap, most especially in terms of the foci on resource extraction and violence monopoly. One could certainly argue that there should be a close relationship between political institution quality and coherence and legitimacy as well. But this degree of overlap, while certainly welcome, is not the reason for interjecting a summary of Hendrix's review at this juncture. Rather, the point of Hendrix's review was to draw some conclusions about the "state of the measurement art." At the risk of oversimplifying, Hendrix concludes three things: (1) State capacity is a multivariate concept and should be measured with some combination of multiple indicators; (2) in addition to avoiding indicators that are influenced by ongoing conflict, analysts should avoid indicators that also capture processes other than state capacity; and (3) in this context, the best foci are those associated with bureaucratic quality and tax extraction.

What this means is that we should be reluctant to substitute GDP per capita for violence monopoly or oil exports for bureaucratic quality. Arguments can be made that link these indicators to the concepts, but they involve rather indirect efforts to capture what state strength is all about and will definitely introduce various types of error. Some poor states are able to control violence while some rich states have problems doing so. Resource curses may or may not retard state development, but that is an analytical question that should proceed separately. There is no reason to make very strong measurement assumptions if we can avoid them with more direct and more narrowly focused indicators. As for which emphases are most desirable, that depends on the concepts being measured. Hendrix did not start with a conceptual definition of state capacity. His task was to survey the different ways analysts had attempted to measure concepts more or less related to state capacity. Our task is different. We start with the Holsti definition and attempt to find indicators that fit what he is talking about. In that respect, we can hardly throw out the idea of violence monopoly. We can try, though, to avoid using indicators that have serious interpretation problems.[4]

Table 3.2. Measures of State Capacity in the Civil-Conflict Context

Concept	Indicators	Examples
Military capacity	Military personnel per capita; military spending; GDP per capita	Mason and Fett (1996), Balch-Lindsay and Enterline (2000), Fearon and Laitin (2003), DeRouen and Sobek (2004), Walter (2006), Balch-Lindsay, Enterline, and Joyce (2008), Buhaug (2010)
Bureaucratic/administrative capacity	1. Survey measures of bureaucratic quality 2. Risk of expropriation 3. Export profiles 4. Revenue extraction 5. Relative political capacity	DeRouen and Sobek (2004), Fearon (2005), Collier and Hoeffler (2004), Humphreys (2005), Buhaug (2010), Thies (2004, 2005, 2007, 2010), Kugler and Arbetman (1997), Buhaug (2010)
Political institution quality and coherence	Anocracy, institutional consolidation, democracy	Hegre et al. (2001), Fearon and Laitin (2003), DeRouen and Sobek (2004), Gates et al. (2006), Vreeland (2008), Marshall and Jaggers (2009)

Note: The examples mentioned are Dylan Balch-Lindsay and Andrew J. Enterline, "Killing Time: The World Politics of Civil War Duration, 1820–1992," *International Studies Quarterly* 44, no. 4 (2000): 615–642; Dylan Balch-Lindsay, Andrew J. Enterline, and Kyle A. Joyce, "Third-Party Intervention and the Civil War Process," *Journal of Peace Research* 45, no. 3 (2008): 345–363; Halvard Buhaug, "Dude: Where's My Conflict? LSG, Relative Strength, and the Location of Civil War," *Conflict Management and Peace Science* 27, no. 2 (2010): 107–128; Paul Collier and Anke Hoeffler, "Greed and Grievance in Civil War," *Oxford Economic Papers* 56 (2004): 563–595; Karl R. DeRouen and David Sobek, "The Dynamics of Civil War Duration and Outcome," *Journal of Peace Research* 41, no. 3 (2004): 303–320; James D. Fearon, "Primary Commodity Exports and Civil War," *Journal of Conflict Resolution* 49, no. 4 (2005): 483–507; James D. Fearon and David D. Laitin, "Ethnicity, Insurgency, and Civil War," *American Political Science Review* 97, no. 1 (2003): 75–90; Scott Gates, Havard Hegre, Mark P. Jones, and Havard Strand, "Institutional Inconsistency and Political Instability: Polity Duration, 1800–2000," *American Journal of Political Science* 50, no. 4 (2006): 893–908; Havard Hegre, Tanja Ellingsen, Scott Gates, and Nils Petter Gleditsch, "Toward a Democratic Civil Peace? Democracy, Political Change, and Civil War, 1816–1992," *American Political Science Review* 95, no. 1 (2001): 33–48; Macartan Humphreys, "Natural Resources, Conflict, and Conflict Resolution," *Journal of Conflict Resolution* 49, no. 4 (2005): 508–537; Jacek Kugler and Marina Arbetman, "Relative Political Capacity: Political Extraction and Political Research," in *Political Capacity and Economic Behavior*, ed. Marina Arbetman and Jacek Kugler (Boulder, CO: Westview, 1997); Monty J. Marshall and Keith Jaggers, *Polity IV Project: Political Regime Characteristics and Transitions, 1800–2008* (College Park, MD: University of Maryland, 2009), at http://www.cidcm.umd.edu/inscr/polity/index.htm; T. David Mason and Patrick Fett, "How Civil Wars End: A Rational Choice Approach," *Journal of Conflict Resolution* 40, no. 4 (1996): 546–568; Cameron G. Thies, "State Building: A Study of Post-Colonial Developing Country Extractive Efforts, 1975–2000," *International Studies Quarterly* 48, no. 1 (2004): 53–72; Cameron G. Thies, "War, Rivalry, and State Building in Latin America," *American Journal of Political Science* 49, no. 3 (2005): 451–465; Cameron G. Thies, "The Political Economy of State Building in sub-Saharan Africa," *Journal of Politics* 69, no. 3 (2007): 716–731; Cameron G. Thies, "Of Rulers, Rebels, and Revenue: State Capacity, Civil War Onset, and Primary Commodities," *Journal of Peace Research* 47, no. 3 (2010): 321–332; James R. Vreeland, "The Effect of Political Regime on Civil War: Unpacking Anocracy," *Journal of Conflict Resolution* 52, no. 3 (2008): 401–425; Barbara F. Walter, "Building Reputation: Why Governments Fight Some Separatists but Not Others," *American Journal of Political Science* 50, no. 2 (2006): 313–330.

Source: Based on the discussion in Cullen S. Hendrix, "Measuring State Capacity: Theoretical and Empirical Implications for the Study of Civil Conflict," *Journal of Peace Research* 47, no. 3 (2010): 273–285.

RESOURCE EXTRACTION

Appropriate data exist, or can be assembled, for each of the three main Holsti foci (as specified later in table 3.5). For resource extraction, there are two emphases. The classical approach to capturing resource extraction is to measure government revenues as a proportion of gross domestic product. It is possible to take this approach one step further and focus specifically on revenue garnered by income tax collection. Different types of governments have various sources of revenues, and it is better to avoid rewarding states that have "easy" access to, say, natural resources that can be taxed or sold. Voluntary participation in income tax collection probably says something about governmental legitimacy as well, but the primary emphasis is placed on the proportional amount of resources that the state can raise through this avenue. Weaker states generally are restricted in the extent to which they can extract revenue resources directly from their population.

To index the coercive side of state extractive capability, Levitsky and Way's scale (see table 3.3), designed just for this purpose, can be pressed into service. The scale has three principal foci: internal security apparatus, single party, and state control of the economy. The stronger and more cohesive the domestic security forces and ruling party, the higher a state falls on the coercive-capacity scale. If the state also controls the economy, it moves even higher on the scale.

LEGITIMACY

There appear to be several ways to gauge legitimacy. One remarkable source of information on this component is provided by the World Bank's annual assessment of governance, in which a large number of indicators, many of them subjective and based on surveys, commercial business information services, and NGO/public-sector rankings, are assembled into four categories of interest:

> Voice and accountability—extent of popular participation in politics and the degree of various related freedoms;
>
> Government effectiveness—quality and independence of bureaucratic services;

Rule of law—public confidence in state institutions proceeding fairly;

Control of corruption—suppression of the use of government positions for private gain.

Table 3.4 provides a longer specification of what exactly the indexes encompass.[5]

Our expectation is that individuals are more likely to identify with their state and accept its authority to the extent that the state is perceived to be effective, accountable, and fair. There is an underlying exchange dynamic at work. States that work and that are responsive (the two dimensions do not necessarily work hand in glove) are more likely to be appreciated by the public and accepted as appropriate institutions. Nonresponsive and/or ineffective institutions tend to alienate individuals who will distance themselves as much as possible from nonperforming state institutions.[6]

In some respects, the four indicators are redundant in the sense that states tend to score highly or not on all four measures. But since we have information on all four, there is little incentive to privilege one or two over the others. Our legitimacy score will be based on the mean score generated by aggregating all four annual scores. Higher scores reflect governments that provide services effectively and fairly; low scores suggest the reverse.

VIOLENCE MONOPOLY

As in the case of the other components, measuring the extent of the state's monopoly on armed force might be accomplished in various ways. However, there is a fifth World Bank indicator that focuses on perceptions about the likelihood that a government will be destabilized or overthrown by domestic violence. To create this index, the World Bank authors combine information on the frequency of armed conflict, political killings, violent demonstrations, torture, disappearances, and terrorism. While it is not perfect, because it does not distinguish between governmental and nongovernmental sources of violence, it would seem to capture subjective assessments of not so much the stability of

Table 3.3. Levitsky and Way Measuring State Coercive Capacity

State Coercive Capacity Scope

High: Large, well-trained, and well-equipped internal security apparatus with an effective presence across the national territory. Existence of specialized intelligence or internal security agencies with demonstrated capacity to penetrate civil society and monitor and repress opposition activities at the village and/or neighborhood level across the country.

Medium: Criteria for high scope are not met, but security forces maintain a minimally effective presence across virtually the entire national territory. No evidence of severe deficits of funding, equipment, and training.

Low: Unusually small/underdeveloped security apparatus. Evidence of a lack of minimally effective state presence in significant parts of the national territory or severe deficits of funding, equipment, and training.

State Coercive Capacity Cohesion

High: Evidence of nonmaterial sources of cohesion, including: (a) recent history of military conflict (leading security officials must be drawn from the generation that participated in the conflict), including large-scale external war (without defeat), or intense and enduring military competition or threat, or successful revolutionary or anticolonial struggle; or (b) pervasive ethnic ties between incumbent party and security forces, in a society that is deeply divided along those ethnic lines; or (c) shared ideology in a context in which this ideological cleavage is dominant; or (d) evidence of consistent ability to use high-intensity coercion in recent past.

Medium: No evidence of nonmaterial sources of cohesion and no evidence of previous insubordination, recent defeat in military conflict, or significant wage arrears to security officials.

Low: (a) No evidence of nonmaterial sources of cohesion and evidence from the decade prior to the period under analysis of significant insubordination by state officials, including attempted coups, open rebellion, large-scale desertion, and refusal to carry out major executive orders; or (b) recent decisive defeat in a major military conflict; or (c) persistent and substantial wage arrears to security officials.

Party Strength Scope

High: Mass organization that penetrates virtually all population centers down to village and neighborhood level and/or civil society and/or workplace. Evidence of significant grassroots activity—during and between elections—across the national territory.

(*continued*)

Medium: Party does not meet the criteria for high scope but possesses a national organization that penetrates most population centers and is capable of carrying out election campaigns and fielding candidates across the national territory.

Low: No party or little or no party organization outside of the capital/major urban centers.

Party Strength Cohesion

High: (a) Single governing party that achieved power via violent conflict, including revolution or national liberation struggle in which much of the current leadership participated; or (b) established single party (has participated in at least two national multiparty elections) with evidence of nonmaterial source of cohesion, including shared ideology in a context in which this ideological cleavage is dominant, and shared ethnicity in a context in which ethnic cleavage is dominant.

Medium: (a) Established single party (has participated in at least two national elections) that does not meet the criteria for high cohesion; or (b) new party (has participated in fewer than two national elections) with evidence of shared ideology or ethnicity in a context in which that ideological or ethnic cleavage is predominant.

Low: (a) Incumbent rules with no party; or (b) incumbent rules without a single party but is supported by multiple and competing parties; or (c) new party (has participated in fewer than two national multiparty elections) and for which there is no evidence of nonmaterial sources of cohesion.

Discretionary State Control of the Economy

1. State-controlled mineral sector accounts for more than 50 percent of export revenue or
2. centrally planned economy that does not undergo large-scale privatization.

Scores: If one of the discretionary criteria for state control of the economy are satisfied, the state coercive-capacity score is increased by one full level. Otherwise, scores for scope and cohesion (low = 0, medium = 1, high = 2) are summed up into a single composite score in which 6–8 is high, 5 is medium high, 4 is medium, 3 is medium low, 0–2 is low. To make these scores more compatible with the other scores, each composite score is multiplied by 10.

Source: Steven Levitsky and Lucan A. Way, Competitive Authoritarianism: Hybrid Regimes After the Cold War *(Cambridge: Cambridge University Press, 2010), 376–378.*

Table 3.4. World Bank Governance Indicators

Indicator	Description
Voice and accountability	Perceptions of the extent to which a country's citizens are able to participate in selecting their government, as well as freedom of expression, freedom of association, and a free media
Government effectiveness	Perceptions of the quality of public services, the quality of the civil service and the degree of its independence from political pressures, the quality of policy formulation and implementation, and the credibility of the government's commitment to such policies
Rule of law	Perceptions of the extent to which agents have confidence in and abide by the rule of society, and in particular the quality of contract enforcement, property rights, the police, and the courts, as well as the likelihood of crime and violence
Control of corruption	Perceptions of the extent to which public power is exercised for private gain, including both petty and grand forms of corruption, as well as "capture" of the state by elites and private interests

Source: World Bank, Worldwide Governance Indicators, at http://info.worldbank.org/governance/wgi/index.aspx#home.

the government per se but, rather, political and societal stability in general. Presumably, the more a state monopolizes armed force, the less likely it is that members of the population will oppose the state with violence. Hence, the more violent unrest is, the less evident is the state's monopoly of armed force.[7]

State Strength

These four indicators—one each for fiscal capacity, internal coercive capacity, legitimacy, and monopoly of violence—can be summed up to create one index of state strength, presented conceptually in table 3.5.

Table 3.5. Components and Measures of State Strength

Concept	Rationale	Measure
State fiscal capacity	Some minimal level of resource extraction is necessary for state survival. Higher levels of state activity require higher levels of state fiscal capacity.	Income tax revenue as a proportion of gross domestic product
State coercive capacity	States can survive and function on the basis of brute force and centralized monitoring, decision-making, and enforcement.	Levitsky and Way coercive-capacity scale
Legitimacy	Populations that perceive that they possess "voice" and that their governments are "accountable" and also "effective" are more likely to identify with, and evaluate positively, their states than are populations that feel that they lack voice and that their governments are not accountable or effective.	World Bank subjective indicators on "voice and accountability," "effectiveness," "rule of law," and "control of corruption"
Armed force monopoly	Governments that cannot maintain some level of internal control over weapons and insecurity are weaker, and are perceived to be weaker, than governments that can.	World Bank subjective indicator on "political stability," which actually focuses on and measures the individual sense of security and the level of conflict in the society that might destabilize government

However, several problems are encountered when aggregating these types of scores. One is that data on state strength indicators are especially subject to missing data and slow reporting. A second problem concerns interpreting extraction scores, since these percentages reflect different kinds of governmental structure (most importantly whether governments subordinate to the central government also collect taxes) and different state priorities (namely, welfare commitments). Extraction scores are also dependent on economic size. Ten percent of trillions is a bit different than 20 percent of a few billion. Finally, relying on the World Bank governance data restricts empirical analyses to the post-1995 era. There are other indicators that can be employed for legitimacy and violence monopoly that are less restrictive in terms of time coverage, and scholars with foci in mind that go beyond the past twenty years or so may wish to substitute other indicators. Therefore, there are good reasons for not aggregating to create a single score. More information can be conveyed, in any event, by treating the three categories separately.[8] Still, there are also some advantages to producing a single score for state strength. If nothing else, it simplifies comparison across a list of countries. We restrict this examination primarily to the four main BRICs, as before. To further assist the interpretation, however, information on three non-BRIC, major powers (France, the United Kingdom, and the United States) is presented as well.

BRICs, Other States, and Comparative State Strength

Table 3.6 lists income tax revenue as a proportion of GDP for the four BRICs and focuses on the period for which the World Bank governance and tax revenue data are available (1996–2012). Earlier data on Russia are missing, but both Brazil and China have expanded their extractive capability. China has roughly doubled its income tax capability. India's capability has remained quite stationary in this period. Moreover, the fiscal extraction capability of India and China lags behind those of Brazil and Russia. For comparative reference, France's percentage extraction rate in the same time period hovered around 22 percent and Britain's percentage was around 27 percent. Yet, the U.S. ratio resembles the Indian figures, averaging about 10 percent in this period. As we have

Table 3.6. Tax Revenues as Percentage of GDP

	Brazil	Russia	India	China	France	U.K.	U.S.A.
1996			9.3	4.7	19.9	26.3	
1998	12.2		8.2	5.7	22.7	27.8	
2000	14		9	6.8	23.2	28.4	
2002	15.8	13.6	8.8	8.5	22.5	27.1	10.4
2003	15.4	13.3	9.2	8.5	22.1	26.5	9.8
2004	15.9	13.2	9.4	8.9	22.3	26.6	10
2005	16.7	16.6	9.9	8.7	22.4	27.2	11.2
2006	16.5	16.6	11	9.2	22.5	28	11.9
2007	16.8	16.6	11.9	9.9	21.9	27.6	11.9
2008	16.7	15.8	10.8	10.3	21.7	28.8	10.3
2009	15.6	13	9.7	10.5	19.8	26	8.5
2010	15.3	13.4	9.5	10.5	21.3	26.7	9.3
2011	15.7	15	10.4		21.3	27	9.7
2012	14.4	15.1	10.8		21.4	25.3	10.2

Source: World Bank, Data, Tax Revenue, at http://data.worldbank.org/indicator/GC.TAX.TOTL.GD.ZS.

noted, the tax revenue ratio can be tricky to interpret, given much different types and sizes of economies as well as different kinds of targets to tax.

Unlike the other indicators, Levitsky and Way's scale information on coercive capability is not archived and must be developed on a case-by-case approach. Table 3.7 lists an application of the scale to the seven states in which we are most interested, again for the 1996–2010 period. The first four items are coded low, medium, or high based on the criteria reported in table 3.3; the fifth item is coded present or absent. Only China receives the maximum number of points. Most of the other states score about the same, with the exception of Russia, which is slightly higher on the scale, reflecting the direction of reforms instituted under the first Putin regime.

There is much more variation in the legitimacy summation scores reported in table 3.8. Among the BRICs, Brazil and India rank in the

Table 3.7. Assessing the Sample on the Levitsky and Way Authoritarian Scale (1996–2012)

	India	China	Russia	Brazil	U.K.	France	U.S.A.
State capacity scope	M (1)	H (2)	H (2)	M (1)	M (1)	M (1)	M (1)
State capacity cohesion	M (1)	H (2)	M (1)	M (1)	M (1)	M (1)	M (1)
Party strength scope	M (1)	H (2)	M (1)	M (1)	M (1)	M (1)	M (1)
Party strength cohesion	L (0)	H (2)	L (0)	L (0)	L (0)	L (0)	L (L)
State control of economy, present (yes) or absent (no)	No	Yes	No	No	No	No	No
Total score	30	80	40	30	30	30	30

middle of the full array of states (averaging low to middle 50s). Their scores are roughly similar across the four subindicators (not shown on the table), although Brazil improves in all four subindexes while India does somewhat less well in accountability, rule of law, and corruption over time. China scores lower than Brazil and India in most of the four subindicators, especially on the voice and accountability dimension. Its overall score stays about the same over time largely due to increasing perceptions of corruption and declining accountability being matched by improvements in governmental effectiveness and rule of law. In contrast, Russia scores least well in terms of the quality of government, and its scores are also similar across all four subindicators—although it does better in government effectiveness than it does in the other indicators. France, the United Kingdom, and the United States are in a different legitimacy bracket altogether, with scores ranging between 85.9 and 94. Their scores are also consistently the same across all four subindicators.

Table 3.8. Legitimacy Summation Scores for
BRICs and Three Western Major Powers

	Brazil	Russia	India	China	France	U.K.	U.S.A.
1996	50.7	28.2	53.8	34.6	89	93.5	91.8
1998	52.2	23	53.8	37.1	89.5	93.8	92.3
2000	53.2	22.6	53.3	38.1	88.9	93.8	92.5
2002	55.8	31.9	49.7	33.6	85.9	93.3	92.5
2003	55.4	29.7	53	36.9	89.4	93.8	92
2004	54.3	29.6	53.2	35.1	91.6	94	91.3
2005	51.3	27.5	54.2	32.5	91.9	93.5	91
2006	52.2	24.7	54	34.3	91.3	94	88.8
2007	53	24.1	53.2	35.3	90.6	93	89.5
2008	54.4	24.4	53.2	36.1	91.1	92.5	90.3
2009	56	25.4	51.9	36.7	90.4	92	88
2010	59.1	25.5	51.4	35.4	89.5	92.2	88.5
2011	58	27.4	50.1	35.9	88.7	92.2	87.9
2012	54.8	25.1	48.3	34.7	89.3	92.4	89.4

By and large, the four BRIC states do less well on the state monopoly of armed force indicator (violence ratings) than they do on governmental quality issues. India scores least well, followed by Russia, China, and Brazil—in that order. But the BRIC scores, at least, are still higher than those associated with the weakest states in the system (not shown on the table), which tend to score at the very bottom of the scale on this dimension.[9] Roughly speaking, and as demonstrated in table 3.9, the BRIC scores average about half the rankings achieved by France, the United Kingdom, and the United States. Note, however, that the U.K. and the U.S. rankings have deteriorated in the last decade or so.[10] Even so, they remain considerably higher than the BRIC scores.

To be as transparent as possible, table 3.10 shows one way to aggregate the separate scores into a single score for 2012 data. First the initial scores are arrayed in the left-hand part of the table. These initial scores are then translated into ordinal scores based on the following scales: for

Table 3.9. World Bank Violence Ratings

	Brazil	Russia	India	China	France	U.K.	U.S.A.
1996	31	16	15	33	78	77	78
1998	30	23	21	38	74	74	78
2000	53	24	25	36	74	79	87
2002	42	30	19	40	80	73	57
2003	48	23	17	32	62	63	55
2004	42	17	24	39	63	61	51
2005	44	20	26	35	63	59	49
2006	42	23	21	32	64	67	60
2007	37	23	19	30	65	66	56
2008	38	25	18	31	67	63	65
2009	54	22	13	30	66	55	59
2010	50	19	11	24	70	61	57
2011	42	18	11	28	65	59	66
2012	48	21	12	28	64	60	68

Table 3.10. Aggregated State Strength or Capacity Scores for 2012

	Extract.	Auth.	Legit.	Viol.	Extract.	Auth.	Legit.	Viol.	Agg. Score
Brazil	14.4	30	54.8	48	M	L	M	M	6/3=2
Russia	15.1	40	25.1	21	M	M	L	L	4/3=1.33
India	10.8	30	48.3	12	M	L	M	L	5/3=1.67
China	10.5	80	34.7	28	M+1	H	M	L	6/3=2
France	21.4	30	89.3	64	H	L	H	M	8/3=2.67
U.K.	25.3	30	92.4	60	H	L	H	M	8/3=2.67
U.S.A.	10.2	30	89.4	68	M	L	H	H	8/3=2.67

Note: China's extraction score is based on 2010 data and is augmented by 1 point on the extraction scale for being a highly authoritarian state.

tax collection, less than 10 percent is considered low, 10–19.9 percent medium, and 20 percent or higher is counted as high; for the other scores, 33.3 percent or less is low, 33.4–66.7 percent is medium, and 66.8 percent or higher is treated as a high score. Additionally, we have to do something with the authoritarian score. It does not make sense to penalize a country for not being sufficiently authoritarian, which would occur if we counted the Levitsky and Way score the same way we do legitimacy or violence monopoly. What we were trying to do was to acknowledge that more-authoritarian states could extract various things from their population that less-authoritarian states could not. Consequently, our inclination is to "reward" highly authoritarian states with an extra point in the extraction column. States receiving a less-than-high score on authoritarianism earn no extra points. For instance, China in table 3.10 is scored as a medium on the extraction indicator but high on the authoritarian index. Thus, China is considered a high extractor when we aggregate the three extraction, legitimacy, and violence monopoly scores.

In general, then, different BRICs do better on some of the components than they do on others. But considering the full array of states, the established major powers tend to score highest on most of the indicators. Weak states score consistently across the board at the very bottom. The BRICs tend to fall in between. India is above Russia, which is at the bottom of table 3.10's aggregate scores, although there are quite a few states not shown that score less well, including Somalia and Afghanistan, which tend to hover at the very bottom of the state strength index. Of the BRICs, Brazil and China do best, on the state strength score, albeit for different reasons.

Another way of examining India's comparative position is to contrast it with other states in South Asia and selected states elsewhere. Table 3.11 lists 2010 state strength scores for five South Asian countries and two other states of interest. India's state strength score is superior to Afghanistan, Pakistan, and Bangladesh, but similar to Egypt's and Sri Lanka's aggregate score. Turkey's state strength score, in turn, is higher than the other six states. This outcome suggests a tripartite division of states in the world. At the bottom of the scale, there are a number of weak

Table 3.11. Selected State Strength Scores for 2010

	Extraction	Legitimacy	Violence	Agg. Score
Afghanistan	Low	Low	Low	1
Bangladesh	Low	Low	Low	1
Egypt	Medium	Medium	Low	1.67
India	Medium	Medium	Low	1.67
Pakistan	Medium	Low	Low	1.33
Sri Lanka	Medium	Medium	Low	1.67
Turkey	High	Medium	Low	2

Note: None of these states received a sufficiently high score on authoritarianism to justify modifying the extraction score.

and failed states. Exactly where the threshold is for these weaker states is difficult to establish with any sense of precision. We might tentatively view state strength scores up to 1.33 as the upper limit for distinguishing weak from moderately strong (medium) states. At the other end of the scale are strong states scoring 2.5 or better. In between 1.33 and 2.5 are a number of moderately strong states. Many of these states probably have some potential for improving on their state strength, but there may be some restrictions on how high they can expect to reach in the immediate future and whether they can exceed the threshold for the next highest capacity category.

Most, if not all, of the scores depicted in tables 3.10 and 3.11 stayed about the same between 1996 and 2012. In most cases, that is about what we should expect—a fair amount of inertia in state strength. In a few cases, a state might plunge abruptly into a lower category. Russia at the end of the Cold War comes to mind. Somalia in the late 1980s/early 1990s is another case. Once they descend, it may be difficult to climb back out of the weaker category, as has been demonstrated by the Somalia case, which may eventually reemerge as several smaller states with variable strengths. Russia, on the other hand, managed to reemerge to a moderate level fairly quickly thanks to its resource wealth. At the same time, the dependence on the resource wealth among other things, probably limits, paradoxically, the ability of Russia to score high on the state strength index.

India is also something of an exception to the generalization that state-capacity scores tend to remain about the same. It improved on tax extraction, moving from 9.1 percent in 1996 to 10.8 percent in 2012. Its percentile scores on the legitimacy components (1996–2013) tended to decline somewhat (governmental effectiveness: 53.7 to 47.4, rule of law 64.3 to 52.6, control of corruption 40 to 35.9, while voice and effectiveness moved in the opposite direction from 62 to 66). Its violence monopoly percentile ranking also deteriorated (19.2 to 12.3) in the same time period. However, if we stick to the ordinal scoring, the above movements actually translate to some improvement, largely due to the improvement in tax extraction (from high at the low end of the continuum to marginally medium). The point is more one of directional tendency. As a candidate for major power status, we might expect India to be at least slowly improving its state strength. Intervally, there is some deterioration; ordinally, there is some improvement. Perhaps the best characterization of the Indian state over the past two decades is that in all of the index categories, India declined slightly or stayed about the same over the past two decades. The metaphor that comes most readily to a mind is a swimmer treading in deep water. The Indian state, faced with quite major problems, is managing to keep its head above water, but only barely. Higher waves in the future, to continue the metaphor, might make it extremely difficult to stay afloat.

At the same time, one encouraging aspect of this problem is that state-capacity scores tend to correspond to data on gross domestic product per capita, as shown in table 3.12. The relationship is not perfect, but it is highly linear. More affluent states are associated with stronger states. Strong states, of course, have long histories. It has been argued that strong states owe some respectable proportion of their strength to surviving the world wars of the twentieth century. War makes states, but it is not the only influence on enhancing state strength. Affluence matters as well. States have become more affluent in the contemporary era due largely to industrialization. As we have seen in chapter 2, early industrialization encouraged the expansion of the states that became major powers in the late nineteenth to early twentieth centuries

Table 3.12. Gross Domestic Product
per Capita and State Capacity

State	GDP per capita	State capacity score
Afghanistan	415.0	1
Bangladesh	750.4	1
Pakistan	818.9	1.33
India	1,262.6	1.67
Egypt	1,575.9	1.67
Sri Lanka	2,135.7	1.67
China	3,865.9	2
Brazil	5,900.5	2
Russia	6,843.9	2
Turkey	8,871.9	2
France	35,669.6	2.67
United Kingdom	40,967.7	2.67
United States	46,405.3	2.67

Note: GDP per capita for 2012 values expressed in 2005 U.S. dollars and taken from the World Bank data bank.

as well. Thus, there cannot be any guarantee that industrialization will continue or that continued industrialization will ensure corresponding improvements in state strength. But industrialization does appear to provide more resources and incentive to improve state strength. It may work that way for the states currently possessing an intermediate position in state strength—neither weak/failed nor strong.[11]

Be that as it may, we need to look more closely at the extraction, legitimacy, and violence components of our (and Holsti's) state strength conceptualization. In the next two chapters, we devote more attention to the two primary questions: (1) How have earlier major powers fared on these dimensions early on in their ascents to elite status in world politics? and (2) How has India fared on these dimensions over time? Is its state doing better. worse, or about the same?

F·O·U·R

Extraction and Legitimacy

In this chapter and the one that follows it, our intention is to look more closely at the three Holsti subconcepts of state capacity: extraction, legitimacy, and violence monopoly. Extraction is about the state's ability to acquire the resources it needs to carry out its designated tasks. Whereas extraction tends to focus on material resources, legitimacy is an attitudinal resource for (or against) the state. Does the population regard the state as an appropriate set of institutions for resolving political problems? The more legitimacy a state possesses, presumably, the easier it is to call on its population for support. If the state must allocate all or most of its resources to simply staying in power by brute force, there is also less left to allocate to other problems. Ample attitudinal support therefore reduces the costs of state maintenance.

Finally, violence monopoly refers to whether the state is capable of establishing an order in which its claim to be the ultimate and principal employer of coercion goes largely unchallenged. The more often states are challenged, and the more intense the nature of the challengers, the less likely the state is to survive as the central institution of a political system.

There is no natural order to or hierarchy among these three components of state capacity. We choose to discuss extraction and legitimacy comparatively in this chapter because they are both eliciting something from a state's population. Violence monopoly is examined in chapter 5. But first we need to consider how strong states emerge in the first place. War is a critical but not the only possible stimulus.

Underlying our interest in the Indian state are two fundamental puzzles about state-making, which we equate with expanding state capacity. One is a legacy left by the late Charles Tilly's well-known argument that states made war and war made states.[1] Tilly, of course, was not the first to make this argument, but he can certainly be given credit for popularizing the war emphasis interpretation. The puzzle, though, is that the argument works best for European and North American state-making experiences prior to 1945. Post-1945 wars in the third world do not seem to have the same type of impact. Either the argument is wrong, it needs greater specification, or something has basically changed. Our answer is a combination of all three. It is not war per se that makes strong states. Rather, it was the half millennium of an upward spiral in war and state-making, beginning in the early modern European era, that created strong states among the survivors of the process. States that did not participate in this 1494–1945 process can still engage in warfare (and do on occasion), but the war impacts are much different and are less likely to contribute to state-making. India is an excellent example of this phenomenon.

Early modern Europe was a highly competitive region in which defeat in war could mean the loss of independence. Success in war usually meant an expansion of the agrarian home base. The victor could absorb the loser in a lethal game in which control of more territory and people meant more relative power in the European region, as long as each surviving state could keep up with the gains of its nearby competitors. Boundaries remained flexible and subject to force, negotiation, and inheritance. Early modern Europe also enjoyed a fair amount of autonomy. European states intervened in other regions, but non-European states did not have the power to intervene in Europe until U.S. intervention in and throughout the twentieth century.

In these circumstances, warfare was nearly continuous somewhere in the European region (and increasingly outside of it as well, as European states sought extraregional resources for its own sake as well as for their intraregional competitions). Given plenty of ambition, rough capability symmetries, and initially weak financing, wars could persist for many years. Increasingly, they affected a greater proportion of the populations at war. At the same time, the mobilization of human and material resources for war became more total.

The nature of Europe's external threat environment (as well as its internal structure of multiple independent actors that had not been coercively unified in a single overarching empire) allowed the coevolution of war, political and military organizations, political economy, and weapons to proceed without much in the way of constraints, and in fact it contributed to the acceleration of that coevolution.[2] The survivors of these processes, by and large, were states that were successful at making war. They had to be. Their military organizations became increasingly professional and efficient. Their weaponry became increasingly lethal. Their populations were increasingly drawn into war preparations and making war. Along the way, these populations were transformed into national citizens with the intense sense of identification with their mother- and fatherlands, whereas before they had been mere subjects and occasional cannon fodder. That is to say, principal political organizations became strong states.

In contrast, most of the new states in the modern, largely post–World War II era (outside of Latin America) have been exposed to much different external environments (while sharing some aspects of the internal structure in terms of multiple independent state actors). Geopolitical competition has certainly existed in regions outside of Europe. Throughout the nineteenth and twentieth centuries, Latin American states fought occasional wars that reflected external expansion ambitions. Yet no state in South America ever sought to conquer the entire region.[3] Territorial conflict was usually over adjacent territories with or without some valued resource (oil, nitrates) or with access to the sea or the Amazon. Boundary lines were inherited from the days of Iberian Empire, but they were often fuzzy due in part to limited penetration and population of the interiors. As South American states developed and pushed inward on their allocated territory, they tended to collide with other states doing the same thing. Brief wars sometimes clarified who should control which space. Sometimes the warring states withdrew from their encounter without fully resolving the boundary demarcations.

The territory of African states was demarcated frequently in nonsensical ways and often reflecting European imperial convenience more than ethnic/economic realities. At the same time, African decision-makers so far have been reluctant to contest state boundaries for fear of opening up a Pandora's box of uncertainties and escalating conflict. The regional norm of avoiding clashes over boundary claims may be in the process of disintegrating, but so far most of the fighting in sub-Saharan Africa has been internal to states, as opposed to between states.[4]

The Middle East is of course a much different story given the ongoing Arab-Israeli conflict—with its occasional interstate wars and ongoing border conflicts and insurgencies—and with Arab-Persian and intra-Arab conflicts as well. Yet, as in Latin America and sub-Saharan Africa, war losers continue to exist as sovereign states. Moreover, with the exception of the Iran-Iraq war in the 1980s, Middle Eastern wars tend to be very short and subject to less than total mobilization outside of Israel. Material losses have been made up by major power patrons external to the region. Most radical efforts to reorganize the region, similarly, have been curtailed by the same external major powers.[5]

South Asia seems little different. India and Pakistan have gone to war on four occasions. In the third war, Pakistan lost considerable territory but not to its principal enemy, India. The advent of nuclear weapons on both sides may contribute further to the maintenance of the territorial status quo. Nuclear-armed states can flirt with escalation but only up to a point. More importantly, South Asian states fight short wars that do not lead to widespread mobilization of the population and economy. Nor are taxes raised to pay for past and future belligerence.

To be sure, differences characterize the Middle East, sub-Saharan Africa, South Asia, Latin America, or, for that matter, early modern Europe. Our main point is only that vastly different external environments in the contemporary era have led to various restrictions on the interactions between war and political organizations. Since war has been restricted, so too have the implications for the other processes. The principal message is that political organizations and economies in

Africa, the Middle East, and Latin America (and elsewhere) are weaker, in part, because they did not experience the same type of high threat, or continuous and escalating warfare, in the external environment that characterized early modern and modern Europe.[6] Whether or not one laments this missed "opportunity," the ways in which processes have worked outside the West have differed from those in early modern Europe. Political organizations are weaker in terms of extractive capability and popular identification with the state than they might otherwise have been.

But if states south of the equator have missed out on the historical upward spiral of war and state-making, does that mean that they are doomed to limited extractions and weak states forever? The answer is no, or at least not necessarily. It means that they are unlikely to experience the horrors of total war and thus also experience the abrupt ratcheting upward of state revenues, expenditures, and general extractive capabilities. It may mean that states that have not gone through the upward spiral of modern and industrialized interstate warfare will not attain the types of state strength achieved by those that did. The reason that it does not mean that limited extractions are foreordained forever is that there is a second historically based hypothesis. States that enjoy economic growth can also anticipate some increases in extractive capability as their domestic environments become more complex.

Skowronek argues that extraction capability can be stimulated by three types of changes.[7] The first one is crisis—as in a war—which requires governmental elites to respond to the demands of the disruptive challenge in new ways. For instance, wars demand increased volumes of revenues and military manpower. States and their leaders must devise new ways of mobilizing the resources required to remain competitive political organizations. If they fail, they are more likely to lose their wars and possibly their existence or autonomy.

A second type of environmental stimulus is class conflict. Labor and capital compete for shares of business profit. Corporations compete with other corporations for market share. Poor and rich struggle for and against redistribution and ameliorating inequalities. Within these warring factions, a government is expected to serve as a mediator/referee and/or as a suppressor of disorder that might interfere with economic growth. If economic growth is rapid, it is likely that a government will need to expand its mediation/suppressor role and the capabilities needed to perform this function. In this respect, economic growth creates new or more intense problems, which lead to expanded government mediation.

The third type of change could easily overlap with the second type. When economies expand significantly, they become more complex with a number of implications. Economic growth is likely to lead to population growth and movement away from rural areas to urban concentrations. New skills are required. Old skills are depreciated. An increase in economic complexity therefore means that the society as a whole is likely to become more complex. There is no reason to assume that greater governmental complexity must follow greater economic and societal complexity, but there does seem some probability of it occurring. If nothing else, a government's revenue stream should expand as the society becomes more affluent. The demand for various government services in police, welfare, and education spheres are also likely to spiral upward. Depending on the history of governance, there is also some likelihood that local power centers will be forced to surrender some political-economic space to expanded central government activity. This surrender is not guaranteed, either, but it is made more probable by the nature of some or all of the new problems that emerge. These problems are less likely to be attacked successfully by local governments with limited territorial scope and variable fiscal reach. Significant economic change, especially along the lines of industrialization, is thus likely to be correlated with significant growth of a central government oriented toward coping with at least some of the problems stimulated by major economic growth.

Skowronek's argument gives us two foci to look at when it comes to assessing extraction capability. Military crises are well known to have a ratchetlike effect on government revenues in some parts of the world. Revenues increase to deal with wartime demands, and when the war is over, the revenues may decline but never quite decline to the prewar level. At the same time, however, we have reason to expect that these revenue ratchets were more likely to be observed in the fiscal histories of older major powers because they were the ones that fought the increasingly total wars associated with the advent of industrialization. So, we should expect to see ratchets in the nineteenth-century class of emerging major powers (Italy, Germany, the United States, and Japan) and less likely to see them in India's record.

The second focus is geared to expansions of central governments associated with economic growth. Assuming some increase in industrialization and economic growth, this type of expansion should be manifested in peaceful years by a gradual, if slow, growth in governmental size—more revenues, more expenditures, more bureaucrats, more governmental services, and so forth. It is possible that political sentiments could emerge that would ensure central governments stay small and limited as a matter of governmental/ruling party/elite philosophy. Britain, in the eighteenth and nineteenth centuries, is well known for just this approach. Warfare had its ratcheting effects, but British politicians would scramble in the postwar era to ratchet government operations back down as much as possible in order to keep governmental costs low. Ultimately, British governmental philosophies changed—after radical changes in the economic and societal order altered the political environment. A second caveat is that extraction capability expansions associated with economic growth probably will not compare well in size with capability expansions associated with major war military crises. Economic growth-stimulated expansions should be more gradual, while military crises tend to be abrupt and radical in effect.

Figures 4.1–4.4 facilitate a quick look at the revenue records of four earlier emerging great powers. The United States' record supports many of our expectations. Three wars—the American Civil War and World Wars I and II—stand out as major stimulators of revenue increases. The increases associated with the Civil War were not sustained in part because politicians preferred to limit the size of government and in part because rapid growth bestowed more revenues to the central government without the need to increase taxes. That is, revenues increased while the relative size of governmental revenues in proportion to the gross national product (GNP) actually decreased in the nineteenth century. This characteristic changed fundamentally in the twentieth century. Two world wars had their more-permanent effects in increasing revenue levels via new taxes. Note, however, that the relative size of

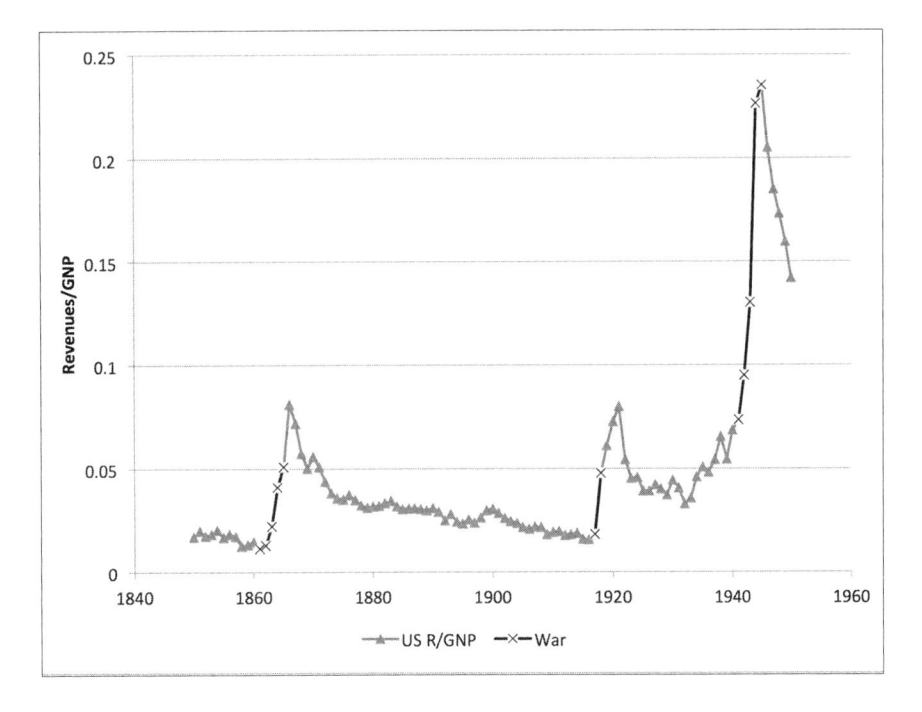

Fig. 4.1. U.S. Government Revenues/GNP

revenues had begun to climb in response to the economic depression that occurred between the two world wars. Again, this change reflected both declining GNP and also the demands for government intervention in the economy. Even so, the U.S. revenue share, and thus its apparent extraction capability, remains relatively low by European standards. The anomaly is a function of the huge size of the U.S. economy and the relatively conservative nature of the U.S. political system.

Figure 4.2 gives an overview of the truncated German revenue experience. Central government revenues grew slowly after 1870 and were changed radically first by World War I and later the world economic Depression of the 1930s. Problems with inflation make it difficult to show these changes more precisely.

Figure 4.3 looks at Italian revenue extraction. Most of Italy's smaller wars preceded the creation of the Italian state. Nonetheless, we find a noticeable World War I impact. Equally prominent, however, is the expansion of extraction in the years preceding 1914–1915. Revenue

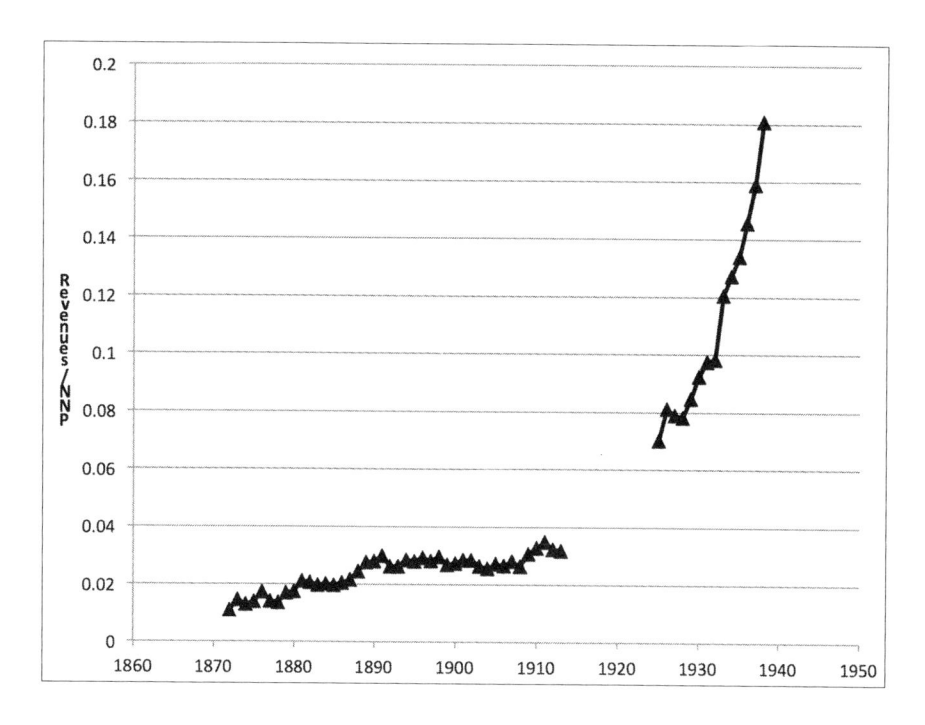

Fig. 4.2. German State Revenues/NNP

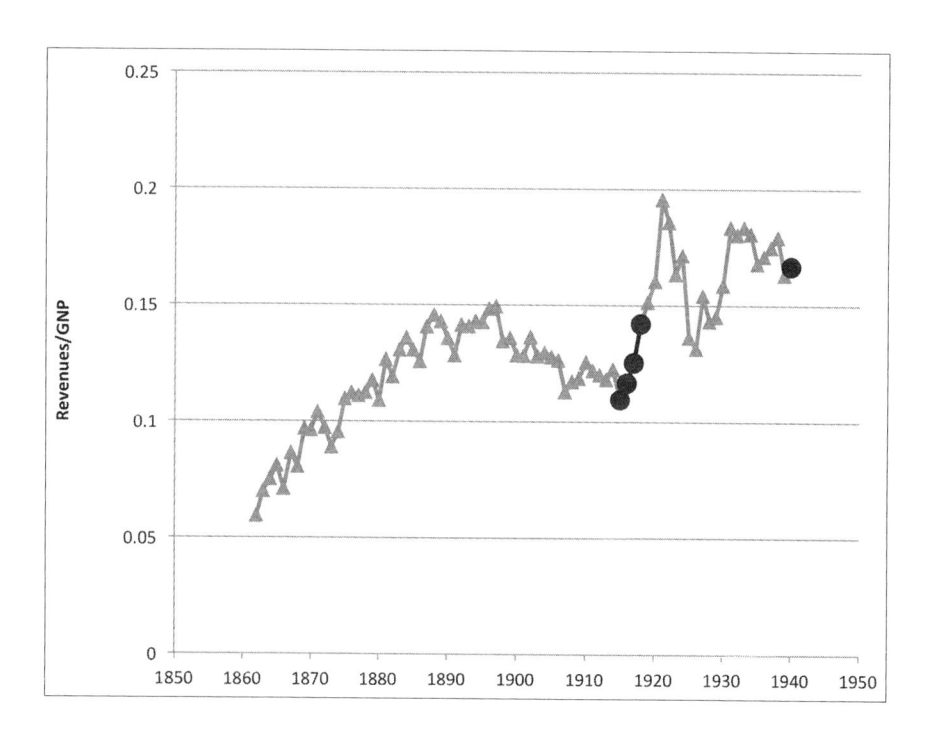

Fig. 4.3. Italian State Revenues/GDP

extraction more than doubled between 1860 and 1895 before leveling off and declining somewhat at the end of the century. Revenue extraction capability continued to ascend after the First World War but then declined back to prewar levels before beginning to climb again in the late 1920s under Fascist direction. As in the other cases examined previously, the Italian record shows a mixture of military crisis, economic crisis, economic growth, and prevailing political philosophy.

Figure 4.4 shows the Japanese revenue history during its great power interval. In this case, the limited Japanese participation in World War I is linked to the relative absence of change in extraction capability after 1914–1918. But the impact of military crises in 1904–1905 and the wars in China are clearly manifested. So was some presumed economic growth-related expansion in the late nineteenth century.

Summarizing these brief examinations, we have some casual support for all three of Skowronek's types of extraction capability. Military crises have their expected effect in all four cases. The 1930s Depression

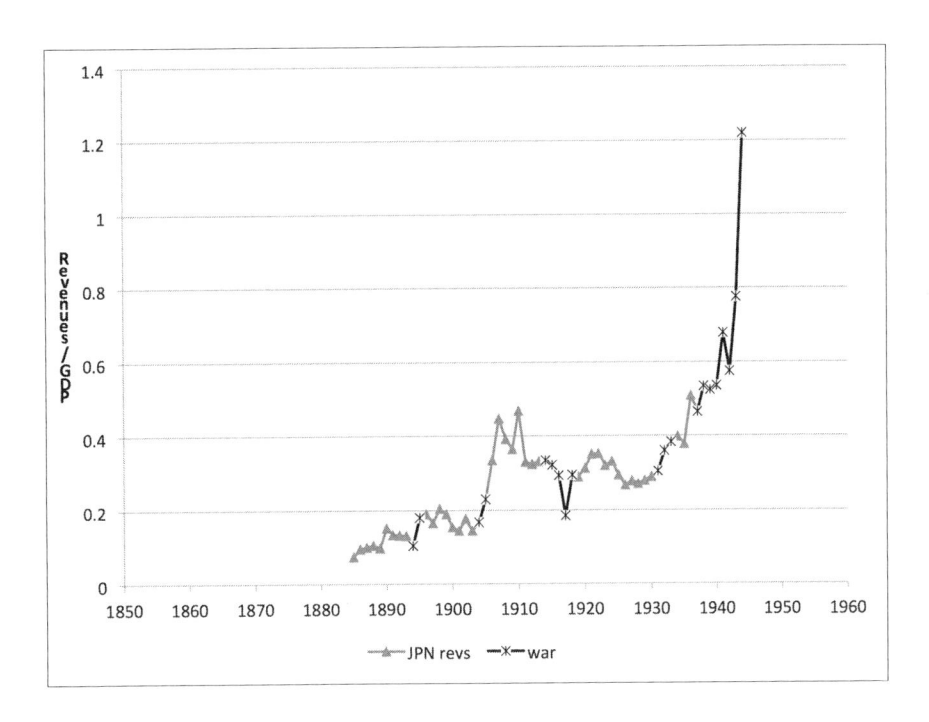

Fig. 4.4. Japanese State Revenues/GDP

accentuates the effect of economic crisis. Usually more modest economic growth—related expansions show up in different ways. In the United States case, more revenues were gained with fewer taxes. In two of the other three cases (Germany and Japan), more gradual increases were associated with economic growth prior to World War I. Italy, on the other hand, experienced prior to World War I considerable extraction capability expansion that cannot be attributed to military or economic crises.

These fiscal histories set the stage for an examination of the Indian record demonstrated in figure 4.5. Two characteristics of the Indian record stand out. First, wars do not appear to have much, if any, discernible effect. This outcome was anticipated. India's limited wars are expected to have had only limited fiscal effects, and that appears to be the case. Second, India resembles nineteenth-century Italy in managing to more than double its extraction capability over fifty-five years. The trend line shown in figure 4.5 is clearly positive, although one could

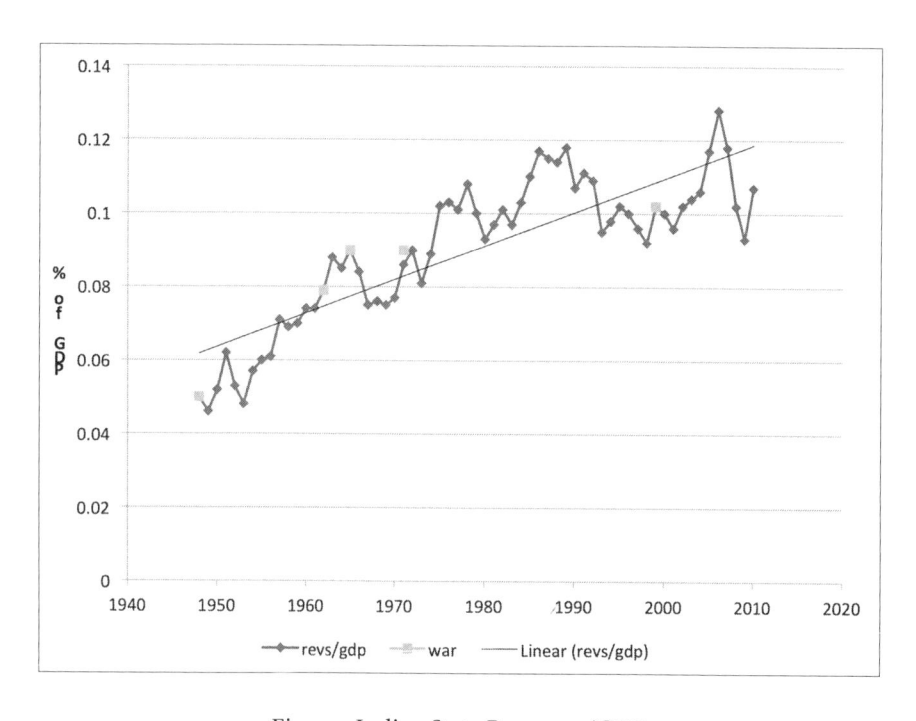

Fig. 4.5. Indian State Revenues/GDP

argue that extraction capability seems to have plateaued since 1980, fluctuating between .1 and .13 in comparison to the gross domestic product. Since this period also overlaps with rapid economic growth, the apparent plateau is misleading. Central government revenues continue to climb even though their proportional size in comparison to the size of the economy remains roughly the same.[8]

Extraction works better when the population is favorably disposed toward the political system in general—regardless of how they may perceive the incumbent government. We turn now to Holsti's second state-capacity component—legitimacy. States can extract legitimacy just as they extract taxes, but while governments can demand that taxes be paid, it is much less likely that demands for legitimacy will be heeded. Legitimacy usually has to be earned.

Legitimacy

India's high legitimacy scores suggest that it is "playing out of its league." That is, India's state enjoys more legitimacy than one would expect given India's level of economic development. India even does well when compared to much wealthier countries. Table 4.1 compares citizen trust levels in eleven federal democracies. On average, India outscored Switzerland, Canada, Austria, the United States, Belgium, Spain, Germany, and Australia. India also outscored Brazil and Argentina. Other things being equal, one might have expected India's trust scores to be similar to those of Brazil or Argentina. Obviously, other things are not equal in this case. India is something of an anomaly when it comes to legitimacy (and democracy) because it does unusually well in these categories.

Of course, the figures reported in table 4.1 are now roughly twenty years old. A number of things have happened since the mid-1990s. Table 4.2 looks at Indian responses between the 1995–1997 survey and one done in 2005. There is some fluctuation. Political parties, the civil service, and possibly the legal system are less trusted, but trust in the Parliament and police is slightly up. The central government fares better a decade later. The general point is that these attitudes are not carved in stone but seem to be holding up reasonably well, with some institutions

Table 4.1. Federal Democracy Citizen Trust in Major State Institutions

	Legal system	Legislature	Political parties	Central government	Civil service	Police
India	67	53	39	48	53	36
Switzerland	65	41	25	50	43	67
Canada	54	38	n/a	38	50	84
Brazil	55	33	32	48	59	45
Austria	58	41	n/a	n/a	42	68
United States	36	30	21	31	52	71
Belgium	45	43	n/a	n/a	43	51
Spain	45	35	18	30	40	61
Germany	54	28	14	24	47	70
Australia	35	31	16	26	38	76
Argentina	27	16	8	27	8	23

Note: The countries are listed in descending order of average trust.
Sources: Based on Alfred Stepan, Juan J. Linz, and Yogendra Yadav, Crafting State-Nations: India and Other Multinational Democracies *(Baltimore, MD: Johns Hopkins University Press, 2011), 76. Most of the data are from Ronald Inglehart et al.,* World Values Survey, 1995–97 *(Ann Arbor, MI: Inter-University Consortium for Political and Social Research). Canada, Belgium, and Austria were not included in the 1995–1997 survey; their data are taken from Ronald Inglehart et al.,* World Values Survey, 1990–93 *(Ann Arbor, MI: Inter-University Consortium for Political and Social Research).*

Table 4.2. Indian Trust in Major State Institutions Over Time

Institutions	ca. 1996	2001	2005
Legal system	67	59	n/a
Legislature	53	43	55
Political parties	39	36	34
Central government	48	62	56
Civil service	53	47	49
Police	36	42	38

Source: Based on Alfred Stepan, Juan J. Linz, and Yogendra Yadav, Crafting State-Nations: India and Other Multinational Democracies *(Baltimore, MD: Johns Hopkins University Press, 2011), 76–77.*

Table 4.3. Trust in Government Percentages

	India	Brazil	Russia	China	United States	Germany	Canada	Global average
2014	53	34	27	76	37	49	51	48
2013	57	33	29	81	53	48	58	44
2012	53	32	26	75	43	33	56	52
2011	44	85	39	88	40	33	52	43
2010	43	39	38	74	46	43	n/a	n/a
2009	43	n/a	43	79	30	35	51	44
2008	49	22	39	80	39	27	39	43

Source: The data were taken from multiple Web displays. See, for instance, the 2014 results at www.edelman.com/insights/intellectual-property/2014-edelman-trust-barometer.

improving while others decline in the way they are perceived by the population.

Over time, it is possible that India still leads federal democracies in terms of institutional trust. Some data on this question is shown in table 4.3. The Edelman Trust Barometer is an annual survey administered by a public relations firm designed to compare popular distrust of business, media, and government. It is not clear how much faith we should put in this barometer, but it does display some interesting comparisons. One of the more dubious aspects of the data is that it has Indian trust in government increasing over time—which seems most unlikely.[9] Yet it also shows Indian trust levels as being above average in most years and variably better than the levels found in other federal democracies (the United States, Germany, and Canada). India does much better than two of the BRICs, Brazil and Russia, but much worse than the surprisingly high levels of China, another reason to be careful in interpreting the data.

Another indicator in which India does quite well is voting turnout for parliamentary elections. Declining legitimacy might be indexed by declining participation in elections. Figure 4.6 indicates no long-term decline. On the contrary, the most recent election is associated with the highest turnout in India's history (70.3 percent). The high turnout in

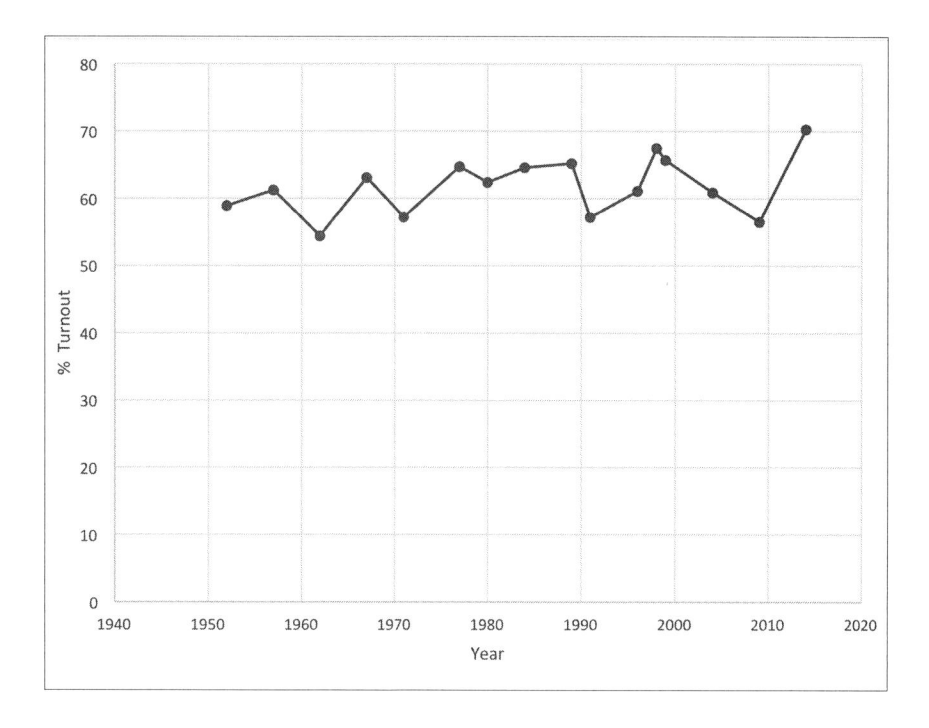

Fig. 4.6. Voting Turnout in India's Parliamentary Elections

2014 does not necessarily mean that legitimacy is increasing, but it does suggest that voters saw the election as a chance to change the government, which in turn implies some belief in the appropriate authority of Indian governments in general, if not the incumbent government voted out of office.

Data that conform somewhat better with less rosy expectations, however, are found in the World Bank's governance surveys. Over the last decade and a half, attitudes toward the political system have largely declined in India. Corruption is perceived as greater, and governmental effectiveness and the rule of law are judged to be decreasing. Only voice/accountability, oddly enough, is quite stable in table 4.4. As far as these data go, one must conclude that governmental legitimacy in India is deteriorating but not all that greatly or quickly.

Why this high legitimacy level is anomalous can be elaborated by considering Gilley's work on state legitimacy.[10] Gilley has developed a very precise definition of what "legitimacy" means. A state is legitimate

Table 4.4. Indian Scores on Selected Governance Items

	Control of corruption	Governmental effectiveness	Rule of law	Voice/ accountability	Mean
1996	40	54	59	62	54
1998	44	54	60	57	54
2000	46	51	60	56	53
2002	38	52	51	58	50
2003	43	55	55	59	53
2004	43	55	54	61	53
2005	43	55	58	60	54
2006	46	54	57	59	54
2007	41	57	56	59	53
2008	44	54	56	60	54
2009	39	56	55	60	53
2010	36	56	55	60	52
2011	33	55	52	61	50
2012	35	47	53	59	49
2013	36	47	53	61	49

Note: Scores are rounded percentile ranks ranging from 0 to 100, with higher scores reflecting stronger governance perceptions.
Source: World Bank, World Governance Indicators, at info.worldbank.org/governance/wgi/index .aspx#reports.

if it is considered to be engaged in rightful rule. Rightful, in turn, refers to legality, justification, and consent. "Legality" means that the state behaves in accordance with explicit rules and customs. Legality makes its behavior predictable and its activities equally applicable to all subjects of the law. "Justification" is more abstract. This dimension refers to states behaving in conformity with society's moral consensus and seems to approximate trust in institutions and political leaders as doing things that benefit citizenry. "Consent," in contrast, is about citizens choosing to demonstrate their support for state institutions and leaders. Do they bother to vote? Do they enlist in the military? Do they pay their taxes?

Gilley operationalizes this complex definition in terms of eight indicators summarized in the left-hand side of table 4.5. The first two

Table 4.5. Gilley Legitimacy Measure and Correlations

Legitimacy	Legitimacy correlations	R
State law abidedness • Citizen confidence in human-rights performance • Citizen confidence in police performance • Citizen confidence in civil-service performance	General governance (effectiveness, corruption control, and rule of law) Income level (gross domestic product per capita) Gender equality (gender empowerment measure) Welfare level (human-development index) Economic governance (economic-freedom index) National happiness (aggregated personal happiness)	.73 .69 .69 .68 .67 .65
Majority/minority justification • Satisfaction with democratic development • Evaluation of current political system • Satisfaction with operation of democracy Consent • Reliance on quasi-voluntary taxes • Voter turnout in national legislature elections	Anti-authoritarian attitudes (attitudes toward strong leadership and democratic opposition) Democratic rights (Freedom House civil-liberties index) Welfare gains (change in human-development index)	.62 .62 .60

Note: R = Pearson correlation coefficient. Gender equality is a composite index based on combining scores on maternal mortality, adolescent fertility, parliamentary representation, secondary-level education attainment, and labor-force participation. Human development is a composite index based on combining scores on life expectancy at birth, mean years of schooling, expected years of schooling, and national income level.

Sources: Based on information in Bruce Gilley, "The Determinants of State Legitimacy: Results for 72 Countries," International Political Science Review 27, 1 (2006): 47–71; and Bruce Gilley, *The Right to Rule: How States Win and Lose Legitimacy* (New York: Columbia University, 2009), 39.

dimensions are captured by attitudinal surveys that measure citizens' perceptions of their state. Consent is represented by national tax paying and voting behavioral tendencies. Gilley's combined measure is different than the one we employ in chapter 3. Yet there is also substantial overlap. Using the World Bank survey data, we have a rule-of-law component that corresponds to Gilley's legality dimension. The voice/accountability data seems to encompass all three Gilley dimensions. Government effectiveness might be said to be the other side of the consent coin. Corruption control fits both legality and justification.

Yet it is neither Gilley's alternative approach to legitimacy nor the substantial, if perhaps not surprising, overlap between his measures and our own that we wish to emphasize. One of the analyses that Gilley undertook was to correlate his legitimacy measure with other variables—shown in the right-hand side of table 4.5. Given the overlap in emphases, it should not be startling to learn that the highest correlation with the Gilley legitimacy measure is something called "general governance," with three of our own World Bank measures.

Most of the other variables that are highly correlated (and only the most highly correlated variables are shown in table 4.5) have something to do with wealth, industrialization, and standards of living. Income levels (wealth) and the level of, and change in, the human development indexes (standards of living) are one-third of the top nine correlates. Anti-authoritarianism, civil liberties, economic governance, and gender empowerment are readily associated with Western liberal preferences most often found in the most industrialized states. Whether these tendencies should be expected to be correlated with national happiness can be left to debate. Yet it is certainly easier to be happy if one is relatively affluent and enjoying a high standard of living than the other way around.

All this would suggest that higher legitimacy scores should be the province of older, more affluent, Western states. Farther away from Europe, North America, and Japan, legitimacy need not be nonexistent, but average scores should be lower. States that are neither old, affluent, nor Western—call them Northern—should have lower scores, other things being equal. As most definitely a non-Northern state, India's relatively high legitimacy scores are anomalous.

India has certainly improved its ranking on income/welfare matters, but it remains fairly low ranked on economic welfare. In 2014, it ranked 160th on gross domestic product per capita (purchasing power parity).[11] On the human-development index, a type of living-standards measure, India scored 135th (of 186 ranked states).[12] That put India in the top 73 percent of the world. In 1980, it had scored 45th (of 65 ranked states), which put it in the top 69 percent of the world over thirty years ago. Technically, that represents a deterioration in relative position, but it probably should be read as little relative change. In 2015, India ranked 128th on the economic-freedom index, which put it into the "mostly unfree" category.[13] India does not appear to be ranked on the gender-empowerment scale due to missing data, but it is unlikely to fare well on that index either.[14]

What is even more remarkable is that the popular support for the political system in India seems to be pervasive throughout the population. Table 4.6 breaks down the support among an amazing variety of different subgroups. There are differences. The table is arrayed in descending rank order on the dated 2004 values. People with college experience are considerably more likely to support democratic politics in India than are groups that have encountered centuries of discrimination (scheduled castes and tribes). Yet all three groups are still highly supportive. Religious identity does not seem to matter much. Neither does affluence, gender, age, or rural/urban residence. People who cannot read are the least supportive, but even their responses have become fairly supportive.

Moreover, the amount of support manifested tends to be increasing over time, especially in terms of the 1971 figures. In some cases, the level of support in 1996 and 2004 was twice as strong as it was in 1971. In every case for which we have data, levels of support are substantially greater in more-recent years than they were in 1971. On this criterion, India does unusually well. While we would certainly expect the latest data to show declines in legitimacy, at least prior to the Modi regime, India has had an unusual record on the legitimacy front. Given India's many political and economic problems, it tends to do better than one would anticipate.

Some of this anomaly may be due to what Gilley has more recently referred to as the Asian "legitimacy premium."[15] He has found

Table 4.6. Support for Indian Democratic Politics

Support	1971	1996	2004
College and above	n/a	74	85
Upper class	n/a	77	82
Male	n/a	73	77
Upper caste	n/a	74	76
Christian	n/a	73	73
Muslim	40	72	73
Hindu	n/a	68	73
National average	43	69	72
Poor	37	68	71
Rural	39	69	70
25 yrs. or older	n/a	69	70
Scheduled caste	38	67	69
56 yrs. or older	n/a	63	69
Scheduled tribe	41	66	68
Women	32	64	67
Very poor	32	64	66
Sikh	n/a	63	66
Nonliterates	31	62	61

Survey Question: Do you think that the government in this country can be run better if there are no parties or assemblies? No responses are considered supportive.

Sources: National Election Study (India) 1971, 1996, 2004 (Delhi: Centre for the Study of Developing Socieites), as reported in Subrata K. Mitra, Politics in India: Structure, Process and Policy *(London: Routledge, 2011), 61; and Alfred Stepan, Juan J. Linz, and Yogendra Yahav,* Crafting State-Nations: India and Other Multinational Democracies *(Baltimore, MD: Johns Hopkins University Press, 2011), 79.*

that Asian states enjoy more legitimacy than expected in comparison to the rest of the world. Gilley traces the general development of this premium back to medieval times, when Asian states were accorded primacy and authoritativeness over society, the reverse of what he believes happened in the West. That may be the case, but states that emerged after World War II in different forms than had existed earlier or before European subordination should not have been expected to enjoy the full premium.[16] India in 1948 was just such a case. An Asian legitimacy premium therefore is unlikely to account for all of India's anomalous status when it comes to the persistence of high legitimacy scores.

Summary

Not surprisingly, India's extraction capacity is not well developed. But then neither were the extraction capacities of states that became great powers in the past two centuries. Older great powers were able to expand their extraction capability, often abruptly, in circumstances of dire societal crises involving intensive warfare. India has not been a stranger to warfare, but the impacts of these wars have been much more limited vis-à-vis India's fiscal capabilities. More promising is the more gradual impact of industrialization and economic growth, which also tends to expand fiscal capability, albeit slowly and haltingly—which appears to be the Indian case.

More unusual is India's high scores on legitimacy, which so far are not deteriorating greatly. While India no doubt benefits from fairly consistent democratic institutions—which have been maintained in a less-than-conducive environment of societal heterogeneity, poverty, and international conflict—Indian scores on this criterion put it among far more affluent states. It is one of India's definite strengths and highlights the "mixed bag" capacities of states falling in between strong and failed states.[17]

In contrast, India does much less well on violence monopoly, our third main area of state capacity. Indian political history since independence has been rife with separatism, insurgencies, and intermittent communal rioting. In many respects, it is remarkable that India has neither transformed itself into a garrison state nor lost territory to breakaway movements. It helps a great deal, of course, that many of these problems are concentrated on India's periphery. Still, the Indian political-violence record is almost as persistent as its legitimacy scores, which, somewhat paradoxical in this respect, have been unusually high. We turn to violence monopoly in the next chapter.

F · I · V · E

Violence Monopoly

Internal violence is no stranger to states ascending to great power status. All four of the states in the second half of the nineteenth century that attained great power status underwent something like a major and formative civil war prior to their attainment of greater status. The U.S. Civil War, the harbinger of industrialized warfare, is perhaps the best known. It did not fully resolve sectional differences stemming largely from different political-economic orientations (industrial in the North versus plantation in the South). Yet it precluded the emergence of two or more rival states in the North American space, which could only have reduced the probability of later great power status for the United States. Italy fought a series of wars, both before and after its great power anointment in 1861 to create a unified Italy. The wars were no more effective in ameliorating the differences between north and south than was the case in the U.S. experience, but they were essential to reducing the political influence of Austria-Hungary and the papacy within the Italian peninsula. Similarly, Prussia, already a weak great power in the mid-nineteenth century, fought a series of wars (the two Schleswig-Holstein Wars, the Austro-Prussian War in 1866, and the Franco-Prussian War of 1870–1871) to solidify its core leadership of the many German states and to incorporate them into a unified Germany. It is hard to imagine the consequent history of the first half of the twentieth century in the absence of this critical state-making prerequisite. Japan also fought a critical civil war in 1868–1869, which was necessary to centralize government authority in the Meiji Restoration. To these cases, we could add Portugal's 1383–1385 monarchical revolution, which facilitated that state's voyages of discovery; France's involvement in the Hundred Years' War and subsequent bloodletting; and England's mid-seventeenth-century civil war and the later Dutch invasion of England in 1688. The formation of the United Provinces of the Netherlands in the late sixteenth century also possessed some civil war overtones in terms of the cleavages between north and south in the Netherlands. Finally, it is difficult to overlook Russia's early twentieth-century civil war, which served as a crucible for the shaping of the Soviet Union, or China's long civil war that preceded the victory of the Chinese Communist Party shortly after World War II.

Most (but not all) great powers thus went through significant episodes of internal war, sometimes intermingled with external war, that either facilitated or influenced their status in world politics.[1] In many respects and in most cases, the internal violence made great power status possible. Larger, more-centralized and more-powerful states were the outcomes. Smaller and less-centralized states tended to be less powerful and, therefore, less likely to qualify for elite status.

India has considerable experience with internal violence at multiple levels. At the macro level, several parts of India have attempted to secede and have experienced insurgency and terrorism. At a meso level, ethnic violence, often taking the form of riots, is no stranger to modern Indian history. At a micro level, a record of poor state protection for weaker segments of the Indian population, especially women and children, is a cause of major embarrassment. Unlike what happened in other ascending states, none of this violence appears to be facilitative for India's aspirations for great power status. They are unlikely to prevent upward mobility. Yet their persistence has to act at least as a drag on ascending status. All three levels of violence also underscore weaknesses in state capacity and the Weberian emphasis on violence monopoly as a major hallmark of state strength.

At the macro level, India operates in the shadow of a well-entrenched form of path dependency. The governance of India has been intermittent but fairly consistent in pattern. Nehru possessed a strong appreciation for the pattern. Chadda derives four broad Nehruvian principles of historical Indian governance:[2]

1. . . . each unified formation in India . . . had created a universal order that transcended specific ideologies and beliefs but did not seek to eliminate or merge them. Instead the empires created an overarching ideology that was both tolerant and inclusive.
2. The legacy of history to the modern Indian state was the notion of layered order, and a central state that limited itself to the public domain. . . . Separate caste and religious communities were accommodated within the broad framework of the overarching ideology, where each maintained its distinctive identity but derived it, in large part, through reference to the whole.
3. . . . each imperial ruler . . . enjoyed a degree of autonomy from India's existing social order [which] meant that it could transcend particular interests; it neither represented such interests exclusively nor allowed such interests to claim the state. . . . Autonomy gave the state the flexibility that it needed to integrate the nation, develop the economy, create new economic and political opportunities, and to equalize society. . . .
4. [Unlike in earlier Hindu and Muslim epochs] . . . the British . . . introduced the notion of fixed boundaries that were clearly demarcated on the ground and drawn in maps. . . .

Other great powers ruled over conglomerate societies but either had the time and/or the ruthlessness to take care of minorities that might cause political trouble. Jews, Muslims, Protestants, Catholics, Huguenots, Native Americans, and Cossacks were encouraged to leave, moved, or were neutralized as political threats. Political integration of the home society did not always precede great power attainment. The political integration of France awaited Napoleon, and Italian decision-makers have yet to pull the disparate parts of its country into one whole. But at least coercive options were available. India has coercive options as well, but to use them fully would undermine the overarching ideology that helps hold a highly heterogeneous society together.

The main point is that Indian governance is predicated on a layered state that is accustomed to tolerating local "deviance" and amorphous boundaries.[3] Yet there are limits to how much local deviation can be sustained, particularly in an era characterized by fixed borders. In earlier times, it was always possible for imperial centers to retreat or withdraw from intensive resistance. Even British rule, which introduced the notion of fixed boundaries, distinguished between areas that were worth controlling and areas that were to be given considerable autonomy. Now, local challenges to the state can neither be ignored or tolerated without some cost to the perceived strength of the state. Some political autonomy may be acceptable, but only some. The problem is that local actors, for various reasons, often want more autonomy than the center deems advisable. As a consequence, one of the rules developed by Indian decision-makers early on was to suppress any attempts at secession. Regional and tribal groups could press for more autonomy and linguistic centralization, but if they went over the line and attempted to leave the Indian Union they should anticipate the full weight of the state's coercive power.[4] This position may have deterred some groups from pressing too hard. It did not stop all groups.

Ironically, then, India emerged into independence greatly violating these historical principles of ruling in South Asia. But it was independence (impending and after the fact) that encouraged the violence that occurred between 1946 and 1950. Ostensibly intercommunal conflict departed from the usual patterns of religious conflict. Talbot and Singh see these kinds of conflicts as contests for group control of territory and relative power that occur as one empire ends and a new state is about to emerge or is emerging.[5] The basic idea was to reduce the number of minorities in one space through various types of violence that terrify people into fleeing. As a form of ethnic cleansing, this violence was not restricted to males, involved terrorism, torture, and maiming, and was carried out like military campaigns by paramilitary groups that had been facilitated by the World War II experience.[6]

How and when such violence broke out varied from region to region, depending on the mix of majority-minorities and the degree of collusion by local state agents (police and railway workers). Yet, overall, the use of violence anticipated independence and its implications and sought to shape it in a way that favored local political power. The level of violence attained encouraged the British desire to withdraw quickly and, thereby, made partition more likely because it appeared to be satisfactory to Hindu and Muslim leaders, in contrast to the postindependence structure advocated by British planners. British advocacy of a loose confederation with a weak central government and strong regions was initially acceptable to the Muslim League but not to the Congress Party. Congress's opposition apparently encouraged Muslim distancing from the proposal in order to get the more-preferred two-state solution. British officials switched their proposal to a two-state solution when it became apparent that the two major camps were prepared to accept it. No one seemed to worry too much about the ongoing ethnic cleansing or the possibility that partition would exacerbate the machinations to create more easily controlled, local political structures. Thus the violence served as both cause and effect. The outcome was large-scale migrations of Muslims, Hindus, and Sikhs to and from India and Pakistan, with a death toll estimated to fall somewhere between a couple hundred thousand and two million.

The sheer and horrific magnitude of the violence was one thing. For our purposes, the political effects of partition, it is argued, were quite comprehensive. Talbot and Singh propose (see figure 5.1) that partition had pervasive effects on India's subsequent political orientation and the nature of its violence.[7] Most obviously, it set up what has become an immediate and long-running interstate rivalry between India and Pakistan, in part because their national foundation myths are totally contradictory. One insists that religion does not matter, while the other insists that it has first priority in establishing the identity of the nation. Several wars have ensued, and external support for domestic rebellion has been persistent as well.

As indicated in the summary of the partition-related violence, local states were politically reconfigured to facilitate majority political control. One very clear manifestation of this phenomena involved Pun-

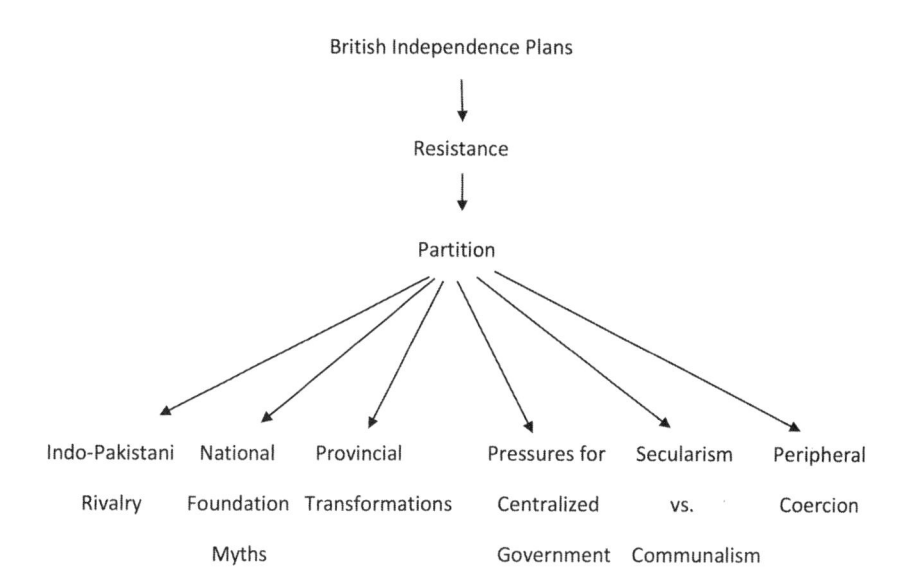

```
                    British Independence Plans
                              │
                              ▼
                         Resistance
                              │
                              ▼
                          Partition
              ╱     ╱     ╱    │    ╲     ╲      ╲
             ╱     ╱     ╱     │     ╲     ╲      ╲
            ▼     ▼     ▼      ▼      ▼     ▼      ▼
```

Indo-Pakistani   National   Provincial   Pressures for   Secularism   Peripheral
Rivalry   Foundation   Transformations Centralized   vs.   Coercion
                 Myths   Government   Communalism

Fig. 5.1. Talbot-Singh Partition-Effects Model *Source: Based on the discussion in Ian Talbot and Gurharpal Singh,* The Partition of India *(Cambridge: Cambridge University Press, 2009), 127–153.*

jab and attempts to create a Sikh majority in an area where it had not existed previously. In a number of places, especially in the northeast, incoming migrants associated with partition flows upset local political economies with new skills and talent looking for employment. Based on their personal experiences, some partition refugees also became radical supporters of harsh treatment of minorities.

Communalism came to be perceived by the Indian political leadership as even more of a political evil than before. It was something to be opposed strenuously to communalism in order to support the secularism needed to govern a heterogeneous society. That way of thought implied the necessity of repression and coercive tactics in order to suppress any manifestations. The same approach was increasingly applied to the peripheral protests for greater autonomy, which escalated in part as a consequence to militant separatist movements. In sum, partition at independence made the subsequent manifestations of political violence much more probable.

Indian Internal Warfare

At the macro level, India's internal wars can be divided into four categories. If one can envision a north-central Hindi heartland, the activities in all four clusters have taken place on the margins of the center. In the far north is predominantly Muslim Kashmir. Not too far removed in location but not as far north are the Sikhs in northwestern Punjab. Farther away to the east but still in the north are the many tribal groups located in northeast India. Stretching from the north down the eastern Indian coast and inland, as well as to parts of southern India, is the "red corridor" in which Communists, Maoists, and Naxalites do battle with landlords, state police, and the army. The first three categories have tended toward separatism; the fourth has not. No single activity is all that threatening to the continued existence of the Indian central state, although decision-makers talk as if the loss of Kashmir would undermine the state's secular raison d'être. But the overlapping occurrence of multiple insurgencies sometimes gives the impression of imminent fragmentation even when that does not seem to be all that probable.

Table 5.1 lists the more significant conflicts that are recognized to have cost twenty-five deaths or more. From the onset of independence, India fought over princely states that were reluctant to join the Union (Hyderabad and Kashmir). Combat with Communists also began early but changed its shape over the decades. Violent tribal resistance to Indian centralization began in the 1950s, continued through the 1960s, and then spread in the 1980s and 1990s. By the late 1990s and early 2000s, there were as many as seven different insurgencies underway at the same time. More recently, as shown in figure 5.2, the frequency of insurgencies has waned, but it would be difficult to argue that the threat of insurgency has run its course.[8]

Frequencies can be misleading, however. If the number of battle deaths is a better indicator of seriousness, insurgent activity is better described as cyclical than as a matter of having peaked and now in decline. We lack systematic evidence for the number of insurgency battle deaths since independence, but the data that we do have since 1989 shows two peaks—the first one driven by Kashmir and the Sikhs, and the second one primarily a Kashmiri affair—followed by marked de-

Table 5.1. More Significant Insurgencies
and Other Conflicts in India, 1948–2011

Area	Years
Kashmir	1948, 1964–1965, 1971, 1984, 1987, 1989–2014
Hyderabad	1948
Communist/Maoist/Naxalite	1948–1951, 1969–1971, 1990–1994, 1996–2014
Nagaland	1955–2000
Mizoram	1966–1968
Tripura	1979–1988, 1992–1993, 1995, 1997–2004
Manipur	1982–1988, 1992–2000, 2003–2009
Sikh	1983–1993
Bodoland	1989–1990, 1993–2014
ULFA-Assam	1990–1991, 1994–2010
Kukiland	1993–1997
Islamic State	2000–2008
Garoland	2010–2014

Source: Based on data found in UCDP/PRIO Armed Conflict Dataset, vol. 5-2015, 1946–2014 (Sweden: Uppsala University). See, for example, Therese Petterson and Peter Wallensteen, "Armed Conflict, 1946–2014," Journal of Peace Research 54, no. 4 (2015).

clines in the number of deaths. Table 5.2 suggests that the northeastern separatist conflicts tend to persist but do not compare in significance to the main shows in the north. In contrast, the Communist/Maoist/Naxalite conflicts fluctuate in severity and register in battle deaths in between the Kashmiri/Sikh and northeastern tribal categories. Overall, however, insurgency deaths appear to be spiraling downward, as depicted in figure 5.3.

While we have separated the insurgencies into four largely geographical categories, it is possible to draw attention to their common denominators. They all represent insurgencies that are forms of internal warfare distinguished by the tactical avoidance of assembling dissident armies to engage the armies of the state in a conventional format, best illustrated by the American Civil War. Too weak to pursue this approach,

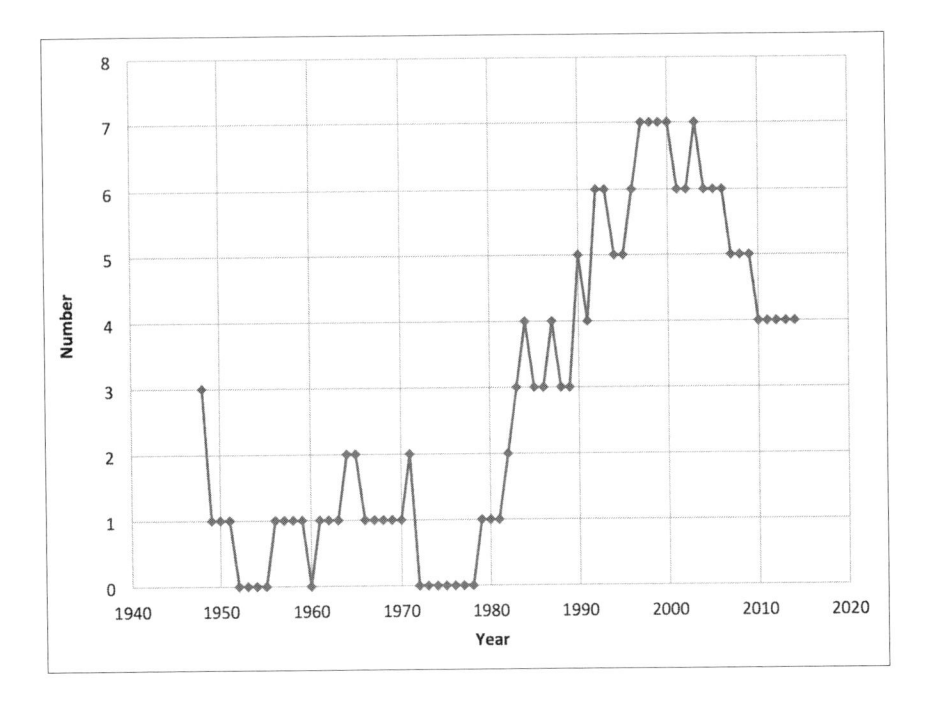

Fig. 5.2. Number of Insurgencies Under Way in India

insurgencies fight guerrilla wars, attacking federal state forces at vulnerable points, and withdraw when they encounter serious resistance or superior coercive power. The next step down the escalatory ladder, terrorism, involves individual and small group tactics designed to demonstrate the state's weaknesses without direct engagement of their forces. This can be done by attacking civilians and/or state agents. By and large, armed dissidents would prefer to fight the state conventionally, but reality often means that they are not strong enough to contemplate this type of warfare and are forced to fall back on insurgency and terrorism.[9]

Beyond the tactical form they take, the insurgencies share other features, as brought out in Chadha's analysis summarized in table 5.3. All seek increased autonomy or independence. All reflect political leadership decisions to escalate the issues beyond more normal political mobilization and contestation to armed conflict. All of the activities take place in political contexts characterized by bureaucratic corruption and the neglect of local and federal states. In part as a consequence, economic

Table 5.2. Estimated Indian Insurgency Battle Deaths, 1989–2014

	Kashmir A	Kashmir B	Sikh	Bodo	ULFA	Tripura	Manipur	Nagaland	C/M/N	Garoland	Total
1989	25	26	1,086	33							1,170
1990	1,086	26	1,035	25	26				25		2,198
1991	1,007	26	1,489		25				53		2,547
1992	1,061	26	1,096			29	25	47	341		2,625
1993	1,163		68	25	25	25	25	92	205		1,603
1994	935			25	25		25	60	54		1,124
1995	686			25	25	25	25	97			883
1996	493	26		25	48		28	90	84		794
1997	553	26		34	114	85	25	37	105		979
1998	339	26		31	55	50	25	40	102		668
1999	1,981	1,174		38	57	63	31	37	99		3,480
2000	1,157	26		27	94	44	61	40	305		1,754
2001	1,163	26		77	124	28			127		1,545
2002	1,500	350		44	59	39			188		2,180
2003	1,246	211		102	42	78	27		99		1,805
2004	1,134			30	74	28	60		71		1,397
2005	1,046				56		35	38	199		1,374

(*continued*)

Table 5.2. (*continued*)

	Kashmir A	Kashmir B	Sikh	Bodo	ULFA	Tripura	Manipur	Nagaland	C/M/N	Garoland	Total
2006	702				50	26	68	42	426		1,314
2007	549				113		57	105	345		1,169
2008	458				75		99		378		1,010
2009	360			83	61		96		549		1,149
2010	370			57	30				570		1,027
2011	140								293		433
2012	141								241	27	409
2013	146			34					210		390
2014	177			28						26	231

Note: The first column (Kashmir A) denotes battle deaths associated with the local insurgency. The second column (Kashmir B) counts battle deaths linked to Pakistani interventions into the Kashmir conflict. Bodo, ULFA, Tripura, Manipur, Nagaland, and Garoland are all northeast Indian tribal/separatist conflicts. The label C/M/N refers to Communist, Maoist, and Naxalite activities.

Source: UCDP Battle-Related Deaths Dataset, vol. 5–2015, 1989–2014 (Sweden: Uppsala University). See, for example, Ralph Sundberg, "Collective Violence, 2002–2007: Global and Regional Trends," in States in Armed Conflict 2007, ed. Lotta Herbom and Ralph Sundberg (Uppsala, Sweden: Universitetstryekeriet, 2008), 165–190.

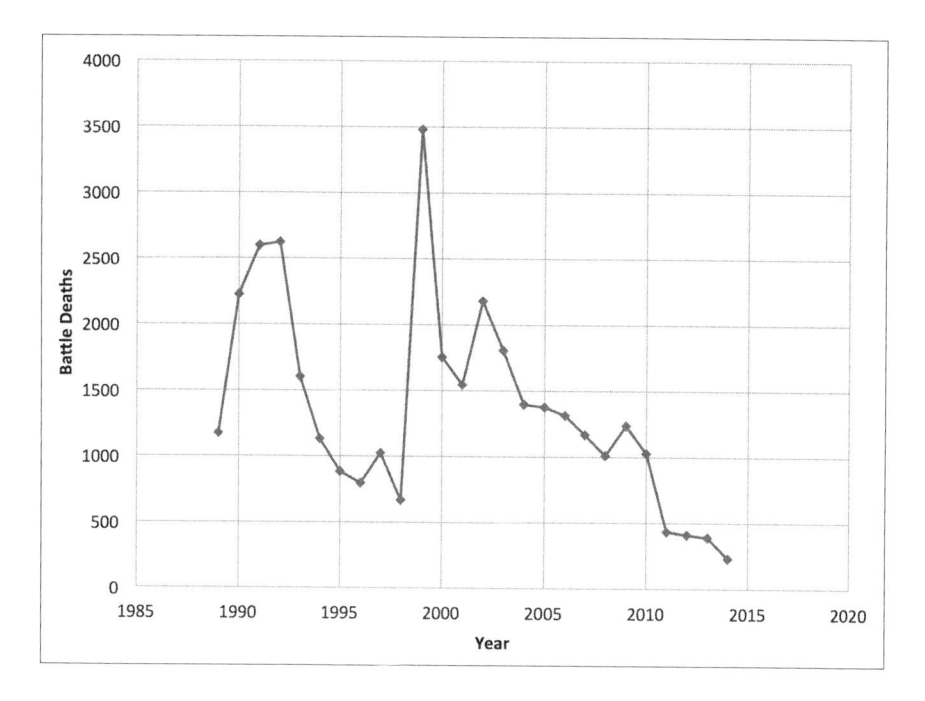

Fig. 5.3. Indian Insurgency Battle Deaths

development has been limited (jobs are lacking). Most of them have historical roots and receive foreign support. Once one moves beyond these descriptors, differences become more noticeable. Some involve specific tribes that perceive their identities and ways of life under attack. Others focus on defending linguistic sovereignty—that is, the freedom to speak their own language in commerce and education without being forced to use some other language by the state. In related fashion, some cases involve reactions to the in-migration of what are viewed as alien groups and the consequent increased competition with these migrants for land and jobs. Similarly, ethnicity, ideology, and religious differences have been more prominent in some conflicts than in others.

There is no denying common denominators in Indian insurgencies. The real problem is the appearance that all of the descriptors listed in table 5.3 have equal explanatory weight. Even if they are present or absent differentially and more or less primary (three asterisks versus one), a list of factors glosses over some distinctive differences that are

Table 5.3. Factors Involved in Indian Insurgencies

	Jammu/ Kashmir	Punjab	Assam ULFA	Assam Bodo	Nagaland	Manipur	Mizoram	Tripura	Gorkhaland	Naxalism
Autonomy/ independence	★★★	★★★	★	★	★★★	★	★	★	★★★	★
Political opportunism	★	★★★	★	★★★	★	★	★★★	★	★	★
Neglect	★	★	★	★	★	★	★	★	★	★
Corruption	★	★	★	★	★	★★★	★★★	★★★	★	★★★
Jobs	★	★	★	★	★	★	★	★	★	★
Historical	★	★	★	★	★	★	★	★	★	
Foreign support	★	★	★	★	★	★	★	★		
Linguistic		★	★	★		★	★	★	★★★	
Tribalism		★	★	★	★	★	★	★		★★★
Ethnic divide				★★★	★	★★★	★	★★★	★	
Religion	★	★	★	★		★		★		
Immigration			★★★			★		★★★	★	★
Educational	★								★	★
Ideological			★			★		★		★★★
Exploitation				★					★	

Note: A single asterisk indicates that, according to the author, the factor was present in the conflict. Triple asterisks indicate that the factor was believed to be a primary cause.

Source: Based on Vivek Chadha, Low Intensity Conflicts in India: An Analysis (New Delhi: Sage Publications, 2005), 422–423.

better emphasized by distinguishing them geographically and, to some extent, historically.[10]

KASHMIR

Jammu and Kashmir is the northernmost Indian state. It is the only state in the union with a Muslim majority. As a general piece of real estate, it can also claim to have been conquered by nearly everybody at some point in time. At different historical intervals, it has been controlled by Hindus, Muslims, and Sikhs coming into the area from different directions. For raiders coming from the north, it was often the first target of predation. Only Britain's control was indirect. It is perhaps not surprising that it remains a contested prize in the postindependence era. Kashmir is highly significant ideologically to the Indo-Pakistani rivals. For India, it constitutes a major challenge to its national premise of secularity. Can it successfully integrate a territory with a Muslim majority? For Pakistan, adjacent Kashmir constitutes a major challenge to its national premise of creating a homeland for Muslims. It does not help that both states consider the area to have important strategic value in its own right or that it has been the principal battleground for the Indo-Pakistani rivalry. Abandoning Kashmir completely, among other things, would mean that one side had lost the rivalry contest.

Jammu and Kashmir became a focal point for the rivalry when the princely states, mainly in the northern part of South Asia, were required to choose between joining India or Pakistan. Other things being equal, they were expected to join the state to which they were contiguous if the local population was compatible with the adjacent state's approach to religion. Two problems, however, were that in some cases, the prince's religion did not align with the majority of the population, and some of the princes strongly preferred independence to adhering to either larger state. Kashmir was a case in point—with a majority of Muslims and a non-Muslim ruler who preferred independence. As a consequence, the Kashmir maharajah delayed making a choice until his kingdom came under attack by invading Pakistani tribal elements and irregulars in 1947. Indian troops were sent in once the Kashmiri ruler had consented to joining India, subject to a later popular plebiscite. Early Indian military successes led to more formal Pakistani intervention and a later cease-fire, with Pakistan retaining control of a limited part of Kashmir. Most subsequent crises and wars between the two rivals, almost invariably, have involved the control of Kashmir, either directly or indirectly.

Part of the overall Kashmir body count in table 5.2 is related to these Indo-Pakistani skirmishes. Another column, however, is related to an insurgency that began only in the late 1980s. Prior to that time, the Kashmiri population had been noticeably uninvolved in the combat over control of the state. At the outset in the late 1940s there is no evidence that the majority Muslim population sought incorporation into Pakistan. While independence and/or certainly a great deal of autonomy within the Indian Union was preferred, most of the local population seemed prepared to accept Indian control.[11] That changed over time.

Improvements in education and economic development to a certain level created a growing problem in which better educated youth found themselves unemployed or underemployed—and thereby more open to recruitment by political and insurgent organizations. Ethnic violence in Assam and civil war in what was to become Bangladesh sent less-quiescent Muslim refugees to Kashmir after the early 1970s. Mujahideen resistance in Afghanistan, the overthrow of the shah in Iran, Pakistani support, and a general movement toward intensified fundamentalism within Muslim, Hindu, and Sikh communities all worked together to encourage more-aggressive stances in defending Muslim rights and preferences. It did not help that the traditional Muslim political organization in Kashmir dated back to the 1930s and was highly resistant to change. While the longtime political leader of the Muslim community died in the early 1980s, his replacement by his politically adept son also encouraged Kashmiris to look elsewhere for political leadership. Nor did the Indian central government's approach to responding to calls for greater autonomy with repression help much, either. In contrast to earlier regimes, Indira Gandhi regarded increased autonomy demands as treasonable activity that required quick and decisive suppression. In 1984, one state government was replaced on dubious grounds by a group that was more accommodating to the Indian central government, which in turn was later succeeded by the leader, now seemingly co-opted by the Gandhi regime, who had been ousted in

1984. Yet by the late 1980s, the central government's attention was fully absorbed by non-Kashmir problems.[12]

Increasing tensions between Muslim and Hindu communities led to some Hindu migration to Jammu. Demonstrations, riots, and strikes had become more common by 1988. Insurgent and terrorist activity became more evident, as did overt calls for Kashmir secession from India. Brutal counterinsurgent activity added more fuel to the violence flames. Ultimately, army and police control regained the upper hand but without completely extinguishing the continuing insurgency.[13]

SIKH INSURGENCY

Sikhism began as a Hindu reform movement some five hundred years ago. While it represented a threat to the Indian stratification scheme by preaching equality, it was not until it backed a losing faction in a Mughal succession contest in the early seventeenth century that imperial forces attempted to suppress it. Resistance to the suppression effort transformed the Sikh movement into a militarized phenomenon. But Sikh militancy did not preclude its eventual defeat (but not extinction) by Mughal forces just before the empire began to fall apart in the early eighteenth century. Intermittent combat with northern raiders encouraged Sikh militancy and eventually led to Sikh military expansion in its own right from its Punjabi territorial base. In the mid-nineteenth century, British forces defeated the Sikhs just in time for them to be rewarded for their loyalty in the 1857 mutiny. Thus began a pattern of British encouragement of Sikh distinctiveness and political rewards for military services, which persisted through World War I and exacerbated communal competition in the Punjabi area without resolving Sikh insecurities. These insecurities were further accentuated by the partition proposal, which threatened to divide Sikh territory between India and Pakistan and to dilute Sikh political power. Calls for a separate Punjab state within the Indian Union were put forward as a way to preserve a Sikh political majority somewhere. This effort was unsuccessful for nearly two decades. Once a separate Punjab came into being, the political emphasis was transferred to efforts to enlarge the state by incorporating Punjabi-speaking territory outside its boundaries. Greater autonomy was also sought in a competitive context among communal groups for converts. Throughout, the main Sikh fear has been the possibility of being reduced to a minority in its own homeland.[14]

NORTHEAST INDIA TRIBAL INSURGENCIES

There have been multiple insurgencies in the northeast, but they all possess some features in common. These are groups that have regarded themselves as non-Indian in ethnicity in part due to their migration into the Indian subcontinent from Southeast and East Asia in centuries past and in part to their subsequent treatment by South Asian empires. At best, some of the tribal areas were incorporated into the Mughal Empire in a marginal way. Some were not. The British continued this pattern by granting more autonomy to the hill dwellers so that they could concentrate on the more-profitable plains dwellers. When Indian independence loomed, various independence movements became increasingly militarized after gaining little or no traction in regular political contestation.

Northeast Indian insurgencies tend to be reactions to perceptions of increased threat within contexts characterized by underdevelopment, scarcity, and limited returns from governmental services. Nagaland and Manipur had been relatively autonomous areas before independence and were forced to give up some of their customary self-governance when absorbed into the Indian Union. In Assam, the main issue has been the in-migration of people from adjacent states (in and out of India) and increased competition between local groups and perceived interlopers for employment and status. The in-migration began long before Indian independence, but subsequent events have accentuated the problem, as illustrated by the population movements associated with partition and the civil war in what was to become Bangladesh. In Tripura, the main issue was the loss of tribal lands to government projects, Bengali in-migration, and industrialization's search for raw materials. Mizoram focused on protecting minority languages.[15]

There are of course a large number of tribes in India. Some have pressed for secession, others seek more autonomy, while the demands of many tribal groups have not escalated to the insurgency level. In the cases that have, the militarized efforts were facilitated by World War II arming (by both sides) and combat experience (Nagaland) and continue to be encouraged by various types of support provided by adjacent states (Pakistan, Bangladesh, Burma/Myanmar, Bhutan, and China).[16] The fact that the insurgencies broke out with nearby sanctuaries in foreign countries makes them difficult to suppress. They have often proved very difficult to handle by local state police forces and required Indian Army intervention. Given the timing of many of the escalations, the charge that Indian central government policies have something to do with encouraging greater conflict is also plausible. Figure 5.2 shows the frequency of insurgencies spiraled upward after 1980 and only began to move downward quite recently. Some of the explanation may be attributable to the shift from Nehru's strong efforts to promote pluralism to Indira Gandhi's tougher approach to dealing with secession/autonomy threats.[17]

COMMUNISTS/MAOISTS/NAXALITES

Communist violence goes back to the early independence years, but in the mid-1960s transformed into something different when it began to be framed as a struggle between rural peasants (assisted by Maoist insurgents) and their landlords.[18] In addition to the usual inequalities prevailing between poor agrarian labor and landlords, rural populations have been subject to widespread displacement and the privatization of what had been common resources, thanks to various types of development projects. Forests have been entered on a more intensive scale to harvest timber and to gain access to mineral resources. Dams have been built to control rivers and to create energy supply. The brunt of much of this activity has been borne by forest-dwelling, tribal populations who are moved or intruded upon without much effective assistance from governments or corporations. Maoist groups offer support and some immediate retaliation against targets considered to be agents of oppression.

Initially, the Maoist efforts were fragmented and different groups competed with one another. In the late 1990s and early 2000s, the Naxalite movement became better organized and the number of competing groups was reduced. The activities have spread through an extensive area that stretches in a broad corridor from Nepal to the south in

Andhra Pradesh. The main efforts remain concentrated in Jarkhand, Chhattisgarh, and Andhra Pradesh—the so-called "Red Corridor" running down the eastern coast of India. In 2004, Naxalite activity was manifested in nine states. By 2010, it had spread to twenty of the twenty-eight federal states.[19] As noted in the number of deaths associated with insurgent fighting in table 5.2, the Naxalite insurgency has become the leading manifestation of Indian internal war.

The Indian Insurgency Problem in General

Insurgencies have become increasingly common, both in India and elsewhere. They last for several years and are usually defeated by governments that are stronger than the insurgents.[20] Yet while governments usually win, it is not uncommon for insurgencies to come back after several years of inactivity. Governmental victory does not necessarily mean the termination of the insurgency. However, insurgencies represent armed challenges of the state's existence, stability, and legitimacy. They are not common in the history of major powers. They divert resources to their suppression. They are embarrassing as long as they persist. Moreover, multiple insurgencies ongoing simultaneously, as in the case of India, is especially embarrassing and suggests that the state is struggling to find a way to suppress such challenges (or else changes in governmental policies may be provoking challenges). Such insurgencies are all the more problematic in a state that prides itself on its commitment to pluralism. Insurgencies often reflect attempts to secede from the pluralistic arrangement and overtly signify that the insurgent groups at least are not buying the state's official rationale or its effectiveness. Although Naxalite efforts are not oriented toward secession, where they are most effective they have taken political control away from the conventional authorities—which could be said to be a form of secession.

In general, then, insurgencies detract from state strength, both materially and perceptually. Left undefeated, they can potentially lead to the state's defeat. Connable and Libicki refer to the tipping point at which "an insurgent victory appears ever more probable, a 'negative bandwagon' effect takes hold, and previously neutral elements among the population, as well as governmental supporters fearful of being caught on the wrong side, support the opposition at an accelerating rate."[21] As these tipping points are reached, a host of additional problems are likely to surface. Internal and external support for the embattled regime fades away. Financial and intellectual capital flees. Military desertions increase. Governments become successively less effective and less likely to survive.

India is nowhere near an insurgency tipping point. At the same time, it has had rather clear problems managing the many insurgencies that it has experienced. Presumably, India will continue to experience insurgencies. To the extent that it does, the country's claim to a monopoly on the legitimate use of force must be questioned. If nothing else, such challenges give external rivals recurring opportunities to contribute to the further weakening of the Indian state.

Communal Violence and Human Rights

We have emphasized macro-level violence in this chapter, but other levels of conflict are germane and not altogether unrelated as well. In some respects, intercommunal violence is very old in South Asia, with warfare between and among Hindu, Muslims, and Sikhs going back many centuries. Yet the historical warfare is just that—warfare between invading and defending armies. Aside from the Indo-Pakistani wars, this type of combat is no more. One of its legacies, however, are Muslim and Sikh minorities within a state that is majority Hindu (approximately 82 percent). In the modern era, wars have been replaced by intermittent riots, involving confrontations between members of different religions, which were increasing in frequency and intensity in the 1980s and 1990s but now have subsided somewhat.

The evidence suggests that these riots tend not to be unplanned outbreaks of primordial hatred.[22] Overwhelmingly, they take place in cities and primarily in only a few cities.[23] Exactly what drives this behavior is debated. Wilkinson sees them as forms of electoral competition.[24] Politicians seek popular identification with their political parties by provoking countermobilizations of minority religious groups. Perceptions of threat lead voters to reward parties that are seen as most militant in dealing with disruptive minorities. We might then expect this form of electoral outbidding in highly competitive electoral districts, but Wilkinson argues that it works the opposite way. Highly competitive venues give politicians incentives to protect minorities in order to obtain their votes in the present or in the future. It is in the least competitive venues that politicians have few incentives to protect minorities. It is in these same least competitive venues that state governments are likely to expend the least police effort in heading off riots. Hence, riots are seen as a function of electoral incentives and police disincentives. Since the police sometimes join the majority rioters, we need to keep in mind that it is not just rioters who are responsible for riots.[25]

But there are other possible factors—none of which seem incompatible with the electoral competition argument. Varshney thinks it has to do with the presence and absence of intercommunal interactions.[26] Where religious groups routinely interact in civic life, riots are less common. Where religious groups are more isolated from one another, there are fewer incentives and resources for communal elites to negotiate differences of opinion. Shani argues that intercommunal riots reflect tensions within Hindu groups and especially conflict over the caste hierarchies.[27] Several authors stress the negative relationships between economic growth and riot behavior.[28]

We have also seen how insurgencies expanded in the 1980s in part due to intransigent governmental attitudes toward the threat of secession. Ganguly and Mukherji attribute a deterioration in the governmental commitment to secularism to a series of event that began in the 1980s.[29] First, Indira Gandhi's regime attempted to undermine the leading Sikh political party by cultivating Sikh extremists. Following Indira Gandhi's assassination by Sikh bodyguards, a court ruling during Rajiv Gandhi's regime threatened to impose Hindu customs on Muslims. Muslims reacted strongly to this threat to their communal prerogatives. The central government responded with a willingness to exempt Muslim marriage and divorce processes from the court edict. This, in turn, inflamed Hindu opinion as a prime illustration of pandering to minorities. Part of the fallout from this affair was a 1985 Hindu demand for access to a Muslim mosque (Babri Masjid) believed to have been built atop a Hindu temple. The demands escalated to an insistence on the destruction of the mosque, which actually took place at the hands of a

Hindu mob unfettered by any police preventative efforts. Here again, we see something of a sea change in the transition from Nehruvian founding principles to the practices of the Gandhi regimes of the 1980s.

Figure 5.4 indicates that after a turbulent beginning, Hindu-Muslim rioting was not all that frequent prior to the 1980s. In that decade, it

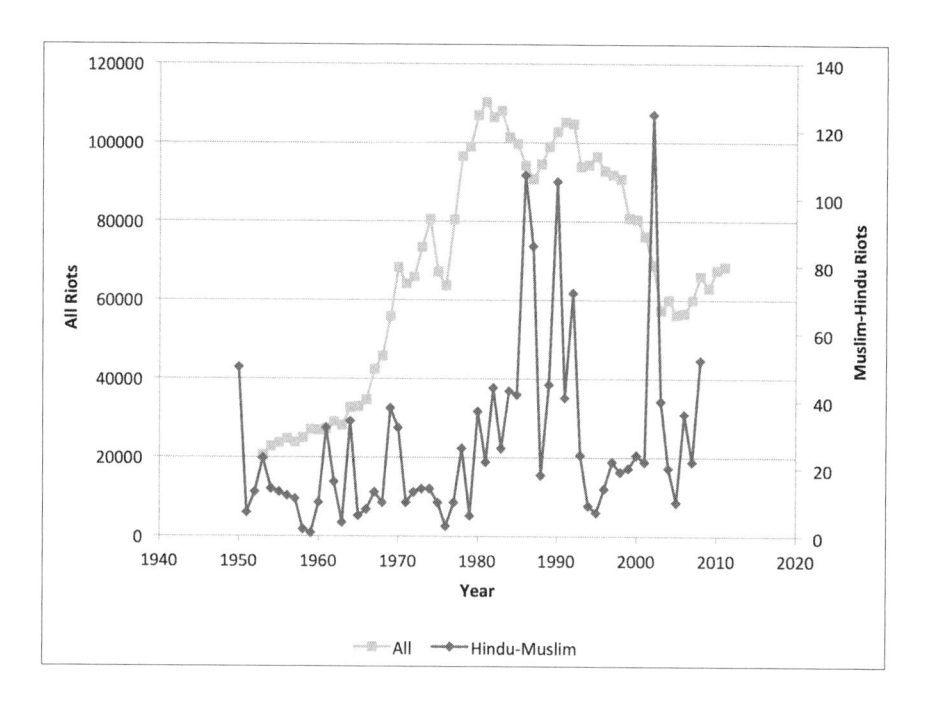

Fig. 5.4. The Indian Riot Record. *Sources: Based on data extracted from governmental figures for all riots reported in Government of India, Ministry of Home Affairs,* Crime in India 2013, *at ncrb.nic.in/crimeinindia.htm, accessed February 24, 2016; and for Hindu-Muslim rioting from Ahutosh Varshney and Steven Wilkinson,* Codebook: Varshney-Wilkinson Dataset on Hindu-Muslim Violence in India, 1950–1995, Version 2 *(Ann Arbor: Inter-University Consortium for Political and Social Research—ICPSR 4342, 2004); and updated Varshney-Wilkinson data reported in Sonia Bhalotra, Irma Clots-Figueras, and Lakshmir Iyer, "Political Identity and Religious Conflict in India," at www.Isid.ac.in/~pu/seminar/20_04_2012_paper1.pdf, accessed February 24, 2016. The updated data, in turn, are credited to Anirban Mitra and Debraj Ray; see their 2012 paper "Implications of an Economic Theory of Conflict: Hindu-Muslim Violence in India," at www.econ.nyu.edu/user/debraj/Papers/hm.pdf.*

escalated and did not subside until the early 1990s. If the data series had ended in 1995, it might have looked as if Hindu-Muslim conflict was dying out. Another spike in 2002, however, suggests that was not quite the case. Rising conflict in 2008 is another indicator. Indeed, the general pattern is for intermittent spikes in Hindu-Muslim conflict. Note as well that the very high level of all-riot frequency in India dwarfs the frequency of Hindu-Muslim riots, but the overall shape of the behaviors are similar subject to a bit of a lag. All-riot frequency began to climb in the 1970s and peaked in 1978. Riot numbers remained high into the late 1990s before they began to de-escalate, only to begin rising again in the past decade. The overlap in configuration (except in 2002) may hint at a common cause, such as economic welfare, but there is no reason to suppose that the drivers of such behavior are singular.

Our task here is not to explain communal violence and the decline of secularist principles in India. However, the Nehruvian idea of developing an overarching approach to governance that was inclusive and tolerant of local autonomies (and discussed earlier in this chapter) has been a cornerstone of the modern Indian ruling political formula. To the extent that it has decayed, the ability of the central state to manage problems in a highly heterogeneous setting has been affected negatively. A decaying ruling formula is unlikely to block great power aspirations. It is likely to constitute a significant drain of resources at the very least, though. More maximally, it could lead to the unraveling of what makes heterogeneous India work politically. In this respect, both macro-level insurgencies and meso-level violence are potentially threatening to the ability of the central state to function. Given the relatively high level of challenges to the state's violence monopoly in Indian contemporary history, it is testimony to the state's ability to operate in adverse conditions. But, at the same time, there is no guarantee that these challenges will never escalate in overlapping fashion and overwhelm the state's weathering capabilities and its basic unity. An Indian state that has lost political control over Jammu and Kashmir, Punjab, northwest India, the spreading Red Corridor in eastern and central India, as well as states in the west, such as Gujarat, with sizeable Muslim minorities, along with a revived Dravidian separatism in the south would be a much different organization than the one that exists now. There is little reason to anticipate a "little" India.[30] Still, there is no reason to rule out such a possibility as an extreme worst-case scenario in a context of increased scarcities due to, say, harsh environmental deterioration and water shortages.

Other dimensions of political violence are also worrying. The lethality of terrorist attacks inflicting high casualties (fifteen or more deaths) has increased in the past two decades. Table 5.4 indicates the widespread nature of these attacks. The trend line shown in Figure 5.5 suggests that the deadliness of the incidents has increased by a factor of greater than two, although no cases are reported for 2012 and 2013.

One could add micro-level violence to individuals, as in murder, kidnappings/abductions, and women gang-raped in public settings recently made more prominent, to this context of increasing violence. Table 5.5 simplifies the analysis by looking only at data on murder, rape, and kidnappings for two years: 1953 and 2013. All three forms of personal violence increase over time (see figure 5.6), but then so too has population (which quadrupled between 1953 and 2013). If we control for population growth, the murder rate per capita has remained constant. Reported cases of rape have increased at a rate far greater than the population increase. Kidnappings have also expanded faster than population

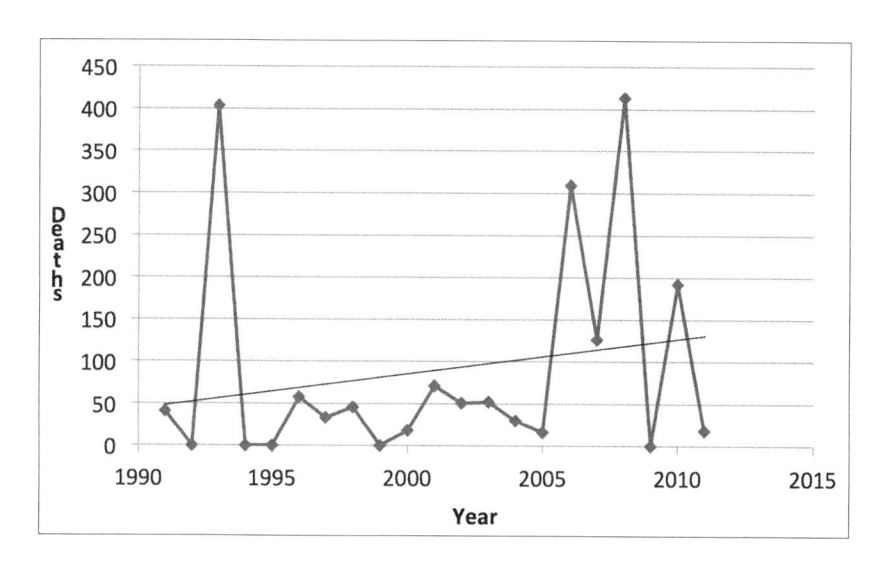

Fig. 5.5. Terrorism Incidents Involving High Deaths *Source: Based on information summarized in table 5.4.*

Table 5.4. High Death Terrorist Attacks, India, 1991–2014

Date	Location	Deaths
10/18/1991	Rudrapur	41
3/12/1993	Mumbai	317
3/16/1993	Calcutta	86
7/20/1995	Jammu	17
8/31/1995	Chandigarh	16
3/21/1996	Delhi	25
12/30/1996	Brahmaputra Mail (Assam)	33
7/8/1997	Bhatinda	33
2/14/1998	Coimbatore	46
1/3/2000	Sringar	18
2/27/2001	Doda (Kashmir)	15
10/1/2001	Sringar	40
12/13/2001	New Delhi	16
9/24/2002	Gandhinagar	32
11/23/2002	Lower Munda (Kashmir)	19
8/25/2003	Mumbai	52
5/23/2004	Lower Munda (Kashmir)	30
6/13/2005	Pulwama	16
2/28/2006	Damagua, Chhattisgarh	55
3/7/2006	Varanasi	21
7/11/2006	Mumbai	181
9/8/2006	Malegnon	37
11/5/2006	Guwahati	15
2/18/2007	Diwana	68
8/25/2007	Hyderabad	43
11/23/2007	Varanasi, Faizabad, Lucknow	15
5/13/2008	Jaipur	80
7/26/2008	Ahmedabad	55
7/26/2008	Mumbai	166
9/13/2008	New Delhi	25
10/30/2008	Assam, Gauhati, others	87
5/172010	Dantewada	44
5/28/2010	Jhargram	148
7/13/2011	Mumbai	18

Source: The Indian information has been extracted from a high-casualty terrorism list found at the Center for Systemic Peace, Vienna, VA, www.systemicpeace.org/inscrdata.html.

Table 5.5. Murders, Rape, and Kidnappings, 1953 and 2013

	Murder	Rape	Kidnappings
1953	9,802	2,487	5,261
	(.026)	(.007)	(.014)
2013	33,201	33,707	65,461
	(.026)	(.027)	(.052)

Note: per capita figures (in parentheses) calculated by the authors.
Source: Based on data reported in India Ministry of Home Affairs, National Crime Records Bureau, Crime in India 2014, at ncrb.gov.in.

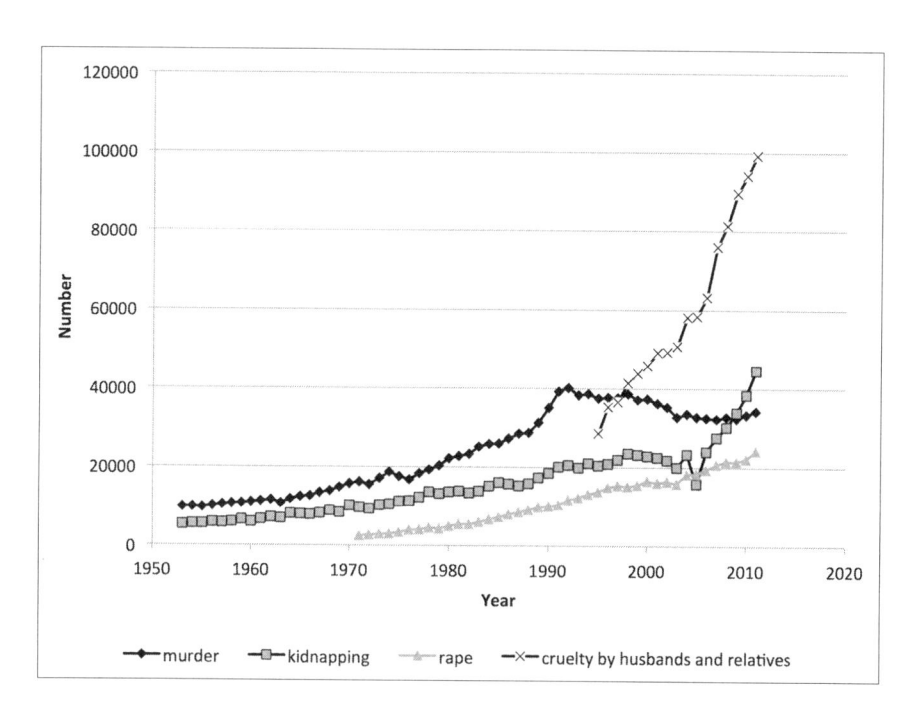

Fig. 5.6. Selected Crimes Against Persons in India *Source: Information extracted from Government of India, Ministry of Home Affairs, Crime in India 2013, at ncrb.nic.in/crimeindia.htm, accessed February 24, 2016.*

growth. These numbers suggest that more people are being exposed to personal attacks even if the probability of dying from them has not become any greater. No doubt, such statistics bring little comfort to the victims.

Summary

No state monopolizes violence completely. India is no exception, but it is also below average in its ability to manage nonstate violence. It is also above average in the factors that lead to challenges of the state's authority. The modern state of India could be said to have been born in an unintended paroxysm of violence, as millions of Hindus and Muslims were encouraged to flee their homes to areas presumed to be more secure. Conflict over the status of Jammu and Kashmir was also part of the birthright of India (and Pakistan). Scattered but difficult-to-suppress-quickly separatist insurgencies in various corners of India have characterized the last sixty-five years of independence. So far, the state has won all of these asymmetrical challenges but not easily. There is every reason to anticipate that India will persist in defeating peripheral separatist attempts. Naxalite violence appears to be another story. It is not that Naxalite groups cannot be beaten. It is more a matter of their threat not being beaten and eliminated. To the contrary, the phenomenon is spreading much more widely than any of the separatist challenges could claim. Part of this problem is that federal state forces are more likely to be outgunned by the Maoist groups. Another part of the problem is a matter of addressing the grievances that stimulate rural protest and rebellion. But other trends contribute to the expectation that violence monopoly is not something that is just around the corner in India. Terrorism lethality is increasing. Kidnappings are increasing. Crimes against women are increasingly reported.

A poor showing in the violence monopoly category is one of the Indian state's greatest vulnerabilities in terms of state capacity. It will need to be improved upon simply to maintain order. Yet it is doubtful that the Indian state will improve in this area rapidly. The scope of the problems are broad; the challenge is immense. The resources to deal with the problems are limited and strained. For these very reasons, the movement toward (or away from) greater degrees of violence monopoly may prove to be the best single barometer of Indian state strength in the years to come.

Even so, there are other areas and arenas of state strength that need to be examined. The next six chapters look at what we call "corollaries" of state capacity. Whereas extraction, legitimacy, and violence are the core components of our interpretation of state strength, the corollaries are areas of application of state strength. Yet the influence is two-way: the corollaries influence state strength as well. Economy and infrastructure (chapters 6 and 7) are critical to sustained economic growth on which the extraction capability depends and, in turn, highly dependent on state action at multiple levels. Inequality (chapter 8) and democracy (chapter 9) are fundamental to the maintenance of both legitimacy and violence. Grand strategy (chapter 10) also undergirds state capacity to the extent that Indian foreign policy is characterized by some semblance of a plan. Yet grand strategy, like defense and security policies (chapter 11), also manifests the expansion of state capacity—especially in the context of ascendance to the elite ranks in world politics.

State-Capacity Corollaries

S · I · X

The Economy

A state's economy is an important factor in assessing possibilities of ascent to great power status.[1] For some, it is the only or at least the main consideration. The reasoning goes something like this: A state with a weak economy is highly vulnerable to external pressure. To gain more autonomy and insulation from external pressures, one must develop the economy so that resources are available for both resisting other states' influence and pursuing one's own state goals. If those goals include gaining membership in the elite club of states, considerable resources are needed to pay for the requisite military-political capabilities (power projection, nuclear deterrence). If the starting point is far behind the competition, that means that the catch-up will require considerable and rapid economic growth.

There is also, of course, a specific Indian twist to this argument. As the largest state in South Asia, India is the natural candidate for becoming a regional hegemon. Yet much of its foreign-policy concerns are preoccupied with its two main rivals. On the one hand, there is nearby Pakistan, a state that has been able to engage India sort of competitively since the end of their mutual colonial statuses, in spite of Pakistan's increasingly weaker capabilities and inability to hold its own on Indo-Pakistani battlefields. China is nearby as well, but its rivalry is also both territorial and positional in nature. India needs to be able to withstand Chinese territorial claims along an extremely extended border and, at the same time, to avoid becoming subordinated to an ascending China within a super-Asia.[2] In both cases, a strong economic foundation is considered desirable. If India became a major power with a major power's economy, so the reasoning goes, it could expect to subordinate Pakistan and compete more evenly with China within the larger (and expanding) Asian region. Moreover, as oil and water become increasingly scarce, an added bonus is that a stronger India might expect to more than hold its own in coming resource wars.

Hence, either because Indian decision-makers want to operate beyond their home region or because they feel they must do so, the problem of India's underdeveloped economy must be addressed as a national security priority.[3] Either economic growth will proceed at an above-average pace (circa 7 percent per year is the threshold usually cited) or it will not. If it sustains such rapid growth, India can expect to become a great power according to some observers.[4] Sustaining anything less than above average may lead to increased political-economic salience but will fall short of being able to address simultaneously developmental concerns (poverty, industrialization) and the ability to operate as a military-political elite power beyond the home region.

The argument certainly has validity, but it conflates what is necessary for attaining great power status with being able to function successfully as a great power. As we argued in chapter 2, there is no discernible threshold of criteria for great power status. States have been accepted into the major power club for a variety of reasons, some of which pertain to possessing elite power attributes. Germany and Japan, for instance, developed elite economies during and immediately after the Cold War without being considered great powers.[5] The obvious and appropriate retort is that these two states have so far chosen not to develop their military capabilities to correspond to their economic standing. If they had (or when they choose to do so), great power status probably would have been, or will be, forthcoming.

That may well be true, but in the last cluster of states promoted to major power status (Italy, the United States, Japan, and, more recently, China), markedly differential economic prowesses were on display. Figure 6.1 captures the lags and leads in nineteenth-century industrialization by examining the rate at which economies became increasingly dependent on coal—a proxy for industrialization prior to the advent of petroleum. Several comments seem to be in order. There was a long lag between Britain, the first site of the industrial revolution, and the other major powers of the period. According to this indicator, no one had caught up to Britain before 1900, although several states were converging on the British position (Germany, France, and the United States)—one of which was anointed as a great power just before the turn of the century. But others (Italy, shown; Austria-Hungary, Russia, and Japan, not shown) were much further behind in the approach to World War I. There is also the separate issue of China's ascent to great power status long in advance of its more-recent improvements in economic standing. None of this discussion is meant to deny that some respectable level of industrialization is desirable as a prerequisite to elite promotion in the twenty-first century. But history would suggest that it is neither necessary nor sufficient for great power promotion per se.

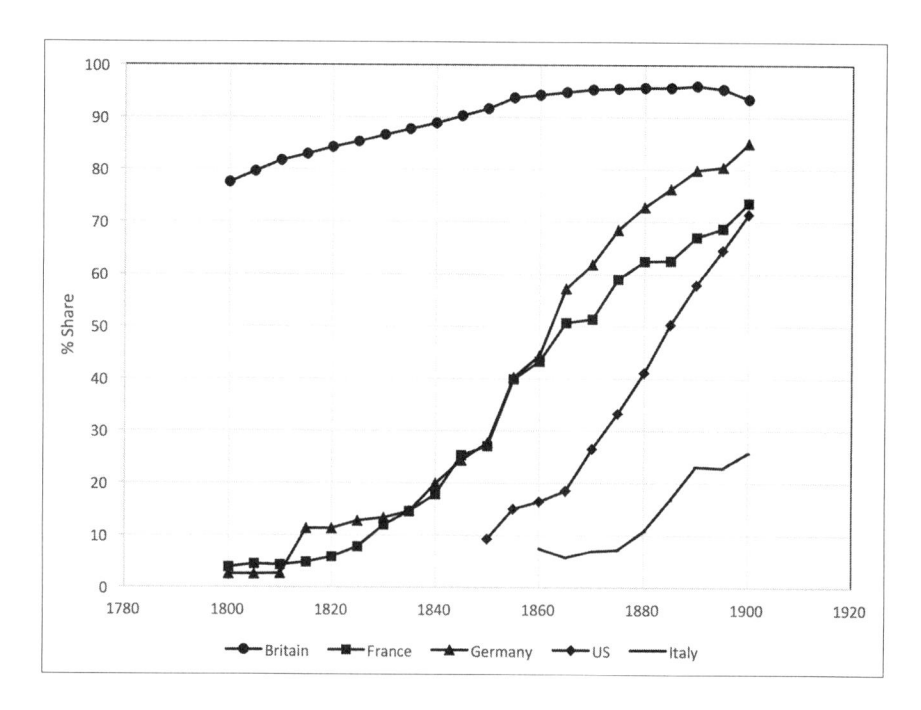

Fig. 6.1. Commitment to Coal as Primary Energy Source in the Nineteenth Century. *Note:* "% Share" *means the percentage for coal of total energy.*

Economic development, however, is a crucial prerequisite to successful maneuvering as a great power. Being able to move beyond the "South Asian box" is very much dependent on overcoming India's weak starting point at independence. As Nayar aptly describes the problem, "India's dominant economic characteristic at Independence in 1947 was a backward economy, heavily dependent on agriculture, yet deficient in food, lacking in a capital goods industry to provide the means for industrialization, and tied to a dependency relationship with the former colonial ruler, Great Britain."[6]

Nayar goes on to recount how India's first three economic plans were designed to develop the heavy industry necessary to break the dependency relationship. Yet the outcome did not quite work out as intended in the five-year plans. In the 1960s and early 1970s India encountered a series of economic problems—some of which were of their own making. Food shortages, due in part to privileging industry over agriculture, led to increased reliance on foreign aid or more dependency. Economic stagnation, inflation, and increased prices for petroleum after the first oil price shock combined to marginalize the Indian economy.

Economic circumstances improved in the late 1970s to early 1980s, as evidenced in figure 6.2's economic-growth-rate series. Another crisis in 1991, this time brought on by a series of politically motivated fiscal deficits, led to an opportunity to continue moving away from state ownership and highly centralized economic decision-making. India had experimented with relaxing some of its controls on business in the early 1980s but was virtually compelled to develop a less closed approach to economic planning by the embarrassment of receiving badly needed International Monetary Fund (IMF) loans in the early 1990s to cope with a series of economic shocks. The First Gulf War had increased oil prices and reduced remittances from gulf workers simultaneously. Export earnings were down. Debt payments were high. A downgrading of India's credit rating made it difficult to borrow more. IMF assistance was thus essential to resolving a balance of payments crisis in 1991. Although the IMF did not insist upon economic reforms, as it usually has in recent decades, Indian decision-makers realized that it was a window of opportunity to introduce major policy changes.[7]

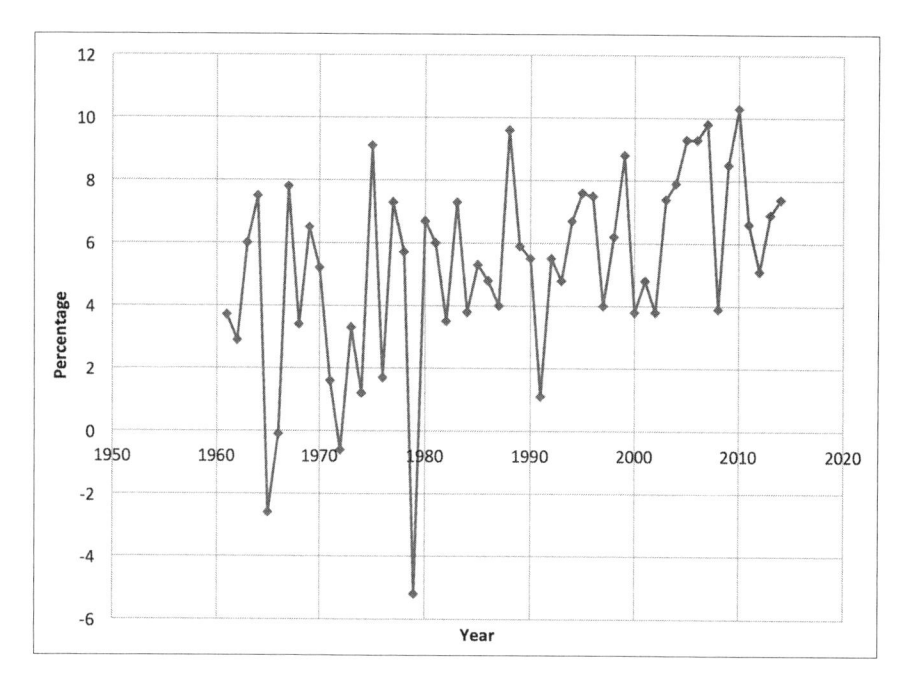

Fig. 6.2. India's GDP Growth Rate. *Note: Percentage is GDP growth rate.*

In any event, the annual economic growth rates since 2001 (through 2014) have exceeded 7 percent on average.[8] Whether this pace can be sustained into the future remains to be seen. But we agree with Sanjaya Baru that more than just a rapid rate of economic growth would be helpful for promotion to, and successful functioning within, the elite ranks of world politics.[9] India faces a number of economic challenges that must be overcome in some fashion for economic development to sustain political-military ascendance. These challenges, on the other hand, also address whether or to what extent the rapid rate of economic growth is likely to be sustained as well.

Our take on the economic challenges confronting India in the context of great powerhood and strengthening the state encompasses the following topics. At the top of the list is the perennial quality-versus-quantity issue. The size of the economy is not irrelevant. Possessing one of the largest economies in the world (GDP) gives some distinction to

India, but its quality (often expressed in GDP per capita terms) may end up mattering more. India will always have a large economy. Whether that large economy is truly powerful is a much different matter.

In some respects, it is the difference between GDP and GDP per capita that leads to a variety of other considerations. Leading the list of other considerations is the specific growth strategy pursued by India. There seems to be some expectation that India will do what China has done, with only a lag of a decade or more, given India's later takeoff. But Indian economic development strategy shares little with China's. China has pursued the classical movement from agrarian to industrial economy by making its agriculture more efficient, thereby releasing agrarian labor for manufacturing purposes. India's agriculture has not been made more efficient. Nor has its manufacturing expanded. India has instead capitalized on expanding its service productivity, especially in information technology (IT).[10] Why should we expect the development outcome to be similar if the approaches differ so substantially?

There are some definite risks that Indian growth could stall. A principal source is the middle income trap, in which economies grow to a point and then find it difficult to grow further into advanced economies capable of developing new technology, as opposed to utilizing technology developed earlier elsewhere. India's growth strategy may make that more likely rather than less likely. But there are other sources of risk. India's postindependence history of economic activity has been unusually insular. It needs capital from abroad. It also needs to develop a more globally competitive orientation that would expand Indian exports as well as make the Indian economy more receptive to foreign investment.[11]

Indian agriculture once benefited from a Green Revolution that expanded its productivity. Many more mouths to feed in the coming years will require more productivity expansion, which is by no means guaranteed to be forthcoming. Another advantage attributed to India is its young population in a world in which most other states, including China, are characterized by aging populations. India's demographic dividend might prove beneficial, but that outcome is also somewhat less than guaranteed.

Finally, improvements to India's economic infrastructure—its roads, ports, railroads, health care, energy resources, and so forth—

which facilitate (or not) the functioning of the economy, will prove critical. Infrastructural problems could easily choke future growth.[12] Unfortunately, the problems of infrastructure are so many that we will devote a separate chapter to their consideration.

The Quality-Quantity Conundrum

Jim O'Neill, the economist who coined the term "BRIC," relates how it dawned on him back in the early 2000s that several large economies were on the threshold of opening up their economies "to the same technology and advantages enjoyed in the West," and that their likely progress "would be prodigious."[13] In the next several decades, the size of the economies of Brazil, Russia, India, and China would grow to surpass the established large economies (the United States, the United Kingdom, France, Germany, Italy, and Japan). India, in particular, was forecast to pass Italy, France, Germany, and Japan by 2035 and to become the world's third largest economy by 2050.[14] While BRIC economic growth has since had its ups and downs, each of the four have exceeded to date the growth forecasts made by Goldman Sachs in 2003.[15]

Attention is drawn to BRIC economic growth for its revolutionary implications. For the past two centuries, economic power has been concentrated in northern economies (Western Europe, North America, and Japan). Now, it seems as if they are about to be eclipsed by southern economies, a variation on turning the world upside down. Yet there are some problems associated with this perspective. One concerns the emphasis on economic size. Another is the implication that the BRICs are doing similar things in their quest for economic growth. The first issue is misleading, while the second one is simply wrong. Both inform how we should look at the Indian economy as an important foundation for great geopolitical power and building stronger states.

Size alone is not the main issue. The Indian economy has been the largest in the world before, but that did not prevent its absorption into the British Empire. Then too the Indian economic growth is often described as being ten years behind Chinese growth rates, not inaccurately, but the implication that India will follow the Chinese ascent trajectory assumes that Indian economic actors are doing something similar to what the Chinese have done. If they have not, as will be shown later in this chapter, markedly different expectations emerge.

THE QUESTION OF SIZE

Tables 6.1 and 6.2 array selected gross domestic product figures based on observed and forecasted numbers for the traditional powerhouses

Table 6.1. GDP Expansion, 1980–2050 (in 2010 U.S. Dollars, Selected States)

	1980	1990	2000	2010	2020	2030	2040	2050
United States	6,462	8,891	12,423	14,658	18,100	22,288	27,742	34,582
Japan	2,482	4,687	5,827	5,459	5,874	6,295	6,707	7,366
Germany	1,915	2,371	2,379	3,316	3,534	3,947	4,457	5,218
France	1,602	1,914	1,664	2,583	2,839	3,477	4,277	5,365
United Kingdom	1,257	1,560	1,848	2,247	2,786	3,604	4,539	5,686
Italy	1,068	1,740	1,374	2,035	2,197	2,580	2,917	3,418
Canada	623	893	905	1,574	1,940	2,282	2,801	3,473
Russia			324	1,465	2,895	4,706	6,563	8,011
Mexico	525	441	839	1,039	1,913	3,212	4,894	6,947
China	469	598	1,496	5,878	13,817	25,584	37,716	52,619
India	423	500	599	1,538	3,477	7,174	13,896	24,984
Brazil	377	778	802	2,090	3,268	4,944	7,178	9,713
Indonesia	221	193	207	707	1,296	2,272	3,809	6,037
Turkey	218	310	333	742	1,260	2,115	3,215	4,451
Iran	217	130	120	357	742	1,435	2,352	3,194
Korea	149	414	666	1,007	1,561	2,068	2,536	3,030
Nigeria	140	48	58	217	434	952	2,179	4,906
Philippines	75	68	95	189	401	839	1,680	3,166
Pakistan	66	74	92	175	380	836	1,743	3,328
Vietnam	65	10	39	104	258	612	1,248	2,183
Egypt	52	140	124	218	500	1,100	2,125	3,606
Bangladesh	45	47	59	105	217	451	892	1,631

Source: Dominic Wilson, Kamakshya Trivedi, Stacy Carlson, and Josip Urua, "The BRICs 10 Years On: Halfway Through the Great Transformation," Global Economics Paper No. 208, Goldman Sachs Global Economics, December 7, 2011.

Table 6.2. GDP Size Rank Order –
1980 versus 2050 (selected states)

Rank order	1980	2050
1	United States	China
2	Japan	United States
3	Germany	India
4	France	Brazil
5	United Kingdom	Russia
6	Italy	Japan
7	Canada	Mexico
8	Mexico	Indonesia
9	China	United Kingdom
10	India	France
11	Brazil	Germany
12	Indonesia	Nigeria
13	Turkey	Turkey
14	Iran	Egypt
15	Korea	Canada
16	Nigeria	Italy
17	Philippines	Pakistan
18	Pakistan	Iran
19	Vietnam	Philippines
20	Egypt	Korea
21	Bangladesh	Bangladesh
22		Vietnam

Source: based on the information reported in table 6.1

of the world economy and a group of states that have been anointed (by the same people who initially brought us the BRICs) as the most likely economies to grow quickly in coming decades. Table 6.2 provides the easiest-to-grasp information. In this grouping, India was the tenth largest economy in 1980. By 2050, it is expected to be the third largest economy. In 2050, the tenth or eleventh largest economies are forecast to be a mix of the traditional and BRIC leaders (plus Mexico and Indonesia). Some seventy years earlier, Mexico, China, and India managed to make the top ten but only because they were not too much smaller than Canada's economy.

Economic size is not insignificant. The undergirding of a large economy can be most helpful in domestic and international politics. Larger populations can mean larger tax bases, military conscription pools, and significant material consumption of the world's goods. Yet economic quantity is not the same thing as economic quality. Gross domestic product per capita is a better measure of economic quality. Not only does this measure suggest something about average quality of life, it also taps into the sophistication of the economy, which is also important for tax bases and consumption. Tables 6.3 and 6.4 look at the same group of states as found in the last two tables but add the control for population size. On this count, the BRICs are located in the lower half of the group in 1980. India and China were at or near the very bottom of the pack. In the forecasted 2050 group, India remains near the bottom in spite of a remarkable improvement in GDP per capita (US$604 in 1980 and $14,766 in 2050, in table 6.3). That puts India's 2050 GDP per capita at about 78 percent of Italy's 1980 GDP per capita. The change, if realized, would be quite impressive but would still leave a number of other states ahead of India (for example, Nigeria, the Philippines, Indonesia, Vietnam, Iran, Mexico). Many of the states in this forecasted future ranking are unlikely to be candidates for great power. Whether they are all likely to have strong states may be equally unlikely.

The differences between GDP and GDP per capita suggest, if nothing else, some caution in perceiving economic growth as one of the drivers of India's ascent to greater status in world politics. Even if the future evolves as forecasted, India will not have one of the world's more affluent or developed economies any time soon. Qualitatively, it will still be stuck at best somewhere in the middle of the overall population of states with a very large and uneven economy.

Table 6.3. GDP per Capita, 1980–2050 (2010 U.S. Dollars, Selected States)

	1980	1990	2000	2010	2020	2030	2040	2050
France	29,732	33,746	28,187	41,132	43,097	50,789	60,515	74,058
United States	28,115	35,094	43,975	47,225	53,693	61,625	72,347	85,791
Canada	25,418	32,243	29,509	46,272	52,191	57,276	66,867	79,575
Germany	24,456	29,977	28,890	40,286	43,637	49,663	57,656	69,782
United Kingdom	22,328	27,266	31,393	36,228	42,336	51,992	63,457	78,091
Japan	21,413	38,340	46,346	43,141	47,070	52,362	58,661	67,860
Italy	18,988	30,625	24,109	33,940	35,840	42,395	48,476	57,781
Russia			2,209	10,248	20,528	34,491	49,995	63,486
Mexico	7,634	5,232	8,391	9,161	15,193	23,719	34,581	48,268
Iran	5,633	2,374	1,842	4,829	9,153	16,990	27,386	37,423
Turkey	4,953	5,730	5,227	10,197	15,606	24,400	35,599	48,577
Korea	3,983	9,643	14,479	20,901	31,334	41,084	51,382	64,393
Brazil	3,096	5,201	4,598	10,723	15,531	22,421	31,983	43,586
Nigeria	1,859	495	468	1,369	2,129	3,692	6,802	12,591
Philippines	1,598	1,098	1,226	2,024	3,657	6,639	11,859	20,433
Indonesia	1,466	1,045	968	2,946	4,936	8,125	13,125	20,571
Vietnam	1,195	148	494	1,179	2,681	6,032	11,999	20,996
Egypt	1,153	2,464	1,830	2,693	5,278	10,334	18,280	29,212
Pakistan	824	664	640	1,007	1,852	3,568	6763	12,106
India	604	572	568	1,256	2,507	4,709	8,541	14,766
Bangladesh	561	444	453	706	1,299	2,481	4,673	8,392
China	477	522	1,179	4,382	9,956	18,365	27,714	40,614

Source: Dominic Wilson, Kamakshya Trivedi, Stacy Carlson, and Josip Urua, "The BRICs 10 Years On: Halfway Through the Great Transformation," Global Economics Paper No. 208, Goldman Sachs Global Economics, December 7, 2011.

Table 6.4. GDP per Capita Rank Order,
1980 and 2050 (Selected States)

Rank order	1980	2050
1	France	United States
2	United States	Canada
3	Canada	United Kingdom
4	Germany	France
5	United Kingdom	Germany
6	Japan	Japan
7	Italy	Korea
8	Mexico	Russia
9	Iran	Italy
10	Turkey	Turkey
11	Korea	Mexico
12	Brazil	Brazil
13	Nigeria	China
14	Philippines	Iran
15	Indonesia	Egypt
16	Vietnam	Vietnam
17	Egypt	Indonesia
18	Pakistan	Philippines
19	India	Nigeria
20	Bangladesh	Indonesia
21	China	Pakistan
22		Bangladesh

Source: Based on information reported in table 6.3.

The China-India Difference

Homi Kharas notes that if one plots Chinese GDP per capita for 1981–1998 with Indian GDP per capita for 1991–2008, essentially lagging Indian economic performance ten years behind Chinese activity, the trajectory of the two series behave very similarly.[16] Figure 6.3 attempts to replicate this observation. Our results show a slightly different path than the one found in Kharas, but the interpretation is similar. Both lines move along similar tracks, moving slightly upward for the first twelve years and then breaking upward more markedly. The impression one gets is that India is following almost identically the path blazed by China's well-known ascent.

If one continues the Chinese series another sixteen years (1997–2012), the outcome is all the more welcome to Indian prospects. We do this in figure 6.4. China's GDP per capita ascent began to accelerate around the turn of the century. If the lagged relationship holds up, India's economic fortunes should be about to improve rapidly. But there are reasons to think that this might not be the case. The lagged relationship makes most sense if the two countries are similar in size, starting point, and economic strategy. China and India are similar in size and starting point but considerably different in terms of economic strategy. China's strategy for economic growth led to a major transformation of

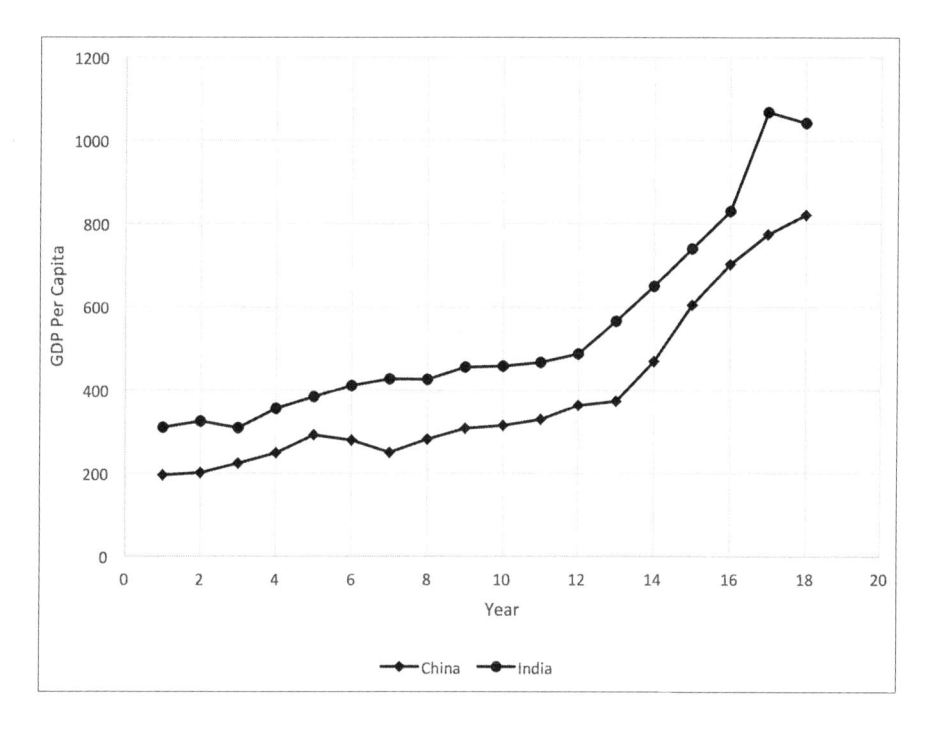

Fig. 6.3. Lagging Indian GDP per Capita Ten Years Behind China's GDP per Capita

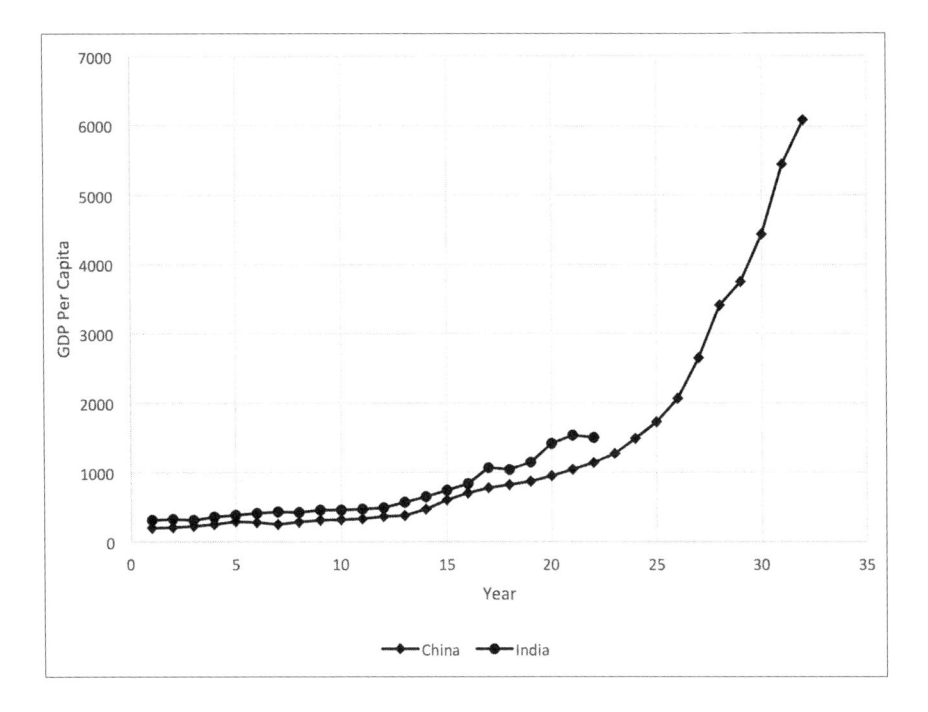

Fig. 6.4. Lagging Indian GDP per Capita Behind Chinese GDP per Capita for Additional Years

the economy and society; the same cannot be said for India. Without the major transformation, there is much less reason to anticipate an Indian acceleration in economic growth. Instead, one might expect more gradual growth in India than in China—which seems to be the case.

How have the two states pursued different growth strategies? The two BRIC states did begin their respective ascents from similar starting points. Both are unusually large states located in Asia that missed out on many of the technological advances of the nineteenth and first half of the twentieth centuries. Both initially adopted development strategies that stressed central planning and insularity from the world economy. Both sought and received Soviet aid at different times. As shown in table 6.5, that is where the initial similarities end and the differences begin to emerge.

While the respective political systems of China and India are vastly different, and so are the circumstances in which the two economies began

Table 6.5. Two BRICs, Two Different Growth Strategies

China differences	China-India common denominators	India differences
	Initially pursued inward/autarkic development strategy	
	Initially employed variations on strong centralized planning before opening up gradually	
	Drew on earlier technology belatedly to pursue rapid catch-up	
Autocracy, consistent one party state: strong governance		Democracy, intermittent, one-party state alternating with weak coalition governments most of the time: weak governance
Began opening gradually in late 1970s in voluntary fashion		Began opening gradually in 1980s but especially in early 1990s after a political-macroeconomic crisis
Greater movement of labor from agriculture to industry		Less movement of labor from agriculture to industry
Early investment in education across the board		Early investment in engineer training
Strong emphasis on expanded manufacturing for export		Strong emphasis on expanded IT service sector for export

(*continued*)

Table 6.5. (*continued*)

China differences	China-India common denominators	India differences
Growth rates roughly three times faster than world average		Growth rates roughly two times faster than world average
Massive transformation of the nature of the economy		Limited transformation of the nature of the economy
	Income and regional inequalities	
	Corruption	
	Environmental pollution	

Source: Based selectively on Carl J. Dahlman, The World Under Pressure: How China and India are Influencing the Global Economy and Environment *(Stanford, CA: Stanford University Press, 2012)*, 45–111.

to expand their participation in the outside world, the main difference in economic strategy is that China opted for becoming a manufacturing center for the west while India focused largely on developing a niche in exporting information technology services to the west. China chose to begin experimenting in the late 1970s with greater participation in the capitalist world economy by first establishing limited coastal zones for exports and then later expanding the proportion of the economy that was involved in manufacturing exports. One of the implications of the Chinese strategy is that large numbers of agricultural workers had to be transformed into industrial workers, and this also meant large-scale migration from rural to urban areas. Another implication is that Chinese agriculture needed to be made more efficient to accommodate the loss of labor. Popular education also had to be improved so that the newly industrialized workers would be prepared to play their role in manufacturing processes.

Partially as a consequence of these very different strategies, India's employment structure has not changed all that much since the 1980s. In

1983, 63.4 percent of the working population were employed in agriculture, while 11.8 percent were found in manufacturing. In 2004–2005, the comparable numbers were 54.9 percent and 12.8 percent respectively. As demonstrated in table 6.6, the agricultural GDP contribution has declined somewhat but the manufacturing share has changed little. While agricultural employment has continued to decline proportionately, more workers are now found in the service sector than in industrial employment.

Corbridge, Harriss, and Jeffrey rightly put considerable stress on this facet of Indian economic development: "One of the most fundamental assumptions about economic development is that it must entail a major transformation in the structure of an economy. In the early stages of development, it is usually the case that the primary agricultural sector is overwhelmingly dominant, and the great majority of the population is engaged directly in agricultural production. The process of development involves an historic shift away from agriculture to industry and a wide range of service activities, and labour out of agriculture and into employment in these sectors."[17] Without the major transformation, can India hope to aspire to Chinese-like, rapid growth rates and continued movement up the development ladder? Or, is it more likely that Indian economic development will move forward more intermittently? If we are forced to choose between these two alternatives, the latter seems more probable.

India did not entirely neglect improving education but focused largely on turning out more students with engineering degrees. This approach was fortuitous for IT purposes but did little to tackle illiteracy in rural India.[18] Since IT services have not required a large labor pool, India's urban-rural gap has also experienced much less transformation than has been the case in China. The lack of employment possibilities in new technology has not halted rural migration to urban centers; it simply means that reducing the urban-rural gap moves more slowly in India than it has in China. It also implies greater persistence for poverty and inequality to the extent that these problems are concentrated in rural areas.

Both approaches have produced unusually high growth rates according to world averages. China's growth rates are roughly three times

Table 6.6. Sectoral Value Added to India's GDP

Year	Agriculture	Services	Industry	Manufacturing
1970	42	37.6	20.5	13.7
1971	40.3	38.5	21.2	14.3
1972	40.3	38.4	21.3	14.4
1973	43.3	36.5	20.2	14.3
1974	40.3	38.2	21.5	15.6
1975	37.6	40.2	22.2	15.2
1976	35.8	40.8	23.4	15.7
1977	37.1	39.7	23.2	15.4
1978	39.5	40.3	24.3	16.5
1979	33.6	41.4	25	17.3
1980	35.4	40.3	24.3	16.2
1981	34.1	40.8	25.1	16.3
1982	32.9	41.9	25.2	15.9
1983	33.5	41.2	25.6	16.1
1984	32.2	42.2	25.7	16.1
1985	30.9	43.4	25.9	16
1986	29.7	44.4	25.9	15.8
1987	29.2	44.9	25.8	15.9
1988	30.2	44	26.5	15.7
1989	29	44.5	26.5	16.4
1990	29	44.5	26.5	16.2
1991	29.4	45.2	25.4	15.2
1992	28.7	45.5	25.8	15.4
1993	28.7	45.8	25.5	15.3
1994	28.3	45.3	26.4	16.2
1995	26.3	46.3	27.4	17.3
1996	27.1	46.3	26.6	16.9
1997	25.9	47.7	26.4	15.8
1998	25.8	48.5	25.7	15
1999	24.5	50.3	25.2	14.6
2000	23	51	26	15.3
2001	22.9	52	25.1	14.6

(*continued*)

Year	Agriculture	Services	Industry	Manufacturing
2002	20.7	53.1	26.2	14.9
2003	20.7	53.2	26	14.9
2004	19	53	27.9	15.3
2005	18.8	53.1	28.1	15.4
2006	18.3	52.9	28.8	16.1
2007	18.3	52.7	29	16
2008	17.8	53.9	28.3	15.4
2009	17.7	54.5	27.8	15.1
2010	18.2	54.6	27.2	14.8
2011	17.9	54.9	27.2	14.7
2012	17.5	56.3	26.2	14.1

Source: World Bank, *World Development Indicators* (Washington, DC: 2015), available at data.worldbank.org/data-catalog/world-development-indicators.

the world average. India's growth rates have been about twice as fast as the average. The question, though, is whether the fast pace of these growth rates can be maintained. It may well be that both economies will slow down, but the more limited transformation (and more infrastructural problems, discussed in the next chapter) in India suggest slower growth prospects for India than for China. In other words, there is little reason to assume that India's growth trajectory will continue to parallel China's. This statement is not advanced solely because the two states' growth strategies are so different. Other areas, in addition to critical infrastructural problems, that suggest more "headwinds" for Indian growth include three that are linked to the differences in growth strategies (the middle-income trap, global competitiveness / foreign investment, and agricultural problems) and one that is not (demographics).

The Middle-Income Trap

Linear forecasts are easy to make. But they are always subject to the *ceteris paribus*—all other things equal or held constant—assumption.

Those other things, unfortunately, do not always behave. One problem with contemporary growth trajectories is called the middle-income trap. An economy can grow quickly, given the right circumstances and especially when it starts from a low point of development with considerable growth potential. At some point in the growth trajectory, however, the economy in question needs to shift from copying and borrowing technology developed elsewhere to being able to develop its own technological solutions. In the Indian case, the obvious example is shifting from serving other economies as an outcall center to developing new IT software and hardware that can be adopted throughout the Indian economy and abroad. These types of shifts are difficult and cannot be assumed, because few states so far have been able to make the transition from low-income to high-income societies.

Figure 6.5 illustrates this problem. The South Korean ascent would have been difficult to predict in the 1950s or 1960s. Yet, with some dips

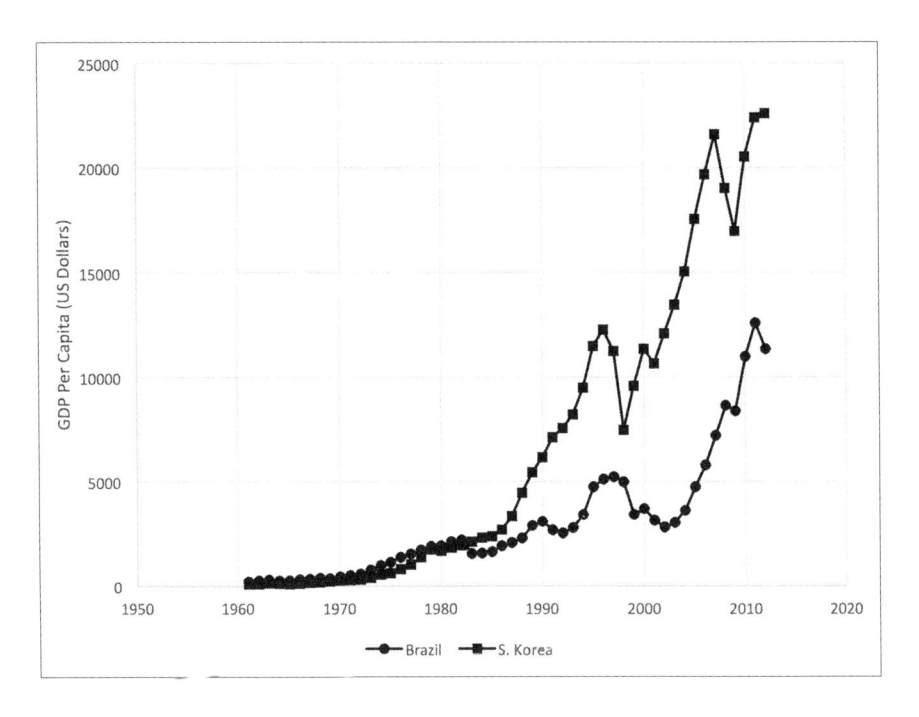

Fig. 6.5. Brazilian and South Korean Economic Growth
Source: Data from World Development Indicators, World Bank

it has been a fairly steady climb upward based on planning and taking advantage of local (for example, Asian war profits) and global (for example, specialization niches) opportunities. Contrast this record with Brazil's slower ascent. Between the 1980s and the early half of the 2000s first decade, Brazilian GDP per capita made little headway. This problem is so common in Latin America that it is sometimes referred to as the "Latin Americanization" model, as in table 6.7. Yet it is a truly global phenomenon. The economic successes of Japan, South Korea, Taiwan, and Singapore are hardly the standard economic growth story.

Walton's model, summarized in table 6.7, offers one way to explain the middle-income trap phenomenon. It represents a combination of business group cronyism, societal/spatial divisions, and poor educational infrastructure that all work toward suppressing income growth. Business groups make arrangements that protect themselves at the expense of competition. Societies are polarized by conflict between groups that have real and imagined reasons to dislike and distrust one another.

Table 6.7. Walton's Model for Middle-Income Traps

Components	"Latin Americanization" model	Transformative model
Capitalism	Oligarchic: major business groups wield disproportionate influence	Competitive: firm innovation more important than group influence
Group-based conflicts	Intensification	Reduced polarization of group-based identities
Spatial inequality	Deepening	Economic and social convergence of poorer regions
Education	Continuing sites for inequality reproduction	Increasingly meritocratic with full access
Outcome	Middle-income trap	High-income society

Source: Based on Michael Walton, "Inequities and India's Long-term Growth: Tackling Structural Inequities," in India 2039: An Affluent Society in One Generation, *ed. Harinder S. Kohli and Anil Sood (New Delhi: Sage Publications, 2010), 89.*

Societies also reflect uneven development with some areas much richer than others, leading to have-versus-have-not conflicts over societal redistribution policies. Education has less impact than it should because its product fails to impart new skills to its consumers. The outcome is economic stagnation, with some people getting very rich while most people just get by. Although Walton calls it the Latin Americanization model, the model components are hardly restricted to one part of the world. India has some potential for all four components corresponding more closely to the left-hand column of table 6.7 than to the right-hand side. Presumably, the greater the movement in the direction of the Latin Americanization model, the less likely linear forecasts of optimistic economic growth are to be realized. Yet figure 6.5 also suggests that middle-income traps do not have to be terminal roadblocks. Economic growth may stall and/or plateau for extended periods of time before resuming.

Global Competitiveness

Given less emphasis on expanding manufacturing facilities, India has benefited less from foreign direct investment (FDI) than China has. Figure 6.6 highlights this difference. China, of course, has been the contemporary leader in receiving this type of external assistance. One might argue that as long as the Chinese economy was favored as a prime place for investment, other places would be hard pressed to compete. India, however, has handicapped itself further by being less bureaucratically receptive to incoming FDI. While some of the lack of receptiveness has been reduced, the problem represents a two-way street. Not only does the Indian economy need to be open to foreign investment, India also needs to be viewed as an attractive place in which to invest.

One quick way to evaluate India's perceived attractiveness is to examine its ranking on a competitiveness index designed to assess a variety of dimensions or attributes of the Indian market environment. India's score has not changed too much between the origins of the index in 2006–2007 and its 2013–2014 score (see table 6.8). It may be more telling that it has not improved. On the contrary, it has declined slightly (4.5 to 4.3). Perhaps the best way to evaluate its position is that its ranking places it in a middle zone that is not first-world but, at the same

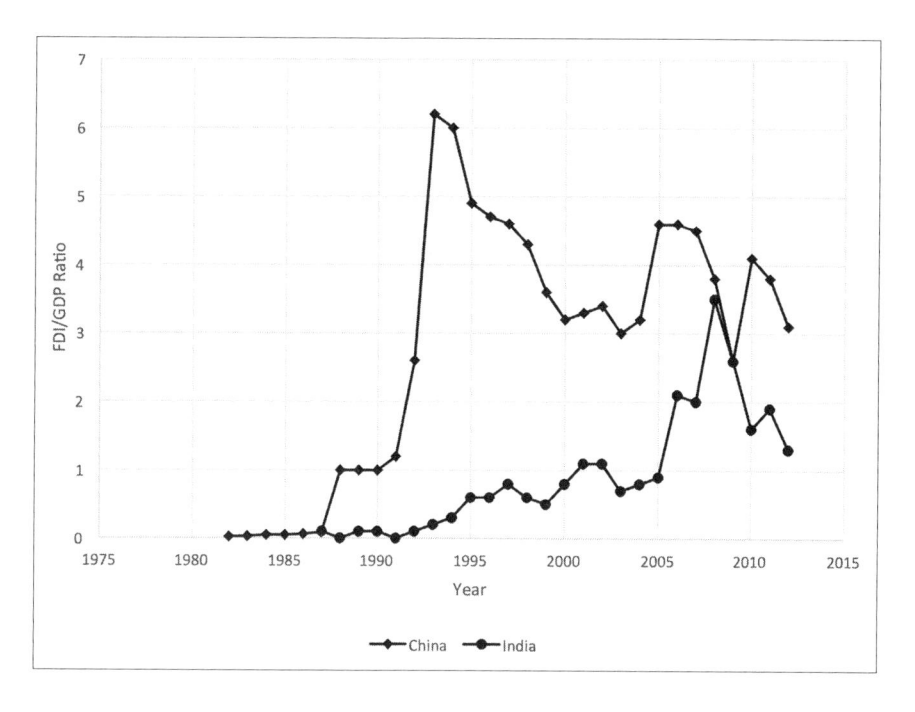

Fig. 6.6. Chinese and Indian Foreign Direct
Investment / Gross Domestic Product

time, is neither third- nor fourth-world. India's 2013–2014 score is in fact exactly the same as Brazil's and Russia's but not quite as good as China's. If nothing else, that outcome suggests Indian competitiveness can be improved.

Table 6.9 specifies the areas that need to be improved for India's global competitiveness score to increase. The table is brief but the areas specified entail rather broad changes. Inflation, corruption, and deficit spending are major features of Indian political-economic culture. Infrastructural problems (examined more closely in the next chapter), ranging from transportation to health and education, are legendary. The third column takes us back to Indian political-economic culture, with an emphasis on the slow pace of change in institutions and gender rights. We might well ask, Which immediate future is more probable? Will there be radical change eliminating some of these reasons for negative evaluations or roughly more of the same? One does not have to be

Table 6.8. Global Competitiveness Scores,
2006–2007 versus 2013–2014

2006–2007		2013–2014	
United States	5.8	Switzerland	5.7
United Kingdom	5.6	Singapore	5.6
Denmark	5.5	Finland	5.5
Switzerland	5.5	Germany	5.5
Japan	5.5	United States	5.5
Finland	5.5	Sweden	5.5
Germany	5.5	Netherlands	5.4
Singapore	5.5	Japan	5.4
Sweden	5.4	United Kingdom	5.4
Netherlands	5.4	Norway	5.3
Canada	5.4	Taiwan	5.3
Taiwan	5.4	Qatar	5.2
Israel	5.3	Canada	5.2
France	5.2	Denmark	5.2
Australia	5.2	Austria	5.2
Norway	5.2	Belgium	5.1
Austria	5.2	New Zealand	5.1
Malaysia	5.2	U.A.E.	5.1
Iceland	5.1	S. Arabia	5.1
New Zealand	5.1	Australia	5.1
Ireland	5.1	Luxembourg	5.1
S. Korea	5.1	France	5.1
Belgium	5.1	Malaysia	5.0
Luxembourg	5.0	S. Korea	5.0
Estonia	4.8	Brunei	5.0
Chile	4.8	Israel	4.9
Thailand	4.8	Ireland	4.9
Spain	4.7	China	4.8
Kuwait	4.7	Iceland	4.7
Czechoslovakia	4.7	Estonia	4.7
Qatar	4.6	Oman	4.6
Tunisia	4.6	Chile	4.6
China	4.6	Spain	4.6

(*continued*)

2006–2007		2013–2014	
S. Africa	4.5	Kuwait	4.6
U.A.E.	4.5	Thailand	4.5
Hungary	4.5	Indonesia	4.5
Lithuania	4.5	Azerbaijan	4.5
Slovenia	4.5	Panama	4.5
Barbados	4.5	Malta	4.5
India	**4.5**	Poland	4.5
Portugal	4.5	Bahrain	4.5
Latvia	4.5	Turkey	4.5
		Mauritania	4.5
		Czechoslovakia	4.4
		Barbados	4.4
		Lithuania	4.4
		Italy	4.4
		Kazakhstan	4.4
		Portugal	4.4
		Latvia	4.4
		S. Africa	4.4
		Costa Rica	4.4
		Mexico	4.3
		Brazil	4.3
		Bulgaria	4.3
		Cyprus	4.3
		Philippines	4.3
		India	**4.3**
		Peru	4.3
		Slovenia	4.3
		Hungary	4.3
		Russia	4.3

Note: States ranking below India are not listed.

Source: World Economic Forum, The Global Competiveness Report, 2013–2014, at www.weforum.org/reports/global-competitiveness-report-2013-2014/.

Table 6.9. Reasons for India's Low Rankings
in Global Competitiveness Scores

Economic	Infrastructure	Politics and society
Inflation	Transportation supply	Lack of institutional reforms
Bribery	IT	Public trust in politics
Public deficits	Energy	Low participation of women in workplace
Public debt	Public health	
Technological readiness	Education	
	Telephony penetration	

Source: World Economic Forum, The Global Competiveness Report, 2013–2014, p. 10, at www.weforum.org/reports/global-competitiveness-report-2013-2014/.

cynical to see the latter as more conceivable than the former. Path dependencies, the socioeconomic and political constraints established in the past and continuing to have effect, are likely to prove strong in the Indian case.

Agricultural Problems

The amount of food needed to feed the Indian population is expected to double by 2050, yet Indian agriculture is already struggling to provide enough food for the current population in which half of the children under the age of five currently are classified as malnourished.[19] Other Asian agrarian producers have done much better in improving their yields. Chinese wheat yields in 2009 were 1.7 times greater than in India. Chinese rice yields are 3 times the amounts produced in India. But these shortfalls are not simply a function of earlier Chinese commitments to making their agriculture more efficient. Rice yields in Vietnam and Indonesia are also twice as productive as those in India.[20]

Baldwin and Bonarriva attribute Indian agricultural problems in part to political problems. Indian farmers are described as a highly unified voting bloc that have pressed for short-term governmental support in contrast to lobbying for long-run changes in research, irrigation, and rural infrastructure.[21] But Chinese agriculture, for instance, is more likely to use fertilizer, to have more agrarian workers available because the amount of arable land is much smaller in China, and to have much better access to water.[22] Indian farmers are more dependent on highly variable monsoon rains. Less water means less agrarian yield, less predictability, and a greater probability of crop failure.

As economic growth continues, more food will be needed for a larger population in general but also for more urban dwellers. Greater affluence also tends to change tastes and diets. Indian agrarian productivity will have to become both more efficient and more diversified. Yet India's rural areas, where agriculture takes place, are characterized by widespread poverty and insufficient water and electricity. Climate change and increased water shortages in the future seem unlikely to facilitate the types of reforms that will be needed. Expanding the food supply and food security will be a major challenge and one that has to compete with a large number of other major challenges.

The Demographic Dividend

One of the areas in which India is supposed to have an advantage over its Chinese rival is in the realm of population dynamics. By 2050, India should have a larger population than China (1.69 billion for India and 1.31 billion for China).[23] Moreover, India will be characterized by a demographic dividend in having a large number of young people when much of the rest of the world, including China, will have large proportions of their populations growing older.

> India is in a demographic-economic sweet spot, with large numbers of young people coming into the work force, and an economy growing fast enough to employ them. Nearly one-third of the Indian population is fourteen years of age or younger. Until the 1990s, India's growth was too anemic to make use of its rapidly growing population, and GDP per capita grew only slightly. Now, however, India's

turbo-charged economy has not only absorbed its growing population, but also turned them into consumers that fuel additional growth. India's demographics have become one of its great advantages.[24]

In the second half of the twentieth century, demographic dividends were credited with a substantial proportion of the economic growth of the Asian Tigers (Japan, South Korea, and Taiwan) and are therefore thought to be a highly significant component in contributing to upward economic mobility. Yet Nicholas Eberstadt underlines what he sees as a fundamental mismatch between where most Indian population growth will occur and where it will be most needed. Northern India is characterized by relatively high fertility levels (4–5 children per woman) but it is in southern India (Bangalore, Chennai, Kolkata, Mumbai) that the economic growth is concentrated. Fertility levels in the south are already at or below replacement levels (2.1 children per woman). As Eberstadt concludes, "This demographic divergence could make sustaining rapid economic growth a trickier proposition than it might seem at first. [Add to this problem the fact that one-third of the working age population has no education and India possesses a serious] material constraint for sustaining a rapid rate of growth."[25] In other words, the demographic dividend could work either way, either for or against more economic growth, depending on changes in other parts of Indian society.

Conclusion

The Indian economy could be braced for a runaway explosion to the top or near the top of the economic hierarchy. Or maybe not. The linear forecasts are rosy, but linear forecasts often do not work out the way people thought they might. Too many factors can intervene. In the Indian case, the likelihood of a rapid ascent with few detours and setbacks seems improbable. Its achievements to date have been impressive. In the first half of the twentieth century, the average economic growth rate was roughly 1 percent per year. Since independence, India has done much better than that and now is being touted as a good candidate to vault to the top of economic system, with substantial political privileges to follow its upward mobility. Yet there are reasons to be cautious about the pace or even the likelihood of this coming about.

India's large size (and location) once made it a dominant part of the world economy.[26] The size facet has not gone away but it connotes both advantages and disadvantages. Large size leads to the probability of a large economy. However, it does not mean that the economy is either complex or well developed. Given the fact that India currently represents the strongest concentration of impoverished people in the world, size can be a hurdle that has to be overcome in some way(s).

India attempted to break free of its former colonial dependency status via a heavy industry/import substitution strategy that was less than completely successful. While the colonial dependency status was reduced, the economy did not become an industrial powerhouse. Trade is not expanding very quickly. Manufacturing remains restricted. Agriculture has become more productive but needs the equivalent of another Green Revolution. Even the bright spot of information technology hinges on whether Indian firms can break free of being just an inexpensive call center for more-advanced economies. It needs instead to become a full-fledged competitor in producing information technology as part of a bid to overcoming the middle-income trap.

There are other handicaps—some of which we will review in the next chapter. The point is not that India is doomed to remaining a less developed economy. Those days are gone. Nor is our argument that India cannot hope to be a great power with a less-than-great economy. What happens to the Indian economy in the next several decades probably will not dictate what happens to India's aspirations for elite status. Such a generalization assumes that the Indian economy will not grow at an average rate of say 7–10 percent a year for the next quarter century. If it does, great power status is quite likely. But if it falls short of 7–10 percent a year, which seems likely, the outcome is much more variable.[27]

What is less variable is that economic weaknesses in India will likely work similarly to state weaknesses in hobbling Indian operations in and outside the South Asian "box." The hobbling metaphor seems most apt. When one hobbles horses, movement is still allowed at a relatively slow pace. Galloping is precluded altogether. If economic prosperity and strength are considered desirable to avoid vulnerability to outside threats and pressures, to improve standards of living, and to facilitate the development of a strong state, it is likely that a range of vulnerabilities will persist in spite of continued economic growth, at whatever pace that can be sustained—and this statement assumes that some, if not all, of the many handicaps are addressed seriously. There are so many hurdles to overcome that it seems unlikely that they will disappear entirely no matter how heroic the effort. Nonetheless, a truly heroic effort may well be needed to merely make a respectable dent in the barriers to economic growth and the creation of a high-income society.

S · E · V · E · N

Infrastructure

Infrastructure refers to the basic physical structures needed for a society to operate and the services and facilities that are essential for the functioning of an economy. Infrastructure consists of transport facilities, utilities, catastrophic risk management and telecommunication networks, which are all key elements of economic growth. The availability and the quality of the infrastructure landscape in a given country or region impact the success of its manufacturing and agricultural activities. By reducing logistical costs and increasing productivity, it is a key pillar of international competitiveness. Investments in infrastructure, particularly in water, sanitation, energy, housing and transport, contribute to poverty reduction and improved quality of life. . . .

Across the world, more than 1 billion people lack access to roads, 1.2 billion do not have safe drinking water, 2.3 billion have no reliable source of energy, 2.4 billion lack sanitation facilities and 4 billion are without modern communication services.[1]

The above passage summarizes India's double infrastructural dilemma. Economic growth is vitally dependent on a structure that facilitates, as opposed to restricts, expanded activity. The ability to move goods more effectively through improved transportation systems (sea- and airports, rails, roads) reduces transaction costs and contributes to lower prices and more competitiveness. These effects are manifested within a country and between countries. Poor infrastructure chokes production, trade, and, therefore, economic growth.[2] Good infrastructure, in contrast, has been shown to have a direct and positive impact on gross domestic product per capita. At the same time, the amount of infrastructural improvement must be fairly substantial. For example, a 10 percent increase in the infrastructural base has been found to be associated with a 0.7–1 percent increase in GDP per capita in general.[3] More specifically, "Hindered by an uncertain policy environment, subdued investor sentiment, red tape and inadequate infrastructure, the [Indian] economy has decelerated from a high of 9 percent growth in 2010 to 5 percent growth in the fiscal year that ended last March."[4]

Poor infrastructure also sustains poverty, disease, and a low-level quality of life, which, in turn, are important foci in their own rights and in the ways that they feed back into economic growth. The empirical evidence supports the proposition that improved infrastructure (in particular, electrification and paved roads) can contribute to urban and rural poverty reduction and better quality of life.[5] Improved infrastructure enhances productivity and expands unemployment. Wages can improve. Prices can decrease if transportation enhancements make the movement of goods more efficient. Moreover, access to unemployment and social services (health and education) is expanded. Better communication systems enhance information levels, enabling people to take advantage of opportunities as they arise. Thus, if India seeks upward mobility in the world economy, it must have a much better infrastructure than it has now. It would not be much of an overstatement to say that Indian economic growth to date has occurred in spite of India's generally poor infrastructure. Further gains will depend increasingly on the ability to improve transportation, energy, water, and communication structures.

India's first infrastructural dilemma revolves around the changes that any initially less developed economy, state, and society must make to become more developed, competitive, and affluent. The existing economic structure was designed for much less ambitious activities. A new foundation has to be constructed that can sustain greater complexity and scale of operations. That the pace of economic growth is so fast only makes it more likely that growth will outpace infrastructural improvements—at least for a while.[6] But the second dilemma is that India has very far to go and little time to make the transition if it hopes to bolster major power claims in the immediate future. In terms of the specific problems noted in the opening passage, India is the home for a disproportionate share of the population characterized by major infrastructural problems. Forty percent of Indian villages have no access to all-weather roads. Eight percent of the population does not have access to "improved" water, which is not quite the same thing as drinkable water. About one-third of the population has no access to electricity, and more than two-thirds rely on traditional fuels (wood and organic) for cooking and heating purposes. Roughly half of the population (49 percent) lack access to sanitation facilities, especially in rural areas where the numbers are much higher (67 percent compared to 14 percent of the urban population). Communication structures are better in India, in comparison to the other types of infrastructure, thanks to the diffusion of inexpensive cell phones. Sixty-five percent of the urban population now has access, in contrast to about 35 percent of the rural population. But only 11 percent of the population has access to the Internet, and some 40 percent of this access is achieved only through cell phones.[7]

In sum, Indian infrastructure is highly uneven, but overall it has one of the weakest infrastructures in the developing world. To move up the status hierarchy rapidly, India has no choice but to attempt to improve its infrastructure as quickly as feasible, but it has a very long way to go in order to accomplish what must be done. The barriers to successfully upgrading its infrastructure in the near future are many. A large and expanding population resident within a large state generates many economic demands. Those demands expand and intensify as some portion of the population moves up the income scale. Yet the difficulties of dealing with demands associated with increased affluence are not made any easier when a sizable proportion of the population remains impoverished and still seeking quite basic needs in a large democracy committed to universal access to economic activities and services. Then too there are additional political problems, only some of which are transitional in nature. Various reports enumerate the following kinds of political-economic barriers to improving India's energy platform (but certainly applicable to all infrastructural foci):

- An uneven and ongoing transition from central planning to a liberalized economy
- An absence of prioritizing and strong political leadership
- Investment shortfalls
- Land acquisition and inadequate compensation disputes
- Implementation problems (slow bureaucracy, difficulties in attaining inter-ministerial and inter-governmental coordination)
- Evolving and changing regulatory rules
- A shortage of private companies with the competency and capacity to execute infrastructural projects[8]

To these complaints, we can add aging equipment, cost overruns, incomplete projects, and corruption.

Observers do not agree on which problems should be given the highest priority.[9] Moreover, one might say—albeit incorrectly—that there is no single Indian problem. The quality of infrastructure and, therefore, the nature of infrastructural problems vary greatly from state to state within the larger federal structure. As if that were not enough, it will also cost a great deal to make even marginal dents in the problems at hand. Because there is so much to do and because the instruments with which to accomplish it are so imperfect, the task is genuinely overwhelming and, as a consequence, is not likely to prove entirely successful in the foreseeable future. Indian infrastructural problems will persist for some time to come. The real question is not whether they will be fully overcome in the next generation, but to what extent true progress can be made when it is proving so difficult simply to keep up with current demands. At the same time, there is a limit to how far economic growth can get ahead of its infrastructural base. Eventually, a restricted foundation will rein in growth possibilities. Hence, an upgraded infrastructural base is vital to continued Indian ascent.

In the remainder of this chapter we try to reinforce these observations with more information about the Herculean nature of overcoming Indian infrastructural problems. Infrastructure is divided into several subfoci: transportation, energy, water, telecommunications, and social services. In turn, these categories are subdivided as appropriate. In some instances, it will be necessary to go beyond strictly infrastructural considerations to make full sense of the issues involved.

Transportation

Transportation infrastructural problems are mainly about major strains placed on inadequate roads, rails, and sea- and airports by a combination of population and economic growth, outmoded equipment, poor management, and responses to improve and expand infrastructure that are proving too slow.

> Rail: The railroad system is huge and one of the largest in the world but essentially constructed prior to independence.[10] Table 7.1 shows that the amount of goods carried by Indian rails almost doubled between 1980 and 2000 and then doubled again between 2000 and 2010. The same doubling pattern applies even more strongly to the number of passengers carried. Even so, high freight charges in order to subsidize passenger traffic have had the unintended consequence of encouraging reliance on less expensive trucks and the highway system to move goods without necessarily increasing passenger traffic.[11]

> Roads: Roads currently handle as much as 60 percent of the freight and 85 percent of Indian passenger traffic.[12] National highways constitute less than 2 percent of the total road network but account for some 40 percent of the traffic. Yet only one-fourth of the national highways have four lanes. Slightly less than half (47.3 percent) of all types of roads are paved, and one-third of Indian villages do not have all-weather roads, and the need for them becomes critical in monsoon

Table 7.1. Railway Goods Transported

	Brazil	China	India	Russia
	Freight			
1980	40,603	570,732	158,474	2,316,000
1990	120,432	1,060,100	235,765	2,523,000
2000	153,863	1,333,606	305,201	1,373,200
2010	267,700	2,451,185	600,548	2,011,308
2012	267,700	2,518,310	625,723	2,222,388
	Passengers			
1980	2,407	138,037	208,558	227,300
1990	2,740	263,530	295,644	274,000
2000	n.d.	441,468	430,666	167,100
2010	n.d.	791,158	903,465	139,028
2012	n.d.	795,639	978,508	144,612

Note: Railway goods transported measure in million tons-km; passengers carried is enumerated in millions.

Source: World Bank, *World Development Indicators* (Washington, DC: 2015), available at data.worldbank.org/data-catalog/world-development-indicators.

season, especially in northern and northeast India. Urban traffic is highly congested and perhaps a bit more manic than in other places.

Ports: Ports are numerous, thanks to a very long coastline, but they tend to be small and antiquated.[13] None of these inadequacies preclude greatly expanded port traffic, as suggested in table 7.2. The ability of port facilities to unload goods, however, is slow enough (three days) to encourage shippers to go elsewhere, where goods can be unloaded and moved inland within one day. As ships become larger, especially in terms of petroleum imports, there is some concern that Indian ports will simply not be able to service them at all without extensive port reconstruction.[14]

INFRASTRUCTURE 163

Airports: Airports share the same problems characterizing seaports. They are numerous but mainly small, poorly managed, and often outdated.[15] As in the case of trains and seaports, airports are also stretched to their limits by greatly increased traffic loads (table 7.3). In the case of air

Table 7.2. Port Container Traffic

	Brazil	China	India	Russia
2000	2.413	41.000	2.245	0.316
2010	8.138	130.290	9.752	3.199
2013	10.176	174.08	10.653	3.968

Note: Indexed in millions.
Source: World Bank, World Development Indicators (Washington, DC: 2015), available at data.worldbank.org/data-catalog/world-development-indicators.

Table 7.3. Air Transport

	Brazil	China	India	Russia
	Freight			
1980	588.2	120.9	366	n.d.
1990	1,082	818.3	664	n.d.
2000	1,728	3,900	548	1,041
2010	1,303	17,194	1,751	3,532
2014	1,597	17,823	1,739	4,414
	Passengers			
1980	13.008	2.568	6.603	n.d.
1990	19.149	16.596	10.862	n.d.
2000	31.287	61.891	17.299	17.687
2010	74.627	266.293	64.687	43.855

Note: Passengers indexed in millions of people.
Source: World Bank, World Development Indicators (Washington, DC: 2015), available at data.worldbank.org/data-catalog/world-development-indicators.

transportation, though, the movement of freight nearly doubled from 1980 to 1990 and nearly tripled from 1990 to 2010. Passenger traffic almost tripled between 1980 and 2000 and then approached a quadrupling between 2000 and 2010. One 2007 forecast called for a 20 percent annual growth in air passengers through 2012 and then a 12 percent annual increase for the next fifteen years.[16]

Energy

India's energy platform is undergoing major changes. In 1990, biomass (for instance, wood and animal waste) generated 42 percent of India's total energy consumption. By 2009, the proportion was down to 25 percent. Over the next two decades, its share is expected to decline to 15 percent. Coal has been and is likely to continue to be the mainstay of the economy. Crude oil, increasingly imported, has bypassed the biomass share and will become increasingly important as Indian consumers make the switch from bicycles and motorbikes to automobiles.[17] Natural gas currently accounts for a fairly small share of total energy consumption, but its share is expected to expand in the future. Barring major new discoveries of domestic gas, an expanding share should also lead to more imports. Nuclear plants have come online but so far tend to operate at suboptimal capacity due to uranium fuel shortages. Renewables (solar and wind) have fair potential but remain in an early stage of development.

Two of the more striking aspects of Indian power consumption is (a) its expansion rate, and (b) its very low level compared to that of the other BRICs. It almost doubled between 1980 and 1990 and then more than doubled between 1990 and 2010. Yet even by 2010, the Indian per capita power consumption remained only a fraction of the usage in the other BRICs—a fourth of Brazil's, a fifth of China's and a tenth of Russia's—as shown in table 7.4. That comparison strongly hints at major problems for India ahead, in the sense that the demand for Indian power consumption can be expected to expand quite considerably in the future. Yet India is already struggling to deal with its current energy problems.

Table 7.4. Per Capita Electric Power Consumption

	Brazil	China	India	Russia
1980	1,007.9	281.6	140.1	
1990	1,454.5	510.5	269.6	6,673.2
2000	1,900.5	993.3	391.0	5,208.8
2010	2,380.5	2,943.8	625.9	6,430.8
2012	2,509	3,475	760	6,617

Note: Indexed in KWh.
Source: World Bank, World Development Indicators (Washington, DC: 2015), available at data.worldbank.org/data-catalog/world-development-indicators.

India's current energy problems are many. The very fact that the per capita consumption is so low compared to consumption in Brazil or China is telling in itself.[18] But perhaps the ultimate expression of these problems was the record blackout that encompassed a two-thousand-mile-long strip of northern India in the summer of 2012 and deprived 670 million people of electricity for two days.[19] A number of coal miners were stuck in mines, train passengers were stranded, hospitals and hotels could only operate on generators if they had them, and traffic ground to a halt in New Delhi.[20] As one source put it, "for an aspiring economic superpower, there can be few more chastening events than electricity cuts as massive as [the July 2012 blackout]."[21] The reasons for the blackout were multiple. Climate seems to have played some role. A weak monsoon season created unusually warm and dry conditions that encouraged increased groundwater pumping for irrigation purposes and the use of air conditioners. The increased demand temporarily overwhelmed India's capacity for generating electricity. But there was much more involved: "India's basic power problem is that the country's rapid development has led demand to far outstrip supply. That means power officials must manage the grid by shutting down power to small sectors of the country on a rotating basis. But doing so requires quick action from government officials who are often loath to shut off power to important constituencies."[22]

Blackouts thus have immediate and underlying, structural causes. Climate problems and air conditioners are immediate causes. Rapid economic growth and a lagging and inadequate power infrastructure are structural causes. The latter, of course, are more germane for our examination—all the more so since energy infrastructure problems are closely entwined with politics and political leadership. An important part of the core energy problem is the political commitment to expand access to energy to all members of the Indian population within the larger context of rapid economic growth. An autocracy could contemplate privileging the needs of rapid economic growth over what is sometimes described as "energy poverty." A quarter of the population still has no access to energy. An equal number have only sporadic access. Even more (roughly 836 million) use traditional fuels (biomass, wood, animal waste) for cooking and heating. Nonetheless, it is conceivable that the energy platform could be channeled primarily into industrial expansion. But in a democracy, there are strong institutional incentives to provide services to voters. As a consequence, energy access is one of the leading priorities of the Indian political system. This objective includes expanding access, but it also has led to the provision of free and subsidized energy to various groups, which distorts energy costs and also encourages the diversion of free energy to commercial enterprises.[23]

However the electrical grid has other problems. Aging equipment must be periodically (but not necessarily conforming to any explicit schedule) shut down for maintenance. Fuel to run the equipment is in short supply. The national grid that is supposed to integrate a number of regional grids is not yet functional. Lines are tapped into illegally. Meters work imperfectly. Customers decline to pay. Nonsubsidized customers are miscategorized as subsidized users. Power outages can be both short and long.[24] All of these problems mean that the electrical system loses as much as nearly one-third of its generation efficiency (31 percent in 2010/2011). Efficiency losses are normal but typically on a much smaller scale. Consequently, potential investors greatly needed to expand the electrical capacity are reluctant to put money into an unprofitable enterprise.[25] Despite these problems, the generation of electricity managed to triple between 1990 and 2009. However, governmental projections expect it to triple again by 2030.[26]

One of the principal problems underlying electricity supply is fuel problems. Coal is the main fuel for electricity plants. India has ample coal reserves, but the coal is not the best quality and requires intermediate processing to increase its utility. The importation of better quality coal from abroad has increased but has proven to be very expensive. The coal deposits in India are located far from where coal is most needed. The rail connections needed to move the coal from where it is extracted to where it is processed into fuel are underdeveloped. Indian mining practices rely on surface extraction, whereas deeper mining would be more effective. Moreover, coal mining until fairly recently has long been as close to a governmental monopoly as is possible in spite of liberalization throughout the rest of the economy. Private investment was once not permitted.

Despite these multiple handicaps, the coal supply was doubled between 1990 and 2010. The problem is that the rate of expansion seems to have peaked and may have hit a ceiling without altering current extraction practices. As a consequence, electrical plants have suffered fuel shortages, which mean that the plants operate at less than optimal levels or do not operate at all, thereby exacerbating the sporadic supply of electricity. The sporadic supply, in turn, is not only inconvenient for individual consumers, it also undermines the foundation for the expansion of manufacturing capabilities and, ultimately, economic growth.[27]

Water

The water issue is rather fundamental since life is dependent on some minimal level of supply. Water concerns encompass availability, potability, and management issues. Is there (will there be) enough water? What shares are needed by different sectors of the economy and society? Is it clean enough to drink? If not, what are the costs? What needs to be done to improve water availability? It is estimated that India's water demands will increase by 89 percent, while its water supply will decline by 44 percent in the next four decades (to 2050).[28] As recently as 1975, India was considered a state with abundant water. Since at least 2000, India has been rated a country characterized by water stress. For many of those for whom water is available, it often is accessible only at certain times during the day.[29] By 2050, it is conceivable that water demands could well exceed what is available.[30]

India receives considerable rain in the monsoon season, but too little of it is saved for redistribution in dryer times.[31] Rivers fed by melting snow flow from the north to the south, but climate change is melting Tibetan glaciers, which could lead to too much water initially and much less later on—a possibility likely to be aggravated severely by global warming and fluctuating rainfall and droughts. A very large number of dams function to control river flows, but some are quite old.[32] Moreover, one-third of the length of India's rivers is considered moderately to severely polluted by sewage, fertilizers, and industrial waste. Population growth, irrigation for agricultural productivity, increased consumption with greater affluence, and industrial demands have expanded water consumption rates. Some of this same expanded activity is responsible for reducing the utility of the water that is available—much of which is greatly contaminated. Half of the water available to rural consumers is considered toxic. Some six hundred thousand children die each year due to diarrhea or pneumonia; both types of death are linked to consuming contaminated water and related hygiene practices.[33] For instance, something like half of the Indian population is believed to engage in open defecation.[34] But agricultural chemicals and industrial waste are also significant contributors to the ongoing contamination. For some time, industrial and agrarian expansion have been given priority over water conservation considerations. Little effective governmental management has taken place, and only in part is this due to the main responsibility that falls to the federal states to regulate water consumption. While state water problems vary greatly, little in the way of coordinating the water management that does occur takes place.[35] Most sources present water problems as largely a man-made problem. Water is likely to become both more demanded and more scarce, but much of the incipient crisis can be traced to governmental mismanagement and neglect. More water could be saved, and the water that is available could be made less hazardous to the population's health.

The Asian Development Bank has generated an index of water security for Asian states. It combines evaluations for five clusters of concern: household usage, economic production, urban access, river basin management, and resilience to water-related disasters. Table 7.5 arrays the averaged security index scores for selected Asian countries. The scores range in the abstract between 1 and 5 but no state has earned a 5. While there are Asian states with higher scores than those shown in table 7.5, the basic pattern is that South Asian states score between 1.4 (Bangladesh) and 2.0 (Nepal), while East and Southeast Asian countries tend to rate more highly (1.8 for Vietnam to 3.4 for Malaysia). Some of this outcome is due to the relative availability of rivers flowing out of Tibet and the size of the respective populations—geography and demography—but it also reflects differences in how water supply is

Table 7.5. Selected Indexes of Asian Water Problems

	National water-security index	Piped water access	Piped urban water access	Improved sanitation access	Daly
Afghanistan	1.4	4	16	37	5,289
Bangladesh	1.4	6	20	56	1,217
China	2.6	68	95	64	324
India	1.6	23	48	34	1,246
Indonesia	2.6	20	36	54	483
Malaysia	3.4	97	99	96	181
Myanmar	2.2	8	19	76	1,551
Nepal	2.0	18	53	31	1,345
Pakistan	1.6	36	58	48	1,072
Philippines	2.2	43	61	74	528
Thailand	2.2	48	80	96	504
Vietnam	1.8	23	59	76	206

Notes: The national water-security index can range from 1 to 5. Access figures refer to percentages of the population with access. Daly is age-standardized "disability-adjusted life years," or an index that calculates years lost to health and premature death causes.

Source: Selectively extracted from Asian Development Bank, *Asian Water Development Outlook 2013: Measuring Water Security in Asia and the Pacific* (Manila, Philippines: Asian Development Bank, 2013), 96, 100.

managed. South Asian populations have severe restrictions on their access to piped water, more so outside cities, but also in urban areas. India is no exception to the South Asian norm, as also is shown in table 7.5. India does better than Afghanistan and Bangladesh (although not as well as Pakistan) on water-access figures but nothing comparable to, say, the Philippines or Thailand. Poor access to reasonably clean water leads to high Daly scores (one measure of diarrheal incidence and population health) for India, the fourth highest in table 7.5. It also costs the Indian economy (and its population) some 73 million working days a year due to waterborne diseases.[36]

India's status on national water security is rated at 1.6—roughly halfway between categories 1 and 2 on the ADB index scale listed in table 7.6. The scale is provided in detail because it underlines where India is and where it is not. Falling between "hazardous" and "engaged," Indian governance has a considerable way to go to attain minimal "capability," let alone "effectiveness" in coping with a situation that is moving toward a national emergency. Climate change could well accelerate the trends toward greater demand and declining supply. High contamination rates are already responsible for major public health problems. Less water for agriculture will threaten food security and the ability to feed the Indian population. Less water for industry will mean less economic growth. Less water for urban areas will mean even greater public health problems and conflict over how what remains is distributed within the country. Since many of India's rivers start outside of Indian territory, increased international conflict over water management disputes can also be anticipated.

Telecommunications

India rates reasonably well in terms of telephones (see table 7.7), thanks to a flood of inexpensive mobile technology in recent years. It lags considerably in landline technology, but this may prove to be an eroding liability as that form of technology gradually declines in utility.

A fairly high receptiveness to cell phones, however, does not carry over to the Internet. Table 7.8 shows that Indian use of the Web is markedly less than the levels attained by the other BRICs.

Table 7.6. ADB National Water-Security Index

National water-security index	National water-security stage	Description
5	Model	Sustainable local agencies and services, sustained sources of public financing for water and environmental protection and management; sustainable levels of public water consumption; and government demonstrating new models of water governance, supporting advanced technology, supporting research and development, and initiating or lending international partnerships
4	Effective	Water-security initiatives built into key national, urban, basin, and rural development master plans; higher priority on national development agenda; public investment reaching appropriate levels; effective regulation; and public awareness and behavioral change as a governmental priority
3	Capable	Continuous capacity building; improving rates of public investment; stronger regulation and enforcement; national development agenda prioritizing water and environment; and focus shifting toward improving local technology and finance capability
2	Engaged	Legislation and policy supported by government capacity building programs; institutional arrangements improving; and levels of public investment increasing (although these rates may still be inadequate)
1	Hazardous	Some legislation and policy on water and environment, and inadequate levels of public investment, regulations, and enforcement

Source: Asian Development Bank, Asian Water Development Outlook 2013: Measuring Water Security in Asia and the Pacific (Manila, Philippines: Asian Development Bank, 2013), 8.

Table 7.7. Telephones (per 100 people)

	Brazil	China	India	Russia
		Landline		
1980	4.1	0.2	0.3	n.d.
1990	6.3	0.6	0.6	14
2000	17.7	11.4	3.1	21.9
2010	21.6	21.9	2.9	31.4
2014	22	18	2	28
		Mobile		
2000	13.3	6.7	0.3	2.2
2010	101	64	61.4	166.3
2012	139	92	74	155

Source: World Bank, World Development Indicators (Washington, DC: 2015), available at data.worldbank.org/data-catalog/world-development-indicators.

Table 7.8. Internet Users (per 100 people)

	Brazil	China	India	Russia
2000	2.9	1.8	0.5	2
2010	40.7	34.3	7.5	43
2014	57.6	49.3	18.0	70.5

Source: World Bank, World Development Indicators (Washington, DC: 2015), available at data.worldbank.org/data-catalog/world-development-indicators.

Social Services

Why include social services in a chapter on infrastructure? The answer is that these services can be viewed from a number of perspectives. One of them is that education, health, and judiciary functions serve not only people but also the economy. A literate population can perform various roles in economic development that are barred to nonliterate populations. Something similar can be said about workers with some math or English background. An unhealthy population cannot be expected to be competitive. If civil disputes do not get resolved by a well-functioning court system, a fast-developing economy becomes less likely. We include social services because they are part of the economic infrastructure, just as roads, ports, and airports are.[37]

EDUCATION

Evaluating an education system is a complex undertaking, but that is not our focus here. Suffice it to say that no one gives the Indian education system high marks. Progress has been made in getting primary students into schools. Literacy rates, up roughly 10 percent in the first decade of this century, have improved as a consequence.[38] Much less progress has been made in improving their skills or in retaining them in school beyond the primary years.[39] Nor need we dwell on the supportive role of education in facilitating economic and political ascent. The ability to read, write, and do math are critical skills for an adaptive workforce, especially in a world in which information technology is becoming a standard underpinning. The basic story of Indian education is much like what we have seen for transportation and energy. A very large, underdeveloped society transiting toward something else is attempting to improve educational access and quality. The numbers and barriers to rapid improvement are great. India has done better on improving access, at least at the primary level, than it has on improving quality at any level. Student skill levels do not appear to be on the upswing. One response has been a marked increase in private schools designed to overcome the problems encountered in public education, ranging from teacher absenteeism to crowded classrooms. Nonetheless, privatization of education is most unlikely to encompass a large proportion of the ever-growing student population.

But evaluating the shortcomings of the Indian education system is not our focus here. Our questions in this chapter have to do with infrastructure. How does the Indian educational infrastructure compare to that of other BRICs? Is progress being made in improving the

Table 7.9. Secondary Pupil-to-Teacher Ratio

	Brazil	China	India	Russia
1980	n.d.	18.9	n.d.	n.d.
1990	n.d.	14.6	n.d.	n.d.
2000	n.d.	17.1	33.6	n.d.
2010	16.7	15.5	25.32	18*
2013	17	15	n.d.	9*

*Note: The 2010 entry for Russia is for 2009; the 2013 entry is for 2012.

Source: World Bank, World Development Indicators (Washington, DC: 2013), available at data.worldbank.org/data-catalog/world-development-indicators.

infrastructure, which, no doubt, is experiencing the same sort of stress and strain found in the transportation and energy sectors? Table 7.9 offers a quick comparison with other BRICs. One of the standard infrastructure indicators in education is the pupil-to-teacher ratio. As one might anticipate, India lags behind the three other BRICs in this important area, facilitating instruction. It should not come as a surprise if we say that many more teachers are needed.

Similarly, more schools are needed, but so are items that help them function. Table 7.10 is especially revealing about the infrastructural problems of schools in India. Note that, in general, some movement in the right direction is discernible where multiple years are reported, but rural school facilities remain fairly underdeveloped.[40] Urban schools are better off than rural ones on average, but their status hardly gives grounds for complacency. The classroom-teacher ratio in rural areas suggests that the number of students is growing faster than the number of schools or classrooms available. Supporting facilities (toilets, libraries, blackboards) are too often not sufficiently available, unusable, or simply unused. There is much to do in improving educational infrastructure in India, just as there is much that needs changing in the overall education system. As in so many other sectors in India, the numbers

Table 7.10. Education Infrastructure Indicators (Percentages)

	Rural			Urban Primary
Indicators	2010	2011	2012	2010–2011
Pupil-teacher ratio*	38.9	40.8	42.8	31.0
Classroom-teacher ratio**	76.2	74.3	73.7	n.d.
Playgrounds	62.0	62.8	61.1	66.0
Boundary wall / fencing	51.0	53.9	54.7	80.8
Drinking water	72.7	73.5	73.0	96.7
Useable toilets	47.2	49.0	56.5	n.d.
Girls' toilets	68.8	77.3	78.7	74.1
Girls' useable toilets	32.9	43.7	48.2	n.d.
Libraries	62.6	71.3	76.1	n.d.
Libraries being used	37.9	42.2	43.9	n.d.
Computers	n.d.	n.d.	n.d.	46.3
Blackboards	n.d.	n.d.	n.d.	45.9
Midday meal served	84.6	87.5	87.1	n.d.

Notes: *Pupil-teacher ratios vary by level of schooling. The asterisked percentages in the first row refer to the extent to which norms at each level are attained.
**The percentages in the double-asterisked row refer to the extent to which the norm of one teacher per classroom is attained.
Sources: *The rural data are extracted from* Annual Status of Education Report (Rural) 2012, *provisional* (New Delhi: ASER Centre, January 17, 2013), 56. *The urban primary data are taken from* National University of Educational Planning and Administration, "Elementary Education in Urban India: Where Do We Stand?" *New Delhi, available at* http://www.dise.in/Downloads/Publications/Publications%202010-11/Urban2010_11.pdf.

of people involved and the cost of altering and upgrading the poor and deteriorating infrastructure are staggering.

The preceding paragraphs have focused exclusively on the primary and secondary sectors, but the tertiary sector is not so different. Something on the order of half of India's population is twenty-five or younger. The potential for a huge supply of people with high skills is an advantage India possesses over its competitors, but it remains a potential if students do not have access to institutions of higher education and if those institutions fail to inculcate the appropriate skills. Enrollment in higher education institutions has quadrupled in the past twenty years, while the number of institutions of various types has increased almost eightfold in the same time period.[41] Nonetheless, few of these institutions appear in global rankings of the best universities.[42] As Goswami notes, the current Twelfth Five Year Plan talks about expansion in student volume, the number of institutions, and the level of public funding but says nothing about an expansion in the quality of the institutions.[43] Even the previous prime minister of India (Singh) has publicly complained about the mediocrity of most of India's colleges and faculty.[44]

The central government plan is to double the number of students enrolled in institutions of higher education in a very short period of time. Yet while the potential pool for students is quite large, the pool of available faculty is not. Even if the number of enrolled students is increased considerably, it will still be below the world average, and there is also the question of whether the subsequent graduates will have employable skills. While there are many schools, there are only a few rated as high quality and, not surprisingly, access to them is very difficult.[45] The obvious solution is to create more high quality institutions but that is much easier said than done in a system that encourages time in the classroom over the research opportunities that might attract stronger faculty. In the interim, shortages in an appropriately skilled population should be expected to carry some negative consequences for sustained economic growth.

HEALTH

India has a large and expanding population, many of whom are poor and most of whom reside in subtropical climate conditions and thereby are highly susceptible to communicable diseases and other health problems. India also possesses a large number of institutions training physicians and nurses (not all of whom, of course, remain in India); it also has a large number of public hospitals. Two-thirds of the hospitals are located in rural areas, which corresponds to the 70 percent of the population that also lives in rural areas. Yet only some 27 percent of the total hospital beds are in the rural hospitals.[46] Moreover, given the size of the population, India does quite poorly in providing hospital beds in general (see table 7.11)—the main indicator of hospital capacity. Catching up with either Brazil or China seems most unlikely. One estimate is that it would require 100 billion U.S. dollars to double India's current hospital capacity.[47] Even were that large a sum to be invested, India would still remain well below the world average.

Nevertheless, statistics cannot capture everything that is important about health infrastructure in India. In 2007, a major accounting firm, admittedly primarily interested in investment opportunities, had this to say about Indian health care: "When it comes to healthcare, there are two Indias: the country . . . that provides high-quality medical care to middle-class Indians and medical tourists, and the India in which the majority of the population lives—a country whose residents have limited or no access to quality care. Today only 25% of the Indian population has access to Western . . . medicine which is provided mainly in

Table 7.11. Hospital Beds per Thousand

	Brazil	China	India	Russia
1980	n.d.	2.2	.8	n.d.
1990	3.3	2.6	.8	n.d.
2000	n.d.	2.5	.7	n.d.
2010	2.4	3.6	1.1	9.66

Sources: World Bank, World Development Indicators (Washington, DC: 2015), available at data.worldbank.org/data-catalog/world-development-indicators; the 1990 and 2000 Indian entries are from IndexMundi, at www.indexmundi.com/facts/India/hospital-beds, accessed February 18, 2016; the 2010 Indian entry is from Abantika Ghosh, "Healthcare Woes: India Has 1 Govt Hospital Bed for 879 People," The Indian Express, updated April 8, 2014, available at http://indianexpress.com/article/india/india-others/healthcare-woes-india-has-1-govt-hospital-bed-for-879-people/; the Russian 2010 entry is from CIA, The World Factbook, and is for 2006, available at https://www.cia.gov/library/publications/the-world-factbook/geos/rs.html.

urban areas.... Many of the rural poor must rely on alternative forms of treatment, such as Ayurvedic medicine, Unani, and acupuncture."[48]

The official data on village access looks somewhat better than 75 percent without access to Western medicine. In 2004, 68 percent of all villages had access to a primary health center and some 77–79 percent had access to a public or private hospital.[49] Yet professional absenteeism is even more prevalent in rural health facilities than it is in rural schools. Blood, vaccines, laboratories, and medical equipment are often in short supply. Nurses tend to be undertrained. Public hospitals in general tend to be significantly understaffed.[50] Undoubtedly, there are major exceptions in major cities, but, overall, access to and the quality of health care in India is clearly far less than desirable.

JUDICIARY

India possesses a large and multi-tiered judicial system with some sixteen thousand judges. But it is estimated that it will need more than four and one-half times as many judges (seventy-five thousand) within the next three decades in order to provide roughly half the judicial service functioning (fifty judges per million people) that is customary in more-developed societies.[51] It is not simply a matter of future population growth and the presumption that affluence and literacy gains will lead to more suits being filed—although both influences are likely to be factors. However, the legal system is already overwhelmed. In the 1980s, the number of cases was approximately three per thousand population. In 2012, it was about fifteen cases per thousand, or a quintupling of the case load. Yet there are many other problems as well. About 20 percent of the current judge positions are vacant—in part due to judges being overworked and underpaid. A sufficient number of courtrooms to hear cases does not exist. Most paperwork is done by hand. Information technology has yet to be applied to managing the flow of documentation. Even if it were, no single standard governs all of the different judicial tiers, so that transferring information between courts can be awkward. Basic data on the level of workload is equally difficult to collect. Federal and state budgets allocate very little money for judicial activities. The general legal system suffers from the same type of corruption that exists elsewhere in Indian society. Not surprising, perhaps, more than one-quarter of the existing cases being managed throughout the entire judicial system are older than five years. A quick resolution of disputes is hardly the norm.

Conclusions

An unsigned editorial in *The Economist* once stated, "The general rottenness of India's infrastructure has long been recognized as the likeliest constraint on the country's economy."[52] Whether we refer to Indian infrastructure as rotten or simply woefully inadequate should not matter all that much. It should be clear that there are many problems in every sector imaginable. Many of the problems overlap in terms of causality and impact. Myrdal, writing about development in general, captures this problem well: "By *development* I mean the *movement upward of the entire social system*. . . . This social system encloses, besides the so-called economic factors . . . the distribution of power in society; and more generally, economic, social and political stratification; broadly speaking, institutions and attitudes. . . . The dynamics of the system are determined by the fact that among all the endogenous conditions there is *circular causation*, implying that if one changes, others will change in response, and those secondary changes in their turn cause new changes all around, and so forth."[53]

There is ample circular causation at work in Indian infrastructure. As a consequence, it is hard to expect improvements in one area without improvements across the board. Yet it is also hard to imagine radical improvements across the board taking place quickly or soon. Roads, trains, and ports all compete with one another. Water and health interact tremendously. Energy and education impose major constraints on what can be done within the economy. Legal system constraints interfere with taking care of disputes within both the society and the economy. All of these systems interact. All add up to an infrastructure that holds back economic growth and improvements in lifestyle.

Still, the problems are addressable. It is even conceivable that they will all be resolved someday down the road. But it is not conceivable that they will be addressed and resolved in the near future. For instance, the International Energy Agency estimates that 10 percent of the population will still lack access to electricity by 2030. Sixty-three percent of the population may still lack access to nonbiomass cooking fuel by that date.[54]

India's energy, education, and health problems are not going to go away anytime soon. In the interim, India's infrastructure cannot help but be a drag on Indian economic ascent, no matter how much money central and state governments throw at the various and sundry problems.[55] Still, the one thing perhaps most absent in infrastructural reforms is concerted political leadership with clear and unwavering priorities and follow-through. It is not simply a matter of political leadership deciding to act on prioritized problems. It is also a matter of making people— inside and outside India—believe that the problems need to be tackled and are being tackled with meaningful results.

A *New York Times* story on the conjunction of a number of setbacks in India in the summer of 2013 is illustrative of this last point. The article noted that one of India's most advanced submarines exploded at its dock, fighting had broken out on the Indo-Pakistani border in Kashmir, and both the Indian stock-exchange index and the value of the rupee had declined rapidly—all within the same week. None of these developments were related. Nor are things not going well hardly unique to India. But when a number of different things go poorly at the same time, especially including faltering economic growth, people no longer can assume that trends will continue to be positive and in their favor. They will find it harder to believe that massive problems can be overcome. As the *New York Times* story suggests, "For the last 10 years, India seemed poised to take its place alongside China as one of the dominant economic and strategic powerhouses of Asia. Its economy was surging, its military was strengthening, and its leaders were striding across the world stage. But a summer of difficulties has dented India's confidence and a growing chorus of critics is starting to ask whether India's rise may take years, and perhaps decades, longer than many had hoped."[56]

As the same article observed, part of the problem is "creaky" infrastructure (along with too much red tape and the lack of follow-through). Another part of the problem is corruption and rising energy costs. These problems can do more than simply sap confidence. They can also constitute major drags on ascent trajectories. In many respects, no other major power has faced such handicaps in developing competitive economic and military power. Certainly, other states have had to overcome economic development liabilities in order to attain elite status. But few were as impoverished and underdeveloped as India once was. Even fewer possessed nearly 15 percent of the world's population. Only China, India's rival, comes close on both counts. China's approach to overcoming infrastructural barriers, however, is to India's as night is to day. Nonetheless, observers started acknowledging China as a great power prior to its infrastructural and economic growth successes. The same could happen to India, but the difference is that India's handicaps are likely to be both more persistent and more overt than they were in Mao's China. Moreover, even China's current claim to elite status can be said to remain fragile.[57]

E·I·G·H·T

Inequality

Inequality can thwart economic growth. An economy in a society populated by a small and wealthy elite and a large mass of impoverished people is much less capable of sustained growth than one in which the poorest echelons are giving way to some upward mobility and moderate affluence. Analysts since Aristotle have praised the utility of middle classes for a variety of benefits. One of them is anchoring modern economic growth. Another benefit often attributed to an expanded middle class is political stability and decreased violence. Yet only the most conservative economists would expect inequality reforms to take place entirely naturally. Economic growth can be expected to reduce some types of inequality (and thereby beget more economic growth), but there are limits to how much and how fast inequalities can be diminished without state intervention. This is where state capacity enters the picture. States intervene in inequality by mandating and providing literacy, education, and employment opportunities to discriminated minorities. State taxation policies can take more from the rich than the poor. States can also choose to pursue undeclared income ("black money") with vigor or a lack of enthusiasm. Extraction will benefit or suffer as a consequence. If states are characterized by high incquality and it is widely perceived that government policy favors the rich, then legitimacy, from the perspective of the poor at least, is apt to deteriorate. Naxalite-type violence may also be expected, thereby detracting from state attempts at monopolizing violence.

Thus, inequality is likely to detract from economic performance and state capacity. Our main questions about Indian economic inequality are whether it is increasing or decreasing, why, and what difference it might make in the Indian case.

Disagreements about Inequality

A vigorous debate is currently underway in India and abroad about the question of economic inequality, especially in the wake of spectacular economic growth in the aftermath of the country's fitful embrace of liberal economic policies. The debate, especially between two economic stalwarts and their allies—Amartya Sen and his coauthor Jean Dreze, and Jagdish Bhagwati and his colleague and coauthor Arvind Panagariya—has focused on whether or not growth should be seen as the principal engine for reducing inequalities.[1] Atul Kohli, a noted political scientist, who had previously written on poverty alleviation in India, proffers a third view.[2] He focuses on the shift to more market-oriented policies and their myriad shortcomings. According to Kohli, the persistence of poverty and the growth in inequality stem from the policy choices of a number of regimes, starting in the 1990s, to favor corporate entities at the cost of addressing public and social needs.

Sen, who has long believed in and written extensively on the role of state-led social action, has argued that without substantial interventions and investments in health care, primary education, and infrastructure, growth will do little to address endemic poverty and may even deepen inequality. Bhagwati, who was long the standard-bearer for the adoption of more market-friendly approaches to economic growth and poverty reduction, has argued that in the absence of a focus on growth, other issues simply cannot be addressed. The debate, beyond a point, has failed to address the more-substantive issues that each contributor has emphasized and has assumed a slightly shrill quality.[3]

Ironically, a closer examination of the polarized arguments suggests that they may have more in common than they realize or are willing to credit one another for. Neither side believes that the market left wholly to itself can solve all issues of poverty and inequality. Nor do they suggest that the state should entirely abandon its regulatory role. Sen and Dreze, in particular, make a limited, clear, and cogent case for particular forms of state intervention while decrying others. The real differences that separate the two analyses have far more to do with questions of emphasis and nuance. It is apparent that Dreze and Sen see a greater role for the state but with a number of qualifications and with an important set of nuances. Bhagwati and Panagariya, on the other hand, would like to see less state intervention and would prefer the emergence of more unshackled private enterprise in a range of areas.

A third view of the questions of growth, poverty, and inequality, especially in the postliberalization era, can be gleaned from a recent work by Atul Kohli.[4] In this book, Kohli, argues that the reforms of the 1990s are neither wholly responsible for the surge of economic growth nor have they contributed significantly to poverty alleviation. More to the point, he contends that they have worsened existing inequalities owing to a number of compelling reasons. His argument and evidence bear both summarization and discussion.

At the outset, Kohli contends that growth had actually started to show signs of improvement in the 1980s and should not be entirely attributed to the post-1991 structural reforms in the aftermath of the fiscal crisis. This proposition, obviously, is the subject of considerable debate, as the consensus view holds that it was the reforms of 1991 in the wake of an unprecedented fiscal crisis that led to the embrace of more market-friendly policies and concomitant higher rates of growth.[5] In any case, this debate on the precise timing of economic growth, which is far from central to the concerns of this chapter, need not detain us further. Instead it is more important to summarize and explore the argument and evidence that Kohli musters to support the proposition that particular policy choices have actually contributed to increasing inequality in the country.

Kohli's central argument is that the reforms that have been undertaken are not so much market-friendly as they are pro-business. A pro-market strategy, he argues, helps out new entrants and consumers. A pro-business strategy, however, tends to benefit more established players in the existing marketplace. Even within this pro-business orientation there was distinct bias in favor of larger firms rather than smaller or medium-size enterprises. These policies involved an anti-labor bias (within the limits of India's democratic polity), a pro-business tilt, and an emphasis on growth over redistribution. The inherent weakness of the Indian state also ensured that direct taxes were not expanded, and so the treasury failed to take in much additional revenue. Since the state continued to make public investments in support of big business houses, especially in infrastructure to reduce various bottlenecks, the lack of revenue generation would help contribute to the fiscal crisis of 1991.

The shift in public expenditure to infrastructural projects away from various redistributive schemes combined with a pro-business, pro-growth orientation, Kohli argues, has contributed to at least three forms of inequality in India. These are inequalities across various states, inequalities across social classes, and across the urban-rural divide.[6]

The Role of Legacies

Inequality, of course, is hardly new to the country. Neither precolonial nor colonial legacies left the country in a particularly egalitarian condition. Recent scholarship, however, has demonstrated that British colonial rule was particularly pernicious in failing to promote growth, did little or nothing to alleviate let alone eradicate poverty, and probably deepened endemic inequalities. In this context it is useful to cite a small body of statistical evidence of India's socioeconomic conditions at the time of British colonial withdrawal and India's independence. The statistics are far from flattering. Life expectancy at birth in 1947 was thirty-two years (in 2012 it was sixty-five); literacy in 1951 (the first year of the postindependence census) was 16 percent (as of 2011 it was 74 percent); and per capita GDP grew at 0.1 percent in 1946–1947 (it grew 4.5 percent in the second quarter of 2013 after a dramatic economic slowdown).[7]

Colonial and precolonial legacies alone, of course, do not explain the existence and perpetuation of gross inequality in India. Apart from existing social hierarchies stemming from monarchial rule, the existence of the caste system in Hinduism not only ensured but justified inequality. To use the evocative term from William Blake, caste served as a "mind-forg'd manacle" throughout much of Indian society, thereby entrenching inequality throughout the social system.[8] With the passage of India's postindependence constitution in 1950, the practice of untouchability, a cornerstone of the caste system, was formally abolished. Despite this sweeping provision, the legacy of centuries has continued to prevail. In fairness, caste and social class are no longer coterminous, and lower castes have indeed made much progress in India's democratic political order.[9] However, social inequality, though difficult to measure quantitatively, nevertheless continues to afflict Indian society.

After independence, in an attempt to also address harsh inequalities, the Indian state adopted a strategy of state-led industrialization.[10] Despite this stated commitment to reducing inequality, as many thoughtful observers have argued, the state failed to address two major sources of inequality. The first, of course, was the issue of land reform. Despite an interest in promoting land reform, owing to the social composition of the dominant political party—the Indian National Congress (popularly and henceforward referred to as Congress)—and its political base, the state was unable to make sweeping changes in land tenure and return "land to the tiller."[11] The second was the country's abject failure to invest in primary and tertiary education. This neglect of primary and tertiary education in effect blocked an important avenue of advancement for significant numbers of India's poor.[12] The evidence from many, more authoritarian East Asian states suggests that the substantial investments that they made in primary education (and in land reform) played a vital role in their later rapid growth and industrialization.[13]

India's emphasis on state-led industrialization, though not bereft of benefits, led to a neglect of agriculture, leaving the country acutely dependent on both imported food as well as foreign assistance to obtain basic foodstuffs.[14] Under considerable pressure from both within and without, and especially after being subjected to the "short tether" policy of the Johnson administration in the United States, India changed its agricultural policies in the late 1960s and early 1970s.[15] These changes helped usher in the country's "green revolution" thereby holding out the prospect of ending the specter of famine. However, as thoughtful observers have discussed at some length, the changes in the socio-economic landscape were neither scale neutral nor value free.[16] There is no question that the transformation of India's agriculture through the utilization of modern technology, the reliance on hybrid, disease-resistant seeds and the use of petrochemical fertilizers dramatically increased the aggregate output of agricultural production in India. However, the social effects of the Green Revolution were not entirely salubrious. Farmers of large- to medium-size landholdings, who had access to agricultural credits were the principal beneficiaries, and small stakeholders were mostly forced off the land.[17] Some scholars have, in fact, argued that the Green Revolution contributed to the rise of a violent, ethno-religious separatist movement in the Punjab in the early 1980s.[18]

About the same time, Prime Minister Indira Gandhi, in a populist turn, and in an attempt to bolster her political base, had resorted to a deft political slogan, *Garibi hatao* (literally "abolish poverty"), during a national election campaign in 1971. Her coterie of advisers and political confidants were firmly in the left wing of the Congress Party and wanted to steer the country away from the reliance on market mechanisms. These political advisers were not only keen on turning the party in a specific ideological direction but were also prepared to use its apparatus as a vehicle for political mobilization. The process through which she chose to carry out these policies, however, was fraught with adverse consequences for the country's democratic political institutions. As Francine Frankel, an authority on India's political economy in the postindependence era, has written:

> Plans committed to paper for creating an ideological and cadre-based party were discarded. Instead, Mrs. Gandhi took a diametrically opposite direction. She adopted a strategy of deinstitutionalization which ensured that control over the organization would remain in her own hands. Worse still, it undermined institutional efficacy as capricious decisions made on political considerations increasingly shaped the structure of India's administrative apparatus. This politicization of India's bureaucracy would have significant adverse consequences for the long term capacity of the Indian state.[19]

Another noted observer of India's political economy, Atul Kohli, echoes Frankel's sentiments in a more recent work. A substantial quotation from his work is apposite, as it succinctly summarizes her strategy and its perverse consequences for growth, poverty alleviation, and the quality of India's democracy.

> Indira Gandhi raised the expectation that her policies would help alleviate poverty—a demanding task that would have required high rates of economic growth, some effective redistribution, and the capacity to penetrate and reorganize rural society. This demanding task, in turn, would have required a cohesive political party and bureaucracy. Indira Gandhi, however, achieved nearly the opposite by further deinstitutionalizing the Congress Party, further fragmenting the state's authority structure, and undermining the professionalism of the bureaucracy. Rather than going to enhanced public investment in agriculture, infrastructure, public sector industries, education, and health, the state's resources were increasingly directed at buying political support. With growing politicization, the bureaucracy and public enterprises simply deteriorated. And finally, the state simply did not support the private sector and became increasingly anticapital, with predictable negative results for investment and growth.[20]

The hollowing out of India's institutional capacity that took place during Gandhi's time in office would have serious adverse consequences for the efficacy of the Indian state in the years and decades ahead. Much of this has been documented elsewhere and consequently does not merit much elaboration.[21] Suffice it to say that the reduced institutional capacity coupled with growing political mobilization produced a predictable outcome of political instability. As Samuel Huntington had long argued, such rapid and dramatic political mobilization against a backdrop of institutional decay can have significant consequences for political stability and order.[22]

The State of Emergency and Beyond

In the wake of this effort, Indira Gandhi embarked upon a series of populist measures, including the nationalization of India's banking system and the abolition of the so-called Privy Purses, a commitment that the postindependence regime had made to the rulers of India's princely states as a condition of their accession to the country following the end of British colonial rule. It is far from clear that these measures, though popular, actually contributed to the economic betterment of India's poor. Subsequently, as is well known, she became embroiled in a significant political controversy over some minor electoral malfeasances leading to a lower-court conviction. Faced with this adverse judgment, she obtained a stay order and then declared a "state of emergency" that lasted the better part of two years. After declaring elections in 1977 she was ousted, and a disparate political coalition largely committed to more market-based approaches to poverty reduction assumed office. This regime proved short-lived, as their internal differences soon came to the fore, thereby paving the way for her return in 1980.

In the 1980s, as the Indian economy stalled, Gandhi undertook some limited reforms to stimulate growth and deal with endemic poverty. Following her assassination in 1984 her son, Rajiv Gandhi, a political neophyte, assumed office. Free from significant ideological predilections and enjoying a substantial political mandate, he continued many of the market-oriented reforms that his mother had tentatively initiated. However, it was not until his death and the emergence of a new regime under Prime Minister Narasimha Rao, that when faced with an unprecedented fiscal crisis the Indian state chose to undertake substantial market-friendly reforms designed to both promote growth and reduce poverty.[23] Since the initiation of these reforms the country has seen both a reduction in poverty and substantial economic growth. Whether inequality has been reduced is less obvious.

The information that we have on Indian poverty figures is relatively straightforward to interpret.[24] Following fluctuations in the 1950s and an early peak in the mid-1950s, the proportion of the population living below the poverty line peaked again in the late 1960s at about 62 percent of the population. Since then, the proportional numbers have demonstrated a linear decline: by 1980, less than 50 percent; by 1990 less than 40 percent; by 2000, less than 30 percent; and by 2006, roughly 20 percent. However, these figures need to be offset by four other considerations. First, the size of the population has expanded considerably over the last sixty years. The total number of people living below the poverty line remained relatively constant between roughly 1975 and 1995, before declining from over 300 million to about 250 million in the mid-2000s. A second factor is that the proportion of poor people living in urban areas has increased over this same time period—nearly doubling from about 15 percent of the total population to about 28 percent, and these numbers are expected to continue climbing. Thus, poverty reduction has been more successful in rural areas. However, a third factor is that most Indians remain impoverished, with 830 million living on less than two dollars a day (in 2005). That means that there are fewer people living on about a dollar a day (US$1.25) than was once the case but that the income levels of the majority of the country have not improved all that much.

The fourth caveat is that minorities are more likely to fall below the poverty line but not as much as they once were. Table 8.1 contrasts the changes in impoverishment among different groups in Indian society. The historically most deprived groups have been the Hindu scheduled tribes and castes, and they continue to be counted among the most poor in Indian society even though steady improvements have been registered. They, along with Muslims, another minority, have decreased their tendency to be concentrated in the most poor by about one-third over the last twenty-five years or so. Still, poverty reduction has been more successful for nonminorities. The overall official calculation shows movement from 45.2 percent to 27.5 percent in the same time period, or about a 40 percent reduction rate.

As for inequality, it appears to have declined somewhat in recent decades, only to have increased again. The Gini inequality indexes in table 8.2 show some decline of roughly 5 percent over the 1980s and 1990s in rural areas before returning to about the same levels in 2004–2005 as they had been in 1983. In urban areas, there has been less decline and more increase—a small decline (less than 2 percent) comparing the period immediately before and after the reforms (1987–1988 versus

Table 8.1. Poverty and Minority Status

	1983	1993–1994	2004–2005
Scheduled Hindu tribe	65.3	51.3	46.5
Scheduled Hindu caste	59.0	49.2	38.5
Hindu: others	39.0	28.6	20.6
Hindu: all	45.3	35.1	26.9
Muslim	53.0	45.9	35.5
Scheduled Christian tribe	41.7	32.8	20.2
Christian: others	31.7	25.0	11.2
Other religions	25.3	23.7	17.6
All	45.2	35.9	27.5

Note: This table uses official, current poverty thresholds, while our textual discussion relies on real over time estimates, which give different calculations of the proportion of the population that is considered poor.

Source: Michael Walton, "Inequities and India's Long-term Growth: Tackling Structural Inequities," in India 2039: An Affluent Society in One Generation, ed. Harinder S. Kohli and Anil Sood (New Delhi: Sage, 2010), 75.

Table 8.2. Changes in Indian Inequality, 1983–2005 (Gini Indexes)

	1983	1987–1988	1993–1994	2004–2005
Rural	30.0	29.9	28.6	30.5
Urban	33.9	35.0	34.4	37.6

Source: Taken from tables in Stuart Corbridge, John Harriss, and Craig Jeffrey, India Today: Economy, Politics & Society (Cambridge: Polity, 2013), 62–64.

1993–1994), but the 2004–2005 inequality metric is nearly 11 percent higher than the 1983 index.

To complicate matters more, the inequality measures vary across India, as is observable in table 8.3 which compares Gini indexes by state immediately before the economic reforms with 2004–2005 figures. In

Table 8.3. Changes in Indian Inequality by State, 1988–2005 (Gini Indexes)

	Urban		Rural	
	1987–1988	2004–2005	1987–1988	2004–2005
Andhra Pradesh	36.1	37.6	30.9	29.4
Assam	31.0	32.1	23.0	19.9
Jharkhand	32.1	35.5	26.6	20.7
Bihar	26.6	33.3	25.2	22.7
Gujarat	27.8	31.0	26.1	27.3
Haryana	28.7	36.5	29.2	34.0
Himachal Pradesh	29.2	32.6	27.1	31.1
Karnataka	34.9	36.8	29.7	26.5
Kerala	36.9	41.0	32.1	38.3
Chhattisgarh	32.1	44.0	24.5	29.8
Madhya Pradesh	33.3	39.7	30.6	26.8
Maharashtra	34.8	37.8	31.2	31.2
Orissa	31.0	35.1	26.9	28.5
Punjab	28.8	40.3	29.7	29.5
Rajasthan	34.6	37.2	31.5	25.1
Tamil Nadu	35.8	36.1	33.0	32.2
Uttarakhand	35.1	32.9	28.3	28.5
Uttar Pradesh	33.5	36.9	28.5	29.0
West Bengal	34.6	38.3	25.8	27.4
All India	35.0	37.6	29.9	30.5

Source: Taken from tables in Corbridge, Harriss, and Jeffrey, India Today, *61–64.*

urban areas, sixteen of twenty states registered Gini index increases of 5 percent or higher, and as many as twelve showed increases greater than 10 percent. Punjab led the list with an especially impressive increase of almost 40 percent. In rural areas, however, inequality decreased or stayed about the same (less than 5 percent) in sixteen states.

Recent Efforts

In 2006, in the aftermath of the general election of 2004, a Congress-led government, under the aegis of the United Progressive Alliance (UPA) came to office. Their assumption of office came after the BJP-dominated National Progressive Alliance (NDA) had campaigned on the theme of "Shining India." Some analysts within the Congress had concluded that this slogan may have indeed reflected the status of a segment of the electorate. Under the NDA, a portion of the population had clearly been the most significant beneficiary of economic liberalization. However, the vast majority of the populace has not seen a perceptible improvement in their well-being.

Not surprisingly, the new regime chose to implement a major welfare provision under the terms of the Mahatma Gandhi National Rural Employment Guarantee Scheme (NREGA). In 2005 it passed this act, and it subsumed at least two prior schemes the Sampoorna Grameen Rozgar Yojana (SGRY), or Universal Rural Earning Scheme, and the National Food for Work Programme. (NFFWP). The provisions of this act are straightforward.

It guarantees every household in India the right to at least one hundred days of work for at least one adult member of a family and guarantees payment at the prevailing minimum wage. The wages can be paid in either cash or kind, and the area of employment is restricted to within five kilometers of the village from where the applicant submits the request for employment. In an attempt to ensure gender equity, the act requires that at least one-third of the program must be composed of women. The act also stipulates that when there are at least twenty women at a work site, provisions have to be made for any children under six that they bring with them. The individual designated to mind the children is also guaranteed the prevailing minimum wage. Finally, it requires that wages to be paid within the fifteen days of when the work was performed.

The act also states that the public works programs that NREGA promotes should not siphon away labor from agriculture and that the programs should result in assets that promote agriculture. However, as two Indian economists have correctly emphasized, agriculture in India is highly seasonal. In a lean season (as opposed to the time of the harvest) the demand for agricultural labor is low, and that is when the hundred days of guaranteed work can prove to be most useful.[25]

What does the available evidence suggest about the utility of this effort in addressing chronic problems of rural poverty? It is beyond the scope of this chapter to provide a complete summary and evaluation of the accumulated evidence. That would entail an enterprise of a wholly different order of magnitude. Instead, an attempt will be made here to glean some key findings based upon large-scale studies that have been conducted. The preliminary evidence seems to suggest that the impact of NREGA has varied considerably across India's states and reflects both historical legacies as well as extant state capacities. Some of the evidence also supports the conclusion that even with the presence of state capacity the perspective of the regime in power can influence the outcomes of the program.

One important and early discussion by the noted Belgian-Indian economist Jean Dreze and a colleague revealed some intriguing results. Some states, they report, have been high performers. For example, the western Indian state of Rajasthan, in the first year of the implementation of the program, provided seventy-seven days of employment to those seeking assistance. They attribute the state's success to a high level of preparedness and prior experience in organizing massive public works programs. They also report some apparently counterintuitive findings. For example, the southern state of Kerala, which has long been known and celebrated for its social welfare measures, had a distinctly poor record of generating employment, offering a mere three days of work per rural household. They attribute this low number not to a lack of effort on the part of state authorities but possibly a low demand for the program. On the other hand, they argue that the same explanation does not hold true for the western state of Maharashtra and the eastern state of West Bengal. In both cases, they argue that the failure to utilize the program can be attributed to the lack of interest in it on the part of local governments.

Does ideological preference make a difference? Their preliminary findings do not seem to lend support to the proposition that particular political parties in power might be more or less prone to promoting the program. Finally, their research also indicated that the all-India figures for the employment of women in this program was downright encouraging, as it was as high as 40 percent on a national basis. In the southern state of Tamil Nadu, it was an astonishing 81 percent.[26] They do not comment on or explain the very high participation of women in Tamil Nadu. However, the higher rate can be attributed to two possible factors. First, it may reflect the availability of work for men in other sectors. Second, it may also suggest that there are fewer barriers for women to work outside the home given the social mores of the state. Finally, given the history of institutional slackness, the prevalence of predatory landlords, and the pervasiveness of corruption at local levels, they reported that in many states the statutory minimum wage was not paid as stipulated.[27]

What other and more recent evidence can be adduced about the working of this program? A study published in 2012, which primarily examines the labor-market impact of the program, has also generated some intriguing findings. Among other matters, it does confirm the early evidence that the program has improved the employment prospects of rural women. It also shows that the program has indirectly contributed to ensuring that minimum wages in the private sector are paid during the agricultural season. However, apparently it has been less successful in providing adequate employment during the agricultural off-season. This latter finding is quite disturbing because one of the principal goals of the program was to ensure employment of those in need during that that season.[28]

Finally, an unpublished study of 2013 provides other useful data from a survey of 184 early-implementation districts and control group of 209 late-implementation districts. Its central findings are clearly worth noting. It concludes that the program has led to an overall increase in consumption, and this holds true for those who belong to the lowest consumption quintile. Even more interesting is the evidence that the most marginalized caste groups have benefited from the program, thereby demonstrating that even the most discriminated segments of Indian society have been able to breach certain barriers.[29]

Obviously, the data on the impact of the program on rural welfare is partial and incomplete. However, a variety of analyses conducted at particular sites and stages seem to indicate that the program, its critics notwithstanding, is accomplishing at least some of its stated goals and may have also generated some unanticipated positive outcomes. In this context it is perhaps important to emphasize the counterfactual: How might have the poor and the marginalized fared in substantial parts of rural India in the absence of this program or other viable alternatives?

Expanding Rights

In 2012, however, growth stalled as a consequence of a host of factors, among them being the revelation of a spate of corruption scandals that paralyzed the ruling regime, the United Progressive Alliance (UPA). The opposition, bereft of ideas, sought to make as much political capital out of them as possible. To its credit, the UPA regime managed to successfully pass the National Food Security Act. Pared to the bone, the act guarantees five kilograms of food grains a month at highly subsidized prices to nearly two-thirds of India's population. Quite apart from the costs to the exchequer, which are quite substantial, questions remain about how effectively the Indian state will be able to administer this vast program. According to one source, the bill is likely to cost the Indian treasury up to 1.67 percent of the country's current GDP.[30]

Despite a professed commitment toward creating a "socialist pattern of society," the Indian state, for all practical purposes did little to tackle the underlying sources of poverty and inequality. Indeed this failure to devote adequate resources to primary education has left India with a disproportionate number of individuals lacking the necessary skills to improve their existing socioeconomic conditions.

Ironically, some recent efforts to redress this critical shortcoming may have had some adverse unintended consequences. Bhagwati and Panagariya, in their discussion of the Right of Children to Free and Compulsory Education (RTE) of 2010 argue that this well-meaning legislation has some unintended perverse results. They correctly identify a number of provisions in the RTE, which, though designed to assist the poor and the disadvantaged, may actually end up causing them harm. Several of these features need to be highlighted.

First, the act provides that every child between the ages of six and fourteen years is guaranteed access to education. Yet the enforcement of this "right" is placed on state governments. In cities it is the responsibility of the municipal corporation, and in rural areas, the *panchayat* (local self-government entity). However, as they correctly argue, hardly all such bodies have the requisite capacity to enforce such a requirement.

Second, the act also requires all private, unaided schools to reserve at least 25 percent of seats in the first grade to students from disadvantaged backgrounds. The act also provides for the state to reimburse the school at the same rate that it spends in public schools. This, they argue, will have the effect of crowding out a substantial number of students from more secure economic backgrounds. In turn, because the state is only required to reimburse the school at the rate it spends on pupils at a state-run institution, it will have the effect of raising the costs to fee-paying students.

Third, the poor and the disadvantaged who are fortunate enough to live in an area where desirable private schools exist may well benefit from the same provision. However, those who do not live in or near such privileged neighborhoods will not stand to benefit from the provision discussed above.

Fourth and finally, the act decrees some minimum standards that all schools must meet. These, however, do not focus on student learning outcomes or achievements. Instead they deal with student-teacher ratios, an all-weather building with one classroom per teacher, a kitchen for midday meals, a playground, a well-equipped library, games, and sports equipment. The costs that these features entail will be beyond the reach of most schools, thereby forcing them to close.[31]

The motivations underlying the RTE are no doubt laudable. However, as discussed above, many of the features of the act may actually leave its intended targets no better off and in some cases may even worsen their existing plight. Therefore, despite its commitment to ensuring that elementary and primary education is accessible, some of its central elements virtually guarantee that it is far from clear that it will produce the sought-after outcomes.

Conclusions

It is evident that the Indian state is moving, albeit quite fitfully, toward enshrining a series of rights for the bulk of its citizenry. The motivations underlying these efforts to expand the scope and dimensions of these rights are indeed varied. They stem from the pressures of various social movements; they reflect attempts to seek political quiescence; and they also involve electoral concerns. Regardless of these diverse incentives, five observations about this broadening of rights are in order.

First, they do represent in many ways a deepening of India's democracy. For example, the RTE, without question, had made significant segments of India's administrative apparatus more responsive to the citizenry despite misuse on the part of some and the efforts of the bureaucracy to thwart its goals of greater transparency. Second, the success or failure of many of these programs designed to make government more accountable, to raise socioeconomic standards, and thereby to provide a minimal level of welfare will depend in considerable measure on institutional efficacy. As argued in this chapter, India's institutions were severely denuded during Mrs. Gandhi's term in office. Her successors, despite some efforts, have not been able to restore them to their past levels of probity and usefulness. Consequently, their ability to implement many of these sweeping programs is at question. Third, the Indian state needs to be mindful of the fiscal consequences of some of these programs. NREGA, as noted earlier, costs the Indian exchequer at least 1 percent of the country's GDP.[32] Fourth, taken together these programs and initiatives can raise popular expectations that may not be fulfilled. Such an outcome could contribute to both distrust in the state and, worse still, social unrest. Fifth and finally, unless economic growth can be restored to the levels that it had reached in the early days of the new century, it is far from clear that these programs can be sustained without significantly adverse inflationary consequences. In this context, there is little question that Bhagwati and Panagariya are correct that in the absence of sustained economic growth, these programs, however well meaning, are unmaintainable. How the Indian state negotiates its way through this thicket of expectations that it has raised, and delivers on them, will in considerable measure affect the future of social stability in the country.

More generally, though, it should be clear that there is no genuine choice between economic growth and governmental intervention as paths to greater equality. Both are necessary. Growth may or may have not have some trickle-down effect, but it certainly helps pay for governmental intervention. Without government intervention, it is unlikely that some of the traditional rigidities in inequality patterns will be overcome. Yet neither may be sufficient, or, better yet, neither may have sufficed to date in overwhelming entrenched poverty and various types of inequalities. It is one thing to elevate standards of living from a dollar a day to two dollars a day; it is quite another to create a genuine middle class. Making a few people very rich is also not quite the same thing as expanding income levels systematically.[33] So far, Indian economic growth and governmental intervention have managed to reduce extreme poverty without yet making much of a dent in inequality. More growth and intervention can be expected to make more inroads into these obstacles, but it will probably require much more economic growth and intervention than has been witnessed to date.

N · I · N · E

Democratic Institutions

In his justly famed 1968 book, *Political Order in Changing Societies*, Samuel Huntington quite deftly separated political and economic development. Political development, as he had argued then, deals with the quality of the institutions of a state. States that had robust institutions could be deemed to be models of political development even though they could not produce widespread prosperity. Indeed he argued that rapid economic development with the concomitant unleashing of social expectations could lead to widespread political disorder. In the closing chapters of the book, he cogently argued why it may be even desirable to limit political participation, because an overly rapid expansion of participation could easily overwhelm the capacity of fragile states to channel them into the institutional arena.

Huntington's work was not without its critics. They accused him of privileging order over social change and accused him of masking his conservative ideological predilections in theoretical garb.[1] This normative critique of Huntington need not detain us at this stage, even though the debate continues apace. Without dwelling on the relative merits of the competing arguments, it is possible to tease out a fundamental proposition from his work: namely, the importance of institutional capacity in any society but especially ones undergoing substantial transition. Viable institutions can deliver a host of public goods and services, fairly adjudicate claims, and maintain minimal political order functions that all modern states are expected to perform.

In some ways, Huntington's pessimistic prophecy has emerged in India. Today the country can justly claim that it has successfully mobilized large segments of its population and enabled them to enter the political arena. India's democracy is far more representative of its citizenry than in the first few decades of the republic. One noted scholar of Indian politics has aptly referred to this phenomenon as India's "silent revolution."[2] However, this mobilization has come at a substantial cost. It has taken place against a backdrop of considerable institutional decay. As a consequence, the capacity of India's institutions, despite the renewal of some, is increasingly under strain. Yet, as this chapter will show, the condition is not one of unrelieved gloom and doom. Some institutions have indeed shown signs of decay. Others, however, have helped bolster democratic practices and thereby portend well for the country's future.[3]

In this chapter we will examine a set of key institutions in India to assess how they have performed and have attempted to address a set of key functions. It does not, however, purport to provide a comprehensive assessment of every public institution in India. Such an effort would indeed be Herculean and would in all likelihood require a separate book. The discussion here instead is focused on a set of institutions that have a particular significance for the argument of this book dealing with the capacity and efficacy of the Indian state to perform a set of vital functions.[4] The first half of the chapter's discussion will focus on how various entities have sought to assess government performance and probity. The latter issue is of particular significance, given that corruption has been rife in postindependence India and has assumed staggering dimensions in recent decades.[5] Indeed as one scholar has cogently argued, corruption is starting to undermine the quality of governance that democratic politics has produced.[6] In the second half of the chapter we move away from specific institutions and turn to the democratic record in general. Throughout the chapter, nonetheless, the focus is on Indian democratic institutions.

India's first prime minister, Jawaharlal Nehru, clearly understood the significance of building and nurturing a range of capable institutions to support the country's nascent democracy. His efforts, of course, benefited substantially from the country's nationalist heritage, which had bequeathed a number of working institutions, most notably the INC.[7]

It is ironic that one of his successors, and no less his daughter, Indira Gandhi, is widely seen as the individual who was responsible for the dismantling of her father's substantial institutional legacy. A number of scholars of Indian politics have quite cogently argued that a number of India's political institutions underwent severe decay during the long rule of Prime Minister Indira Gandhi. According to them she politicized the bureaucracy, sought to undermine the independence of the judiciary, ossified the political base of the Indian National Congress, the dominant political party, and steadily centralized political power in New Delhi. Worse still, until Sanjay Gandhi's death in a plane crash in 1980, she allowed her son to bring in large numbers of individuals into the Congress Party who had little or no use for established norms, procedures, and principles of a working democracy. In the process institutional pathways were either bypassed or undermined.[8]

There is little question that many of these charges have some veracity. However, it is equally important to underscore that India's political system has demonstrated a capacity for institutional renewal. A number of developments in the wake of her departure from political office suggest that although her legacy was certainly corrosive, it did not wholly undermine the prospects of institutional resurgence.

Decline and Renewal

The political decay that took place during the decades of the 1960s and 1970s was significant. However, the polity nevertheless demonstrated a capacity for institutional renewal. More to the point, not only were existing institutions which had fallen into desuetude strengthened and bolstered, but new institutional mechanisms were created, especially in the first decade of the twenty-first century. Consequently, the workings of India's governing institutions have a distinctly uneven quality. The limitations of the country's institutional capacity, while not crippling, are nevertheless serious enough to warrant concern about its putative rise.

There is little or no question that all of India's political parties have witnessed varying degrees of decline. The most dramatic, of course, has been the deterioration of the Indian National Congress. Founded in 1885, it spearheaded the Indian nationalist movement and for at least the first thirty years of India's independence it had a coherent ideology and enjoyed a wide measure of internal democracy. From the time of Indira Gandhi it witnessed a growing ideological incoherence and ended its commitment to internal democracy. Since then, despite periodic calls for the restoration of its internal organization, few, if any, such measures have been implemented. Instead the party remains wedded to the Nehru-Gandhi lineage, has lost its ideological moorings, and has all but dispensed with internal democracy.

The principal opposition party until the 2014 election (when it obtained a clear-cut majority in Parliament), the right-of-center Bharatiya Janata Party (BJP), is also not known for its commitment to regular, internal elections. Instead, it has tended to coalesce around powerful personalities and regional stalwarts. Unlike Congress, however, which appears to have lost its ideological lodestars, the BJP at least can claim to have an ideological corpus. It is favorably disposed toward free markets, has a strong pro-Hindu orientation, and believes in the pursuit of a muscular foreign policy.

Beyond these two national parties, the vast majority of India's political parties, barring the two Communist parties (which are in a state of terminal decline), are focused on regional issues and concerns and woven around the personalities of particular leaders. Several of them, ranging from Mamata Banerjee of the Trinamool Congress in West Bengal to Jayalalitha Jayaram of the All India Anna Dravida Munnetra Kazhagam in Tamil Nadu, are known for their imperious, idiosyncratic modes of governance and have evinced scant interest in building their parties as working institutions with routinized procedures and programs. Of course, these are not the most egregious cases. In the state of Bihar, a local politician, Laloo Prasad Yadav, of the Rashtriya Janata Dal, had managed to remain in power for the better part of a decade on the basis of rank populism, a flagrant disregard for any and all institutional procedures, and with scant regard for personal probity. Finally, indicted in a massive public scandal, he was forced out of office but nevertheless remains a political force. In sum, the state of political parties in the country reflects, for the most part, a spectacular process of political decay.

Mirroring the decline of political parties is the state of India's Parliament. Once again, the roots of this decline can be traced to the tenure of Prime Minister Indira Gandhi. Her father, Jawaharlal Nehru, and his successor Lal Bahadur Shastri, used Parliament as an arena for discussion, debate, and deliberation and emphasized respect for and decorum within the institution. She, however, treated it with a mixture of fear or contempt, depending on the status of her party's parliamentary strength.[9] Her successors, including her son, Rajiv Gandhi, continued to flout the initial norms and expectations that had made the Indian Parliament a viable deliberative body. Recent developments have not provided any reason to believe that the organization is about to resuscitate itself.

What are the principal charges that both analysts and scholars have leveled against the current working of the Parliament? A former secretary-general of the Lok Sabha (Lower House) of the Indian Parliament, writing in 2005, Subhash Kashyap had the following lament: "Parliament was conceived as the legislature or the law-making body, but of late law-making has ceased to be even the most important of its functions either qualitatively or quantitatively. From about 48 percent, it has come down to occupy less than 13 percent of its time. The character of Parliament has also changed as a result of changes in membership composition."[10] The final statement, which alludes to the composition of Parliament, is actually quite telling. It is a disturbing fact that in the fifteenth Lok Sabha, as many as 150 members had criminal backgrounds.[11] Admittedly, many of these criminal charges, upon closer examination, may not be wholly disturbing and in some cases reflective of India's complex judicial system. Nevertheless, as a recent analysis shows, some of the charges pending against elected lawmakers are far from frivolous.[12]

The decline in the membership of Parliament is reflected in the functioning of the body. Two well-known political scientists have conducted a study that reaches come deeply disturbing conclusions about the state of India's Parliament. The full results of this analysis cannot be summarized here. Instead, a few of their salient findings will be highlighted, as they represent a disturbing coda about the condition of India's Parliament. According to this study, Parliament has abnegated most of its duties related to effective surveillance of the executive. There is a growing gap between the complexity of modern legislation and the capacity and inclination of members to effectively tackle such demands. Finally, the sheer growth of political parties, many of which are institutionally weak, has also enhanced the hurdles to collective action.[13]

Another institution of considerable significance that remains efficacious but has important limitations is the Indian Administrative Service (IAS), the successor to the colonial-era Indian Civil Service (ICS). Entry into this body is strictly through competitive examinations. Once selected through a rigorous procedure the entrant, along with those of a host of other national services, is put through a standard training process and begins his or her professional career at the lowest rung of the administrative ladder in the state to which the individual is assigned.

According to a former IAS officer, there are important elements of continuity to the service, though some changes have come about in its composition and functions. Today the service is more broadly representative of Indian society, it draws individuals with a greater dispersion of professional backgrounds (as opposed to those from the humanities and the social sciences), and has been forced to be more responsive to the emergence of mass media and participatory democracy. The officer, however, challenges the popular view that the service is today more politicized than its predecessor. However, he does not provide sufficient evidence to bolster this assertion,[14] nor does he deal with the frequent charges of the decline in probity within the organization.[15]

Systematic evidence of corruption in the IAS is not easy to locate. Anecdotal evidence based upon internal reports does, however, persist.[16] Furthermore, to ensure the compliance of civil servants to the dictates and preferences of local and regional political leadership, it appears that they are frequently subjected to being transferred to other jurisdictions. These transfers, according to more than one source, are often made in flagrant violation of the rules and regulations of the service.[17]

Institutional Renewal

One of the most successful examples of institutional renewal involves the Election Commission of India (EC). Until the early 1990s, the body had become a mostly somnolent entity unwilling or unable to enforce its writ. As a consequence, widespread fraud, voter intimidation, and other forms of chicanery had come to characterize India's elections at both national and state levels. A fundamental transformation came about under the tutelage of the tenth chief election commissioner, T. N. Seshan, who assumed office in December 1990. Unlike his predecessors, who had not used the powers that had been reposed in the office, Seshan chose to use them, and to considerable effect.[18] He enforced a range of existing strictures designed to limit campaign spending, ensured the protection of voters, and prevented politicians from abusing government resources for electoral purposes.

Though he was not without his critics within India's political class, Seshan's moves proved, for the most part, to be widely popular with the electorate.[19] Also, his reforms did not prove to be dependent solely on his presence in office. His successors, though less flamboyant and self-aggrandizing, upheld the norms and procedures that he had sought to implement, and a largely somnolent organization became transformed into a viable watchdog determined to eradicate electoral fraud and abuse.[20] Indeed, it is safe to argue that the institution has now acquired a standing in India's electoral system that will make it extremely difficult to dislodge or undermine.

The resurrection of the Election Commission is an obvious example of the possible resuscitation of a near-moribund body. For the myriad shortcomings of India's democracy, its electorate can nevertheless take comfort from the fact that a vital rite of any democratic state, free and fair elections, can be mostly taken for granted. During the sixteenth general election, held between April and May of 2014, the commission reprimanded a number of candidates for breaching established electoral norms. Even the Bharatiya Janata Party's successful candidate for the office of prime minister, Narendra Modi, did not escape censure.[21]

The EC alone, however, is not the only example of institutional regeneration. Other institutions too have shown signs of revitalization. Among them is the government's watchdog, the Comptroller and Account-General of India (CAG). This institution, in an incipient form, had existed even during the British colonial era. It was revived in postindependence India's constitutional order, and its powers were codified some twenty years later in an act of Parliament in 1971. Today it has close to sixty thousand employees. It has, on a number of occasions, sought and revealed questionable government choices and acquisitions. A complete account thereof obviously is well beyond the scope of this chapter.

Within the last three decades the organization has come into public prominence. It first drew popular attention in the late 1980s when it revealed that there were serious irregularities involved in the purchase of the Swedish Bofors field gun for the Indian Army.[22] Subsequently, in the wake of the Kargil War of 1999, the CAG came into the limelight when it issued a report that had questioned the probity of the purchase of body bags and coffins for soldiers killed in the conflict. The case was handed to the Central Bureau of Investigation (CBI), which leveled charges against three army officers. After extensive investigations that lasted well over a decade, the CBI concluded that there was insufficient evidence to prosecute any of the individuals who had been initially charged with paying an inflated price for the coffins.[23]

The disturbing charges and the long investigation into the purchase of the coffins ended without any prosecutions. However, some recent actions of the CAG have not only attracted considerable public attention but have also led to a series of court cases, the resignation and incarceration of several prominent politicians, and forced the United Progressive Alliance (UPA) government to overturn important prior decisions. One of the most prominent of these involved the CAG's scathing report on the cost overruns and the dubious purchases in the lead-up to the nineteenth Commonwealth Games (CWG) in New Delhi.[24] This report eventually led to the prosecution of Suresh Kalmadi, a Congress politician and senior official connected with the CWG.

In addition to unearthing possible malfeasances in the acquisition of equipment for the CWG, as well as significant cost overruns, the CWG the CAG also released a report in 2011 that estimated a loss of US$40 billion to the exchequer owing to a flawed auction of the 2G electromagnetic spectrum. Even though some observers challenged the CAG's estimate of the loss, it forced the government nevertheless to cancel the vast majority of the licenses that had been issued owing to a Supreme Court judgment.[25] Parenthetically, it might be added that the court's decision to cancel the licenses stemmed from a Public Interest Litigation (PIL) application, thereby demonstrating the power and utility of the PIL mechanism. In 2012 the CAG also called the government to account on the allocation of coal seams.[26] Once again, faced with both parliamentary pressure and adverse public opinion, the government was forced to cancel the initial allocation.

The CAG's recent record in auditing questionable government spending choices and allocation decisions may lead to the conclusion that this watchdog body has been mostly successful in bringing most wrongdoing to heel. Such a conclusion, however, could be somewhat misleading. A number of ancillary institutions, which are charged with ensuring governmental probity, have not functioned with similar efficacy. More to the point, it could be argued that some of them suffer from inherent design flaws that limit their ability to curb various forms of governmental misconduct. In this context it may be worthwhile to examine the record of two organizations, the Central Vigilance Commission (CVC) and the Central Bureau of Investigation.

The CVC was set up as early as 1964. The problem with the organization is that it has always lacked the powers of investigation and has instead had to rely on the CBI and the Enforcement Directorate (ED) for those tasks. This in turn poses its own problems. The CBI lacks real institutional autonomy and can only proceed after it has received the permission of a state government to act. Thus, though the CBI has launched a series of investigations, few actually result in significant prosecutions or convictions. In 2009, for example, it had a conviction rate of a mere 62 percent of those accused.[27] Absent changes in its current organizational structure, it is most unlikely that its ability to bring about more prosecutions and in an expeditious fashion will increase anytime soon.

What explains the abrupt attention that has now been focused in the political and public arenas on the CAG reports on government malfeasance? At least three factors help explain the extraordinary attention that they have commanded. First, the sheer scale of the possible graft involved helped dramatize the investigative reports. The 2G scam, according to the CAG, may have cost the exchequer as much as $40 billion. Second the timing of the release of the reports was critical in focusing public interest on them. They were released at a time when a social activist, Anna Hazare, had already sought to bring the issue of both petty and high-level corruption into the limelight.[28] Third and finally, unlike previous reports, these analyses not only adduced evidence of possible malfeasance but also went ahead to proffer policy prescriptions.[29] The sheer political significance of these CAG reports suggests that in the foreseeable future this organization will continue to play a salutary role in India's political order.[30]

Institutional Innovation

Not only has the country witnessed the restoration of certain institutions but it has also seen some innovative approaches to the improvement of governance. Two of these in particular merit some discussion. The first is the Right to Information Act (RTIA) of 2005. It emerged from the work of a number of key social activists who helped create the National Campaign for (the) People's Right to Information (NCPRI) in 1996.[31] Their activism ultimately culminated in the passage of legislation in 2005. Under its terms, barring certain areas that are deemed to be off limits for reasons of national security, the act mandates that "all citizens shall have the right to information." Furthermore it enjoins all government institutions to take the necessary steps to make such information available and requires governmental bodies to respond within a span of thirty days. A failure to do so permits the petitioner to file a complaint with the state-level Information Commission seeking redress.[32] According to the authors of a field experiment dealing with slum dwellers and their access to the public distribution system in India, the use of the RTIA was at least as effective as bribery to secure access to a basic public service.[33]

Other studies and accounts suggest that the use of RTIA has had important consequences for transparency and has helped reduce corruption and inefficiency in government programs. One study, which synthesized evidence from a number of other analyses, four years after the passage of the legislation, argued that on balance it had produced rather positive results in a number of different areas of governance. Some of its key findings are worth noting. First, fears had been expressed in many quarters that this legislation would lead to a flood of requests for information. Yet these misgivings apparently proved to be unfounded. Second, it also showed that the legislation had revealed corruption in public services, sadly not an especially surprising conclusion. Third, oddly enough, while the Indian media provided much coverage of the new law, few members chose to use it as a tool of investigative journalism.

Apart from these conclusions the study also highlighted some ongoing problems with the RTIA. Members of India's public bureaucracy remained hostile toward RTIA applicants; problems of administrative capacity to enforce the law reduced the level of compliance; and the proactive disclosure features of the law were often honored in the breach.[34] Ironically, the very success of this legislation has led the national government to try to limit its scope to some degree. For example, in 2012, the government issued new regulations that restricted the format of RTIA applications and set a word limit. These attempts to alter the provisions of the act met with understandable criticism from various social activists.[35]

Yet another example of institutional innovation that has had some salutary consequences for public policy is the mechanism of Public Interest Litigation (PIL). It originated in the early 1980s at the instance of a former chief justice of the Indian Supreme Court, P. N. Bhagwati, and his colleague, Krishna Iyer. In their view, far too many aggrieved individuals and groups simply lacked the financial and organizational resources to approach the bench. Accordingly, they devised a system under which a petitioner with a legitimate complaint could approach the court for relief on the basis of a postcard. The court could then take cognizance (or not) of the petition and respond appropriately.

Since it was instituted as a legal principle, the court has passed orders to protect the Taj Mahal from corrosive air pollution, rid the Ganges of industrial effluents, enhance air quality in New Delhi, protect forests and wildlife in various parts of India, and have ordered cities to clear garbage.[36] Despite the obvious attraction of this legal device to address significant failures or lapses of public policy the mechanism is not without its limits or its critics. Among other matters, analysts have argued that its initial purpose, the protection of the public interest, on occasion has been compromised and has been substituted with the pursuit of private concerns under the guise of addressing larger societal ills. Other critics have complained of judicial overreach and have suggested that it has encroached upon the proper functions of the executive and legislative branches of government. It has apparently also led to the inefficient use of judicial resources thanks to frivolous applications, contributed to judicial populism, and on occasion has only yielded outcomes which are mostly symbolic.[37] These criticisms, for the most part, are not bereft of substance. The limitations of PIL are, no doubt, real. That said, there is little question that the device has achieved some of its intended goals.

Faced with crises, the Indian state has also proven to be responsive and has sought to fashion institutional panaceas. In 1993, for example, the government of Prime Minister P. V. Narasimha Rao responded to criticisms from home and abroad about its human rights record in the insurgency-wracked state of Jammu and Kashmir. It created the National Human Rights Commission (NHRC). Critics at first dismissed the NHRC as little more than a token body, yet since its inception it has increasingly asserted institutional autonomy. On a number of occasions it has forced the government to account for its actions or omissions regarding issues as varied as squalid prison conditions, the conduct of drug trials in the country, child trafficking, water quality in the Ganges River and violations of laws banning child labor. The NHRC, despite its efforts to expand its reach, has its limits. It cannot, for example, probe matters that deal with national security in in states in turmoil.

India's institutional capacity is decidedly mixed. At one level, the country has no dearth of working institutions. These range from a professional civil service; an independent and innovative judiciary; an election apparatus that handles the world's largest electoral exercise with skill, dexterity, and more than a modicum of fairness; and a working Parliament. However, many of these institutions either find that the demands placed on them exceed their extant capacity, or they have witnessed a decline in normative standards, or they are subject to political manipulation. These patchy features of India's institutions raise serious questions about the country's ability to meet a number of emerging challenges. Given the slackness of so many institutions, their lack of reliability, and the evident corruption that dogs them, it is far from clear if the country can address the problems of growth, equity, and political stability. Indeed, quite ironically, if India does continue to grow at a rapid pace, it is likely to confront accelerated social demands. These in turn are likely to place increased stress on already overburdened institutions.

Unless existing institutions can be refurbished, with their norms strengthened, their probity restored, and their capacity expanded, they will almost for a certainty hobble the prospects of India's rise. The Indian electorate reposed considerable hopes in the election of a BJP led government in the sixteenth general election of 2014 and especially in the emergence of Prime Minister Narendra Modi. Modi may well possess much drive, charisma, and policy experience. However, he has to work within the constraints of existing institutional legacies. Whether or not he can bring about suitable reforms remains an open question. His initial efforts, in part because of the intransigence of the principal opposition party, the Indian National Congress, have not been significant.

Indian Democracy in General

Whatever one might say about its specific political institutions, the emergence and persistence of Indian democracy are theoretical and historical anomalies. Early theorists of democracy argued that this form of government not only required but was generated by certain social and economic requisites—none of which India possessed.[38] More recent analysts have claimed that particular levels of economic development are crucial for the perpetuation and consolidation of democracy.[39]

India's rapid and successfully consolidated transition to democracy during the years following British withdrawal in 1947—a transition accomplished despite acute and widespread poverty as well as deep and numerous social cleavages—raises doubts about this claim's validity. India has also managed to make its democratic experiment work even though the annual per capita income of its citizens still hovers below the one-thousand-dollar standard deemed critical for democratic consolidation.

The historical origins of India's democracy also present an important puzzle. Contrary to popular belief, the British did little or nothing to promote the growth of democratic institutions in India. Instead, Indian nationalists from the late nineteenth century onward successfully appropriated liberal-democratic principles from the United Kingdom and infused them into the Indian political context. Under the towering influence of Mohandas K. Gandhi in the 1930s, these beliefs and principles were disseminated to a broad swath of India's population via the Indian National Congress, the leading nationalist political party. As this was occurring, the British colonial regime was losing few opportunities to thwart or at least contain the growth of democratic sentiment and practice in India.[40] The Indian nationalists can justifiably claim that each step toward self-rule and democratic governance was the result of sustained and unrelenting political agitation against authoritarian colonial rule.[41]

Indeed, it can be argued that India's transition to and sustenance of democracy have been the fruits of both structure and contingency. The dominant strand of the nationalist movement had been democratic. In keeping with that spirit, the framers who drew up India's constitution in 1950 adopted a democratic structure that sought to represent the views of the many rather than the opinions of the few.[42] Yet the role played by contingent factors—the great "wild cards" of history—cannot be dismissed. Indian democracy and with it the world will always owe a huge debt of thanks to particular nationalist leaders such as Gandhi and Jawaharlal Nehru, the first prime minister. They and their colleagues not only shucked off the dead hand of colonialism but also fostered a nationalist movement and a political elite that have shunned the authoritarian temptation.[43]

That is not to say that Indian democracy's record since the British exit in 1947 is unblemished. On the contrary, that record is distinctly mixed. And yet there can be little question that, despite myriad challenges, India has managed to achieve democratic consolidation. Any dispassionate assessment will run through a familiar litany: the adoption and maintenance of a system of universal adult franchises from the outset, mostly free and fair elections, regular alternation of the parties in power as a result of those elections, a range of viable political parties across a wide ideological spectrum, an open and vibrant press, an apolitical and professional military, and a fiercely independent judiciary.

Moreover, the federal structure that India's constitutional dispensation enshrines has often shown a remarkable capacity for innovation. As early as 1956, the array of states inherited from British India was reorganized along linguistic lines. And as recently as 2000, the new state of Jharkhand was carved out of the northern state of Bihar in order to meet demands for regional autonomy. India's fitful embrace of the market since 1991 will, in all likelihood, continue to reinforce the logic of federalism. As the national government sheds its voluminous regulatory powers, states will be able to pursue more innovative economic policies and diverse strategies of economic development. India's language policy also constitutes a striking success of its federal structure. By means of the three-language formula,[44] the country has fended off the kinds of fratricidal conflicts that led to the 1971 breakup of Pakistan and that until recently continued to wrack Sri Lanka.

Finally, amid intense contestation and debate, India's programs of affirmative action (or "positive discrimination") have made both symbolic and substantive progress toward breaking William Blake's "mind-forg'd manacles" of caste and caste-based discrimination. These are hardly trivial achievements in a vast country that began its democratic career burdened with low literacy, extraordinary ethno-linguistic diversity, highly uneven levels of economic development, widespread poverty, and serious external threats to its territorial integrity.

Yet even if one sets aside the more-polemical critiques of Indian democracy, there is no denying its shortcomings.[45] The country's performance in protecting the rights of ethnic and religious minorities has been flawed; the government has shown scant regard for civil and personal rights when suppressing secessionist movements; the efficacy of many of India's public institutions remains questionable; and its achievements in the area of development are at best anemic, as the quarter of all Indians who still live below the poverty line might attest.

Moreover, it is clear that these shortcomings are neither "ancient history" nor gradually disappearing. For example, figure 9.1 plots two

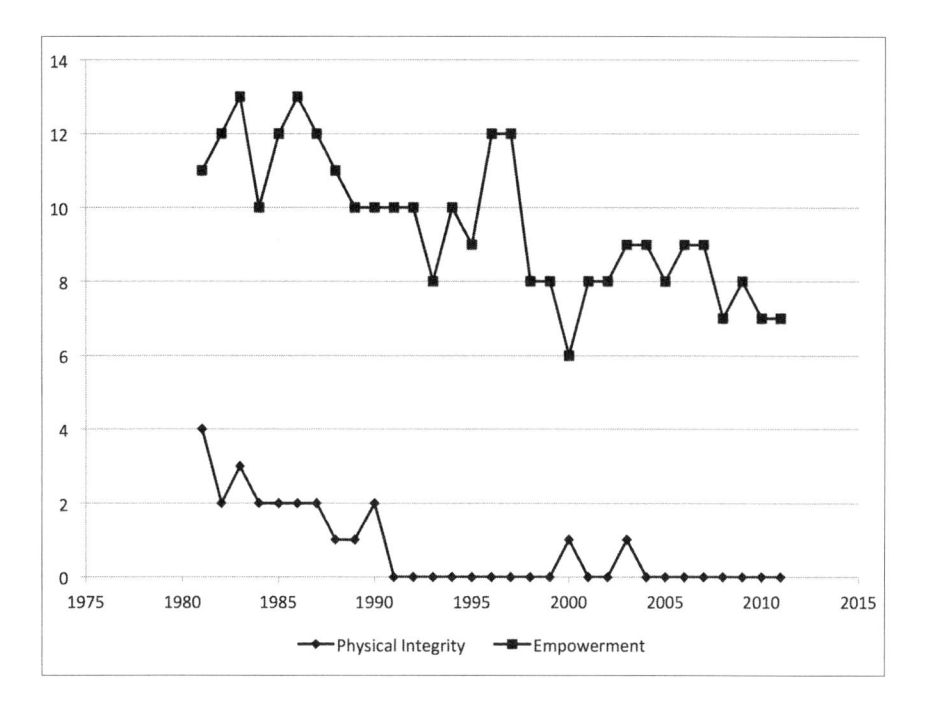

Fig. 9.1. Indian Human Rights Indexes

indexes of human rights over the past several decades.[46] The upper series in the figure has a possible range of 0 to 14 (2 points per right, aggregated in the index) and measures individual empowerment rights, encompassing rights to physical movement, speech, assembly, work, elections, and religion.[47] The trend line of the index is clearly negative, with high values in the early 1980s to substantially lower scores shown since 1999. The bottom series focuses on the physical integrity of individuals.[48] To what extent are people subjected to torture, extrajudicial killing, political imprisonment, and disappearances? This index ranges from 0 to a possible maximum of 8 (2 points per right, aggregated in the index). Its trend line is equally negative, with India receiving a zero score in most years since 1990. No doubt, the low scores are attributable in considerable part to police and army behavior in peripheral separatism and Naxalite conflicts, but that hardly excuses away the persistently low scores.

Would an alternative form of governance be more appropriate for India? The country did, in fact, experiment with a brand of authoritarianism under Prime Minister Indira Gandhi in the late 1970s. The results of this brief undemocratic interlude proved unsatisfactory in many ways, and voters resoundingly rejected it in the 1977 national elections.[49] Since then, the country has witnessed the decline of the once-dominant Congress Party and the rise of a plethora of regional parties, coped with a major economic crisis, and confronted the specter of resurgent Hindu nationalism. Of these, the rise of Hindu chauvinism may pose the greatest threat to democracy's well-being. An extraordinary pluralism of religious beliefs, practices, and identities has long been a basic feature of life on the subcontinent. Any failure or abandonment of India's secular dispensation would sound the death knell of democracy as well.[50] Such threats and difficulties notwithstanding, however, the constitutional structure of democracy in India remains robust.

More to the point, democracy is now the only game in town. The key tenets of democracy are woven firmly into the warp and woof of India's political culture.[51] No political party can expect to make serious headway without a fundamental commitment to democratic procedures. Debate in Parliament may have become less civil and more contentious now that a fuller range of India's social and economic diversity is represented there, but all parties accept the concept of a loyal opposition. Furthermore, India's poor and illiterate participate in national and state-level elections with gusto. Indeed, it is worth reiterating that it was the Indian public that resoundingly rejected Indira Gandhi's authoritarian experiment in the late 1970s.

Challenges and Prospects

Seventy years after independence and sixty-seven years after the adoption of its constitution, how has Indian democracy fared? What are the principal challenges that it confronts? What are the prospects for fuller democratic consolidation? These questions are far from trivial. The successful consolidation of Indian democracy has a range of theoretical and policy-relevant implications. From a theoretical standpoint, India's democratic consolidation challenges the current expert consensus that some "floor" level of economic growth is needed before democracy can consolidate. The policy relevance is equally significant: The continuing success and deepening of democracy in a polyethnic, unevenly developed country could have a potent demonstration effect on prospects for democratic governance elsewhere in the developing world.

Discussing every one of the numerous conceivable challenges that Indian democracy confronts as it enters a new millennium is far beyond the scope of our present undertaking. Three areas, however, do stand out by virtue of the significance that they hold for the future working of Indian democracy: human rights, corruption in public life, and secularism.

HUMAN RIGHTS

Despite the considerable success of the Indian state in holding free and fair elections, sustaining a free press, and dramatically expanding the franchise, the abuse of coercive state power remains a grave problem. All too often, such power is used arbitrarily against the poor, minorities, and those who dare to challenge the state's writ. The police, as a recent tragedy dramatically underscored, evince scant regard for the rights of the poor and dispossessed.[52] All too often, a person's class status has too much to do with whether and how the police respond. Furthermore, police abuses are more pronounced in poorer states such as Bihar or Assam, where standards of accountability are sorely lacking. The evidence from such states of rampant deaths in police custody emphasizes the gravity of this situation.[53]

The state's willingness to uphold human rights has come under the greatest strain whenever it has dealt with substantial challenges to its authority. For example, in its efforts to suppress secessionist movements (whether in the Himalayan state of Jammu and Kashmir to the north, Tamil Nadu in the far south, Punjab in the northwest, or Assam in the far east), the central government in New Delhi has resorted to a panoply of draconian legislation that enables it and its agents to act with virtual impunity. Particularly worth discussing are two laws that together have substantially corroded personal rights and civil liberties, especially under conditions of widespread political instability and institutional duress.

The first is the Armed Forces Special Powers Act (Jammu and Kashmir) of 1990. This law was enacted in order to help deal with the long-standing ethno-religious insurgency in Kashmir, India's only Muslim-majority state and long the bone of contention in a bitter territorial dispute with Pakistan. The act was meant to grant the Indian military and other security forces as much leeway as possible to conduct counterinsurgency operations without fear of punishment. Among other disturbing features, this act permits Indian security forces to use extensive coercive powers (including deadly force) when acting in good faith. Under the aegis of this sweeping legislation, security forces sometimes resorted to deliberate, extrajudicial killings.

The second law that opened the door to systematic human rights abuses was the March 2002 Prevention of Terrorism Activities Act (POTA). Passed in the aftermath of the September 11 attacks in New York and the December 13, 2001, suicide assault on the Indian Parliament (Lok Sabha) building in New Delhi, POTA had a nationwide reach that surpassed that of the Armed Forces Special Powers Act, as the latter law applies only to particular states. Individuals arrested under POTA were legally denied the right of habeas corpus. The legislation had also placed significant curbs on free speech, resulting in its use as a weapon in political vendettas.

It is perhaps a testament to the growing strength of India's civil society and the concomitant regard for democratic norms that the Congress Party—led United Progressive Alliance (UPA) government that came to power in May 2004 felt compelled to repeal POTA in September 2004. Nevertheless, insist human rights activists, POTA's two-year existence saw the law repeatedly misused in a blatantly partisan and arbitrary manner, often as part of efforts to punish minorities and political opponents. Although it is comforting that POTA, under severe public criticism, was eventually overturned, the mere fact that the Indian state was willing and able to encroach upon individual rights and civil liberties with such impunity constitutes a disturbing comment on the state of India's democracy.

CORRUPTION IN PUBLIC LIFE

Another source of concern about the future of India's democracy, already touched upon in chapter 7, stems from the persistence of endemic corruption in public life. In August 2011, these were brought to the fore thanks to the actions of a well-known social activist, Anna Hazare. Hazare, an austere and self-professed Gandhian, had long been known for his social activism in his native state of Maharashtra. However, on this occasion he chose to highlight the problem of pervasive corruption in public life in the national capital undertaking a very public fast and insisting that the government pass a substantial anticorruption measure.[54] Hazare's fast and rally attracted a wide swath of India's citizenry. The crowds that flocked to his cause clearly demonstrated that he had struck a powerful and resonant chord among a wide cross section of India's citizenry. The understandable and growing public frustration with these blatantly corrupt practices may soon turn into cynicism. Such a prospect would be quite corrosive of India's democracy.[55]

That there is a serious corruption problem in India is made clear in tables 9.1 and 9.2. Based on surveys, a considerable proportion of the population has had some experience with paying bribes in order to obtain governmental services (table 9.1), and the practice appears to be fairly widespread throughout the political and economic systems (table 9.2). Only the Indian military almost escape attention on this score. One problem is that corruption is inefficient and raises the costs of governmental services. But the more critical problem is that it erodes the legitimacy of the institutions considered to be corrupt. If all or most institutions are considered corrupt to some extent, perceptions of the value of democracy cannot be expected to go unscathed. But then, as with most generalizations about India, corruption problems are not evenly manifested across India. It is more of a problem in some states than in others. Wealthier states, states with more highly educated populations, and states that are less dependent on federal subsidies tend to be afflicted with corruption.[56]

That this problem of corruption is not merely a mundane feature of Indian life is underlined by table 9.3, which draws attention to India's high ranking on corruption. India is perceived to be the most

Table 9.1. Experience with Paying Bribes
to Public Services in India

Public services	Percent who had paid bribe
Police	62
Registry and permit services	61
Land services	58
Utilities	48
Education	48
Tax revenue and/or customs	41
Judiciary	36
Medical and health	34

Source: Based on Global Corruption Barometer 2013 data in T. Ramachandran, "Global Survey Paints a Dismal Picture of Corruption in India," The Hindu, July 12, 2013, at http://www.thehindu.com/opinion/blogs/blog-datadelve/article4904739.ece.

Table 9.2. Rank Order of Perceived
Indian Institutional Corruption

Institutions	Percent of people who think they are characterized by corruption
Political parties	86
Police	75
Parliament	65
Public officials	65
Education system	61
Medical and health	56
Business/private sector	50
Judiciary	45
Religious bodies	44
Media	41
NGOs	30
Military	20

Source: Based on Global Corruption Barometer 2013 data in T. Ramachandran, "Global Survey Paints a Dismal Picture of Corruption in India," The Hindu, July 12, 2013, at http://www.thehindu.com/opinion/blogs/blog-datadelve/article4904739.ece.

Table 9.3. India's Position in the Worldwide Prevalence of Corruption Ranking

Percent of respondents reporting paying bribes for government services	Applicable countries
Greater/equal 75%	Liberia, Sierra Leone
50–74.9%	Cambodia, Cameroon, Ghana, **India**, Kenya, Libya, Mozambique, Senegal, Tanzania, Uganda, Yemen, Zimbabwe
40–49.9%	Afghanistan, Algeria, DRC, Ethiopia, Kyrgyzstan, Mongolia, Morocco, Niger, South Africa
30–39.9%	Bangladesh, Bolivia, Egypt, Indonesia, Jordan, Kazakhstan, Mexico, Nepal, Pakistan, Solomon Islands, South Sudan, Taiwan, Ukraine, Vietnam
20–29.9%	Bosnia and Herzegovina, Colombia, Greece, Iraq, Lithuania, Madagascar, Moldova, Papua New Guinea, Paraguay, Peru, Serbia, Slovakia, Turkey, Venezuela
15–14.9%	Armenia, Cyprus, Czech Republic, Kosovo, Latvia, Macedonia, Romania, Sri Lanka, Sudan, Thailand, Tunisia
10–14.9%	Argentina, Chile, El Salvador, Hungary, Israel, Jamaica, Palestine, Philippines, Rwanda, Vanuatu
5–9.9%	Bulgaria, Estonia, Italy, Slovenia, Switzerland, United Kingdom, United States
Less than 5%	Australia, Belgium, Canada, Croatia, Denmark, Finland, Georgia, Japan, South Korea, Malaysia, Maldives, New Zealand, Norway, Portugal, Spain, Uruguay

Source: Transparency International, "Global Corruption Barometer 2013," at www.transparency.org/gcb2013/report.

corrupt state in South Asia by this Global Corruption Barometer index. Although not all states are included in the survey, Bangladesh, Pakistan, and Sri Lanka fall several intervals below the Indian position.[57] India also competes for relative position with only a handful of sub-Saharan African states. It is hardly an attractive ranking to possess.

SECULARISM

Human rights and corruption are not the only disturbing aspects of India's democracy. Certain key norms and principles that have undergirded Indian democracy are also at risk. One of them is the vital dimension of Indian secularism, the future of which is fraught with danger. Given the country's multireligious character, the demise of secularism would seriously compromise democracy by consigning a significant share of the populace—mainly belonging to religious groups outside the Hindu majority—to second-class status. This normative concern aside, the dismantling of the secular edifice could also unravel the social compact between the Indian state and minority populations that number in the hundreds of millions (India's Muslim community alone is thought to number as many as 150 million). If minorities were to become targets of systematic, legalized discrimination, would their sense of loyalty to the Indian state remain unweakened? Such a fraying of bonds could in turn fuel movements of subnational self-assertion or even secessionism as minority populations came to feel lastingly disenfranchised.

It is important to underscore that the founders of the Indian state were committed to a vision of civic nationalism.[58] Nevertheless, even at the time of independence and partition, a forerunner of today's Bharatiya Janata Party (BJP), the Hindu Mahasabha, opposed the creation of a secular state. Large sections of the Hindu Mahasabha, seeking an entry into the electoral arena, joined the Bharatiya Jana Sangh, founded shortly after independence by a Bengali politician, Shyama Prasad Mukherjee. Until the 1989 national elections, the heavily upper-caste Hindu nationalists constituted an extremely limited force in parliamentary politics because of their small numbers. In that year, however, they became more formidable, winning more than one-eighth of the seats in the Lok

Sabha. A decade later, they won a parliamentary plurality and managed to forge a coalition government at the national level.

During their time in office, BJP leaders sought systematically to alter the terms of political discourse in India. While professing a commitment to secularism, they argued that the Congress and other political parties had simply appeased religious minorities in pursuit of electoral gains. This charge had some merit, but the BJP was less interested in the principled correction of abuses than it was in finding political cover for a wholesale dismantling of the secular order enshrined in the constitution. The Hindu nationalists' hostility to secularism became evident in a number of different arenas, ranging from a systematic attempt to alter social science and history textbooks to the party leaders' willingness to countenance widespread, state-sanctioned violence against Muslims, especially during the bloody disturbances that rocked the northwestern state of Gujarat (the only BJP-run state in India) in February 2002.[59]

In the 2004 national elections, for complex reasons that included a poor choice of electoral allies and complacency about the benefits of rapid economic growth, the BJP met an electoral rout. The Congress-led coalition that returned to power reaffirmed its commitment to secularism and reversed many antisecular BJP policies. Yet it would be premature to dismiss the challenge that the BJP and its extraparliamentary allies (popularly referred to as the Sangh Parivar, or "family group," and composed of the Bajrang Dal, the Vishwa Hindu Parishad, and the Rashtriya Swayamsevak Sangh) pose to secularism. Their electoral defeat in 2004 led them to reexamine their political strategies, but their commitment to an antisecular agenda remains mostly intact.[60]

It is possible to make this argument even though the BJP and its principal campaigner, Narendra Modi, sought to downplay communal and sectarian rhetoric in the campaign of the sixteenth general election in 2014. It can well be argued that this avoidance of divisive sloganeering was more tactical rather than substantive. Given the near complete economic disarray in the country, with growth faltering, it made eminent sense for Modi to highlight the failures of governance. In the end this tactic certainly worked to BJP's advantage. It swept into power, winning as many as 282 seats in the 545-seat Parliament.[61] How it chooses to govern now that it has a clear-cut mandate remains to be seen.

Its initial days in office have provided some signs that it intends to pursue a long-term agenda toward the cultural transformation of the country. Among other matters, it appears that the government is intent upon appointing individuals with questionable professional qualifications to key historical and cultural institutions. A couple of recent choices are indicative of the government's apparent agenda. There is no question that previous governments, especially under the Indian National Congress, had frequently placed left-wing academics and professionals in key government educational and cultural institutions. However, these individuals had substantial professional accomplishments and enjoyed a degree of intellectual standing. Two key appointments have raised serious concerns about the regime's commitment to intellectual integrity. The first has involved the appointment of Yellapragada Sudershan Rao, a historian of questionable standing, to the directorship of the prestigious Indian Council for Historical Research (ICHR).[62] The second episode that has caused considerable concern among a significant segment of India's cultural world deals with the choice of Gajendra Chauhan, an actor of limited distinction, to the directorship of the highly regarded Film and Television Institute of India (FTII).[63] Both of these developments portend that the BJP remains beholden to its institutional allies and that it has not abandoned its agenda of Hindu cultural nationalism.

In the meantime, if the Congress has any hope of regaining lost ground, it will have to reaffirm its commitment to principles of secular governance without resorting to sleight-of-hand favoritism toward certain minorities when electoral imperatives so demand.[64] Too many compromises by Congress will provide the BJP with fresh ammunition for its charge that Congress and its allies "pamper" minorities, especially Muslims.

Given the country's many religious currents, an Indian democracy cut away from its moorings in secular neutrality would soon come to grief on illiberalism's rocky shores.[65] It might maintain the trappings of procedural democracy, but it would lose one of its sheet anchors—namely, the protection of minority rights.

Portents of Hope and Sources of Concern

The foregoing discussion makes it more than evident that India's democratic record is far from unblemished. Yet it is vital to underscore that an alternative to liberal-democratic procedures were tried between 1976 and 1977 and found to be sorely wanting. If anything, that brief interregnum clearly demonstrated that, contrary to popular belief, India's poor and disenfranchised cared deeply both about bread and ballot. Indeed, as the noted Indian economist and Nobel Laureate Amartya Sen has argued quite persuasively elsewhere, the two are inextricably intertwined.[66]

The power of the ballot, as he has cogently argued, may well help prevent the recurrence of famine as policy-makers can ill afford to ignore the dire plight of their constituents who are faced with the prospect of starvation. Sen's argument, based upon a comparison of evidence drawn from postindependence India and the PRC during its Maoist phase, demonstrated that the lack of any electoral and representative mechanisms in the PRC along with significant barriers to the free flow of information contributed to millions of starvation deaths during the Great Leap Forward.[67]

Furthermore, it is not India's messy, chaotic and noisy democracy that has contributed to various problems of separatism, ethnic conflict, and violence. Instead it is the country's periodic failures to adhere to these norms and procedures that in considerable measure have brought grief to its door. Had India's political leadership steadfastly hewed to a range of democratic and federal norms and statutes, it may have well fended off the emergence of separatist movements in both the Punjab and Kashmir. Similarly, if both the principal national political parties—the Indian National Congress (INC) and the Bharatiya Janata Party (BJP)—had not engaged in a process of ethnic outbidding, a host of ethnic and communal passions might not have been stirred and violence between Hindu and Muslim communities not ensued.

In a closely related vein, despite the outcome of the 2014 national elections, India cannot abandon its commitment to secularism. Not only would the country veer dangerously toward an illiberal political order but, worse still, it could face renewed and even greater political discord and violence. The early portents of such a distressing future are already visible. A small but growing, minority of India's vast Muslim community have already started to respond to the siren call of radical Islam.[68] If this trend toward greater radicalization continues, the country could face social fissures of an unprecedented order.

Finally, this assessment of India's democracy would be incomplete without a brief discussion of the recrudescence of Maoist violence in India (see chapter 5). The sources of Maoist terror in India can be traced to a movement that originally erupted in Naxalbari, a tea-growing area in the northern part of the state of West Bengal in 1967. It initially began as a rural peasant revolt against the exploitative practices of landlords and drew its inspiration from Maoist China. Subsequently, it spread to the state capital of Calcutta, where significant numbers of well-educated, middle- and upper-middle-class college students imbued with ideological fervor joined the fray. As the movement became increasingly violent and elements of it became corrupted with entry of criminal gangs and extortion rackets, the state and national governments moved to effectively if ruthlessly suppress it.[69]

Even though the government's tactics eviscerated the movement, all of its followers did not abandon their commitment to their revolutionary beliefs. Some of them went underground but managed to sustain the movement in embryonic form and recruit a new cohort of supporters. In the 1990s they succeeded in kindling some extant grievances of segments of the population that did not benefit from India's dramatic economic growth, who witnessed the complicity of state and national governments in the exploitation of natural resources, and who did not receive much in the form of state-sponsored schemes of social welfare. These factors, in combination, provided a combustible basis to rekindle the movement to the point that Prime Minister Manmohan Singh actually conceded in 2010 that it was the single gravest internal threat to India's national security.[70]

The state's response to this internal security threat has been uneven. In considerable part the patchy response has stemmed from India's federal structure. Some states, which are better governed, can bring in greater revenues and consequently can field more efficacious police forces. Others, however, have failed to respond with similar vigor and resourcefulness. This varied set of state responses has often enabled the insurgents to flee into ungoverned or poorly administered areas of neighboring states, thereby making it exceedingly difficult to contain and terminate the movement.

India has a mixed if eventually effective record of dealing with insurgencies. Among other matters it has demonstrated an extraordinary ability to simply wear down insurgents and, on occasion, make suitable political concessions, including the creation of new states. However, the vast majority of these movements have been ethnic and separatist.[71] This Maoist movement, however, is class-based and straddles multiple states. Consequently, coping with this movement may require targeted repression, attempts at addressing some underlying grievances, and a strategy that takes into account the limitations of India's federal structure when dealing with the needs of multiple states. Forging such a strategy without corroding fundamental rights and liberties and respecting the limits of the country's federal structure will be a demanding task for any national government. How the Indian state fashions such a response will have a significant impact on the quality of its democratic future.

But how the Indian state deals with any given insurgency is only part of the state-building picture. How or whether the Indian state deals with the multiple problems that require some type of resolution will tell us whether or to what extent it is relatively effective. At some point, a relatively effective state may be needed to cope with great power status. Otherwise, it will be difficult to take advantage of the enhanced status and the greater complexities associated with a global role.

Democratic institutions can contribute to determining which problems are addressed. These same institutions can also shape the policy outcomes. In this respect, Indian democracy becomes both the independent and dependent variable. By addressing problems effectively, Indian decision-makers can reinforce public appreciation for democratic institutions. Whether they choose to address one type of problem or another may in turn hinge on which decision-makers have been selected by competitive processes. Sometimes, perceptions of past effectiveness can play some role in these same selection processes. It is a circular process that is closely linked to state legitimacy. Legitimacy, we have argued (in chapters 3 and 4), is one of the main components of state capacity. Legitimacy therefore undergirds the successful exploitation of any possible improvements in the Indian state's international standing.

T·E·N

Grand Strategy

Grand strategies are like cookbooks that tell people what mix of ingredients are needed to attain selected outcomes. If it's a sheet of cookies that is desired, one needs to mix flour, eggs, sugar, and butter, perhaps with some nuts and chocolate, and bake clusters of the ingredients for a particular length of time at a predesignated heat. In the foreign-policy realm, grand strategies instruct decision-makers how to attain end goals. For instance, one tack that is currently underway is predicated on the notion that Indian security will hinge on "control" of the Indian Ocean. If China controls the Indian Ocean, India will suffer as a consequence. Accordingly, India needs to expand its naval resources considerably to be able to project power throughout the Indian Ocean and to counter the power projection efforts of its rivals. More specifically, it will need blue-water vessels, such as aircraft carriers and nuclear submarines, to carry this out if for no other reason than because the rivals are developing these capabilities and it will be difficult to compete with them without equivalent naval capabilities.

Grand strategies are also important to analyses of state strength. Relatively weak states can develop grand strategies that are improbable in the absence of the requisite capabilities needed to bring them about. Strong states can get on by focusing in the short term on the crisis of the week without any long-range plan. Yet even strong states need blueprints or cookbooks to achieve longer-term goals. Should one concentrate one's military resources in maritime or land capabilities? Should one focus on the immediate region, or is it critical to operate beyond the home region? Should one emphasize coercion or cooperation as the principal tool for dealing with adjacent states?

In-betweeners—states that are neither weak nor strong—must also be concerned about strategies for improving their status and capabilities so that they are better able to achieve whatever goals are thought to need pursuing. That is, grand strategies for the states in the middle must look inward and outward at the same time. They are unlikely to achieve their external goals without also improving their internal resource foundation, which also happens to include a state that is strong enough to formulate, tackle, and attain its goals.

India has long had a grand strategy and a largely stable set of goals. One of its most consistent features has been the quest for great power status. The means to achieve this quest, however, have shifted over time. This chapter will argue that it initially sought to achieve this through the pursuit of an ideational foreign policy. Ideational foreign policies stress leadership in promoting ideas such as nonalignment or third-world solidarity. The attractiveness of these themes is not supposed to depend on how many tanks or bombers its advocates may or may not possess. Subsequently, it adopted a mix of ideational and material approaches in pursuit of those ends. In the wake of the Cold War it has tilted quite significantly toward acquiring the requisite material capabilities to pursue that goal. Nevertheless, a segment of its policy-making apparatus seems unable and indeed unwilling to completely shed its attachment to some ideational concerns, however atavistic and very possibly counterproductive to its goal of achieving great power status.

This element within India's foreign- and security-policy establishments remains alive and well despite the advent of Prime Minister Narendra Modi's regime in 2014, one with a markedly different ideological orientation. Upon assuming office it introduced considerable vigor to India's foreign policy. It has not sought to improve relations with India's immediate neighbors; it has demonstrated a new degree of resolve in dealing with Pakistan (and to a lesser degree, the People's Republic of

China, the PRC); and it has sought to deepen existing ties with countries ranging from the United States, Japan, and Australia. However, it remains unclear if it will be able to sustain the initiatives that it has undertaken and will thereby usher in a markedly new era in India's grand strategy.[1]

In this chapter we will show how structural, domestic, and decision-making factors have all shaped the country's grand strategy. The relative weights that can be assigned to these forces, however, have varied over time. To that end, this chapter will provide an explicit periodization and discuss the specific roles of these factors on the conduct of the country's strategy since independence in 1947. It will argue that a mostly ideational period lasted from 1947 to 1964. This phase drew to a close in the aftermath of the disastrous Sino-Indian border war of 1962 and the death of India's first prime minister, Jawaharlal Nehru. A second phase, which relied on similar rhetoric but diverged quite sharply in the realm of action, began in the aftermath of Nehru's demise and lasted until the eve of the third Indo-Pakistani conflict. A third phase began in 1971 and concluded around the termination of the Cold War. This phase saw much continuity with the previous one. However, it was a period of strategic dependence for the country because of its quasi-alliance with the Soviet Union. In this context it may be useful to underscore that the shock of the 1962 war had already undermined India's attempt to maintain its fierce independence in the conduct of foreign affairs. As will be discussed later in this chapter, fearful of the prospects of renewed intransigence on the part of the PRC, India had unsuccessfully sought a nuclear guarantee from the United States, the United Kingdom, and the Soviet Union.

At the Cold War's end and with the dissolution of the Soviet Union, the country adopted a foreign policy that recognized the significance of harnessing material power to best meet its foreign- and security-policy goals. However, one factor, which had been a leitmotif of India's foreign policy, especially in its early years—the quest for an independent foreign policy—once again, asserted itself.[2] This was almost invariably referred to as the quest for "strategic autonomy."[3] It is possible that India's grand strategy and concomitantly its foreign and security policies will enter a fourth phase with a greater emphasis on the accouterments of national power and increased pragmatism under the leadership of Prime Minister Narendra Modi.[4] In its initial days in office the Modi government has scrupulously avoided any public discussion of the country's historical commitment to nonalignment, nor has it invoked the concept of "strategic autonomy."[5]

We discuss the highlights of each period, analyze the key forces shaping India's current foreign and security policies, and then address some ongoing policy concerns. The implicit questions throughout this chapter are whether and how India's strategies are commensurate with its resources.

In the Wake of Independence

DEFYING SYSTEMIC CONSTRAINTS

British colonial withdrawal from the Indian subcontinent had left the nascent Indian state mostly impoverished. It was sandbagged with a large, poor population and limited industrial capacity and was not blessed with an overabundance of strategic resources. Though the precise reasons remain the subject of continued controversy, even as late as 1943 4 million individuals had perished in a famine in eastern India, and most notably in Bengal.[6] Despite India's very substantial contribution to World War Two, its actual military capabilities were quite limited.[7]

According to realist premises, these material constraints should have hobbled the country from playing a significant role in the emergent global order even if it so aspired.[8] India's state strength at this juncture was indeed quite limited. Table 10.1 provides a comparison of the material capabilities of key states around 1947.

Nevertheless, Indian policy-makers, most notably Jawaharlal Nehru, made a conscious choice not to adhere to such realist expectations and instead sought to pursue a mostly ideational foreign policy. Such a strategy was possible because of his overweening influence and standing within the Indian political arena in the wake of independence. He not only had impeccable nationalist credentials but he was easily the most cosmopolitan member of the Indian nationalist movement.[9] His interest in international affairs was long-standing, and he had written

Table 10.1. Material Capabilities

	India	China	Japan	United Kingdom	United States
GDP (millions of 1990 US$)	213,680 (1947)	244,985 (1950)	120,377 (1947)	327,044 (1947)	1,285,697 (1947)
	215,927 (1948)	273,733 (1951)	138,290 (1948)	337,376 (1948)	1,334,331 (1948)
GDP per capita (1990 US$)	618 (1947)	448 (1950)	1,541 (1947)	6,604 (1947)	8,886 (1947)
	617 (1948)	491 (1951)	1,725 (1948)	6,746 (1948)	9,065 (1948)
Population	346,000,000 (1947)	538,244,000 (1947)	78,119,000 (1947)	49,519,000 (1947)	144,688,000 (1947)
	350,000,000 (1948)	541,085,000 (1948)	80,155,000 (1948)	50,014,000 (1948)	147,203,000 (1948)
Iron and steel production (thousands of tons)	1,277 (1947)	70 (1947)	2,082 (1945)	12,929 (1947)	77,015 (1947)
	1,277 (1948)	606 (1950)	6,988 (1952)	15,116 (1948)	80,413 (1948)

(continued)

Table 10.1. (*continued*)

	India	China	Japan	United Kingdom	United States
Primary energy consumption (thousands of coal-ton equivalents)	33,752 (1947) 34,071 (1948)	18,187 (1947) 29,555 (1950)	34,266 (1945) 48,877 (1952)	223,696 (1947) 233,072 (1948)	1,315,777 (1947) 1,396,394 (1948)
Military expenditure (thousands of current year US$)	218,680 (1947) 275,196 (1948)	257,474 (1947) 2,558,000 (1950)	4,002,481 (1945) 289,212 (1952)	6,656,196 (1947) 3,438,984 (1948)	14,315,999 (1947) 10,960,998 (1948)
Military personnel	311,000 (1947) 311,000 (1948)	4,015,000 (1947) 4,000,000 (1950)	6,095,000 (1945) 119,000 (1952)	1,302,000 (1947) 847,000 (1948)	1,583,000 (1947) 1,446,000 (1948)

Sources: The figures for GDP, GDP per capita, and population are from Angus Maddison, Historical Statistics for the World Economy, A.D. 1–A.D. 2003 (Paris: Organisation for Economic Co-operation and Development, 1995–2003). These figures are available online at http://www.ggdc.net/Maddison/Historical_Statistics/horizontal-file_03-2007.xls, accessed September 15, 2012. All the remaining figures have been taken from the National Material Capabilities (v4.0) dataset of the Correlates of War project, available online at http://www.correlatesofwar.org/, accessed September 15, 2012. Additional indicators are from the following sections of Tim Dyson, Robert Cassen, and Leela Visaria, eds., Twenty-first Century India: Population, Economy, Human Development, and the Environment (New Delhi: Oxford University Press, 2004):

1. Tim Dyson, "India's Population—The Past," pp. 15–31.
   Total fertility per woman (1941–1951): 5.96 (p. 20).
   Literacy in 1951: 7.9 percent for women; 25 percent for men (p. 27).
2. Tim Dyson and Pravin Visaria, "Migration and Urbanization: Retrospect and Prospects," 108–129.
   Percent of population living in the cities (1951): 17.3 percent (p. 116).
3. Shankar Acharya, Robert Cassen, and Kirsty McNay, "The Economy—Past and Future," pp. 202–227.
   Average GDP growth rate 1951/1952–1960/1961: 3.9 percent (p. 206).

with authority about global issues at length prior to India's independence.[10] As a consequence, he easily emerged as the principal architect of India's postindependence foreign policy.

DOMESTIC HURDLES AND CONCERNS

Though unfettered in his ability to forge India's foreign and security policies, Nehru was faced with significant material and organizational constraints.[11] He had inherited not only a truncated state, thanks to the partition of the British Indian Empire, but also lacked a cadre of individuals trained and interested in matters of foreign affairs. Furthermore, at home he was faced with two sets of daunting tasks. The first involved tackling the problem of widespread rural and urban poverty. In an attempt to build the sinews of a modern state, India chose a strategy of economic development and emphasized heavy industrialization and extensive state intervention in the economy.[12] This approach, while it did help create an industrial base, failed to promote rapid economic growth or dramatically reduce poverty.[13]

The second mission involved forging an effective political union from the patchwork quilt of states that he had inherited from the British Indian Empire. This effort, however, at least in its initial stages, was accomplished with much skill. Able Indian civil servants that were inherited from the British Indian Civil Service, most notably under the leadership of a remarkable individual, V. P. Menon, played a vital role in ensuring the accession of the "princely states," which had been nominally independent as long as they had recognized the paramount authority of the British Crown.[14] Despite this initial success throughout much of the first two decades, the Indian state had to cope with what the American journalist referred to as "fissiparous tendencies"—various centrifugal forces stemming from ethnic, linguistic, and class tensions that threatened the viability of the Indian polity.[15]

These domestic infirmities profoundly influenced Nehru's international outlook. Keenly aware of India's material weaknesses but equally desirous of shaping the postwar global order, he envisioned an ideational foreign policy. Such a policy would seek to hobble the use of force in international affairs; it would promote the role of multilateral organizations, end racial discrimination, reduce global inequities, and would hasten decolonization.[16]

Furthermore, because of his concerns about Bonapartism as well as the opportunity costs of defense spending, Nehru sought to limit India's military expenditures.[17] Finally, his fears of external domination, stemming from the long history of British colonial exploitation, led him to enunciate an independent foreign policy for the nascent state, popularly referred to as the "doctrine of nonalignment."[18] Nehru's commitment to nonalignment and its core principles became the cornerstone of India's foreign and security policies.

However, some of its key premises, especially the commitment to limit the use of force to resolve international disputes, were soon put to the test as India became embroiled over a territorial contest involving the status of the princely state of Jammu and Kashmir.[19] When confronted with a Pakistan-based and supported tribal invasion of the state, Nehru authorized the airlift of Indian troops to halt their advance having obtained the imprimatur of the monarch who had sought Indian assistance to fend off the invaders.[20] Nevertheless, reflecting his faith in international organizations, Nehru referred the issue to the United Nations for resolution. At the UN, thanks to deft Pakistani diplomacy and blatant British partisanship, the issue became deeply enmeshed in Cold War politics, and India's original complaint about Pakistan's support for the invaders was lost.[21]

A PLACE IN THE GLOBAL ORDER

Despite problems in the region and India's obvious material limitations, Nehru sought a substantial role for India in global affairs. To that end India became a major advocate for the decolonization process and was an early supporter of United Nations peacekeeping operations.[22] The issue of decolonization, of course, was a significant plank of the Non-Aligned Movement (NAM), one that Nehru, along with Sukarno of Indonesia, Gamal Abdel Nasser of Egypt, and Marshall Tito of Yugoslavia sought to promote. Obviously, the interest in decolonization stemmed from the country's own historical experience. It was also in keeping with

Nehru's ideational worldview. Even India's involvement in early UN peacekeeping operations was related to the decolonization enterprise. To that end, India provided a significant contingent to the UN operations in the former Belgian Congo; it was a member of the International Control Commission (ICC) for Cambodia, Laos, and Vietnam; and it attempted to play a mediatory role in bringing the Korean war to a close.[23] Finally, owing to Nehru's deep-seated aversion to nuclear weapons, India also sought to place the issue of disarmament on the global agenda. To that end he was instrumental in introducing a resolution with Ireland at the United Nations General Assembly in 1954, calling for a "standstill agreement" on all nuclear tests.[24] Obviously, this proposal did not make much headway, but it did ultimately provide the basis for the Partial Test Ban Treaty (PTBT) of 1963.

Nehru's ideational worldview, however, led him to underestimate the differences that he confronted with the PRC closer to home. Specifically, he did not wholly comprehend the emerging rivalry with the PRC.[25] Furthermore, in an attempt to limit defense spending, he also downplayed the significance of the border claims that the PRC asserted in the mid-1950s. Instead, he believed that his diplomatic attempts to conciliate the PRC would succeed. Accordingly, after the PRC's occupation of Tibet in 1950 he avoided any public condemnation of the Chinese occupation and refused to take the matter to the United Nations, despite entreaties from Tibetan exiles.[26] He did, however, grant refuge to the Dalai Lama when he fled from Tibet in 1959 in the wake of the failed Khampa rebellion.[27]

Despite these conciliatory gestures, his willingness to offer refuge to the Dalai Lama and to permit the Tibetans to set up a government in exile caused considerable misgiving in Beijing about New Delhi's intentions. Furthermore, differences over poorly demarcated colonial borders came to the fore around the same time. The subsequent collapse of negotiations over the border dispute in 1960 lead India to adopt the so-called "forward policy," which involved sending in small military contingents into disputed areas to assert India's claims. These units, in the words of a senior retired Indian military officer, had "neither teeth nor tail."[28] Nevertheless, the Chinese deemed them to be provocative, and in October 1962 they launched a well-orchestrated attack on Indian positions. The ill-equipped and outgunned Indian forces were, for the most part, easily routed, resulting in a near-complete military debacle.[29] Simply put, it was a flawed strategy of compellence that brought about this disastrous outcome: India had failed to match its resolve with the requisite capabilities.[30]

After the 1962 Debacle

THE SEARCH FOR MATERIAL POWER

The ideational approach that Nehru had so championed suffered a body blow as a consequence of the Sino-Indian border war. Nehru was forced to concede that gross lack of defense preparedness had brought on the military disaster of 1962. In its wake he authorized the transformation of India's military. His overweening standing in the domestic political arena also took a significant battering as the previously quiescent political opposition came to the fore. Though still unable to dislodge Nehru, his opponents secured the resignation of his minister of defense and alter ego, Krishna Menon. At another level, even his doctrine of nonalignment came under duress.[31] Nevertheless, his critics both within the parliamentary opposition and in the country's nascent civil society were unable to ensure its complete abandonment.

In this connection, external factors also played a role in preventing the wholesale departure from nonalignment. At the peak of the 1962 crisis, Nehru had abandoned his qualms about the United States and had actively sought American military assistance, including air cover. The United States, keen to bolster India as a bulwark against the possibilities of Chinese Communist expansionism in Asia, proved willing to assist India both militarily and diplomatically.[32] To that end, it did collaborate with the Indian Air Force as well as intelligence agencies to embark on a substantial program of aerial intelligence gathering.[33] However, the robust U.S.-Pakistan alliance quickly placed important limits on the scope and extent of American military assistance.[34] Furthermore, the residual commitment to nonalignment, especially after the initial shock of the military debacle started to recede, ensured that policy-makers remained loath to rely inordinately upon the United States for continued military and security assistance.[35]

Since an excessive dependence on a superpower was deemed politically and ideologically unacceptable, India had little or no choice but to resort to a strategy of internal balancing to cope with the emergent security threat from the PRC. To that end, plans were made for raising ten new mountain divisions equipped for high-altitude warfare, a million-man army, a forty-five squadron air force with supersonic aircraft, and modest steps toward naval modernization.[36]

POLITICAL TRANSITIONS

Nehru passed away in 1964. As a consequence of his passing as well as the disastrous effects of the Sino-Indian border war, Indian policymakers were forced to reappraise the ideational approach to foreign and security policies. Some within Parliament openly questioned the value of nonalignment. However, Nehru's successor, Prime Minister Lal Bahadur Shastri, an individual of limited stature within the ruling Congress Party, was hardly in a position to spell out an alternative approach to India's foreign and security policies. That said, despite the professed commitment to the principles of nonalignment, there were perceptible shifts in New Delhi's pursuit of foreign and security policy goals. Obviously, the constraints on defense spending, which were characteristic of the Nehruvian era, fell apart.[37] India nevertheless persisted with Nehruvian goals, such as global nuclear disarmament, in various global forums.

However, these efforts quickly became tempered and increasingly attuned to the structural realities of power. For example, in the discussions on the nonproliferation treaty in Geneva at the Eighteen Nation Disarmament Conference (ENDC), India had sought to link it to plans for the eventual elimination of nuclear weapons. As it became increasingly apparent that no such efforts were in the offing and that the treaty would create a two-tier system, India steadfastly refused to accede to it. India's refusal, in considerable measure, stemmed from its perception of an extant threat from the PRC. Perceptions of this threat dramatically increased in the wake of the first Chinese nuclear test in 1964.[38] Indeed, within a year of this test, Prime Minister Shastri authorized the Subterranean Nuclear Explosions Project (SNEP).[39]

In 1965, a second war with Pakistan over Kashmir ensued and ended in a stalemate. The origins of this conflict have been explored elsewhere.[40] Shortly after the war, Prime Minister Shastri died of a heart attack and Indira Gandhi, Nehru's daughter, succeeded him in office. Even with her assumption of office India could not, at least in the public sphere, abandon its earlier ideational commitments even as it recognized the importance of material power. This tension between two competing organizing principles became evident in its quest for a nuclear guarantee from the great powers to cope with the perceived nuclear threat from the PRC. On the one hand India sought extended deterrence from the Soviet Union, the United Kingdom, and the United States. On the other hand it was unwilling to jettison its nonaligned status.[41] Ultimately, India's fears of Chinese nuclear blackmail, combined with its failure to obtain a nuclear guarantee from the great powers, led it to pursue a nuclear weapons program.[42]

A Period of Strategic Dependence

GLOBAL POWER SHIFTS AND INDIA'S CHOICES

The next phase in India's foreign and security policies can be traced to the third Indo-Pakistani conflict in 1971. The origins of this war did not lie in the Kashmir conflict but stemmed from the exigencies of Pakistani domestic politics.[43] This event can be considered a turning point because it showed that India's policy-makers had effectively shed their Nehru-era inhibitions about the use of force despite their reliance on the rhetoric of an earlier period. When confronted with a regional crisis, the new prime minister, Indira Gandhi, displayed no qualms about the use of force to advance what she deemed to be India's vital security interests. Simultaneously, despite professions of a continuing commitment to nonalignment, she forged a new security partnership with the Soviet Union to safeguard India's security interests along its northern frontier.[44] This partnership, though clearly beneficial to India, especially during the East Pakistan crisis, was not without cost. Admittedly, the Soviets did not manage to penetrate India's policy-making apparatus nor fundamentally alter its policy choices.[45] Nevertheless, there is little question that the relationship did limit India's policy options, particularly in the wake of the Soviet invasion of Afghanistan.[46] This period of Indian strategic dependence on the Soviet Union would last until the latter's dissolution in 1990. In the aftermath of the Soviet collapse the principal successor state, Russia, evinced little or no interest in sustaining the relationship that had been developed and nurtured over nearly the past two decades.

Indira Gandhi's turn to the Soviet Union came when confronted with two important developments. The first was at a global level, with significant potential repercussions for regional security, and the second was at a bilateral level. The first was the beginnings of the U.S.-PRC rapprochement following the visit of the U.S. secretary of state, Henry Kissinger, in July 1971 to the PRC, using Pakistan as an intermediary. The possible entente in Sino-American relations, with Pakistan playing the role of an intercessor, caused grave concern in New Delhi given its strained ties to both capitals.

These fears were highlighted when the East Pakistan crisis, which started in December 1970, placed a massive refugee burden on India in the spring of 1971 following a vicious Pakistani military crackdown on the province's hapless population.[47] After seeking diplomatic solutions to the crisis in East Pakistan, Indian policy-makers concluded that it was cheaper to resort to war and dismember Pakistan than to absorb the refugees into its already turgid population.[48] However, cognizant of the emergent U.S.-PRC-Pakistan nexus, India's policy-makers had to ensure that the PRC would be constrained from opening a second front along its Himalayan borders. To hem in the PRC, Indira Gandhi signed a twenty-year treaty of peace, friendship, and cooperation with the Soviet Union in August 1971. Article IX of this treaty, for all practical purposes, amounted to a security guarantee.

With India's northern front secured and the support of a veto-wielding power in the United Nations Security Council, her government embarked on a strategy that provoked a military attack from Pakistan in early December 1971.[49] Indian forces, which were wholly prepared for war, quickly invaded East Pakistan and brought the conflict to close within two weeks.[50] Even U.S. support for Pakistan during this crisis, including the sailing of a task force into the Bay of Bengal, failed to deter Indira Gandhi from pursuing her stated war aims, which involved a military defeat of Pakistan in the east and the creation of a new state.[51]

CRITICAL CHOICES

India's resort to a careful, deliberate politico-military strategy to deal with this crisis showed that it had all but dispensed with the Nehruvian normative reservations about the use of force.[52] Indeed in the wake of this crisis India clearly emerged as the dominant power on the subcontinent and sought to consolidate its position. To that end it developed a tacit doctrine (popularly referred to as the "Indira Doctrine") that made clear to its smaller neighbors that it would brook no interference on the part of external powers in what India deemed to be its neighborhood.[53]

Professions to the contrary aside, the Indo-Soviet treaty effectively ended India's commitment to nonalignment.[54] Furthermore, in the wake of the successful passage of the Nuclear Nonproliferation Treaty in 1968, India had moved ahead with its quest to develop a nuclear weapons capability. Though the exigencies of domestic politics clearly played a role in terms of its exact timing, within three years of the Indian victory over Pakistan, India tested its first nuclear device. Indian apologists claimed that the nuclear test was for strictly peaceful purposes.[55] However, one of the principal architects of India's nuclear weapons program later conceded that it was an initial attempt to develop nuclear weapons.[56] Faced with a raft of external sanctions that had dire consequences for the continued pursuit of its nuclear weapons program, and fearful of greater economic pressures, India's policy-makers chose not to conduct any further tests, even though the clandestine program was not abandoned.[57]

THE REMNANTS OF IDEATIONAL POLITICS

Some residual commitment to the Nehruvian grand strategy nevertheless continued to animate Indian foreign policy. For example, even though it was contrary to India's material interests, the country became an ardent champion for the call to create a New International Economic

Order (NIEO).[58] In this endeavor, India played a critical role in the Group of 77, an entity composed of seventy-seven developing countries and created in 1964 at the United Nations session that had led to the creation of the United Nations Conference on Trade and Development (UNCTAD).[59] The NIEO was especially damaging to India, as it was then and remains a desperately energy-short country. In this context it needs to be recalled that one of the key weapons that was used to demand the creation of the NIEO was the OPEC price hike. India also sought to play the role of the standard-bearer of the developing world in other international forums. To that end, in 1972, at the Stockholm Conference on the Human Environment, Indira Gandhi chose to highlight the importance of poverty alleviation over emerging environmental concerns.[60]

These attempts on India's part, to play a role larger than what its material capabilities warranted, failed for all practical purposes to amount to much. A domestically weak India coping with endemic problems of poverty and internal discord stemming from class, ethnic, and economic cleavages, could exercise little clout in the global arena. More to the point, in the early Cold War years, India had wielded a degree of normative influence. As a consequence of its own violation of the very principles that it had espoused, not to mention their flagrant disregard within the NAM, India's invocation of normative concerns was deemed to be mostly hollow.[61] Not surprisingly, the great powers largely ignored India's rhetoric at these multilateral forums.

These gestures in international forums aside, when faced with emergent security threats and tough choices India's policy-makers showed little interest in the idealism that had so characterized Nehru's foreign policy. In the wake of the Soviet invasion of Afghanistan in December 1979, Indira Gandhi, who had just returned to office after a brief interregnum, refused to join the global chorus of condemnation. Once again, it was clear that India was balancing against what it deemed to be its most clear-cut threats.[62] With the Soviet invasion of Afghanistan, the Reagan administration had chosen to bolster Pakistan's military capabilities, thereby eroding India's conventional superiority over its long-standing adversary. To help restore its military edge over Pakistan, Indira Gandhi avoided any public criticism of Soviet actions while seeking substantial arms transfers at highly concessional rates.[63]

This need to rely on the Soviet Union as well as India's anodyne position on the invasion and occupation of Afghanistan underscored its strategic dependence on the Soviets and the clear limits of its professed commitment to nonalignment.

In an attempt to reduce India's dependence on the Soviet Union in pursuit of a more robust outcome of the doctrine of containment,[64] the United States under the Reagan administration made some preliminary overtures toward India in the early 1980s. The renewed U.S.-Pakistan military relationship and the memories of American support for Pakistan during the 1971 crisis remained the principal hurdles in any attempt to ameliorate relations. The Reagan administration, obviously unwilling to dilute its security ties to Pakistan, nevertheless found a means to entice Indian policy-makers. To that end they dangled the possibility of Indian access to U.S. dual-use high-technology items on a selected basis.[65] Despite the robust arms-transfer relationship with the Soviet Union, there were some highly sophisticated technologies that India could not obtain from its otherwise reliable partner. As a consequence of these overtures and India's willingness to respond, a mild thaw came about in Indo-U.S. relations under Rajiv Gandhi, Mrs. Gandhi's son and successor. Nevertheless, the "shadow of the past" loomed large in Indo-U.S. relations.[66] Furthermore, given the limited scope of Indo-U.S. economic ties, differences about Pakistan and India's continued dependence on the Soviet Union placed clear limits on any possible rapprochement with the United States.

The dependence on the Soviet Union, it should be emphasized, was not limited to the arms-transfer relationship. In considerable part India had come to rely on a tacit Soviet security guarantee against the PRC. Indeed, though it is poorly recognized, India decided to cross the nuclear Rubicon in 1998 because it had realized in the wake of the Soviet collapse that Russia would not uphold prior security commitments toward India. In a speech that he had delivered in Vladivostok in July 1986 Gorbachev had already made clear that the fundamental changes in Soviet foreign policy were under way. Among other matters, he had outlined a framework for the improvement of relations with the PRC. The latter issue had caused some nervousness in New Delhi. However, those committed to the Indo-Soviet relationship had sought to downplay any possible adverse repercussions for India as a consequence of a possible Sino-Soviet rapprochement.[67]

Coping with the Soviet Collapse and "Enlightened Self-Interest"

ADAPTING TO A NEW GLOBAL ORDER

At the Cold War's end, India's grand strategy underwent drastic changes. The central concern of the country's grand strategy, the quest for a substantial role in global affairs, nevertheless remained. It needs to be underscored, however, that in the absence of structural shifts in global power as well as the end of the Soviet model of economic development, it is questionable if such dramatic changes in India's grand strategy would have materialized. When faced with past crises the Indian state had resorted to ameliorative efforts but had not undertaken fundamental shifts in its foreign and economic policies. For example, in the wake of the 1962 crisis, it had made major changes in its defense policies. However, it had not wholly abandoned its normative worldview in the domain of foreign policy.[68] Also, in the aftermath of a major fiscal crisis in 1966, India had only undertaken incremental changes.[69] Accordingly, it can be argued that while ideational changes in the global arena as well as the presence of reform-minded leaders played a vital role in the foundational shifts that occurred, structural shocks were of the greatest consequence in inducing any discernible shifts in grand strategy.[70] A failure to adapt to the drastic changes in the global order would have left India both economically and diplomatically marginalized.

Both the Cold War's end and the Soviet collapse came as a complete surprise to Indian policy-makers. In the words of a senior Indian diplomat, it was the strategic equivalent of the "collapse of a supernova" as far as India was concerned.[71] Most importantly, it meant that India's implicit security guarantee from the Soviet Union had abruptly ended. Consequently, it would have to either seek a new patron or rely on internal efforts to balance against the threat from the PRC.

Seeking a new security umbrella from the United States was not really a viable option because of the persistence of a range of policy differences. Furthermore, many within India's policy-making community were fearful of the emergence of a unipolar global order. Accordingly, a significant policy debate ensued within its attentive public. Those wedded to Nehruvian ideas of world order continued to insist on their relevance and suggested that India reaffirm its commitment to those principles.[72]

DOMESTIC NEEDS AND POLICY SHIFTS

The Cold War's end also coincided with an unprecedented financial crisis. In the aftermath of the first Gulf war, India's exchequer was virtually facing bankruptcy. The country had purchased petroleum on the global spot market in the run-up to the war, it had helped repatriate over one hundred thousand workers from the region and had also lost their remittances. To compound matters, a series of debt payments to multilateral banks came due in early 1991. This conjunction of forces created a virtual maelstrom for the Indian economy. Faced with similar crises in the past, India's policy-makers had, at best, undertaken piecemeal reforms but had refused to abandon the basic tenets underlying India's policy choices.[73] However, on this occasion, they utilized this crisis to bring about dramatic and indeed far-reaching changes to the country's political economy.[74]

Specifically, Prime Minister Narasimha Rao and his then minister of finance, Manmohan Singh, sought to dramatically alter the course of India's foreign as well as economic policies.[75] In the economic arena, the country abandoned its long-held commitment to import-substituting industrialization (ISI), it shed a labyrinthine set of regulations, and also opened its markets to a considerable degree to foreign investment. In the realm of foreign policy it slowly started to shed its reflexive hostility toward the United States, it made efforts to reduce tensions with the PRC, and it embarked upon a concerted attempt to engage the economically vibrant states of Southeast Asia. Relations with Pakistan, India's nettlesome neighbor, however, showed few signs of improvement. Instead, the outbreak of an indigenous insurgency in the disputed state of Jammu and Kashmir worsened relations, especially as Pakistan sought to exploit extant local grievances.

The failure to improve relations with Pakistan notwithstanding, there is no question that the changes in India's foreign-policy orientation proved to be substantial. The country effectively shed its "bunker mentality" as it sought to play a renewed role in global affairs.[76] It also dropped its willingness to serve as the spokesperson for the developing world as it sought to address the crying needs of domestic economic development and long-term threats to national security. These sweeping changes notwithstanding, its policy-makers nevertheless remained adverse to the prospect of a unipolar global order.[77] Two factors in considerable part explained India's concerns about a unipolar world. One stemmed from a widespread belief that a dominant global power would limit India's scope for maneuvering in the international arena. A second was closely related to the first and was rooted in the belief that an overweening power could impose its will on India in a range of global regimes extending from human rights to nonproliferation. Since India was already at odds with the United States in both these arenas, the concerns about American global dominance took on added significance.

The drastic changes that came about also encompassed India's security policy. Since the 1974 test, India had maintained a policy of nuclear ambiguity.[78] However, with the end of the Soviet nuclear guarantee; multilateral pressures, especially in the wake of the indefinite and unconditional extension of the NPT in 1995; the subsequent efforts to realize a Comprehensive Test Ban Treaty (CTBT); and a deterioration of the security environment in South Asia—all combined to mark a critical change in India's nuclear policy.[79] Accordingly, in May 1998 India tested five nuclear weapons. In their wake the country confronted widespread global disapprobation including a raft of new bilateral and multilateral sanctions. Nevertheless, it steadfastly refused to terminate the program.[80] Even the advent of a markedly different regime in 2004 following the electoral defeat of the right-wing Bharatiya Janata Party (BJP)–led National Democratic Alliance (NDA) had no discernible effect on India's nuclear weapons policies.

Nor, for that matter, were there any dramatic substantive shifts in the realm of foreign policy under the new Congress Party–led United Progressive Alliance (UPA) government. The current regime's emphasis on "enlightened self-interest" as the lodestar of its foreign policy did not differ much in substance from those that the previous regime had pursued.[81] In fact, the improvement in Indo-U.S. relations continued apace despite some ongoing differences in particular areas ranging from the pace of India's domestic economic reforms, to dealing with the question of Iran's apparent clandestine quest for nuclear weapons, over how best to tackle climate change, and how to pursue further trade liberalization. Both sides, however, took these differences in stride.[82]

India's engagement with the states of Southeast Asia, which started in the early 1990s, has also continued to expand. In this connection, even though Indian policy-makers are loath to so admit publicly, one of the key prongs of India's involvement with this region stems from the increasing assertiveness of the PRC.[83] To that end India has stepped up naval cooperation with a number of states in Southeast Asia, Australia, and also with Japan.[84] All these developments evince that India's leadership is acutely cognizant of the significance of material power in global affairs.

However, significant elements within the political leadership as well as its attentive public are seeking to reinforce an earlier principle that had guided India's foreign and security policies. Namely, they are keen on ensuring that the country not be perceived as a U.S. ally despite the growing strength of the relationship.[85]

To that end, India is seeking to shore up its role in various cross-regional forums. It helped create a new entity, India, Brazil and South Africa (IBSA), in 2003 designed to foster economic cooperation and also promote policy coordination in other multilateral arenas. Though some policy coordination has ensued, this trilateral dialogue has not been able to wholly overcome significant differences in both capabilities and interests. India, however, has become a more active participant in the Brazil-Russia-India-China-South Africa (BRICS) forum. Nevertheless, it is far from clear whether bilateral differences can be managed effectively in the latter organization. For example, despite rhetorical attempts to bridge differences, the PRC and India remain at odds over a range of bilateral and regional issues. Finally, India remains fixated on its quest to become a permanent member of the United Nations Security Council (UNSC). Its policy-makers increasingly argue that India should be granted this status to reflect the changed structure of the global order in which India has become a significant player on the basis of its economic clout, its military prowess, and its demographic status. Despite some sympathetic nods from the principal Western powers, the country faces formidable obstacles in this quest.[86] One of the principal roadblocks remains the intransigence of the PRC to any expansion of the UNSC that would include India.

NEW DIRECTIONS OR BACK TO THE FUTURE?

During the early Cold War years, the doctrine of nonalignment provided its policy-makers with a simple organizing principle. Later, despite the mostly rhetorical commitment to nonalignment, the leadership grudgingly recognized the significance of material power. Indeed, as has been argued in this chapter, the country entered into a strategic partnership with the Soviet Union to guarantee its security when reliance on its own internal efforts was deemed inadequate. Subsequently, with the Cold War's end and the termination of the tacit Soviet security guarantee, the country chose to acquire a nuclear weapons capability to fend off the possibility of future nuclear coercion at the hands of the PRC. Furthermore, its adoption of more liberal economic policies and its abandonment of a state-dominated strategy of economic growth had yielded substantial benefits. Significant and mostly sustained economic growth in the wake of its fitful embrace of economic liberalization, a slow but steady rapprochement with the United States after the nuclear tests, and its increasing integration into the global economy has led to a chorus of assessments that India would emerge as a global power in the twenty-first century.[87]

Despite these appraisals of India's imminent rise, as most knowledgeable analysts recognize, the country is still beset with a host of burdens it must shed before it can realize its potential. The domestic constraints that India confronts are substantial, and many have been highlighted in earlier chapters. However, some salient issues can be underlined. The country faces substantial rural and urban poverty, its infrastructure remains highly uneven, it faces a resurgent Maoist insurgency in significant parts of the nation, the quality of its institutions and their efficacy are highly uneven, and it faces the specter of fractious coalition regimes for the foreseeable future. None of these limitations are likely to be addressed swiftly. Beset with these domestic hurdles, the country's ability to project power beyond its immediate shores, to assume new responsibilities in multilateral forums, and to proffer solutions to global challenges may all be hobbled.

Finally, despite the dexterity that its policy-makers had demonstrated both in domestic and foreign-policy realms at the end of the Cold War, they have yet to forge a new intellectual consensus to direct the country's foreign policy.[88] Beyond the insistence on "strategic autonomy," they have failed to develop a coherent set of principles that might enable the country to carve a distinct niche in the emerging global order. Indeed, a number of competing visions now seem to be animating the political debate within India.[89]

The regime of Prime Minister Modi, as argued earlier, has a distinct worldview and deep ideological roots. Despite the prime minister's personal interest in foreign policy and an ideological orientation that has distinctly realist proclivities, the ability to harness India's domestic resources and to forge a new foreign-policy consensus will not be an easy task.[90] Both the existence of alternative visions of global order within India's foreign-policy elite and the limitations of its existing domestic institutions could constrain the fashioning of a new grand strategy. The latter issue is of particular concern: India's state strength today is considerably greater than what it possessed in the first few decades of independence. It has successfully prosecuted several wars, it has weathered a series of natural calamities, and it has successfully fended off all challenges to its territorial integrity. These successes clearly underscore the resilience of the Indian state and its enhanced capacity. However, its extant capacity may not suffice for the purpose of shaping its regional circumstances and then transcending the region to exercise strategic influence across Asia and beyond.[91] And, of course, without the fashioning of a necessary domestic political consensus, India's choices and responses to matters of global, regional, and national concern may remain ad hoc and idiosyncratic.

E·L·E·V·E·N

Defense and Security Policies

India's defense policies have evolved considerably since the early years of the republic. In the initial years after independence, thanks to the dominance of the doctrine of nonalignment, defense expenditures were deliberately held in check.[1] Concomitantly, thanks to the overweening influence of India's first prime minister, Jawaharlal Nehru, there was a pervasive belief that diplomacy could serve as a viable substitute for force in international affairs. The consequences of this neglect of military prowess proved to be disastrous for India in 1962, when a border war with the People's Republic of China (PRC) erupted. The Indian military, caught woefully unprepared, fought with valor but proved utterly incapable of stemming the Chinese onslaught.[2] From India's standpoint, it lost fourteen thousand square miles of territory in this conflict. The border dispute continues to dog Sino-Indian relations.[3]

Only after the shock of the war did India's policy-makers embark upon a strategy of defense modernization.[4] In considerable measure, this effort at bolstering India's military capabilities enabled the country to decisively defeat its other, nettlesome adversary, Pakistan, in the 1971 war.[5] Following Pakistan's military defeat, India emerged as the dominant military power in the region. However, it did not succeed nor did it aspire to extend its military reach much beyond South Asia throughout the next two decades. It did conduct a single nuclear test in May 1974 but chose not to continue an overt nuclear weapons program in the face of costly and significant international sanctions

In considerable part, India's unwillingness and inability to stretch its military ambit beyond its immediate littoral stemmed from three distinct sources. First, the ethos of the Indian military remained mostly focused on territorial defense against Pakistan and the PRC. Second, the anemic growth rates of that the country's economy posted during these years did not provide much leeway for a significant expansion of military capabilities. Third, neither the country's political leadership nor its military planners visualized a larger role for the country's armed forces, because there were few if any interests that had to be secured much beyond India's immediate borders.

It was really not until the advent of India's fitful embrace of a more market-oriented approach toward economic growth in the early 1990s that it could devote more resources to the military, that it saw the necessity to possess capabilities to protect nascent trade and energy interests, and that it recognized the need to compete more effectively with the growing reach of the People's Liberation Army Navy (PLAN). Also, after decades of reliance on a strategy of nuclear ambiguity, owing to a complex convergence of heightened regional threats coupled with emergent global pressures from the nonproliferation regime, India finally became a nuclear power in May 1998.[6] Since the tests, it has been steadily working toward the construction of a nuclear triad, though it faces several organizational and some technological constraints.[7]

What are the principal threats and challenges that the country's defense policy confronts? What are some of the major institutional, technological, and organizational hurdles toward addressing these? What are the prospects of overcoming these limitations?[8] The remainder of this chapter will attempt to answer these questions, as the answers can provide important and invaluable clues about the country's ability not only to shape the political order in its immediate neighborhood but also to shape the milieu beyond its immediate shores to enhance its standing as a power of some consequence.

Internal Threats and Challenges

At the outset it is important to highlight that even after six decades of independence, India faces important challenges of domestic consolidation. It has, for the most part, managed to deal with a series of insurgencies that have wracked the country since the 1950s.[9] Despite its mostly successful efforts to quell challenges to domestic order and territorial integrity, it still confronts a restive population in the disputed state of Jammu and Kashmir and faces a continuing set of challenges from neophyte Maoist (Naxalite) guerillas in significant parts of the country. The then Indian prime minister, Manmohan Singh, in 2010 described the Maoist insurgencies as the single most important internal security threat plaguing the country.[10] According to the Union Ministry of Home Affairs, in 2011, as many as 182 districts in 20 Indian states (out of 640 districts in 28 states and 7 Union territories) were afflicted with Maoist guerilla activity.[11]

Despite the dangers to public order and the costs that these insurgencies have exacted on the country, it has yet to devise a national, coordinated strategy to deal with them. The reasons for the country's inability to fashion an effective strategy are manifold. However, one of the principal barriers to the adoption of a nationwide strategy is structural. Under India's constitutional dispensation, the question of law and order is a state subject. Consequently, the national government cannot impose its writ on a state until such time as the state authorities demonstrate they are simply incapable of maintaining law and order. Consequently, even though a number of states across the country are wracked with Naxalite violence, the national government in New Delhi cannot unilaterally act to suppress the rebels. Individual states are thereby at liberty to request national funds and seek the assistance of central paramilitary forces but are not so obligated.

Given this federal, constitutional design, the responses of particular states, based upon their material and organizational capabilities, have varied considerably. Furthermore, given the porousness of state borders, when faced with the success of a counterinsurgency strategy in one state, the rebels have often sought sanctuaries in adjacent states that lack similar enforcement powers. The ability of the insurgents to effectively exploit such safe havens has significantly hobbled the capacity of the Indian state to end this renewed challenge to the country's political stability.

If the past record of the Indian state in dealing with insurgencies is any guide, the Indian state will eventually prevail over the current rebels. The process will involve an amalgam of coercion, co-optation, and concessions. Several factors confer significant advantages on the state. First, the sheer coercive capacity of the Indian state is much greater than what it possessed three or four decades ago. Second, the diffuse and class-based features of this insurgent movement make it more difficult to target the insurgents. However, unlike insurrections in India's northeast or in the Punjab, these are not movements that seek secession. Consequently, while they do threaten public order and impose both social and economic costs, they do not fundamentally threaten the territorial integrity of the state. Third, and finally, some states, most notably Andhra Pradesh, have already demonstrated an ability to significantly denude the organizational and material capabilities of the insurgents. Through the use of specially trained, well-equipped, and professionally oriented police forces, the state has decimated much of the Naxalite base.[12]

Beyond the Naxalite problem, the Indian state still confronts a Pakistan-aided insurgency in the disputed state of Jammu and Kashmir. The origins of this particular insurgency were indigenous.[13] However, thanks to Pakistan's involvement, it has significantly metamorphosed.[14] A number of Pakistan-based terrorist organizations continue to periodically wreak havoc in the state and stoke extant grievances that the Indian state has yet been unable to fully address.

The Indian state has paid a significant price in suppressing the insurgency in Kashmir. The costs have been moral, material, and human. At an ideational level, the counterinsurgency strategy that the Indian state had mounted involved a scant regard for human rights violations. Not surprisingly, India found itself on trial in the courts of both national and especially international public opinion.[15] Subsequently, the tactics and strategies that the Indian state relied upon became more sophisticated, though occasional abuses of authority did persist.

At a material level, it is difficult to disaggregate the precise costs that the conflict has exacted on the Indian exchequer.[16] The reasons are twofold. First, regardless of the insurgency, India would deploy substantial forces because of ongoing border disputes with Pakistan and the PRC. Consequently, to obtain an accurate estimate of the additional costs, it would be necessary to separate the costs of routine deployments from the forces that have been added to deal with the insurgents. Such an exercise, while not impossible, faces substantial hurdles because adequate data simply does not exist in the public realm. Second, such an effort would also require a careful estimation of the likely loss of investment in the state owing to the prevailing disturbed conditions within it.

Finally, the human toll that the insurgency has exacted is substantial. The precise numbers, however, are the subject of debate. Some estimates place the total deaths to be as high as one hundred thousand. Governmental figures, however, suggest that as of 2011 about forty thousand individuals had perished since the onset of the insurgency.[17] Subsequent reports suggested that the insurgency was still exacting a substantial toll on India's internal security forces.[18]

Two factors will determine the future of Kashmir's long-simmering insurgency. First, the Pakistani military establishment has to conclude that support for the insurgency has not brought it any closer to the realization of its long-standing goal, namely, the acquisition of approximately two-thirds of Kashmir, which remains under Indian control. After three wars, multiple crises, and substantial support for a host of insurgents, it has been unsuccessful in this endeavor. Accordingly, if it were to stop providing sanctuaries and end material and organizational support to the insurgents, the remnants of the uprising would, for the most part, lose its force.

Second, the government of India will also need to address underlying grievances that have long festered. Its ability to do so will be greatly helped when the need to deploy substantial paramilitary forces ends as the insurgency draws to a close. The large repressive apparatus that envelopes the region has, in itself, become a source of grievance to the local population.

Beyond the near-endemic problem that the Indian state confronts in Kashmir, it now faces an emergent internal security threat. This stems from the growth of disaffection with the Indian state among small but significant segments of India's vast Muslim population. A complete sociological analysis of the emergence of this form of alienation from the Indian state is simply beyond the scope of this discussion. However, in considerable part, it can be traced to two important sources. First, there is some evidence that Muslims have faced structural discrimination within India. An important survey that the government of India had commissioned revealed the inadequate representation of Muslims in virtually every arena of educational attainment, social standing, and governmental employment.[19] Second, within the past two decades, with the rise of the Bharatiya Janata Party (BJP), the climate of political opinion in the country has taken on a distinct anti-Muslim tone. The latter, combined with communal riots that have often targeted Muslim communities in various parts of India, has contributed to the rise of a degree of Muslim militancy in the country. Unless both the social roots of this problem are addressed along with appropriate intelligence and policing measures, India may face yet another acute internal security problem, which could have significant adverse consequences for its social and political stability.[20]

External Threats and Challenges

India faces two major external threats: the first is from the PRC, with which it has a long-standing border dispute that has shown little or no prospect of resolution despite multiple attempts. Furthermore, India has had to confront the PRC's growing assertiveness along the disputed border in recent years. The PRC's willingness to flex its capabilities along the border has, in turn, led India to bolster its own existing military capabilities. Apart from the tensions that have increased along the disputed border in the first two decades of the twenty-first century, the PRC's economic growth has also contributed to an expansion of its naval reach. The expanded scope of the PLAN's operations has also caused significant misgivings among defense planners in New Delhi. Finally,

India's policy-makers have also cast a wary eye on the PRC's growing involvement in India's immediate periphery, especially in Pakistan, Sri Lanka, Burma/Myanmar, Nepal, and Bangladesh. The Sino-Pakistani nexus, of course, has been long-standing.[21] Though it has experienced some strains in recent years, it is hard to visualize how the PRC would wholly abandon an ally whose contentious relationship with India has served its own interests well. The only possible circumstance under which the PRC might distance itself from this ally is if the threat of Islamist militancy starts to spill over into its own restive Muslim minorities in Xinjiang.[22]

What has vexed India's policy-makers, well beyond the Sino-Pakistani security partnership, has been the PRC's willingness and ability to increasingly make inroads into India's other, smaller neighbors. The PRC's significantly greater material resources, its superior diplomatic clout, and India's own maladroit handling of various bilateral issues with its smaller neighbors stands to place India at an increasing strategic disadvantage vis-à-vis its behemoth northern neighbor unless it makes significant changes in its foreign and defense policies.[23]

The Indo-Pakistani relationship had shown some signs of limited improvement owing to a concerted attempt on the part of Indian policy-makers across the political spectrum to reduce tensions. However, in the aftermath of a horrific terrorist attack in November 2008 on Bombay/Mumbai, the antecedents of which were traced to the Pakistan-based terrorist organization, the Lashkar-e-Taiba (LeT), despite attempts on the part of New Delhi to resume the peace process, progress has been at best quite fitful.[24] The fundamental issue that has vexed the Indo-Pakistani relationship, that of the status of the disputed state of Jammu and Kashmir, remains unresolved.[25] Multilateral, bilateral, and even unilateral attempts to find a diplomatic resolution have long floundered.[26] Nor, for that matter, has Pakistan's resort to force induced India to make any concessions. Even after three wars (1947–1948, 1965, and 1999), Pakistan has been unable to wrest any portion of Kashmir from India.[27]

Coping with and Responding to Threats

The threats from both Pakistan and the PRC are unlikely to end anytime soon. However, over the medium to long term, the threat that Pakistan poses will in all likelihood diminish. Pakistan is presently besieged with a host of internal problems—institutional, economic, and political. None of these are subject to easy resolution. Consequently, despite its adoption of an asymmetric war strategy using proxy forces it is unlikely that it will make much headway against India. The economic gap between the two states is simply too great and is likely to widen in the future.

Even though in 2013 India's growth rate had faltered, the country's potential for growth remained robust. A shift in the policy mix can easily place the country back on a more steady growth path. Indeed owing to a complex mix of favorable exogenous and endogenous factors, the Indian economy performed markedly better in 2014–2015.[28] The restoration of a more robust growth rate, if sustained, will enable its policy-makers to devote a greater share of resources to defense and thereby cope with any challenge that might emerge from Pakistan.

The more compelling external security threat that India confronts is that from the PRC. Devising a strategy to deal with this threat is likely to tax both the institutional and material resources that India has at its command. Obviously, one strategy that it could embark upon is one of external balancing. To that end it could seek to forge a more viable security partnership with the United States. Such a partnership, especially given the U.S. pivot to Asia, might enable India to address any likely threat from a resurgent and hostile PRC. India's policy-makers, however, are most unlikely to pursue this particular option. The reasons for their unwillingness to adopt such a strategy are not difficult to explain. During much of the Cold War, India had a mostly frosty relationship with the United States. In the Cold War's aftermath, there has been a significant thaw in Indo-U.S. relations.[29]

Despite this growing bonhomie that has been characterized with the steady growth in military-to-military contacts, the expansion of intelligence cooperation, and the purchase of military equipment, India–United States relations remain strained.[30] These developments notwithstanding, a significant segment of India's political elite still deem the United States to be a somewhat unreliable partner. Unlike in the past, much of this distrust does not stem from ideological sources. Instead the misgivings about any inordinate reliance on the United States to guarantee India's security stem from what India's policy-makers perceive to be the vagaries of American policy toward the region as well as toward Asia. Furthermore, others within the policy apparatus fear that such a dependence on the United States is likely to reduce India's freedom to maneuver in the global arena. Given these considerations it is unlikely that the relationship will evolve into a genuine security partnership that guarantees India's security in the face of renewed hostility from the PRC.

However, under the current circumstances, India's policy-makers are unlikely to resort to a strategy of external balancing. How might India cope with the PRC's growing capabilities and assertiveness? Faced with what it deems to be increased probes along the Himalayan border in recent years, India's defense establishment has embarked upon a series of new initiatives to secure the northern border and to address possible military contingencies that might arise.[31]

Even as India bolsters its capabilities along the Himalayan border, it is increasingly likely to find itself in competition with the PRC in the neighboring states of South Asia and not merely Pakistan. The PRC had, of course, long made significant inroads into Burma/Myanmar.[32] India, which had been loath to deal with the military regime in the country, had shunned it until the early 1990s. Since then it has sought, albeit fitfully, to counter the growth of the PRC presence and influence.[33] To that end, India has embarked on a multifaceted approach to deal with Burma/Myanmar, focusing on the expansion of trade and transit links, infrastructural development, investments in human capital building, and bolstering institutional capacity. Whether or not this multipronged strategy will yield the desired results remains an open question.[34]

In addition to its significant presence and influence in Burma/Myanmar, the PRC has also started to extend its reach into states where India had long enjoyed a privileged position. These include Bangladesh, Nepal, and Sri Lanka. In all these three states India has witnessed a steady erosion of its influence. The PRC, for the most part, has been able to limit India's historic standing in these states through an amalgam of deft diplomacy as well as the provision of significant amounts of foreign assistance.

Apart from this competition that India now confronts in its neighborhood, it also faces the possibility of growing naval competition with the PRC in the Indian Ocean. Not surprisingly, the Indian Navy, without explicitly alluding to the expansion of the capabilities and reach of the People's Liberation Army Navy (PLAN), has been steadily expanding its own assets and its areas of operation. To that end, India created a Far Eastern Naval Command (FENC) at Port Blair in the Andaman Islands off its eastern coast in the early part of the first decade of the new century.[35] In considerable part this endeavor was closely tied to its increasing fears about the PLAN's role in Burma/Myanmar as well as India's expanding trade ties to the economically vibrant states of Southeast Asia.[36]

Despite the competitive and even potentially adversarial relationship with the PRC, India's policy-makers still remain loath to rely on the United States to balance the PRC. This unwillingness to turn to the United States to cope with a possibly recalcitrant PRC stems in considerable part from three important sources: they are ideational, historical, and political. At an ideational level, it can be traced to the residual role of India's earlier commitment to nonalignment. Until recently it was referred to as a quest for "strategic autonomy." Since an overt reliance on the United States could compromise this principle, India's policy-makers remain unwilling to rely on the United States despite U.S. efforts to court India.[37] At another level, they also hesitate to dovetail their strategic calculus with that of the United States because of the periodic American involvement with and support for Pakistan. Finally, apart from the quest for strategic autonomy, India's policy-makers also face important domestic constraints: a left-wing constituency in Indian politics has a deep-seated hostility toward any form of strategic partnership with the United States and has sought, albeit with limited degrees of success, to undermine the recent improvement in Indo-U.S. ties.

Consequently, despite the Obama administration's "pivot" to or "rebalancing" strategy toward Asia, it is far from clear that India will readily step up to the plate and work in concert with the United States to balance China. Instead it will continue to build up its own domestic capabilities, will enhance ongoing cooperation with a number of states in both Northeast and Southeast Asia, and will maintain a level of defense cooperation with the United States.[38] To that end, it will expand the band of naval cooperation with Japan, South Korea, and Vietnam and will continue many U.S.-led multilateral naval exercises in which it has been a participant. However, it will not pursue an explicit strategic alignment with the United States designed to hem in China.

The investments that India is now making in the maritime arena suggest that it does see continuing challenges from the PRC in that realm. From India's standpoint the potential threats from China could materialize athwart either coast. The PRC involvement in the development of a Pakistani naval base at Gwadar in Baluchistan had long provoked India's anxieties. To address the possible risk that this naval hub could pose to India, it has started to build a US$8 billion naval base in Karwar south of Goa on its on Arabian Sea coast. When completed it would be able to berth a substantial number of surface vessels, including submarines. The principal task of this naval deployment would be to ward off any efforts on the part of China or Pakistan to block the entrance into the Gulf of Oman and the Strait of Hormuz.[39]

To that end it has been bolstering its capabilities along its eastern seaboard. Among other efforts, India is now building a new naval base in the coastal state of Andhra Pradesh about fifty kilometers from the headquarters of Eastern Naval Command in the port city of Visakhapatnam.[40]

A possible shift in the Indo-U.S. relationship, however, could come about under two conditions: one external and the other internal. The external source could be twofold: a transformation of the U.S.-Pakistan relationship and a further deterioration of the Sino-Indian relationship. An attenuation of the U.S.-Pakistan military nexus would assuage long-standing Indian misgivings about the United States and thereby open up the possibility of an improved Indo-U.S. strategic relationship. Simultaneously, an enhanced threat from the PRC may induce India's policymakers to reassess their unwillingness to align with the United States.

At a domestic level, if the Bharatiya Janata Party manages to consolidate its position, the residual hostility and distrust toward the United States may gradually dissipate in India's foreign-policy establishment.

Such a transformation, of course, would be facilitated if the United States were to simultaneously reduce its military commitment to Pakistan.[41]

Defense Procurement

Faced with what it deems to be a number of external as well as internal security challenges and concerned about its ability to protect vital trade interests, within the past decade India has undertaken a major program of military modernization. To that end there has been a steady expansion of the Indian defense budget. Robust economic growth has made possible this sustained commitment to defense modernization. Indeed between 2008 and 2012, India's acquisitions, listed in table 11.1, amounted to 12 percent of the global arms market, making it the leading arms importer in the world. It is useful to note, however, that this spending spree that the country has embarked upon reveals its failure to develop an indigenous defense industrial base despite a long-standing commitment to self-reliance. In 2013, the Indian minister of defense, A. K. Antony, publicly conceded that 70 percent of India's software and hardware needs were met through imports.[42]

Indeed the vast majority of India's efforts to develop various forms of weaponry, ranging from a main battle tank to a fighter aircraft, have been plagued with cost overruns, technological glitches, and program failures.[43] For example, the pursuit of a Light Combat Aircraft (LCA) has long been plagued with delays and dramatic cost overruns.[44] Two government-run entities, Hindustan Aeronautics Limited (HAL) and the Defense Research and Development Organization (DRDO), have been jointly involved in the development of this aircraft. Originally scheduled for delivery to the Indian Air Force (IAF) in 2008, it finally saw trials at an air exercise in February 2013.[45] In 2016, the first two of these aircraft were delivered to the Indian Air Force. In considerable part these delays could be attributed to the DRDO's failure to develop a viable engine for the aircraft.[46] Owing to its failure to develop an engine requisite to the needs of the aircraft, it had to be fitted with a General Electric F404 engine.[47] This persistent failure to deliver products despite long gestation periods has led to some scrutiny and even public criticism of the performance of these organizations.[48]

Table 11.1. Indian Defense Purchases, 2008–2013

Defense Purchases Country	Year	Defense System	Quantity	Cost (US Dollars)
Brazil	2014	EMB-145 aircraft	3	210 m
France (joint venture)	2012	Scorpene submarine	6	4.3 bn
Israel	2016	Medium-range SAM	18 units	1.4 bn
Israel/Russia	2009	Il-76TD Phalcon AWACS aircraft	3	1 bn
Italy	2012	AW101 Merlin	24	170 m
Russia	2008	Su-30MKI fighter	40	1.6 bn
Russia (joint venture)	2010	Brahmos PJ-10 missiles		2 bn
Russia	2011	Mi-17V-5 Hip	80	1.2 bn
Russia	2012	Talwar II-class frigate	3	1.5 bn
Russia	2013	Kiev-class submarine	1	2.5 bn
Russia (joint venture)	(final delivery due 2015)	Su-30MKI fighter	140	part of deal totaling 8.5 bn
Russia	(final delivery due 2016-2017)	Su-30MKI fighter	42	3.3 bn
Russia	(ordered 2006)	3M14E Klub-S (SS-N-27 Sizzler) missile system	28	182 m
Russia	(ordered 2010)	MiG-29K Fulcrum D Fighter	29	1.5 bn
Russia (joint venture)	(ordered 2010)	Brahmos Block II (Land Attack) Missiles		1.73 bn
Russia (joint venture)	(delivery in progress)	T-90S Bishma tanks	347	1.23 bn

(*continued*)

Table 11.1. (*continued*)

Defense Purchases

Country	Year	Defense System	Quantity	Cost (US Dollars)
Switzerland	2012	PC-7 Turbo Trainer MkII aircraft	75	527 m
United Kingdom	2012	Griffon 8000TD hovercraft	12	52 m
United States	2013	P-81 Poseidon surveillance aircraft	8	2.1 bn
United States	2013	C-17A Globemaster III transport aircraft	10	4.1 bn
United States	(ordered 2010)	AGM-84 Harpoon Block II missiles	24	170 m

Principal Foreign Suppliers Ranking

Ranking	Country	Amount
1	Russia	11.782 bn (26.242 bn including joint projects)
2	United States	6.37 bn
3	France	4.3 bn joint project
4	Israel	1.4 bn (2.4 bn including joint project with Russia)
5	Switzerland	527 m
6	Brazil	210 m
7	Italy	170 m
8	United Kingdom	52 m

Note: Costs and amounts are in millions (m) and billions (bn).

Sources: *based on* The Military Balance 2013 (London: Routledge, 2013): 346–348 *and* Ajai Shukla, "HAL's Trainer Pitted as Rs 4,500 cr Cheaper Than Swiss Pilatus Trainer," Business Standard (April 15, 2013), *at* http://www.business-standard.com/article/economy-policy/hal-s-trainer-pitted-as-rs-4-500-cr-cheaper-than-swiss-pilatus-trainer-113041500059_1.html.

Nevertheless, as a consequence of the forces of path dependence, a bureaucratic-technological momentum, the desire to obtain strategic autonomy, and a concomitant nationalist commitment to the development of an indigenous defense capability, India's policy-makers have proven unwilling to abandon the elusive quest for self-reliance. Given the past performance of the vast majority of India's defense industries, the unwillingness of any government to open most units to the private sector, and the lack of hard budget constraints, it is hard to visualize how the indigenous defense sector can be expected to improve its functioning in the foreseeable future.

In the meantime, India has continued to rely on Russia for major weapons acquisitions even as it seeks to diversify its sources of supply. It has increasingly turned to Israel, among others, especially for the acquisition of airborne warning and control systems (AWACS) and marine aerostat radar.[49] India's continued reliance on Russia, in part, stems from its historic relationship with the Soviet Union, which had proven to be a very reliable supplier during many of the Cold war years.[50] In turn, since a significant portion of India's extant arsenal is of Soviet origin, it has not proven easy to wholly jettison the relationship. Furthermore, as in the Soviet era, Russia remains willing to sell India the vast majority of military equipment without what Indian policy-makers deem to be onerous restrictions. Even when differences have arisen over the sale of high-cost items, the two sides have managed to find ways to compromise and reach an eventual accord. For example, though significant cost escalation characterized the sale of the retrofitted Russian aircraft carrier, the *Admiral Gorshkov*, the two parties managed to reach an accord after protracted negotiations.[51] Finally, much to the liking of Indian policy-makers, Russia has also proven willing to develop a range of weaponry under co-production arrangements. All of these factors explain the continuation of the arms-transfer relationship with Russia.

Despite this continued reliance on Russia, thanks to a thaw in Indo-U.S. relations in the post–Cold War era, and despite persistent anxieties about the reliability of U.S. weapons transfers, the reflexive hostility of left-wing Indian political parties toward any form of strategic partnership with the United States, and the reservations of the indigenous defense production establishment, India is now more willing to acquire weaponry from the United States.[52] To that end it has made a series of high-profile purchases in recent years. Among them are included, the purchase of C-130JS Super Hercules military transport aircraft,[53] Harpoon Block II missiles to improve the air force's air-to-surface warfare capabilities,[54] Boeing P-8Is to replace its aging, Soviet-vintage Tupolev Tu-142s,[55] Pratt and Whitney engines to power the Boeing C-17 Globemaster III aircraft,[56] and Apache multi-role combat helicopters.[57]

Ironically, it was this spate of military acquisitions from the United States combined with some technical assessments that led India's policy-makers to favor the purchase of the French Rafale multi-role fighter aircraft after considering a range of other alternatives.[58] Some informed analysts have argued with considerable force that the decision was made solely on the basis of careful technological comparisons and performance criteria that the IAF had spelled out.[59] However, other well-placed political observers claim that India's policy-makers, especially in the United Progressive Alliance regime (2004–2014), concluded that offering a multibillion-dollar deal for 126 medium multi-role combat aircraft to the United States after the purchase of a range of other equipment was simply too much for the political traffic to bear.[60] Unfortunately, some of the structural vagaries of India's defense procurement system led to the collapse of the US-French agreement on the Rafale fighters.[61]

No discussion of military procurement would be complete without an analysis of India's nuclear weapons program. The program has moved from its "recessed deterrent" posture to one that will inevitably conclude in a nuclear triad.[62] Also, despite an insistence on what its policy-makers term "minimum credible deterrence," the scope of the various strategic programs that are currently underway raise questions about what combination and configuration of nuclear forces would constitute such a status.[63] Nevertheless, progress toward the goal of a limited, triadic, and survivable force, has been fitful and limited.[64]

After sinking considerable effort and resources, in 2009 India managed to develop a prototype nuclear submarine, the *Arihant* (Destroyer of Enemies) based upon a Russian *Charlie*-class submarine that had been loaned to India earlier. According to press reports the nuclear submarine will be equipped with India's indigenous *Sagarika* series of missiles, which are capable of delivering a 500 kilogram payload to distances between 750 and 1,000 kilometers. Such capabilities would place most of Pakistan within range from the Arabian Sea and significant parts of the PRC's most prosperous regions when operating in the South China Sea.[65] As of mid-2016, however, the submarine was yet to be inducted into the Indian Navy, though it had started to undergo "sea acceptance" trials in early 2012 and underwent final sea trials in early 2016.[66]

The other components of the triad—nuclear capable aircraft and ballistic missiles—have also seen some progress. The missile program, which had its origins in the Integrated Guided Missile Development Programme initiated as early as 1983, has produced a suite of missiles, some of which are now operational and capable of carrying nuclear warheads. Since 1989, when the country tested the Agni I, the DRDO has developed four others, ending with the Agni V. All of these are single warhead missiles., Even though the DRDO had not obtained official sanction as of 2013, it had begun preliminary work on the Agni VI, designed to carry multiple warheads and able to strike targets at a distance of 6,000 kilometers.[67] Apart from the development of this range of ballistic missiles, the DRDO has also invested much effort and resources in the development of a ballistic missile defense (BMD) program. This program appears to have made some progress.[68] Even if the program proves successful, policy-makers have yet to clarify how the BMD would be configured into India's emergent nuclear posture.

The final component of India's triad is based on several squadrons of Mirage 2000, Sukhoi Su-30MKI and Jaguar aircraft. In 2010, the tri-services Strategic Forces Command (SFC) sought its own complement of nuclear capable aircraft independent of the air force.[69] However, it remains unclear if this request was eventually granted.

Despite all these hardware acquisitions, the country has yet to formulate a viable nuclear doctrine, even though the National Security Advisory Board had been tasked and did indeed produce a draft nuclear doctrine.[70] One element of the draft doctrine, the principle of "no-first-use," however, seems to be upheld in official circles.[71]

Conclusions

This brief survey suggests that despite institutional slackness and bureaucratic hurdles, India is acquiring significant military might to cope with a range of threats. It is also developing a power-projection capability, as can be inferred from some of its military acquisitions. Unfortunately, cost overruns, poor results, and persistent deals characterize the vast majority of its domestic military programs. Even its foreign-weapons-acquisition process, as underscored with the delays in selecting the medium-range multi-role combat aircraft, evinces a process that is extremely cumbrous and unwieldy.

Despite these shortcomings, India has managed to suppress, or at least contain, all domestic challenges to its security and territorial integrity. Barring its disastrous defeat in 1962 in the Sino-Indian border war, it has also managed to ward off external challenges to its territorial order. Given its extant domestic capabilities as well as its steadily expanding military muscle designed to deal with external threats, it may be able to cope with future challenges from either source. The key question, however, is whether or not its seemingly haphazard, fitful, and uncoordinated efforts will prove sufficient to enable it to transcend the region and become an actor of some consequence in the maintenance of stability and order beyond its immediate neighborhood.

Finally, the lack of doctrinal clarity continues to dog India's nuclear weapons program, despite uneven progress on a number of technological fronts. How are these acquisitions designed to achieve the goals of nuclear deterrence and, if deterrence fails, actual use? No clear-cut answers are yet available to these critical questions. Nor for that matter, despite significant investments in the development and possible deployment of ballistic missile defenses, is any coherent argument available in official circles about how the BMD might play a role in India's nuclear strategy.

Summary and Conclusion

T·W·E·L·V·E

Ascending India–Its State-Capacity Problems and Prospects

We need to first recapitulate our extended argument. In chapter 1 the basic puzzle we outlined was the newfound emphasis on an ascendant India, possibly rising even to great power status in the not-too-distant future. Observers are aware that India has limitations that might impede its ascent, but little explicit attention has been given to India's state. This is odd because the state may prove to be India's primary liability. Moreover, it is central to addressing the other impediments. At the same time, political science tends to focus on the differences between strong states and weak or failing states. India is none of these. It falls in between the extreme points on the state-capacity continuum. In point of fact, we do not really know much about the "in-betweeners" or how best to analyze them. Thus, our central question is, What should we make of India's state? Are its institutions robust and effective? Can the Indian central state get things done? If it has problems getting things done, could the inadequacies of the state thwart the rise of a middle power to higher elite status? Or might it simply mean that an ascendant India would find that it lacked the institutional means to exploit its newly found status?

In tackling these questions, we have not pursued every path conceivable. Public administration and bureaucracy, for example, have not been examined at all. There are many state agencies. We have focused exclusively on the central government without moving down one level of analysis to talk about its specific components. If we had done otherwise, space and attention considerations would have forced us to zero in on a few and ignore the rest.

Something similar can be said about federalism. Since independence India's federal structure has undergone substantial changes.[1] The founders of the modern Indian state, most notably Jawaharlal Nehru, had sought to create a powerful central state for a number of compelling reasons. First and foremost, they had believed that a centralized state was necessary for the tasks of economic development. As the state was expected to play a substantial role in that process, a decentralized polity would prove to be an impediment to the adoption of national economic plans. Second, they had also feared that substantial devolution of power to the constituent states could provide the basis for secession.[2] Third and finally, they were also aware that the passage of key elements of social legislation, such as the abolition of untouchability, would require the exercise of federal (central) power.[3]

In the early years of the Indian republic these extensive constitutional powers of the central government were rarely, if ever, abused. The Congress Party, under Nehru's leadership and tutelage, was prepared to adhere to the expectations of center-state relations as outlined in the constitutional order. The one stark exception was his dismissal of a legitimately elected Communist government in the southern state of Kerala in 1959 on questionable grounds.[4] Subsequently, under one of his successors, his daughter, Indira Gandhi, the powers vested in the central government were routinely abused. As the Congress Party atrophied under her watch and as regional parties came to the fore, she often dismissed state governments without much regard for constitutional proprieties.[5] Following her assassination in 1984 after a brief return of the Congress Party to power, the country saw a series of coalition governments that reflected the rise of regional parties against a backdrop of the decline of the Congress Party.

The abuse of central power since then, for the most part, has ended. Several possible reasons can be adduced for this shift. First, while firm evidence is hard to muster, it can be argued that the rampant misuse of central powers under Indira Gandhi's tenure and the popular backlash that it generated made future regimes hesitant to exercise them in a similar fashion. Second, since a number of national governments were either coalition regimes or were dependent on regional parties for parliamentary support, it became difficult to resort to arbitrary actions against various state governments. Third and finally, after 1991, following India's fitful embrace of the market, states have acquired much greater economic clout and leeway and are less dependent on the central government.[6]

In the absence of a national party that acquires substantial majorities in both houses of Parliament, it can safely be assumed that the devolution of powers that has taken place to India's constituent states will remain mostly intact. The logic of economic liberalization, of course, will bolster this trend as states are given greater leeway to forge their economic strategies. Indeed the task of the central government, unlike in the past, will be to try to persuade India's states to adopt nationwide legislation in a range of areas. Recent parliamentary debates have extended from areas as diverse as the creation of a national anti-terrorism force to the adoption of a goods and services tax.[7]

The relative powers of federal and central governments always proceed subject to some tension. Too much power ceded to the center or not enough can be an additional liability in state making. In India, the question is in flux after a progressive weakening of the center. Whether the center regains some of its former powers or different federal states become stronger remains to be seen. At this point in time, it is hard to forecast which alternative is the more likely, and that is one reason for not saying much about it at this time.

Then too, much of our analysis relies heavily on work already done by others. That is, we discuss topics such as economic infrastructure, inequality, democracy, and foreign/defense policies in terms of our state-making interest. But we did not expect to blaze new trails into elucidating their dynamics. Our focus has been on how these selected processes relate to the strength of the state. We have been somewhat more innovative, we think, in developing new ways to measure state capacity based on a previously existing extended conceptualization. We take K. J. Holsti's definition of state strength and break it down into three components: extraction, violence monopoly, and legitimacy. We then proceed to measure these components for India, other BRICs, and current major powers. Our basic answer, then, as to what to do about the "in-betweeners" is to first be as precise as feasible in identifying where states fall on selected state-capacity measures. Then it is possible to assess whether their positions change over time, and what these movements in position might signify.

In chapter 2 we took a step back from our focus on state capacity and asked whether we had sufficient theory to account for great power ascendance. After some discussion, the answer was negative. This prompted us to bring together, selectively, some different arguments from Choucri and North and Nayar and Paul, along with constructing an auxiliary argument about favorable environments. Earlier forms of our argument were sketched in figures 2.4 and 2.5. We can now integrate these arguments in the form of figure 12.1. We retain a modified version of lateral pressure theory (Choucri and North), combined with the favorable environment insertion, and link it to the relationships among state capacity, leadership/strategy, and governmental problem solving via a linkage through state capabilities. State capacity is a state capability; it also feeds off other state capabilities through extraction and legitimacy. Leadership/strategy utilizes capabilities, just as leadership/strategy is no doubt conditioned to some degree by whatever capabili-

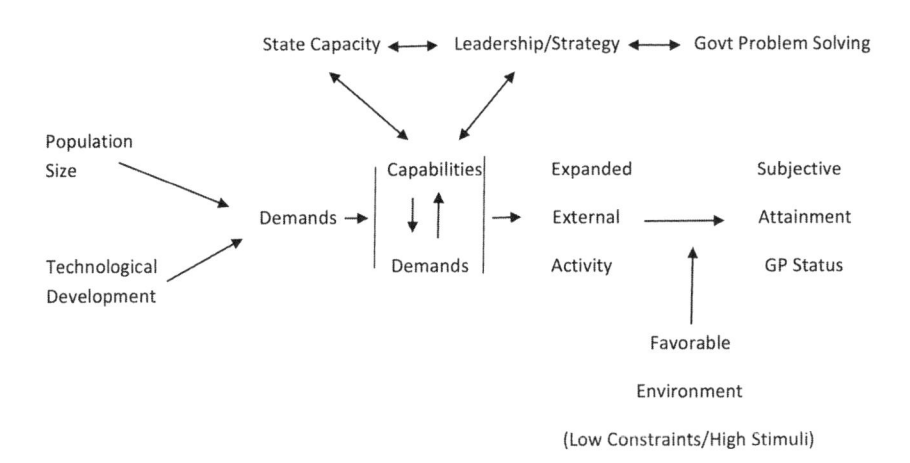

Fig. 12.1. Great Power Ascendance and State Capacity

ties are available. For instance, small and poor states are less likely to adopt the same types of strategies as large and rich states.

While we are quite explicit about the subjective nature of great power ascendancy, in that minimal economic, military, and battlefield strengths historically have not been obvious, figure 12.1 suggests that state capacity is linked to the pursuit of demands, expanded activity, and great power status improvements. It assists these processes, but we do not think a particular level is necessary. Earlier ascending great powers had underdeveloped state capacities as they moved up the ranks. This liability did not seem to hold back their promotions. Underdeveloped state capacity, however, can influence negatively the level and success of the activities that are expanded to satisfy increased demands. So too can the relative absence of political leadership and strategy formulation. One needs policy entrepreneurs that are interested in making use of state capacity and other capabilities to execute decisions that, ideally, are predicated on explicit strategic planning.

At the same time, chapter 2 also discussed the world economy's technological gradient in which states, or at least some states, move up the gradient with underdeveloped economies becoming more-complex enterprises. Some move toward the very apex of the system, and one may become the system leader as the most technologically advanced, lead economy in the world economy.

Movement up and down the technological gradient is not the same thing as ascending to great power status. A state can be a great power without having made much progress up the technological gradient—as China demonstrated in 1950. It is also possible to rank high on the technological gradient, as in the contemporary cases of Japan and Germany, without holding great power rank. Ironically, India's case for great powerhood is often based primarily on the absolute size of its economy and hypothetical extensions of current trends. It is also assumed that other capabilities, such as military power, will follow economic developments. But, there are multiple possibilities. Two BRICs (China and Russia) already possess great power status without parallel elite status on the technological gradient. Both states are working to change that asymmetry. Another possibility is that the states with newly expanding economic growth (as in the cases of Brazil and India) may stall and fall into the middle-income trap without achieving elite positions on the technological gradient. But they could become great powers along the way nonetheless. Or, it may be that BRIC economic growth will slow across the board sufficiently to fall short of radically altering the distribution of economic wealth in the world economy.

We cannot yet be sure which of these scenarios are most likely to come into play for India. We are more sure that state capacity will have some significant role to play in how things work out. In chapters 3–5 we have put forward a new approach to measuring state capacity. This is an area dominated by fairly loose conceptualization and very partial and sometimes far removed operational indicators. If we are most interested in examining states that are neither strong nor weak/failed, it seemed best to be as explicit and specific as possible in capturing state-capacity positioning. Indicating where states fall on the capacity continuum requires first, conceptualization of what state strength is about and, second, appropriate measurement of the conceptualized components. We rely on K. J. Holsti's definition to satisfy the first requirement.[8] The three components of his conceptualization include extraction, monopolizing the legitimate use of force, and legitimacy. We then developed a slate of appropriate indicators for each of these parts of the whole.

Two indicators are advanced for state extraction capability. Fiscal capability is measured in terms of income tax revenue as a proportion of GDP. A second indicator that captures a different dimension of how states mobilize resources is provided by Levitsky and Way's state coercive capability.[9] This measure focuses on the state's brute ability to command resources and acquiescence. The monopoly of armed force is operationalized in terms of a composite World Bank indicator that is termed "political stability," which actually measures the absence of violence in a society.[10] For legitimacy, we utilize four World Bank indicators (voice and accountability, effectiveness, rule of law, and control of corruption). The measures can be treated separately or aggregated to devise a single operationalization of state capacity or strength.

On the tax revenue measure, India lags behind other BRICs and more-established major powers (with the exception of the United States). In terms of coercive capacity, India is comparable to Brazil and the established major powers but far behind Russia and China. The monopoly of the legitimate use of force ranks India far behind most other states in general. On legitimacy, India does much better. While it is not as strong as the established major powers on this score, India is relatively strong and comparable to Brazil and ahead of the other BRICs. Overall, India is ahead of the Russian position, falls behind Brazil and China, and places at a point substantially lower than that of the established and affluent major powers. While this puts India considerably ahead of Pakistan, Bangladesh, and Afghanistan in its home region, it does less well than Turkey and is roughly equivalent to Egypt and Sri Lanka. More importantly, though, India's state capacity, which is good in some areas and poor in others, does not appear to be gaining ground overall. It can only do this by improving in the poor categories while at least holding steady in the areas in which it does better. Extraction inches forward with economic development. Legitimacy persists at a respectable level despite the appearance of increasing public corruption. Public violence wanes in lethality, but violence monopoly continues to elude the Indian central government.

Other major powers initiated their elite trajectories with limited fiscal capabilities, considerable internal violence, and contested legitimacy. These attributes, we repeat, do not necessarily preclude upward movement toward great power status. Weaknesses in these areas, however, suggest that any improvements in status will be handicapped by foundational liabilities. The weaker the state foundation, presumably, the greater will be the handicaps to overcome. In the absence of improvement in international status, many domestic problems remain to be resolved by the Indian state. More state capacity is very much needed to do all that needs to be done.

The long established great powers survived bouts of global warfare and created strong states in the process. Newly emerging aspirants are not likely to have that "opportunity" to bolster their state capacities in crisislike situations. The wars they fight tend to be more limited and therefore have less effect on state-making. But state-making is not exclusively dependent on global warfare. Economic growth is an alternate driver. For instance, India's fiscal extraction rate has doubled since the late 1940s. Economic growth can expand the state's ability to improve its coercive capabilities and limit societal violence. Legitimacy is also linked to positive economic growth, although it is conceivable that rapid growth will aggravate already existing inequalities and work against the maintenance of state legitimacy.

Nonetheless, India's various types of violence problems, ranging from separatism and insurgency to crimes against individuals, are quite distinctive from a major-power-trajectory perspective. At times, it seems as if some of these problems are being put to rest only to see them reemerge (communal rioting, Kashmir and Naxalite insurgencies, in particular). India's ability to create a stable domestic order, one of its major weaknesses, will provide a compelling benchmark of India's ability to improve its state capacity. Paradoxically, of course, India will first have to improve other dimensions of its state capacity in order to create a more orderly domestic system. Nothing is easy when it comes to enhancing state capacity.

The second half of our examination, chapters 6 through 11, adopts a slightly different perspective. Instead of looking at state capacity directly, these chapters pursue more indirect paths by focusing on various areas that either undermine or manifest state capacity. Chapters 6 and 7 spend some time on economic and infrastructural problems—the ways in which production is oriented and the ways in which people and commodities are moved and energized. Economic productivity and growth lay the foundation for improved status in world politics and a better way of life at home. Infrastructure undergirds economic productivity and growth, trade, quality of life, and poverty/disease. Without a functioning and dynamic economy and an adequate infrastructure, basic societal processes simply do not work very well. India's economic growth has improved in recent years, but it remains unclear if it possesses the right ingredients and policies for sustained growth into the future. India clearly lacks an adequate infrastructure, and it has very far to go to be in a position to claim even moderate adequacy in this area. Unfortunately, the odds seem stacked against any major improvements in infrastructure anytime soon, given all that needs to be done. Political leadership has been less than strong and consistent, investment monies are relatively scarce, bureaucracies are slow to act, costs are rising, and construction projects are vulnerable to high levels of corruption. The task is genuinely Herculean and unlike any situation that ever faced other successful major power aspirants—with perhaps the exception of China.

Inequality, the focus of chapter 8, is another complex part of the societal foundation for state capacity and other public and private activities. To some extent, economic growth can be expected to address some aspects of economic inequality, but entrenched inequalities require state intervention. Again, the process is circular. Some level of state capacity is needed to intervene successfully, but, at the same time, some diminishment of inequalities is necessary to avoid stifling or distorting the economic growth required for improvements in state capacity. As noted, moreover, economic growth also has some strong potential for increasing inequalities, with perverse implications for other aspects of state capacity, such as legitimacy and perhaps violent propensities as well.

India has reduced its levels of extreme poverty without yet creating a much more affluent middle class. At the same time, wealthy Indians have become richer. Rural inequalities have decreased while urban inequalities have increased. The income levels of minorities have improved without changing the likelihood of their being the subject of economic discrimination. Some questions naturally arise as to whether the Indian state can continue to attack these problems successfully or otherwise without high levels of economic growth. In general, the numbers suggest that India is becoming less equal, rather than more equal.

Closely linked to the level of inequality are democratic institutions (chapter 9). In this area, India is an anomaly. Despite all the odds against it in terms of development, income levels, and security threats, India has a flourishing democracy. It has had a highly democratic political system most of its existence as an independent state. Elections are free, opposing interests are organized in the form of political parties that alternate in power, the judiciary is independent, and the military stays in the barracks. None of these attributes are all that common in less developed circumstances.

More common in less developed and nondemocratic circumstances are attacks on ethnic/religious minorities and harsh treatments of separatist movements. Human rights are not given consistently high priority. Corruption of public institutions is perceived as widespread.

Public institutions, themselves, are not viewed as very efficacious. Secularism is under attack. Despite more than a half century of democracy, all of these attributes also characterize Indian politics. It is not just that Indian democracy is less than perfect—as if any political system could claim perfection; the real problem is that the corrosive dimensions of Indian institutions and its form of democracy pose some threat to the persistence of the benefits of democracy. To the extent that the corrosive dimensions become more acute or go unaddressed, the basic legitimacy of the system is likely to come under attack. Democracy has been one of the strengths undergirding Indian state capacity. There is no guarantee, however, that it will persist as a strength. It is not an asset that can be taken for granted.

Turning to more externally oriented foci, chapters 10 and 11 look at grand strategies and defense policies. Independent India has had several grand strategies. Each has been undone by external shocks. The Nehruvian ideational emphasis was undermined by India's defeat by China in 1962. The close relationship with the Soviet Union in the 1970s and 1980s was undone by the end of the Cold War and the collapse of the Soviet Union. Since then, India has managed to move away from central planning of its economy—a domestic form of grand strategy—without developing a new plan for dealing with the outside world. In its absence, Indian foreign policy is likely to be ad hoc and less effective at taking advantage of opportunities to attain Indian goals.

Historically, Indian defense preparations have been regionally oriented at best. This approach seemed most appropriate given limited economic surplus, restricted ambitions, and localized threats. But things are changing. More money is available for defense. Foreign-policy ambitions are expanding requiring an extraregional military-power-projection capability. The local threats persist, but new threats appear to be emerging that are no longer restricted to South Asia. The Middle East is increasingly salient for petroleum and employment. Central Asia is increasingly salient as a potential source of new problems for India and another contested arena with Pakistan. The Indian Ocean and Southeast Asia are increasingly important to Indian foreign-policy considerations, in part related to the expansion of Chinese foreign-policy activities.

In conjunction with a changing threat environment, Indian ambitions to play bigger roles in devising rules for the world economy and other global issues, such as nuclear proliferation and environmental protection, are expanding. A desire for a permanent seat in the UN Security Council is a clear manifestation of these expanding horizons in foreign policy. Both the wider scope for the sources of threat and the desire to join the elite states of world politics require an expansion of military capabilities. Military capability expansion is ongoing. The questions are At what pace? and Subject to what planning and what levels of coordination? It is not enough to simply buy more advanced weapons systems. The a priori questions of what is most needed and why must be addressed first. Priorities to attain future goals need to be established and then carried out. Such planning and execution have not been noticeable in Indian defense policy.

Thus, we argue that the Indian state cannot be considered weak. It has too many strengths for that. But it is by no means a strong state, either. Consequently (and like other states), it has some potential of moving in either direction—toward greater weakness or greater strength. It could also stay mired in the middle. Our data suggest, however, that it is, at best, running in place when its state capacity needs to be moving in exactly the opposite direction, especially given the overwhelming array of domestic problems to resolve and/or its expanded external ambitions.

We have not said much about future policy problems. Yet it seems clear that population and temperatures will increase, the supply of water will decrease, and obtaining sufficient energy will remain a serious problem. India's population is expected to continue to grow through the 2050s with a roughly 40 percent increase anticipated between 2010 and 2050. India's population should pass China's as the largest on the planet toward the end of the 2020s.[11] Global warming remains relatively unaddressed, implying that temperatures will likely rise beyond the two degrees Centigrade that policy analysts have sought to head off. Areas that are already warm will become even warmer and increasingly subject to severe weather patterns. The food supply in India, already under considerable stress, will not escape increasing problems with growing food throughout South Asia. Only one Asian state, Afghanistan, ranks lower than India on the Asian Development Bank's National Water Security Index.[12] Access to water will become more problematic, just as too much water in floods and loss of coastal land will cause other kinds of problems, including increased refugees from neighboring countries. Energy supply shortfalls and energy infrastructure inadequacies are already quite noticeable.[13] Future energy problems could easily be worse than those India has experienced in the recent past.

The point of trotting out all of these current and impending woes is that the environment for getting things done by the state will grow more dire in the immediate future. If past state efforts have fallen well short of resolving many of the problems India confronts, one can only wonder what may transpire when those problems become more acute. There is no assumption being made here that only the India central state can or will address these policy problems. But the central state will need to make a highly significant contribution to resolving or coping with them if the population, environment, food, water, and energy problems are not to overwhelm Indian society.

Conclusion

"The long-term challenge for Indian leaders as they contemplate a larger global role also hinges upon how well they negotiate the clash between the demands of two Indias—the rising India as reflected in the country's growing aggregate economic and military power and the developing India characterized by widespread illiteracy, deep-seated poverty, and rising demand for resources."[14]

In many respects, the previous quotation summarizes India's basic dilemma as it rises in the international hierarchy. Its population may become the world's largest, its economy is becoming one of the world's largest, and its military power will probably move along at least a similar upward trajectory. Yet just about everything concerning India is characterized by developmental handicaps of one sort or another. Too many people are poor, infrastructure is woefully lacking, and demands on the state for action to remedy these problems are multiplying. The Indian state, on the other hand, is characterized by a mixture of strengths and weaknesses. It scores high on its democratic attributes but much less so on its overall effectiveness. It has been and continues to be plagued by peripheral insurgencies and separatist movements. Its extraction capacity has improved but still has a long way to go, given the tasks the state needs to undertake.

A dramatic way of communicating the scale of the task ahead can be quickly hinted at by comparing India not to current great powers or even other BRICs, but to a state that was once and not so long ago greatly underdeveloped and that has since made great strides in upgrading its economy, infrastructure, and societal standard of living. Table 12.1 contrasts 2010 figures for the two states. The gaps between South Korean attributes and those possessed by India are considerable. South Korea is of course a smaller country and therefore, it might be argued, more readily susceptible to rapid development. Yet rapid or slow, the Korean transformation is not an unrealistic target, albeit perhaps one for many

Table 12.1. India and South Korea, Selected Comparative Indicators

Indicators	India 2010	South Korea 2010
School enrollment, tertiary (% of relevant age group)	11.8	91
Hospital beds (per 1,000 people)	0.9	7.1
Physicians (per 1,000 people)	0.6	1.6
Urban population (% of total population)	29	81
Electrical outages (days)	67	0.4
Mobile phone subscribers (per 100 people)	15	83
Broadband subscribers (per 100 people)	0.2	29
Research and development expenditure (% of GDP)	0.9	3.2
Scientific and technical journal articles (per million people)	13	341
Researchers in research and development (per million people)	119	3,723

Source: Selectively based on Homi Kharas, "India's Promise: An Affluent Society in One Generation," in India 2039: An Affluent Society in One Generation, *ed. Harinder S. Kohli and Anil Sood (New Delhi: Sage, 2010), 24.*

decades down the road. The real point is not a matter of whether Korea is a good target to emulate. Rather, the point is what combination of economic growth and state intervention will be needed to move India toward the Korean standards?

Table 12.2 gives a slightly different slant on this question. It may seem unfair to compare India to South Korea. South Korea's ascent has not been predicated on population and economy size. Some of the ingredients of its ascent trajectory—Japanese imperial occupation, U.S. aid, and the opportunity to profit from supplying the Korean and Vietnam Wars—are not easily translated into the Indian context. Nor are they

Table 12.2. Infrastructure Indicators: India, China, South Korea

Indicator	India	China	South Korea
Electric power consumption (kWh per capita)	503	2,041	8,063
Value lost due to electrical outages (% of sales)	6.6	1.3	n.d.
Roads, paved (% of total roads)	47	71	89
Air transport, freight per capita (million ton-km)	0.8	8.5	186.6
Container port traffic (TEU: 20-foot equivalent units) per capita	6,283	79,149	343,406
Mobile phone subscribers (per 100 people)	21	42	90
International Internet bandwidth (bits per person)	32	280	1,027
Improved sanitation faciltlies (% of population with access)	28	65	n.d.
Improved water source (% of population with access)	89	88	92

Source: Selectively based 2009 figures from Harinder S. Kohli, "Infrastructure for a Competitive Edge: Overcoming Bottlenecks and Keeping Pace with Exploding Demand," in India 2039: An Affluent Society in One Generation, ed. Harinder S. Kohli and Anil Sood (New Delhi: Sage, 2010), 135.

repeatable. Yet states find themselves caught up in hierarchies, locally and globally, whether they like it or not. In Asia, there are states that are low in the regional hierarchy and states that are relatively higher. India is by no means at the bottom of the Asian hierarchy, but many of its attributes do not compare well with other states in the same region—let alone with the great powers. Table 12.2 compares three Asian states on infrastructural characteristics. On all but the very last item in the list (access to improved water source), India's economic infrastructure places it far behind the two other states selected for comparison.[15] To catch up with China, let alone South Korea, India would have to literally double or more the quality of its economic infrastructure. By the time India catches up to where China is now, China will have moved on its own attempt to catch up with other economic powers.

One of the metaphors employed in these types of analyses is that of preparing for sprinting versus marathon racing. Writing on economic growth, Homi Kharas has suggested that India must avoid preparing for sporadic sprints. What is needed is commitment to the type of performance required to endure much longer contests.

> Despite the strong fundamentals and reasons for optimism, the high growth rates that underpin India's promise are by no means pre-ordained. . . .
>
> India would have to follow the path of a "determined marathoner" rather than that of a "sporadic sprinter." Marathoners build the momentum to grow through traps and challenges that lie in their way. . . . Sprinters become exhausted and pause to catch their breath. Once their growth is slowed, it becomes hard to revive. The main distinction between marathoners and sprinters is in the institutional capabilities to develop long-term strategies and the implementation capabilities to execute their strategies.[16]

This advice may be appropriate for economic growth. It is not as germane to our broader interests in ascendance questions and, in particular, the role of the state in fostering ascendance. The problem is that the metaphorical choice is a false one. The Indian state needs to have the capacity to both sprint and to endure marathons. To continue the metaphor, the Indian state's current capability is more like that of an out-of-shape weekend jogger. Compared to sprinters and marathoners, the leg and heart muscles are underdeveloped. Lung capacity is restricted. The pace is glacial. Such a pace may enable the runner eventually to get from point A to point B. But if the two points are very far apart, getting from start to finish will take a very long time. Such a pace is far too slow to accomplish the type of changes needed for India to become more competitive in world politics in the near future.[17]

Leadership and appropriate strategies are needed to address India's many problems. The Indian state will not improve on its own. That is where reformist leadership enters the picture. Priorities have to be established, goals set, and action plans implemented. Yet, as we have remarked perhaps too often, it is difficult to address adequately the problems when the central instrument for addressing them—state capacity—is as handicapped as it is. India needs not only more concerted leadership and grand strategies for goal attainment, it also needs a vastly enhanced state capacity if it is to cope with its expansive problems and expanding ambitions.

The development problem is thus circular. More capacity is needed to achieve more capacity. This is one of the central reasons that weak states normally remain weak states. They lack the resources to improve their institutions for problem solving. India is not a weak state. As an "in-betweener," it has some resources for capacity development and should be in a position to make a stronger state if decision-makers (and the population) insist on making it one. None of that guarantees, of course, that it will do so. The obstacles are considerable.

Notes

ONE The Indian State's Capacity to Get Things Done

1. By Indo-Pacific Asia, we are referring to the ongoing integration of a number of Asian subsystems, stretching from India to Australia into a new super-Asia.

2. On India's counterinsurgency record, see Sumit Ganguly and David P. Fidler, eds. *India and Counterinsurgency: Lessons Learned* (London: Routledge, 2009); on the dangers to the Indian state from social cleavages, see Selig Harrison, *India: The Most Dangerous Decades* (Princeton, NJ: Princeton University Press, 1960); on the Malthusian fears, see Paul R. Ehrlich, *The Population Bomb* (New York: Ballantine Books, 1968).

3. James Boxell and Carola Hoyos, "India Move Offers Lifeline for Rafale Jet," *Financial Times*, January 31, 2012.

4. Ashley J. Tellis, *Dogfight! India's Medium Multi-Role Combat Aircraft Decision* (Washington, DC: Carnegie Endowment for International Peace, 2011).

5. Unfortunately for the Indian Air Force, which is in dire need of modernization, the defense acquisition saga did not end with the decision to purchase the Rafale. Over the next several months the final negotiations entered troubled waters, with the two sides unable to agree on costs and offsets. During a trip to France in April 2015, Prime Minister Modi decided to acquire thirty-six Rafale fighter jets in "fly-away" condition as part of a government-to-government deal. See Nicola Clark, "France: India Agrees to Buy 36 Rafale Fighter Jets," *New York Times*, April 16, 2015.

6. James Lamont, "India's Schools Fail to Keep Pace with Growth," *Financial Times*, January 31, 2012, at http://www.ft.com/intl/cms/s/0/4b4a1472–47f0–11e1-b1b4 –00144feabdco.html#axzz2r3bA2X7h.

7. Charles A. Goldman, Krishna B. Kumar, and Ying Liu, *Education and the Asian Surge: A Comparison of the Educational Systems in India and China* (Santa Monica, CA: RAND Corporation, 2008).

8. Kalevi J. Holsti, *The State, War, and the State of War* (Cambridge, UK: Cambridge Studies in International Relations, 1996), 88–89.

9. We make no claim that the topics that we choose to write about exhaust the issues that might be considered in the environment of state capacity. For instance, we might have given more attention to ongoing regionalist propensities in which federal states compete with the center for relative power(s), or climate change problems and its links to water and energy security. We might have also spent more time with specific political institutions. But then we might also have continued to write this book for an indefinite time into the future. We do not aim to be the last word on Indian state capacity and would be most disappointed if it turns out that we are wrong on this question.

10. "Progress by Pak in Tackling Terror Not Quick as We Like: Obama," *Indian Express*, November 7, 2010, at http://www.indianexpress.com/news/progress-pak-in-tackling-terror-not-quick-we-like-obama/707820/0, accesses February 20, 2016.

11. "Leon Panetta in Delhi, Says India 'Linchpin' for American Strategy in Asia," *Times of India*, June 6, 2012, at http://timesofindia.indiatimes.com/opinion slogged/13871933.cms?loggedinuser=; and "India, U.S. Forging New Phases of Ties, Says Hilary," *The Hindu*, June 14, 2012..

12. See the full text of the speech by Indian External Affairs Minister Shri Yashwant, September 23, 2003, at http://mea.gov.in/Speeches-Statements.htm?dtl/4744/Speech+by+External+Affairs+Minister+Shri+Yashwant+Sinha+at+Harvard+University.

13. See John D. Ciorciari, "India's Approach to Great Power Status," *Fletcher Forum of World Affairs* 35, no. 1 (2011): 61–89.

14. Council on Foreign Relations, Charlie Rose Interviews Indian PM Manmohan Singh, February 27, 2006, at www.cfr.org/india/charlie-rose-interviews-indian-pm-manmohan-singh/p9986.

15. See the full text of the IISS Fullerton Lecture by Dr. S. Jaishankar, Indian foreign secretary, July 10, 2015, at http://mea.gov.in/Speeches-Statements.htm?dtl/25493/IISS_Fullerton_Lecture_by_Dr_S_Jaishankar_Foreign_Secretary_in_Singapore.

16. See Confederation of Indian Industry-Deloitte, "Prospects of Global Defence Export Industry in Indian Defence Market (2010)" at www.defense-aerospace.com/dae/articles/communiques/ DeloitteIndian Defence.pdf; Abhijit Singh, "INS Vikramaditya and the Aircraft Carrier Debate"; *The Diplomat*, December 10, 2013 at thediplomat.com/2013/12/ins-vikramaditya-and-the-aircraft-carrier-debate/; Zachary Keck, "India's Modi Approves Aircraft Carrier Funding, *The Diplomat*, July 11, 2014, at thediplomat.com/2014/07/ indias-modi-approves-aircraft-carrier-funding/; Rahul Bedi, IHS Jane's 360, "Modi Approves Indian Navy Plan to Build Six Submarines and Seven Frigates," February 19, 2015; David Tweed and N. C. Bipindra, "Submarined Killers Showcase India's $61 Billion Warning to China," *Live Mint*, August 16, 2015.

17. Admittedly, a good portion of this new funding must go toward modernizing a defense force that is less than competitive with other major powers. But India has been the leading importer of military equipment for the past three years. See "Narendra Modi Boosts Indian Defence Spending by 12pc in First Budget," *South China Morn-*

ing Post, August 15, 2015, at www.scmp.com/news/asia/article/1551374/narendra-modi-boosts-indian-defence-spending-12pc-first-budget.

18. See, for instance, Mussarat Jabeen, "Indian Aspirations of Permanent Membership in the UN Security Council and American Stance," *South Asian Studies* 25, no. 2 (2010): 237–253.

19. David Scott, "India's 'Extended Neighborhood' Concept: Power Projections for a Rising Power," *India Review* 8, no. 2: 107–143.

20. See, among others, Barry Buzan, "South Asia Moving Towards Transformation: Emergence of India as a Great Power," *International Studies* 39 (February 2002); 1–24; Balder Nayar and T. V. Paul, *India in the World Order: Searching for Major Power Status* (Cambridge: Cambridge University Press, 2003; Dinshaw Mistry, "A Theoretical Empirical Assessment of India as an Emerging World Power," *India Review* 3, no. 1 (2004): 64–87; Edward Freidman and Bruce Gilley, eds., *Asia's Giants: Comparing China and India* (New York: Palgrave Macmillan, 2005); Leslie E. Armijo, "The BRICs Countries (Brazil, Russia, India, and China) as Analytical Category: Mirage or Insight?" *Asian Perspectives* 31, no. 4 (2007): 7–42; Sumit Ganguly and Manjeet S. Pardesi, "India Rising: What Is New Delhi to Do?" *World Policy Journal* 24, no. 1 (2007): 9–18; David Scott, "The Great Power 'Great Game' between India and China: The Logic of Geography," *Geopolitics* 13, no. 1 (2008): 1–26; Bill Emmott, *Rivals: How the Power Struggle between China, India, and Japan Will Shape Our Next Decade* (Boston: Houghton Mifflin, 2009); Harsh V. Pant, "A Rising India's Search for a Foreign Policy," *Orbis* 53 no. 2 (2009): 250–265; Aseema Sinha and Jon P. Dorschner, "India: Rising Power or a Mere Revolution of Rising Expectations?" *Polity* 42 (2010): 74–99; Sandy Gordon, *India's Rise as an Asian Power: Nation, Neighborhood, and Region* (Washington, DC: Georgetown University Press, 2014). Not surprisingly, there is less than full agreement that India is destined to attain great power status in the near future.

21. Indian National Sample Survey found at www.mospi.nic.in/Mospi_New/site/inner.aspx?status=3&menu_id=3.

22. Ken Rapoza, "Guess Where Coca-Cola Will Invest $5 Billion," *Forbes*, June 26, 2012, at http://www.forbes.com/sites/kenrapoza/2012/06/26/guess-where-coca-cola-will-invest-5-billion/.

23. "Ikea to Invest $1.2 Billion in India to Open 25 Stores," *CBSNews*, June 22, 2012, at http://www.cbsnews.com/news/ikea-to-invest-12b-in-india-to-open-25-stores/.

24. See, for instance, Manoj Kumar Patairiya, "Why India Is Going to Mars," *New York Times*, November 22, 2013, at http://www.nytimes.com/2013/11/23/opinion/india-must-go-to-mars.html; Hartosh Singh Bal, "Indian Craft Is Lofted Toward Mars, Trailed by Pride and Questions," *New York Times*, November 5, 2013, at http://www.nytimes.com/2013/11/06/world/asia/Indian-craft-is-lofted-toward-mars-trailed-by-pride-and-questions.html?ref=Sunday; and Louis Friedman, "The New Space Race: It's Not Just the U.S. and Russia Anymore," *Los Angeles Times*, December 9, 2013, at http://www.latimes.com/opinion/commentary/la-oe-friedman-new-space-race-2013 1209,0,2903110.story#lxzz2nOu7RUf8.

25. Asit K. Biswas and Leong Ching, "That Crooked Carrot Is Also Food," *New York Times*, October 14, 2011, at http://www.nytimes.com/2011/10/15/opinion/15.ht-ed biswas15.html.

26. Swaminathan S. Anklesaria Aiyar, "India Booming: Cyclical or Sustainable?" *India Times*, January 31, 2007, at http://articles.economictimes.indiatimes.com/2007-01-31/news/28438690_1_higher-growth-india-gdp-growth-savings-rate.

27. Ambrosia Sabrina, "Eurozone Crisis to Affect India: Manmohan Singh Urges Strong Agenda for Economic Recovery," *International Business Times*, June 17, 2012, at http://www.ibtimesco.in/articles/353021/20120617/eruozone-crisis-india-manmohan-g20-summit.htm.

28. See the data in CIA World Factbook 2016, at https://www.cia.gov/library/publications/the-world-factbook/geos/in.html.

29. See, for instance, Arvind Subramanian, "Why India's Economy is Stumbling," *New York Times*, August 30, 2013, at http://www.nytimes.com/2013/08/31/opinion/why-indias-economy-is-stumbling.html?_r=0.

30. ET Bureau, "Government Contains Fiscal Deficit at 4 Percent; Beats Its Own Target," *Economic Times*, May 18, 2015.

31. David Pilling, "Indian Makers Are Still the Stuff of Modi's Dreams," *Financial Times*, August 13, 2015.

32. Neha Thirani, "India Companies Spend Overseas for Growth," *International New York Times*, April 17, 2012, at http://india.blogs.nytimes.com/2012/04/17/india-companies-spend-overseas-for-growth.

33. "India's 2G Telecom Scandal Spans the Spectrum of Abuse," *India Knowledge @ Wharton*, December 2, 2010, at http://knowledge.wharton.upenn.edu/india/article.cfm?articleid=4549.

34. "Outrage Over Report that India Lost $210bn in Coal Scam," *BBC News*, March 22, 2012, at http://www.bbc.com/news/world-asia-india-17471359.

35. For an early, thoughtful, and sympathetic critique, see Jagdish Bhagwati and Padma Desai, *Planning for Industrialization* (London: Oxford University Press, 1970).

36. For an analysis of the origins and evolution of the Indo-Soviet relationship, see Robert Horn, *Soviet-Indian Relations: Issues and Influence* (New York: Praeger, 1982).

37. Ramesh Thakur, "India After Nonalignment," *Foreign Affairs* 71, no. 2 (1992), 162–182.

38. On this subject, see Isabelle de Saint-Mezard, *Eastward Bound: India's New Positioning in Asia* (New Delhi: Manohar-CSH, 2005).

39. See Sumit Ganguly, "South Asia After the Cold War," *Washington Quarterly* 15, no. 4 (1992), 173–184.

40. On the Indian nuclear decision, see Sumit Ganguly, "India's Pathway to Pokhran II: The Prospects and Sources of India's Nuclear Weapons Program," *International Security* 23, no. 4 (1999), 148–177.

41. A sense of the American and global reactions to the Indian nuclear tests can be gleaned from Strobe Talbott, *Engaging India: Diplomacy, Democracy, and the Bomb* (Washington, DC: Brookings Institution, 2006).

42. Nitin Gokhale with Janaki Fernandes and Abhinav Bhatt, "How Indian Navy Is Expanding and Modernising," *NDTV*, June 25, 2012, at http://www.ndtv.com/article/india/how-indian-navy-is-expanding-and-modernising-235746.

43. A case for a more negative interpretation is made in Jean Dreze and Amartya Sen, *India, Development and Participation*, 2nd ed. (Oxford: Oxford University Press, 2002), 289–294.

44. See, among many others, Miguel A. Centeno, *Blood and Debt: War and the Nation-State in Latin America* (University Park, PA: Pennsylvania State University Press, 1994); Jeffrey Herbst, *States and Power in Africa: Comparative Lessons in Authority and Control* (Princeton, NJ: Princeton University Press, 1990); Otto Hintze, *The Historical Essays of Otto Hintze*, ed. Felix Gilbert (New York: Oxford University Press, 1975); Victoria Tin-bor Hui, *War and State Formation in Ancient China and Early Modern Europe* (Cambridge: Cambridge University Press, 2005); Samuel P. Huntington, *Political Order in Changing Societies* (New Haven, CT: Yale University Press, 1968); Robert Jackman, *Power without Force: The Political Capacity of Nation-States* (Ann Arbor: University of Michigan Press, 1994); Atul Kohli, "State, Society, and Development," in *Political Science: The State of the Discipline*, ed. Ira Katznelson and Helen V. Milner (New York: W.W. Norton, 2002), 84–117; Margaret Levi, "The State of the Study of the State," in Katznelson Milner, *Political Science*, 33–55; Michael Mann, *The Source of Social Power*, 3 vols. (Cambridge: Cambridge University Press, 1986 and later); Joel Migdal, *Strong Societies and Weak States: State-Society Relations in the Third World* (Princeton, NJ: Princeton University Press, 1988); Joel Migdal, *State in Society: Studying How States and Societies Transform and Constitute One Another* (Cambridge, Cambridge University Press, 2001); Bruce D. Porter, *War and The Rise of the State: The Military Foundations of Modern Politics* (New York: Free Press, 1994); Karen Rasler and William R. Thompson, *War and State Making: The Shaping of the Global Powers* (Boston: Unwin Hyman, 1989); Brian D. Taylor, *State Building in Putin's Russia: Policing and Coercion After Communism* (Cambridge: Cambridge University Press, 2011); Charles Tilly, ed., *The Formation of National States in Western Europe* (Princeton, NJ: Princeton University Press, 1975); Charles Tilly, ed., *Coercion, Capital, and European States*, AD 990–1992 (Cambridge, MA: Blackwell, 1992).

45. Gunnar Myrdal, *Asian Drama: An Inquiry into the Poverty of Nations* (New York: Pantheon, 1968), vol. 2, 895.

46. Bernard D. Nossiter, *Soft State: A Newspaperman's Chronicle of India* (New York: HarperCollins, 1970).

47. Edward Luce, *In Spite of the Gods: The Strange Rise of Modern India* (New York: Doubleday, 2007).

48. Anand Giridharadas, *India Calling: An Intimate Portrait of a Nation's Remaking* (New Delhi: Fourth Estate, 2010).

49. Simon Denyer, *Rogue Elephant: Harnessing the Power of India's Unruly Democracy* (New York: Bloomsbury, 2014).

50. Stephen P. Cohen, *India: Emergent Power* (Washington, DC: Brookings Institution Press, 2001).

51. Dietmar Rothermund, *India: The Rise of an Asian Giant* (New Haven, CT: Yale University Press, 2008).

52. Arvind Panagariya, *India: The Emerging Giant* (New York: Oxford University Press, 2008).

53. Amrita Narlikar, *New Powers: How to Become One and How to Manage Them* (New York: Columbia University Press, 2010).

TWO Ascending Major Powers

1. To render these calculations comparable, all great power capabilities are pooled for the entire period, not just the years in which they were accorded great power status. But since we are focusing on the new great powers of the 1860–1905 class, we exclude Chinese capabilities, which would overwhelm the comparison.

2. We exclude showing China's share when charting population and military personnel because its very large share simply dwarfs the relative size of the other states being examined. That China's very large size prior to 1950 did not matter much when it came to determining which states were great powers underscores the subjectiveness of the status allocations.

3. In this figure, Chinese capabilities are included because energy consumption per capita is very low in the period that we are examining.

4. For a more systematic approach to identifying major power status in the post–World War II era, see Thomas J. Volgy, Renato Corbatta, Keith A. Grant, and Ryan G. Baird, "Major Power Status in World Politics," in *Major Powers and the Quest for Status in International Politics: Global and Regional Perspectives*, ed. Thomas J. Volgy, Renato Corbatta, Keith A. Grant, and Ryan G. Baird (New York: Palgrave-Macmillan, 2011), 1–26.

5. Fareed Zakaria, *From Wealth to Power: The Unusual Origins of America's World Role* (Princeton, NJ: Princeton University Press, 1998).

6. Ibid., 21.

7. Ibid., 19.

8. Nazli Choucri and Robert North, *Nations in Conflict: National Growth and International Violence* (San Francisco: W. H. Freeman, 1975), 1.

9. For instance, giving China veto power in the UN Security Council in the 1940s does not seem to have been based on calculations that China had earlier demonstrated any qualifications for great power status. Similarly, some of the current impetus for bestowing great power status on India seems to be more about encouraging India to join a maritime-rim coalition aligned against China than it does about India having passed some capability threshold.

10. A good example is Sweden, a formidable power prior to the emergence of Russia and Prussia. But Britain and France are more-recent examples.

11. The theory was stimulated by reading the discussion in Richard Rosecrance and Arthur A. Stein, "Beyond Realism: The Study of Grand Strategy," in *The Domestic Bases of Grand Strategy*, ed. Richard Rosecrance and Arthur A. Stein (Ithaca, NY: Cornell University Press, 1993), 3–21.

12. Knox's work is indispensable for both the Italian and German cases, even though his goal is to account for the later emergence of fascist and Nazi states. See MacGregor Knox, *To the Threshold of Power, 1922/33: Origins and Dynamics of the Fascist and National Socialist Dictatorships*, vol. 1 (Cambridge: Cambridge University Press, 2007).

13. Stephen Skowronek, *Building a New American State: The Expansion of National Administrative Capabilities, 1877–1920* (Cambridge: Cambridge University Press, 1982). See as well Richard F. Bensel, *Yankee Leviathan: The Origins of Central State Authority in America, 1859–1877* (Cambridge: Cambridge University Press, 1990); and Richard F. Bensel, *The Political Economy of American Industrialization, 1877–1900* (Cambridge: Cambridge University Press, 2000).

14. Skowronek, *Building a New American State*.

15. William W. Lockwood, "Economic and Political Modernization," in *Political Modernization in Japan and Turkey*, ed. Robert E. Ward and Dankwart A. Rustow (Princeton, NJ: Princeton University Press, 1964), 117–145.

16. Nazli Choucri, Robert C. North, and Susumu Yamakage, *The Challenge of Japan Before World War II: A Study of National Growth and Expansion* (New York: Routledge, 1992), 59.

17. Russia and China both ascended as a consequence of demonstrating military prowess in the eighteenth and twentieth centuries, respectively. Similarly, it makes good sense for relatively weak great powers to draw back from open antagonisms and to focus on developing their own capabilities when their principal opponent's capabilities are strong. China adopted this approach under Deng Xiaoping. Contemporary Russia seems to be following a similar course.

18. Baldev Raj Nayar and T. V. Paul, *India in the World Order: Searching for Major-Power Status* (Cambridge: Cambridge University Press, 2003), 32.

19. More recently, the BRIC group has become the BRICS group with the addition of South Africa. However, South Africa's potential for economic ascent is radically different and much more limited than India's or China's. Its inclusion in the group seems more a matter of politics among the large developing states, and we need not follow their lead in this analysis.

20. The total GDP in figure 2.7 is based on adding GDP estimates for India, China, western Europe, and the United States across approximately the last two thousand years. The western European proportion is not shown because it parallels the U.S. share trajectory—a late rise and more recent decline—and makes it very difficult to interpret the figure. The GDP data are taken from Angus Maddison's GDP project, expressed in 1990 international Geary-Khamis dollars, and is found at http://www.ggdc.net/maddison/maddison-project/home.htm.

21. A case can be made that Song China was the world's leading economy in the period immediately prior to the invasion of the Mongols, but not afterward. See George Modelski and William R. Thompson, *Leading Sectors and World Powers: The Coevolution of Global Politics and Economics* (Columbia, SC: University of South Carolina Press, 1996).

22. Earlier, small size was an advantage for political-economic cohesion. Very small states such as Genoa, Venice, and Portugal were able to assume technological leads for periods of time that were considerably disproportional to their population and territorial sizes. For an elaboration of this argument, see Karen Rasler and William R. Thompson, *War and State Making: The Shaping of the Global Power* (Boston: Unwin Hyman, 1989).

23. These threshold figures are configured around a conservative assumption of 25 percent of the world's lead economy (the United States) GDP per capita levels during these decades. For an argument using this working threshold for distinguishing between global north and south states in the nineteenth and twentieth centuries, see William R. Thompson and Rafael Reuveny, *Limits to Globalization and North-South Divergence* (London: Routledge, 2010).

24. Actually, this tendency is probably already better established than we realize. World Wars I and II, for instance, can be seen as conflicts over whether Germany or the United States would succeed Britain as the system's lead economy. The clarity of what is at stake tends to be made more hazy by all of the sundry motivations for conflict that are activated by periods of technological transition.

25. Homi Kharas, "Realizing the Asian Century: Mega Challenges and Risks," in *Asia 2050: Realizing the Asian Century*, ed. Harinder S. Kohli, Ashok Sharma, and Anil Sood (New Delhi: Sage, 2011). See as well Harinder Kohli and Anil Sood, eds., *India 2039: An Affluent Society in One Generation* (New Delhi: Sage, 2010).

26. Kalevi J. Holsti, *The State, War, and the State of War* (Cambridge: Cambridge Studies in International Relations, 1996).

THREE Conceptualizing and Measuring State Strength

1. Such an observation does not imply that we have consensus on what sorts of resource packages are necessary for elite status—only that we have experience with arguing about these types of credentials.

2. Kalevi J. Holsti, *The State, War, and the State of War* (Cambridge: Cambridge University Press, 1996), 83. The Holsti definition is not the only approach to conceptualizing state strength, but we would suggest that it is quite attractive in the sense that it draws attention to three state attributes that often appear in some fashion in these types of discussions. Compare, for instance, Adam Smith's definition utilized by Besley and Persson: "Little else is required to carry a state to the highest degree of opulence from the lowest barbarism, but peace, easy taxes, and a tolerable administration of justice, all the rest being brought about by the natural course of things"—cited in Timothy Besley and Torsten Persson, *Pillars of Prosperity: The Political Economics of Development Clusters* (Princeton, NJ: Princeton University Press, 2011), 1. While Besley and Persson make interesting use of this definition, and in a way that overlaps to some extent with our own, Smith's argument is not really about state strength per se. Rather, Smith's concern is more about economic growth ("the highest degree of opulence") and a facilitative state that either evades war or minimizes domestic conflict, goes light on taxation, and reduces dispute tendencies with a "tolerable" judiciary. Thus, there certainly are alter-

native approaches to defining state strength, but we need to be careful that the starting point is really about state strength, as opposed to something else, such as economic growth facilitation.

3. Cullen S. Hendrix, "Measuring State Capacity: Theoretical and Empirical Implications for the Study of Civil Conflict," *Journal of Peace Research* 47, no. 3 (2010): 273–285.

4. Hendrix notes that using military size and spending to measure violence monopoly has the problem that states with high rates of rebellion and insurgency are apt to have large militaries. As a consequence, it is not clear that military capability necessarily captures the absence of nonstate violence.

5. Not surprisingly, these indicators are often found in indexes of failed/weak states. See, for instance, Susan E. Rice and Stewart Patrick, *Index of State Weakness in the Developing World* (Washington, DC: Brookings Institution Press, 2008); and Stewart Patrick, *Weak Links: Fragile States, Global Threats, and International Security* (Oxford: Oxford University Press, 2011). One difference in the nature of the undertaking is that we are attempting to operationalize a conceptualization of state strength, while the many indexes of failed/weak states seek to create indicators of something quite similar but in a more ad hoc or inductive way. We do not claim any inherent superiority to our approach. It is more likely that all of these indexes capture fairly similar phenomena. Whether one chooses to emphasize the lower, upper, or middle ranges of these scores depends on one's theoretical question.

6. This process is complicated by trade-offs between effectiveness and responsiveness. With which kind of state—a highly effective but unaccountable state versus a highly responsive but ineffective state—is legitimacy more probable? More work on this problem needs to be done. See as well Bruce Gilley, *The Right to Rule: How States Win and Lose Legitimacy* (New York: Columbia University Press, 2009) for a different and more data-intensive approach to these questions.

7. The problem with this dimension, of course, is that analyses focusing on explaining violence cannot use a state-strength indicator that contains a violence component. Otherwise, one is explaining violence with an indicator partially based on violence. But the same thing could be said about extraction or legitimacy. That is, state strength indexes utilizing information on extraction, and legitimacy cannot be employed to explain extraction and legitimacy processes.

8. One question that remains unresolved is whether all three subcomponents of the Holsti concept should be treated as equal in substantive weight.

9. Somalia's scores for this period range between 0 and 1; Afghanistan scores between 0 and 4.

10. The abrupt decline of the French, British, and U.S. scores in the early part of the twenty-first century are puzzling and may suggest some changes in the sources used by the World Bank to develop composite scores.

11. However, see chapter 2 on what is referred to as the "middle-income trap." If states stall in their drives toward industrialization, might we not expect there to be corresponding problems in the enhancement of state strength?

FOUR Extraction and Legitimacy

1. Charles Tilly, "Reflections on the History of European State Making," in *The Formation of National States in Western Europe*, ed. Charles Tilly (Princeton, NJ: Princeton University Press, 1975).

2. See Jack S. Levy and William R. Thompson, *The Arc of War: Origins, Escalation, and Transformation* (Chicago: University of Chicago Press, 2011) for an elaboration of this interpretation.

3. Relatively weak efforts (that is, short in duration and intensity) were made to conquer Central America in the early nineteenth and twentieth centuries.

4. The Congo War, also known as Africa's World War (1996–2003), which involved eight African states and numerous armed factions within states, is a significant exception. Yet even in this case, the distinctions between internal and external fighting are very difficult to portray as black and white.

5. This process goes back at least to early-nineteenth-century attempts to prop up the Ottoman Empire from external and internal attacks. The 1956 Sinai War demonstrates, in marked contrast to the two Gulf Wars, that major powers have not always agreed on how best to accomplish this role.

6. The argument is expressed in different ways in see Michael N. Barnett, *Confronting the Costs of War: Military Power, State, Society in Egypt and Israel* (Princeton, NJ: Princeton University Press, 1992); Michael C. Desch, "War and Strong States, Peace and Weak States?" *International Organization* 50, no. 2 (Spring 1996): 237–268; Steven Heydemann, "War, Institutions, and Social Change in the Middle East," in *War, Institutions, and Social Change in the Middle East*, ed. Steven Heydemann (Berkeley: University of California Press, 2000); Miguel A. Centano, *Blood and Debt: War and the Nation State in Latin America* (University Park: Pennsylvania State University Press, 2002); Jeffrey A. Herbst, "States and War in Africa," in *The Nation State in Question*, ed. T. V. Paul, G. John Ikenberry, and John A. Hall (Princeton, NJ: Princeton University Press); Ann Hironaka, *Neverending Wars: The International Community, Weak States, and the Perpetuation of Civil War* (Cambridge, MA: Harvard University Press, 2005); and Levy and Thompson, *The Arc of War*.

7. Stephen Skowronek, *Building a New American State: The Expansion of National Administrative Capabilities, 1877–1920* (Cambridge: Cambridge University Press, 1982).

8. Parenthetically, we should also note the existence of "black money," which refers to personal and corporate funds that evade government taxation via nondeclaration. The size of the amount that circumvents taxation certainly relates to state extraction capabilities. In the Indian case, numerous estimates have been made, but there does not seem to be any solid consensus on the scale of the problem. An overview of the estimates that have been advanced can be found in India, Ministry of Finance, "Black Money," white paper, May 2012 (New Delhi: Ministry of Finance), at finmin.nic.in/reports/WhitePaper_BackMoney2012.pdf. Another estimation of the size of "shadow economies" in developing countries ranked India fifteenth of eighty-eight states. The size of India's shadow economy was estimated at around 22.4 percent, which was con-

siderably under the average size of 35–37 percent of GNP. See Friedrich Schneider, Andreas Buehn, and Claudio E. Montenegro, "Shadow Economies All Over the World: New Estimates for 162 Countries for 1999 to 2007" (Policy Research Working Paper, no. WPS 5356, World Bank, Washington, DC, 2010), http://documents.worldbank.org/curated/en/2010/06/12864844/shadow-economies-all-over-world-new-estimates-162-countries-1999–2007.

9. Another facet that raises interpretation doubts are the occasional quick shifts in governmental trust (Brazil in 2010–2012, the United States in 2009–2010 or 2013–2014). One would normally anticipate more gradual rises and declines.

10. Bruce Gilley, *The Right to Rule: How States Win and Lose Legitimacy,* (New York: Columbia University Press, 2009).

11. Central Intelligence Agency, *The World Factbook*: Country Comparison—GDP per capita (PPP), 2016, at https:// www.cia.gov/library/publications/resources/the-world-factbook/geos/in.html.

12. United Nations Development Programme, Human Development Report 2014, at hdr.undp.org/ sites/default/files/hdr14-freport-en-1.pdf.

13. Heritage Organization economic freedom rankings for 2015 are reported at www.heritage.org/index/ranking. This measure focuses on rule of law, limited government, regulatory effectiveness, and open markets.

14. See the most recent rankings reported at United Nations Development Programme, Human Development Reports, hdr.undp.org/en/media/HDR-20072008_GEM.pdf. This index aggregates proportional measures of the number of seats women hold in Parliament; the number of female legislators, senior officials, and managers; the number of female professional and technical workers; and the ratio of estimated female-to-male earned income.

15. Bruce Gilley, *The Nature of Asian Politics* (Cambridge: Cambridge University Press, 2014), 40–41.

16. On this point, see Pierre Englebert, *State Legitimacy and Development in Africa* (Boulder, CO: Lynne Reinner, 2000).

17. The "mixed bag" reference refers to the range of possibilities associated with "in-between" ranks. Medium scores can be earned if a collection of attributes all place a state in roughly the same position. Yet the same medium scores can be gained by a collection of attributes that are mixed in ranks—some high while others are lower. India's state corresponds to the latter situation, with strong scores on legitimacy, middle scores on extraction, and, historically, low scores on violence monopoly. In a mixed-bag situation, the question then becomes whether these capabilities are improving or deteriorating. Ideally, the best circumstances for state-making involves maintaining the high scores while improving on the lower scores.

FIVE Violence Monopoly

1. Sweden, the Netherlands, Spain, and Austria are the exceptions, even though there are ways to view the breakup of the Kalmar Union (Sweden), the Dutch struggle

for independence from Hapsburg Spain, and the Spanish Reconquista—certainly all violent episodes—as approximating violent antecedents to great power status.

2. Maya Chadda, *Ethnicity, Security, and Separatism in India* (New York: Columbia University Press, 1997), 28–29.

3. As one anonymous reviewer noted, this tolerance for multiple identities puts India in a different category than the European states that Charles Tilly was writing about in terms of state-making (see chapter 2).

4. Paul Brass, *The Politics of India Since Independence* (Cambridge: Cambridge University Press, 1990), 149.

5. Ian Talbot and Gurharpal Singh, *The Partition of India* (Cambridge: Cambridge University Press, 2009), 65–66.

6. Former soldiers with the appropriate military training and weapons and demobilized young males were more available than had been the norm.

7. Talbot and Singh, *The Partition of India*, 127–153.

8. Insurgency activity was continuing in 2015 in several cases, although casualty counts have been lower in recent years and therefore do not show in the Uppsala/Prio database.

9. See Stathis Kalyvas, "Warfare in Civil Wars," in *Rethinking the Nature of War*, ed. Isabelle Duyvesteyn and Jan Angstrom (London: Frank Cass, 2004), on these distinctions.

10. By denoting differential presence and whether they are primary or secondary, it should be clear that Chadha is not arguing that all of the factors are equally important.

11. Ajit Bhattacharjea, *Kashmir: The Wounded Valley* (New Delhi: UBS Publishers, 1994); Sumit Ganguly, *The Crisis in Kashmir: Portents of War, Hopes of Peace* (New York: Cambridge University Press, 1999).

12. This account depends heavily on Sumit Ganguly, *The Crisis in Kashmir*.

13. In surveys conducted in 2002 and 2008, roughly three of every four Kashmiris expressed a preference for independence from India. Joining Pakistan was not a popular option (8 percent and 2 percent, respectively). Only 1 percent in both 2002 and 2008 said they wanted to continue the current relationship with India. See Alfred Stepan, Juan J. Linz, and Yogendra Yadav, *Crafting State-Nations: India and Other Multinational Democracies* (Baltimore: Johns Hopkins University Press, 2011), 114.

14. Gurharpal Singh, *Ethnic Conflict in India: A Case-Study of Punjab* (Basingstoke, UK: Palgrave Macmillan, 2000).

15. Sanjib Baruah, *India against Itself: Assam and the Politics of Nationality* (Philadelphia: University of Pennsylvania Press; 1999).

16. A Swedish data set on third-party support for insurgencies lists accusations or evidence for Myanmar, Pakistani, Bangladeshi support for conflict in Manipur; Pakistani, Bangladeshi, Myanamar, and Chinese support for the Nagaland conflict; Bangladeshi support for the Tripura insurgency; Bhutan, Bangladeshi, and Myanmar support for Bodoland; and Pakistani, Bangladeshi, Bhutan, and Myanmar support for Assamese

conflict. See Uppsala Conflict Data Program (UCDP) External Support—Primary Warring Party Dataset, version 1.0; and Stina Hogbladh, Therese Petterson, and Lotta Themner, "External Support in Armed Conflict, 1975–2009: Presenting New Data" (paper presented at the annual meeting of the International Studies Association, Montreal, Canada, March, 2011).

17. Sumit Ganguly and David P. Fidler, eds. *India and Counterinsurgency: Lessons Learned* (New York: Routledge, 2009).

18. According to Dasgupta, Communist leaders were imprisoned by the British government prior to independence, and shortly after independence they attempted armed uprisings that were either suppressed quickly or failed to generate much sustained popular support. See Biplab Dasgupta, *The Naxalite Movement* (Bombay: Allied Publishers, 1974), 15–18.

19. See Stuart Corbridge, John Harriss, and Craig Jeffrey's very useful chapter, "Why Has Maoism Become Such a Force in India," on Maoist insurgency, in *India Today: Economy, Politics, and Society* (Cambridge: Polity Press, 2013), 197–217.

20. For specific information on insurgency duration (a median length of ten years) and outcome probabilities (that vary with duration, among other factors), see Ben Connable and Martin C. Libicki, *How Insurgencies End* (Santa Monica, CA: RAND Corporation, 2010).

21. Ibid., 15.

22. It is conceivable that Indian communal violence was more "politically innocent" prior to World War II. Some authors differentiate between traditional rioting and politicized postwar rioting. Traditional rioting was more likely when Hindu and Muslim religious festivals overlapped and created increased friction between groups that led to some relatively unplanned skirmishing. See Suranjan Das, *Communal Riots in Bengal, 1905–1947* (Delhi: Oxford University Press, 1991); and Talbot and Singh, *The Partition of India*, 65–66.

23. Varshney notes that some two-thirds of the Indian population resides in rural villages but only 4 percent of the rioting occurs outside of cities. Moreover, eight cities account for 46 percent of the rioting. As much as 82 percent of India's urban population has not experienced intercommunal rioting. See Ashutosh Varshney, *Ethnic Conflict and Civic Life: Hindus and Muslims in India* (New Haven, CT: Yale University Press, 2002), 87–118.

24. Steven I. Wilkinson, *Votes and Violence: Electoral Competition and Ethnic Riots in India* (Cambridge: Cambridge University Press, 2004). On this type of explanation, see also Paul R. Brass, *Theft of an Idol: Text and Context in the Study of Collective Violence* (Princeton, NJ: Princeton University Press, 1997); and *The Production of Hindu-Muslim Violence in Contemporary India* (Seattle: University of Washington Press, 2003).

25. There are, of course, analysts who are skeptical of political incentives explaining riot behavior. See Stuart Corbridge, Nihila Kalra, and Kayoko Tatsumi, "The Search for Order: Understanding Hindu-Muslim Violence in Post-Partition India," *Pacific Affairs* 85, no. 2 (2012): 287–311; and Ashutosh Varshney and Joshua R. Gubler, "Does the

State Promote Communal Violence for Electoral Reasons?" *India Review* 11, no. 3 (2012): 191–199.

26. Varshney, *Ethnic Conflict and Civic Life*.

27. Ornit Shani, *Communalism, Caste and Hindu Nationalism: The Violence in Gujarat* (Cambridge: Cambridge University Press, 2007).

28. See, for instance, Anjali T. Bohlken and Ernest J. Sergenti, "Economic Growth and Ethnic Violence: An Empirical Investigation of Hindu-Muslim Riots in India," *Journal of Peace Research* 47, no. 5 (2010): 589–600; Raheel Dhattiwala and Michael Biggs, "Explaining Spatial Variation in Hindu-Muslim Violence in Gujarat, 2002," at http://www.sociology.ox.ac.uk/working-papers/explaining-spatial-variation-in-hindu-muslim-violence-in-gujarat-2002.html; and Anirban Mitra and Debraj Ray, "Implications of an Economic Theory of Conflict: Hindu-Muslim Violence in India," 2012, at www.econ.nyu.edu/user/debraj/Papers/hm.pdf.

29. Sumit Ganguly and Rahul Mukherji, *India Since 1980* (Cambridge: Cambridge University Press, 2011), 141–166.

30. Selig S. Harrison, *India: the Most Dangerous Decades* (Princeton, NJ: Princeton University Press, 1960); Kanti Bajpai, "Diversity, Democracy, and Devolution in India," in *Government Policies and Ethnic Relations in Asia and the Pacific*, ed. Michael Brown and Sumit Ganguly (Cambridge, MA: MIT Press, 1997), 33–82.

SIX The Economy

1. Much the same can be said about the relationship between economic and state strength. A strong state might once have been able to be built with a weak economy—think seventeenth-to-eighteenth-century Prussia, but one of the reasons for building such a powerful state was to acquire a stronger economic foundation. In general, one would anticipate a positive, linear relationship between state strength and how well the economy functions. Therefore, it would also follow that an expanding economy creates potential for strengthening the state.

2. Super-Asia refers to an area with the ongoing tendency for the distinctions among South, Southeast, East/Northeast, and perhaps even Central Asia to be diminishing.

3. See, for instance, K. C. Yeh and Benjamin Zyder, *Asian Economic Trends and Their Security Implications* (Washington, DC: RAND Corporation, 2000); Ashley Tellis, "South Asia," in *Strategic Asia*, ed. Richard J. Ellings and Aaron L. Friedberg (Washington, DC: National Bureau of Asian Research, 2001); Sanjaya Baru, "Strategic Consequences of India's Economic Performance," in *Globalization and Politics in India*, ed. Baldev Raj Nayar (New Delhi: Oxford University Press, 2007).

4. Tellis, "South Asia," 240.

5. When Germany first attained great power status, it was not yet a challenger of Britain's industrial lead. Nor was Japan a leading economic power, as will be demonstrated later in chapter 6, when it received great power recognition in the very late nineteenth century.

6. Baldev Raj Nayar, "Globalization and India's National Autonomy," in Nayar, *Globalization and Politics in India*, 355.

7. See, for example, the discussion of economic transformations in Sumit Ganguly and Rahul Mukherji, *India Since 1980* (New York: Cambridge, 2011), chap. 3; and the economic analyses found in J. Williamson and R. Zagha, *From Slow Growth to Slow Reform* (Washington, DC: Institute for International Economics, 2002); B. DeLong, "India Since Independence: An Analytical Growth Narrative, in *In Search of Prosperity: Analytic Narratives on Economic Growth*, ed. D. Rodrik (Princeton, NJ: Princeton University Press, 2003); Arvind Subramanian, *India's Turn: Understanding the Economic Transformation* (New Delhi: Oxford University Press, 2008); and the long chapter on "When and Why Did India Take Off," in *India Today: Economy, Politics and Society*, ed. Stuart Corbridge, John Harris, and Craig Jeffrey (Cambridge, UK: Polity, 2013).

8. The 2002–2012 average was 7.4 percent. As it happens, if one projects an average 7 percent annual economic growth rate forward twenty years from 2013, India's economy would be approaching China's economic size in 2033.

9. Baru, "Strategic Consequences of India's Economic Performance." Baru puts forward a different list of foci than we do, but some of his interests, such as wealth redistribution and fiscal strength, are examined in other chapters.

10. Barry Bosworth and Susan M. Collins find that industry's share of Indian economic output remained fairly constant at 26 percent from 1980 to 2013, while services' share expanded from 38 percent to 60 percent. Agriculture's share dropped from 36 percent to 14 percent in the same time period. See their "India's Growth Slowdown: End of an Era?" *India Review* 14, no. 1 (2015): 10.

11. Bosworth and Collins, in "India's Growth Slowdown," p. 21, argue that India was much less affected by the 2008 global recession than was the case elsewhere, because it exported little in terms of manufactures and had not been all that successful in drawing in foreign investment.

12. Ironically, Bosworth and Collins, p. 23, also suggest that the early economic growth success discouraged addressing the infrastructural problems and now they need to be addressed to restimulate economic growth success.

13. Jim O'Neill, *The Growth Map: Economic Opportunity in the BRICs and Beyond* (New York: Portfolio/Penguin, 2011), 20.

14. Dominic Wilson and Roopa Purushothamanan, "Dreaming with BRICs: The Path to 2050," Goldman Sachs Global Economics Paper, no. 99, October 2003.

15. Of course, that does not mean that the 2035 or 2050 forecasts will prove to be as accurate.

16. Homi Kharas, "India's Promise: An Affluent Society in One Generation," in *India 2039: An Affluent Society in One Generation*, ed. Harinder S. Kohli and Anil Sood (New Delhi: Sage, 2010), 19.

17. Corbridge, Harriss, and Jeffrey, *India Today*, 81.

18. Nonetheless, solid gains have been made in literacy improvement. According to Bosworth and Collins, *India's Growth Slowdown*, p. 18, the illiteracy rate in 1983–1984 was 55 percent. By 2011–2012, it had been reduced to 28 percent.

19. Vikas Bajang, "Galloping Growth and Hunger in India," *New York Times*, February 11, 2011, at www.nytimes.com/2011/02/12/business/global/12food.html?pagewanted=all&_r=0.

20. World Bank, *India: Issues and Priorities for Agriculture*, May 17, 2012, at www.worldbank.org/en/news/feature/2012.05/17/india-agriculture-issues-priorities.

21. Katherine Baldwin and Joanna Bonarriva, "Feeding the Dragon and the Elephant: How Agricultural Policies and Trading Regimes Influence Consumption in China and India," *Journal of International Commerce and Economics*, published electronically May 2013, at http:www.usitc.gov/journals. Gulati, Fan and Dalafi, however, attribute the more radical approach taken in China to be linked to twenty years of serious mismanagement (combining the years of the Great Leap Forward and the Cultural Revolution) and the fear of peasant revolt if circumstances were not reformed radically. Even so, Chinese reforms proceeded cautiously. See Ashok Gulati, Shenggen Fan and Sara Dalafi, "The Dragon and the Elephant: Agricultural and Rural Reforms in China and India," International Food Policy Research Institute, Washington DC, September, 2005, at www.ifpri.org/sites/default/files/pubs/divs/mtid/dp/papers/mtidp87.pdf. See as well Alejandro Nin-Pratt and Shenggen Fan Yu, "Comparisons of Agricultural Productivity Growth in China and India," *Journal of Productivity Analysis* 33 no. 3 (2010): 209–223.

22. On average, Chinese fertilizer use is close to three times as much as in India. More than half of India is categorized as arable in comparison to about 13 percent of China. At the same time, Chinese agrarian practices also devote more attention to the cultivation of animals for food purposes. Hindu vegetarianism tends to restrict farm animals to milking.

23. Ranjit Goswami, "India's Population in 2050: Extreme Projections Demand Extreme Actions," *East Asia Forum*, April 5, 2013, at www.eastasiaforum.org/2013/04/05/indias-population-in-2050-extreme-projections-demand-extreme-action/.

24. William H. Avery, *China's Nightmare, America's Dream: India as the Next Global* Power (New Delhi: Amaryllis, 2012), 79.

25. Nicholas Eberstadt, "The Demographic Future: What Population Growth—and Decline—Means for the Global Economy," *Foreign Affairs* 89, no. 6 (2010): 54–64.

26. Yet this dominance was manifested in sheer size and not economic dominance or control over the Asian world.

27. Earlier forecasts dealt with a lower range: 7 percent on average guaranteed great power status, while 5–6 percent would not suffice. We are simply pushing up the variability threshold knowing full well than an average 10 percent is quite improbable in India.

SEVEN Infrastructure

1. World Economic Forum, "Global Agenda Council on Infrastructure 2013," at www.weforum.org/content/global-agenda-council-infrastructure.

2. See, for instance, William Easterly and Ross Levine, "Troubles with the Neighbors: Africa's Problem, Africa's Opportunity," *Journal of African Economics* 7,

no. 1 (1998): 120–142; Nuno Limao and Anthony J. Venables, "Infrastructure, Geographical Disadvantage, Transport Costs, and Trade," *World Bank Economic Review* 15, no. 3 (2001): 451–479; Paul Collier and Stephen O'Connell, "Opportunities and Choices," in *The Political Economy of Economic Growth in Africa, 1960–2000*, vol. 1, ed. Benno J. Ndulu, Robert H. Bates, Paul Collier, and Charles C. Soludo (Cambridge: Cambridge University Press, 2007), 76–136; Douglas H. Brooks and Benno Ferrarini, "Changing Trade Costs between People's Republic of China and India," (working paper no. 203, Asian Development Bank, Manila, 2010); Timo Henckel and Warwick McKibbin, "The Economics of Infrastructure in a Globalized World: Issues, Lessons and Future Challenges," Brookings Institution, June 4, 2010, at www.brookings.edu/~/media/research/files/papers/2010/6/04%20infrastructure%20economics%20mckibbin/0604_infrastructure_economics_mckibbin.

3. Cesar Calderon, Enrique Moral-Benito, and Luis Serven, "Is Infrastructure Capital Productive? A Dynamic Heterogenous Approach," World Bank and CEMFI, December 2009, at http://www.moralbenito.com/papers/pmg.pdf.

4. Neha Thirani Bagri, "Increased Global Demand Aids India's Mild Recovery," *New York Times*, November 29, 2013, at http://www.nytimes.com/2013/11/30/business/international/moderate-recovery-is-forecast-for-india.html?_r=0.

5. See Ifzal Ali and Ernesto M. Pernia, "Infrastructure and Poverty Reduction—What is the Connection?" ERD Policy Brief Series, no. 13 (Manila: Asian Development Bank, 2003), available at http://www.adb.org/Economics/default.asp.; Cynthia C. Cook, Tyrell Duncan, Somchai Jitsuchon, and Anul Sharma, *Assessing the Impact of Transport and Energy Infrastructure on Poverty Reduction* (Manila: Asian Development Bank, 2005); and B. Seetanah, S. Ramessur, and S. Rojid, "Does Infrastructure Alleviate Poverty in Developing Countries?" *International Journal of Applied Econometrics and Quantitative Studies* 6, no. 2 (2009): 17–36.

6. One factor to keep in mind is that earlier aspirants to elite status in world politics required a relatively long time to double their per capita GDP. The United Kingdom took 154 years, Germany 65 years, and the United States required 53 years. More recent ascenders have doubled their GDP per capita in much less time. China took 12 years, while India needed 16. In these latter two cases, the great size of the populations involved are difficult to compare with the then much smaller United Kingdom (9 million), Germany (28 million), and the United States (10 million) at the beginning of their rapid growth phases. This point is highlighted in Richard Dobbs, Jeremy Oppenheim, Fraser Thompson, Marcel Brinkman, and Marc Zornes, *Resource Revolution: Meeting the World's Energy, Metals, Food, and Water Needs*, McKinsey Global Institute, November 2011, at www.mckinsey.com/features/resource-revolution. The combination of very rapid growth within the context of huge populations makes the achievements all the greater. It also suggests that growth outpacing the infrastructure should hardly be surprising. Yet the outpacing is much more apparent in the Indian case than it is in the Chinese case.

7. Sridhar Vedachalam, "Water Supply and Sanitation in India: Meeting Targets and Beyond," GWF Discussion Paper 1237, Global Water Forum, Canberra, Australia,

2012, at http://www.globalwaterforum.org/wp-content/uploads/2012/10/Water-supply-and-sanitation-in-India-GWF-1237__.pdf; Telecom Regulatory Authority of India, "Highlights on Telecom Subscription Data as on 31st May 2012," July 4, 2012, available online at http://www.trai.gov.in/WriteReadData/PressRealease/Document/PR-TSD-May12.pdf.

8. Sun-Joo Ahn and Dagmar Graczyk, *Understanding Energy Challenges in India: Policies, Players and Issues* (Paris: International Energy Agency, 2012); FICCI and Ernst & Young, "India Infrastructure Summit 2012: Accelerating Implementation of Infrastructure Projects," 2012, 5–6, available at http://www.ey.com/Publication/vwLUAssets/FICCI_Infra_report_final/$FILE/FICCI_Infra_report_final.pdf.

9. See, for example, Sanjoy Chakravorty, who notes that land acquisition is said to have become the most important problem because industrialization and infrastructure expansion requires land that has been used for agricultural purposes and farmers are becoming more resistant to selling their land. See his *The Price of Land: Acquisition, Conflict, Consequence* (New Delhi: Oxford: Oxford University Press, 2013). While the point is that land is essential for expansion to take place, it is difficult to put this problem at or near the top of the list.

10. FICCI and Ernst & Young, "India Infrastructure Summit 2012," 13, observes that only about ten thousand kilometers of rail line has been added to the system in the past sixty-two years. That sum represents about 17 percent of the rail network.

11. FICCI and Ernst & Young, "India Infrastructure Summit 2012," p. 13, notes that the share of rail passenger traffic declined from 74 percent in the 1950s to 13 percent at present (2012). Rail freight movement declined from 86 percent to 39 percent in the same time period. This same source also criticizes the safety and quality of rail infrastructure, average speed and sanitation practices of the railways, and shortages in the availability of rolling stock. A long list of needed upgrades include modernizing about a third of the existing track, strengthening a large number of bridges, introducing new high-speed locomotives and coaches, installing green toilets, and the construction of dedicated freight corridors. The report concludes (p. 17) that the "development of railway infrastructure, particularly in the last decade, has been deficient due to multiple reasons, with insufficient funds, misplaced investment priorities, lack of organizational reforms and inability to attract private investments being the main ones."

12. FICCI and Ernst & Young, "India Infrastructure Summit 2012," 5.

13. The World Bank counts 199 ports, but most of these are not major ports. See World Bank, "India Transport Sector," 2013, 1, at web.worldbank.org/WBSITE/EXTERNAL/COUNTRIES/SOUTHASIAEXT/EXTSARREGTOPTRANSPORT/0,,contentMDK:20703625~menuPK:868822~pagePK:34004173~piPK:34003707~theSitePK:579598,00.html. FICCI and Ernst & Young, "India Infrastructure Summit 2012," p. 4, refers to thirteen major and sixty nonmajor ports as actually operational.

14. FICCI and Ernst & Young, "India Infrastructure Summit 2012," p. 23, points out that the Indian government's expectation that some 80 percent of the planned port improvements will be financed by private investment seems highly unrealistic given the reluctance of the private sector to participate in limited profit activities. Further delays

in port upgrading thus should be anticipated. See as well Jessica Seldon and N. K. Singh, "Moving India: The Political Economy of Transport Sector Reform," in *Economic Reform in India: Challenges, Prospects and Lessons*, ed. Nicholas C. Hope, Anjini Kichor, Roger Noll, and T. N. Srinivasan (Cambridge: Cambridge University Press, 2013).

15. The World Bank counts 125 airports, of which 11 are international—see World Bank, "India Transport Sector," 1. The Delhi and Mumbai airports account for 40 percent or more of the total traffic.

16. John Kasarda and Ranbabu Vankayalapanti, "India's Aviation Sector: Dynamic Transformation," in *India Economic Superpower: Fiction or Future?* ed. Jayashankar M. Swaminathan (Singapore: World Scientific Publishing, 2009), 136.

17. In 1990, 37 percent of oil was imported. By 2012, the imported proportion had risen to 75 percent. By 2035, 92 percent of oil is expected to be imported. See Ahn and Graczyk, *Understanding Energy Challenges in India*.

18. See Harinder S. Kohli, "Infrastructure for a Competitive Edge: Overcoming Bottlenecks and Keeping Pace with Exploding Demand," in *India 2039: An Affluent Society in One Generation*, ed. Harinder S. Kohli and Anil Sood (New Delhi: Sage, 2010), 134.

19. Jagdish Bhagwati and Arvind Panagariya nominate power shortages as the infrastructure problem that is "most urgent." See their *Why Growth Matters: How Economic Growth in India Reduced Poverty and the Lessons for Other Developing Countries* (New York: Public Affairs, 2013), 131.

20. Simon Denyer and Rami Lakshimi, "India Blackout, on Second Day, Leaves 600 Million without Power," *Washington Post*, August 1, 2012, at http://www.washingtonpost.com/world/asia_pacific/huge-blackout-fuels-doubts-about-indias-economic-ambitions/2012/08/01/gJQA7j1LMX_story.html; Gardiner Harris and Vikas Bajaj, "As Power Is Restored in India, the 'Blame Game' Over Blackouts Heats Up," *New York Times*, August 1, 2012, at www.nytimes.com/2012/08/02/world/Asia/power-restored-after-india-blackout.html?pagewanted=all.

21. "Blackout Nation: Power Cuts in India Show That a Lack of Reform Is Beginning to Hurt Ordinary People," *The Economist*, August 4, 2012, at www.economist.com/node/21559941.

22. Harris and Bajaj, "As Power Is Restored in India." See as well Sunila S. Kale and Sumit Ganguly, "India's Dark Night: The Politics Behind the Power Failure," *Foreign Affairs*, August 8, 2012, at http://www.foreignaffairs.com/articles/137819/sunila-s-kale-and-sumit-ganguly/indias-dark-night.

23. Denyer and Lakshimi, "India Blackout, on Second Day," for instance, suggests free electricity supplied to farmers for irrigation purposes is sold to factories. Kelli L. Joseph, on the other hand, argues that a combination of theft, corruption, and an artificial pricing structure make improvements in the public provision of power most unlikely without radical changes to its operating mode. See her "The Politics of Power: Electricity Reforms in India," *Energy Policy* 38, no. 1 (2010): 503–511.

24. One estimate is that Indian power outages are responsible for as much as 9 percent of lost potential industrial output. See *The Economist*, "Creaking, Groan-

ing: Infrastructure Is India's Biggest Handicap," December 11, 2008, at http://www.economist.com/node/12749787.

25. These problems are discussed in Ahn and Graczyk, *Understanding Energy Challenges in India*, 40. They note that generation efficiency losses are 4 percent in South Korea, 5 percent in Japan and China, 10 percent in Indonesia, and 17 percent in Brazil.

26. A proposed partial solution involves building 292 dams in the Himalayas to expand hydropower capacity, but this proposal has serious implications for biodiversity losses and human dislocation. It also assumes that climate change will not reduce river flow in the future. See Rachel Nuwer, "Hobbled on Energy, India Ponders a Multitude of Dams," *New York Times*, January 7, 2013, at http://green.blogs.nytimes.com/2013/01/07/hobbled-on-energy-india-ponders-a-multitude-of-dams/.

27. Rajiv Biswas, *Future Asia: The New Gold Rush in the East* (New York: Palgrave-Macmillan, 2013), 105–106.

28. Grail Research, "Water—The India Story," March 23, 2009, at http://www.grailresearch.com/pdf/ContenPodsPdf/Water-The_India_Story.pdf.

29. John R. Wennersten reports that 1952 water availability per capita was 3,450 cubic meters. By 2010, it had declined to 1,800 cubic meters and is expected to decline further to 1,200 cubic meters by 2025. See *Global Thirst: Water and Society in the 21st Century* (Atglen, PA.: Schiffer, 2012), 84.

30. Kevin Ferguson, "Report Suggests Water Woes for India," *New York Times*, June 10, 2010, at http://green.blogs.nytimes.com/2009/06/10/report-suggests-water-woes-for-india/.

31. Only 48 percent of the rainfall actually enters Indian rivers, and less than one-quarter (18 percent) of the rainfall is actually usable, according to Nina Brooks, "Imminent Water Crisis in India," August 2007, at www.arlington.institute.org/wbp/global-water-crisis/606. She also draws attention to declining aquifers, leaking pipes, untreated sewage, and crumbling storage devices as additional contributors to the loss of usable water.

32. The oldest dam in operation dates to 1000 C.E., but another 114 are over one hundred years in age. See Srelatha Menon, "The Real Truth about Our Dam Problem," *Business Standard*, December 13, 2011, at http://www.business-standard.com/article/economy-policy/the-real-truth-about-our-dam-problem-111121300092_1.html.

33. Gardiner Harris, "Rains or Not, India is Falling Short on Drinkable Water," *New York Times*, March 12, 2013, at www.nytimes.com/2013/03/13/world/asia/rains-or-not-india-is-falling-short-on-drinkable-water.html?_r=O.

34. UNICEF/WHO, "Diarrhoea: Why Children Are Still Dying and What Can Be Done," 2009, 20—available at http://www.unicef.org/media/files/Final_Diarrhoea_Report_October_2009_final.pdf.

35. Two exceptions are the "Water Policy and Action Plan 2020," which would decentralize water management practices, and "The River Interlinking Project," which would integrate the flow of water of ten major rivers at considerable expense and human displacement. For criticism of the latter, see A. C. Shukla and Vandama Asthana, "Anatomy of Interlinking Rivers in India, A Decision in Doubt," in *Program in Arms Control*

Disarmament and International Security (Champaign-Urbana: University of Illinois at Urbana-Champaign, November 2005); and Wennersten, *Global Thirst*, 92–93. The implication is that all centralized water management is not necessarily a good thing.

36. Vedachalam, "Water Supply and Sanitation in India."

37. Technically, the judiciary is usually categorized as a political institution, but we are not focusing on the functioning of political institutions in this undertaking, and thus we include the judiciary somewhat unconventionally in this chapter.

38. In 2001, about 65 percent of the population was considered literate. By 2011, the literacy rate had improved to 74 percent, largely as a function of providing classrooms to rural areas. Urban literacy is already at 84 percent. See B. Sivakumar, "Literacy Rate Jumps 10% in a Decade in India," *Times of India*, November 23, 2014, at timesofindia.indiatimes.com/india/literacy-rate-jumps-10-in-a-decade-in-india/articleshow/45244626.cms.

39. See Geeta Gandhi Kingdon, "The Progress of School Education in India," Global Poverty Research Group, March 2007, at http://www.gprg.org/pubs/workingpapers/pdfs/gprg-wps-071.pdf; Sonalde Desai, Amaresh Dubey, B. L. Joshi, Mitali Sen, Abusaleh Sheriff, and Reeve Vanneman, *Human Development in India: Challenges for a Society in Transition* (New Delhi: Oxford University Press, 2010), 75–96; Sam Hills and Thomas Chalaux, "Improving Access and Quality in the Indian Educations System," OECD Economics Department Working Papers, no. 885, OECD iLibrary, available at http://www.oecd-ilibrary.org/docserver/download/5kg83k687ng7.pdf?expires=1390426175&id=id&accname=guest&checksum=54B2FD58C58DC57807DF5758BABD7AF3; *Annual Status of Education Report 2012 (Rural)*, provisional (New Delhi: ASER Centre, January 17, 2013).

40. There is empirical evidence, however, to suggest that urban-rural differences on education are narrowing. See Viktoria Hnatkovska and Amartya Lahiri, "The Rural-Urban Divide in India" (working paper, International Growth Centre, London School of Economics and Political Science, London, February, 2013, at www.theige.org/sites/default/files/Rural%20Urban%20Divide%202%20Final.pdf.

41. See Lindsay Daugherty, Trey Miller, Rafiq Dossani, and Megan Clifford, *Building the Links between Funding and Quality in Higher Education: India's Challenge* (Santa Monica, CA: RAND Corporation, 2013). The expansion since independence is even more impressive—one hundred thousand in 1947 to approximately 11 million students in 2011. See Fazal Rizvi and Radhika Gorur, "Challenges Facing Indian Higher Education," vol. 2 (Melbourne: Australia India Institute, 2011), at www.aii.unimelb.edu.au/sites/default/files/Fearless%20nadia%20image%202.pdf.

42. India possesses a few professional schools (business and engineering) that have made some lists. See, for instance, Ernst & Young and FICCI, "FICCI Higher Education Summit 2012: Higher Education in India: Twelfth Five-Year Plan (2012–2017) and Beyond," 25, at http://www.ey.com/Publication/vwLUAssets/Higher_Education_in_India/$File/EY-FICC_Higher_Education_Report_Nov12.pdf, which notes that two Indian schools were included in the QS World University Ranking of the top five hundred global universities for 2011–2012. However, seven Russian, sixteen Chinese, and

four Brazilian universities were also on the list. See also K. C. Chakrabarty, "Indian Education System—Issues and Challenges," Bank for International Settlements, at www.bis.org/review/r110809b.pdf.

43. Ranjit Goswami, "Economic Growth and Higher Education in India and China," East Asia Forum, July 13, 2012, at www.eastasiaforum.org/2012/07/13/economic-growth-and-higher-education-in-india-and-china/.

44. Rizvi and Gorur, "Challenges Facing Indian Higher Education," 3–4.

45. PricewaterhouseCoopers, "India—Higher Education Sector: Opportunities for Private Participation," January, 2012, at http://www.pwc.in/en_IN/in/assets/pdfs/industries/education-services.pdf.

46. The urban hospital beds and other medical facilities tend to be highly concentrated in four large cities, as well. See Avneesh Kumar and Saurau Gupta, "Health Infrastructure in India: Critical Analysis/Policy Gaps in the Indian Healthcare Delivery," occasional paper, Vivekananda International Foundation, July, 2012, at http://www.vifindia.org/occasionalpaper/2012/health-infrastructure-in-india-critical-analysis-of-policy-gaps-in-the-indian-healthcare-delivery.

47. "India Needs $100Bn to Add 1 Bed per 1,000 Population," *Financial Express*, October 21, 2010, at http://www.financialexpress.com/news/india-needs-100-bn-to-add-1-bed-per-1000-population/700704.

48. PricewaterhouseCoopers, "Healthcare in India: Emerging Market Report 2007," at http://www.pwc.com/en_gx/gx/healthcare/pdf/emerging-market-report-hc-in-india.pdf.

49. Laveesh Bhandari and Siddhartha Dutta, "Health Infrastructure in Rural India," India Infrastructure Report 2007, Indian Institute of Technology, Kanpur, at http://www.iitk.ac.in/3inetwork/html/reports/IIR2007/11-Health.pdf.

50. Kumar and Gupta, "Health Infrastructure in India."

51. National Court Management Systems (NCMS), Policy and Action Plan, Supreme Court of India, available at http://supremecourtofindia.nic.in/ncms27092012.pdf.

52. *The Economist*, "Creaking, Groaning."

53. Gunnar Myrdal, "What Is Development?" *Journal of Economic Issues* 8, no. 4 (1974): 729–730; emphasis in original.

54. Ahn and Graczyk, "Understanding Energy Challenges in India."

55. In the current five-year plan (2012–2017), the central Indian government is doubling its infrastructural investment. But that does not mean that all of the investment targets will be realized. See FICCI and Ernst & Young, "India Infrastructure Summit 2012," 5–6.

56. Gardiner Harris and Bettina Wassener, "A Summer of Troubles Saps India's Sense of Confidence," *New York Times*, August 18, 2013, at http://www.nytimes.com/2013/08/19/business/global/a-summer-of-troubles-saps-indias-confidence.html.

57. See Susan L. Shirk, *China: Fragile Superpower* (Oxford: Oxford University Press, 2007).

EIGHT Inequality

1. See Jean Dreze and Amartya Sen, *An Uncertain Glory: India and Its Contradictions* (Princeton, NJ: Princeton University Press, 2013); Jagdish Bhagwati and Arvind Panagariya, *Why Growth Matters: How Economic Growth in India Reduced Poverty and Lessons for Other Developing Countries* (New York: Public Affairs, 2013).

2. Atul Kohli, *Poverty amid Plenty in the New India* (Cambridge: Cambridge University Press, 2012).

3. Gardiner Harris, "Rival Economists in Public Battle Over Cure for India's Poverty," *New York Times*, August 21, 2013, at http://www.nytimes.com/2013/08/22/world/asia/rival-economists-in-public-battle-over-cure-for-indias-poverty.html?pagewanted=all&_r=0.

4. Atul Kohli, *Poverty amid Plenty*.

5. Rahul Mukherji, *India's Economic Transition: The Politics of Reforms* (New Delhi: Oxford University Press, 2010).

6. Atul Kohli, *Poverty amid Plenty*, 111–130.

7. These statistics are derived from Preetika Rana and Joanna Sugden, "India's Record Since Independence," *IndiaRealTime, Wall Street Journal*, August 16, 2013, at http://blogs.wsj.com/indiarealtime/2013/08/15/indias-record-since-independence/.

8. From William Blake, "London," *Songs of Experience*, 1794. For a thoughtful discussion of caste, see Susan Bayly, *Caste, Society and Politics in India: From the Eighteenth Century to the Modern Age* (Cambridge: Cambridge University Press, 1999); for an alternative formulation, see Nicolas B. Dirks, *Castes of Mind: Colonialism and the Making of Modern India* (Princeton, NJ: Princeton University Press, 2001).

9. Christophe Jaffrelot, *India's Silent Revolution: The Rise of Lower Castes in North India* (New York: Columbia University Press, 2003).

10. For two largely sympathetic accounts, see Albert H. Hanson, *The Process of Planning: A Study of India's Five-Year Plans, 1950—1964* (London: Oxford University Press, 1966); and Baldev Raj Nayar, *The Modernization Imperative and Indian Planning* (Delhi: Vikas Publications, 1972).

11. On this issue see Francine Frankel, *India's Political Economy: The Gradual Revolution, 1947–2004* (New York: Oxford University Press, 2009); also see Ronald Herring, *Land to the Tiller: The Political Economy of Agrarian Reform in India* (New Haven, CT: Yale University Press, 1983).

12. Myron Weiner, *The Child and the State in India: Child Labor and Education Policy in Comparative Perspective* (Princeton, NJ: Princeton University Press, 1990).

13. Robert Wade, *Governing the Market: Economic Theory and the Role of Government in East Asian Industrialization* (Princeton, NJ: Princeton University Press, 2003).

14. John P. Lewis, *Quiet Crisis in India* (Washington DC: Brookings Press, 1962).

15. On the sources of Johnson's "short tether" policies, which tied food assistance to India's posture on the Vietnam War, see Sumit Ganguly, "Of Great Expectations and Bitter Disappointments: Indo-U.S. Relations during the Johnson Administration," *Asian Affairs* 15, no. 4 (1988–1989): 212–219.

16. These two terms are derived from the work of the American political scientist, Paul Brass.

17. Much of this is discussed at length in Francine Frankel, *India's Green Revolution: Economic Gains and Social Costs* (Princeton, NJ: Princeton University Press, 1971).

18. Paul Wallace, "Political Violence and Terrorism in India: The Crisis of Identity," in *Terrorism in Context*, ed. Martha Crenshaw (University Park: Pennsylvania State University Press, 1995).

19. Francine R. Frankel, *India's Political Economy, 1947–2004* (New Delhi: Oxford University Press, 2005).

20. Kohli, *Poverty amid Plenty*, 88.

21. On this subject see Paul R. Brass, *The Politics of India Since Independence* (New York: Cambridge University Press, 1994).

22. Samuel Huntington, *Political Order in Changing Societies* (New Haven, CT: Yale University Press, 1968).

23. Many of these developments are discussed in Sumit Ganguly and Rahul Mukherji, *India Since 1980* (New York: Cambridge University Press, 2011).

24. Indian poverty data are characterized by a number of problems pertaining to estimation and reliability. Our interpretation is based on figures put forward and analyzed by, among others, Himanshu, "Recent Trends in Poverty and Inequality: Some Preliminary Results," *Economic and Political Weekly* 42, no. 6 (2007): 497–508; Gaurav Datt and Martin Ravallion, "Shining for the Poor Too?" *Economic and Political Weekly* 65, no. 7 (2010): 55–60; Rukmini Srinivasan, "India Has No Middle Class?" *Times of India*, May 6, 2010, at http://articles.timesofindia.indiatimes.com/2010-05-06/india/28279518_1_middle-class-countries-definition; Stuart Corbridge, John Harriss, and Craig Jeffrey, *India Today: Economics, Politics & Society* (Cambridge: Polity, 2013), 47–79.

25. Diganta Mukherjee and Uday Bhanu Sinha, "Understanding NREGA: A Simple Theory and Some Facts," in *Human Capital and Development: The Indian Experience*, ed. Natteri Siddharthan and Krishnan Narayanan (New Delhi: Springer India, 2013).

26. Jean Dreze and Christian Oldiges, "Commendable Act," *Frontline* 24, no. 14, July 27, 2007, at http://www.hindu.com/thehindu/thscrip/print.pl?file=20070727001804100.htm&date=fl2414/&prd=fline&.

27. Ibid.

28. Laura Zimmermann, "Labor Market Impacts of a Large-Scale Public Works Program: Evidence from the Indian Employment Guarantee Scheme" (working paper no. 6858, Institute for the Study of Labor, Frankfurt, 2012).

29. Nayana Bose, "Raising Consumption through India's National Rural Employment Guarantee Scheme" (unpublished manuscript, Department of Economics, Vanderbilt University, October 2013), at https://my.vanderbilt.edu/nayanabose/files/2013/11/Job-Market-Paper_Nayana-Bose.pdf.

30. Megha Bahree, "How Bad, Really, Is India's New Food Security Bill?" *Forbes*, September 2, 2013, available at http://www.forbes.com/sites/meghabahree/2013/09/02/how-bad-really-is-indias-new-food-security-bill/.

31. Bhagwati and Panagariya, *Why Growth Matters*, 198–199.

32. Zimmerman, *Labor Market Impacts*.

33. India had forty-eight billionaires in 2012, a number exceeded in Asia and the Pacific only by China (which had ninety-five on the mainland and thirty-eight in Hong Kong). See Rajiv Biswas, *Future Asia: The New Gold Rush in the East* (New York: Palgrave MacMillan, 2012), 45.

NINE Democratic Institutions

1. Samuel P. Huntington, *Political Order in Changing Societies* (New Haven, CT: Yale University Press, 1968); Mark Kesselman, "Order or Movement? The Literature of Political Development as Ideology," *World Politics* 26, no. 1 (October 1973): 139–154.

2. Christophe Jaffrelot, *India's Silent Revolution: The Rise of the Lower Castes in North India* (New York: Columbia University Press, 2003).

3. For a judicious assessment, see Niraja Gopal Jayal, "The State and Democracy in India or What Happened to Welfare, Secularism, and Development," in *Democracy in India*, ed. Niraja Gopal Jayal (New Delhi: Oxford University Press, 2011).

4. For a critical discussion of how the institutions of the Indian state has dealt with the poor and especially the rural poor in India, see Stuart Corbridge, Glyn Williams, Manoy Srivastava, and Rene Veron, *Seeing The State: Governance and Governmentality in India* (Cambridge: Cambridge University Press, 2005).

5. Sumit Ganguly, Corruption in India: An Enduring Threat," *Journal of Democracy* 23, no. 1 (January 2012): 138–148.

6. Rob Jenkins, "Civil Society versus Corruption," *Journal of Democracy* 18, no. 2 (April 2007): 55–69.

7. Maya Tudor, *The Promise of Power: the Origins of Democracy in India and Autocracy in Pakistan* (Cambridge: Cambridge University Press, 2013).

8. Henry Hart, ed. *Indira Gandhi's India: A Political System Re-Appraised* (Boulder, CO: Westview Press, 1976); Robert L. Hardgrave, Jr., *India Under Pressure: Prospects for Political Stability* (Boulder, CO: Westview Press, 1984), and Paul Brass, *The Politics of India Since Independence* (New York: Cambridge University Press, 1994).

9. Yubaraj Ghimire, "The Decline of Parliament," *India Today*, July 15, 1994.

10. Subhash C. Kashyap, "Parliament, Reform Thyself," *The Tribune*, September 24, 2005.

11. IANS, "150 newly elected MPs have criminal records," *Hindustan Times*, May 17, 2009.

12. Christophe Jaffrelot and Gilles Verniers, "Lawmakers and Law-Breakers," *Indian Express*, July 2, 2014.

13. Devesh Kapur and Pratap Bhanu Mehta, *The Indian Parliament as an Institution of Accountability* (Geneva: United Nations Research Institute for Social Development, 2006).

14. For charges of political interference in the IAS, see Dalel Benbabaali, "Questioning the Role of the Indian Administrative Service in National Integration,"

South Asia Multidisciplinary Academic Journal, 2008, available at http://samaj.revues.org/633.

15. Anirudh Krishna, "Continuity and Change: the Indian Administrative Service 30 Years Ago and Today," *Commonwealth and Comparative Politics* 48, no. 4 (2010): 433–444.

16. Jayaprakash Narayan, "Corruption in Civil Services," *Times of India*, August 10, 2002.

17. S. K. Das, *Public Office, Private Interest: Bureaucracy and Corruption in India* (New Delhi: Oxford University Press, 2001), 130–131.

18. Sanjoy Hazarika, "India's Election Commissioner Gains a Following," *New York Times*, January 30, 19994.

19. John-Thor Dahlburg, "Election Umpire Calls Them as He Sees Them: Shyness Isn't a Problem for India's T. N. Seshan, Who is Proud of Driving 'The Fear of God' into Law-Breakers," *Los Angeles Times*, January 25, 1994.

20. Manohar Singh Gill, "India: Running the World's Biggest Elections," *Journal of Democracy* 9, no. 1 (January 1998): 164–168.

21. Sanjoy Majumder, "Indian Election: Narendra Modi Accused of Poll Law Violation as Millions Vote," *BBC*, April 30, 2014, available at http://www.bbc.com/news/world-asia-india-27200609.

22. N. Ram, "Know Your Bofors," *Frontline* 16, no. 24 (November 13–26, 1999).

23. PTI (Press Trust of India), "Coffin Scam: Court Discharges Three Former Army officials," *Economic Times*, December 11, 2013.

24. IANS (Indo-Asian News Service), "CAG Report on Commonwealth Games Tabled in Parliament," *Daily News and Analysis*, August 5, 2011.

25. J. Venkatesan, "Supreme Court Scraps UPA's 'Illegal' 2G Sale," *The Hindu*, February 3, 2012.

26. PTI, "Coalgate: CAG report slams UPA government, BJP demands PMs resignation," *Times of India*, August 17, 2012.

27. Aman Sharma, "CBI's Conviction Rate Alarmingly Low," *India Today*, 15 March, 2010, available at http://indiatoday.intoday.in/story/CBI%27s+conviction+rate=low/1/88296.html.

28. Sumit Ganguly, "India's Corruption Problem," *Foreign Affairs*, August 20, 2011, available at http://www.foreignaffairs.com/articles/68219/sumit-ganguly/indias-corruption-problem.

29. Ronojoy Sen, "Going Beyond Mere Accounting: The Changing Role of India's Auditor General," *Journal of Asian Studies* 2, no. 4 (November 2013): 801–811.

30. For a useful overview of the CAG and other institutions in combating corruption, see Shibashis Chatterjee and Sreya Maitra Roychoudhury, "Institutions, Democracy and 'Corruption' in India: Examining Potency and Performance," *Japanese Journal of Political Science* 14, no. 3 (September 2013): 395–419.

31. Chetan Agrawal, "Right to Information: A Tool for Combating Corruption in India," *Journal of Management and Public Policy* 3, no. 2 (June 2012): 26–38; also see

Rob Jenkins and Anne Marie Goetz, "Accounts and Accountability: Theoretical Implications of the Right-to-Information Movement in India," *Third World Quarterly* 20, no. 3 (1999): 603–622.

32. Leonid Peisakhin and Paul Pinto, "Is Transparency an Effective Anti-corruption Strategy? Evidence from a Field Experiment in India," *Regulation and Governance* 4 (2010): 261–280.

33. Ibid., 261.

34. Alasdair Roberts, "A Great and Revolutionary Law? The First Four Years of India's Right to Information Act," *Public Administration Review* 70, no. 6 (November/December 2010):.925–933.

35. Press Trust of India, "Govt. Puts Word Limit on RTI Pleas, Defines Format," *IbnLive*, August 12, 2012, at http://ibnlive.in.com/news/govt-puts-word-limit-on-rti-pleas-defines-format-for-appeal/281605–3.html.

36. Layanya Rajamani, "Public Interest Environmental Litigation in India: Exploring Issues of Access, Participation, Equity, Effectiveness and Sustainability," *Journal of Environmental Law* 19, no. 3 (2007): 293–321.

37. Surya Deva, "Public Interest Litigation in India: A Critical review," *Civil Justice Quarterly* 28, no. 1 (2009).

38. Seymour Martin Lipset, "Some Social and Economic Requisites for Democracy," *American Political Science Review* 53, no. 1 (1959): 69–105.

39. Adam Przeworski and Fernando Limongi, "Modernization: Theories and Facts," *World Politics* 49, no. 2 (1997): 155–183.

40. For example, British colonial officials saw to it that much of the senior Congress Party leadership spent the Second World War in detention even as the leaders of the Muslim League and the Indian Communist Party faced few restrictions. Neither of the latter two entities was known for internal democracy or commitment to liberal-democratic norms.

41. For an articulate exposition of this perspective, see Rajeev Bhargava, "Democratic Vision of a New Republic," in *Transforming India: Social and Political Dynamics of Democracy*, ed. Francine Frankel, Zoya Hasan, Rajeev Bhargava, and Balveer Arora (New Delhi: Oxford University Press, 2000).

42. Granville Austin, *The Indian Constitution: The Cornerstone of a Nation* (Oxford: Clarendon Press, 1966).

43. Consider, for example, the brilliant self-critique that Nehru penned as early as 1937 under a nom de plume. Chanakya [Jawaharlal Nehru], "The Rashtrapati," *Modern Review* (Calcutta), November 1937.

44. All children attending primary school in India are required to learn three languages: their mother tongue, Hindi (the dominant language of northern India), and English. For a particularly thoughtful treatment of this subject, see Jyotindra Das Gupta, "Language Policy and National Development in India," in *Fighting Words: Language Policies and Ethnic Relations in Asia*, ed. Michael E. Brown and Sumit Ganguly (Cambridge: MIT Press, 2003).

45. For an ideologically charged and partisan critique, see Ayesha Jalal, *Democracy and Authoritarianism in South Asia: A Historical and Comparative Perspective* (Cambridge: Cambridge University Press, 1995).

46. The data are taken from the Cingranelli-Richards (CIRI) Human Rights Dataset, found at http://www.humanrightsdata.com.

47. See David L. Cingranelli and David L. Richards, "Measuring the Level, Pattern, and Sequence of Government Respect for Physical Integrity Rights," *International Studies Quarterly* 43, no. 2 (1999): 407–418.

48. See David L. Richards, Ronald Gelleny, and David Sacko, "Money with a Mean Streak? Foreign Economic Penetration and Good Respect for Human Rights in Developing Countries," *International Studies Quarterly* 45, no. 2 (2001): 219–239.

49. Jyotindra Das Gupta, "A Season of Caesars: Emergency Regimes and Development Politics in Asia," *Asian Survey* 18 (1978): 315–349.

50. Sumit Ganguly, "The Crisis of Indian Secularism," *Journal of Democracy* 14, no. 4 (2003): 11–25.

51. For a nuanced discussion of India's democratic political culture and its discontents, see Pratap Bhanu Mehta, *The Burden of Democracy* (New Delhi: Penguin, 2003).

52. Amelia Gentleman, "Killings in Delhi Slum Expose Unequal Justice for India's Poor," *International Herald Tribune*, January 6, 2007, at http://www.nytimes.com/2007/01/06/news/06iht-web.0106india.4121749.html?pagewanted=all&_r=0.

53. On the question of deaths in police custody, see the National Human Rights Commission, "Annual Report 2004–2005", at nhrc.nic.in/Documents/AR/AR04-05 ENG.pdf.

54. Sumit Ganguly, "India's Corruption Problem: Anna Hazare and India's Democracy, *Foreign Affairs*, August 20, 2011, at http://www.foreignaffairs.com/articles/68219/sumit-ganguly/indias-corruption-problem#.

55. In a 2013 article, Debroy and Bhondari note that a content analysis of media coverage increased nearly fourfold in the 2005–2010 period, in part because the foci was increasingly on "big ticket" types of corruption. See Bibek Debroy and Laveesh Bhondari, "Corruption in India," *The World Financial Review*, March 3, 2012, at www.Worldfinancialreview.com/?p=1575.

56. Nicholas Charron, "The Correlates of Corruption in India: Analysis and Evidence from the States," Quality of Government Institute, University of Gothenburg, Sweden, at http://www.eldis.org/vfile/upload/1/document/1112/Charron%20AJPS%20 Forthcoming.pdf.

57. Unfortunately, Brazil, China, and Russia appear to be absent from the survey.

58. A formal commitment to secularism was added to the Constitution of India of 1950 as late as the Forty-Second Amendment, which dates from 1976.

59. On this subject, see Ganguly, "The Crisis of Indian Secularism."

60. For a trenchant discussion of the conditions under which the BJP might moderate its stance, see Subrata K. Mitra, "The Ambivalent Moderation of Hindu Nationalism in India," *Australian Journal of Political Science* 4, no. 3 (2013): 269–285.

61. For a detailed analysis of the defeat of Congress, see Suhas Palshikar, "The Defeat of the Congress," *Economic and Political Weekly*, September 27, 2014.

62. Anita Joshua, "Choice of ICHR Chief Reignites Saffronization Debate," *The Hindu*, July 16, 2014.

63. Abhishek Saha, "FTII: Protests against Chauhan to Continue Despite 'Threat,'" *Hindustan Times*, July 16, 2015.

64. Some of these concerns are dealt with in Jagdish Bhagwati, "Secularism in India: Why Is It Imperiled?" at http://www.columbia.edu/~jb38/papers/pdf/Secularism_in_India.pdf.

65. On this point, see the discussion in Fareed Zakaria, "The Rise of Illiberal Democracy," *Foreign Affairs* 76, no. 6 (1997): 22–43.

66. Amartya Sen, "How Is India Doing?" *New York Review of Books*, December 16, 1982, at http://www.nybooks.com/articles/archives/1982/dec/16/how-is-india-doing/.

67. For a compelling account of the horrors of the Great Leap Forward, see Judith Shapiro, *Mao's War against Nature: Politics and Environment in Revolutionary China* (New York: Cambridge University Press, 2001).

68. Rama Lakshmi, "India's Moderate Muslims See Peril in Growth of Stricter Form of Islam," *Washington Post*, June 29, 2008, at http://www.washingtonpost.com/wp-dyn/content/article/2008/06/28/AR2008062801101.html.

69. Ranjit Kumar Gupta, *The Crimson Agenda: Maoist Protest and Terror* (Delhi: Wordsmiths, 2004).

70. Agencies, "Naxalism Gravest Internal Security Threat to Nation: PM," *Indian Express*, April 21, 2010, at http://indianexpress.com/article/india/latest-news/naxalism-gravest-internal-security-threat-to-nation-pm/; also see Prakash Singh, *The Naxalite Movement in India* (New Delhi: Rupa, 2006).

71. Sumit Ganguly and David P. Fidler, eds., *India and Counterinsurgency: Lessons Learned* (London: Routledge, 2007).

TEN Grand Strategy

1. C. Raja Mohan, *Modi's World: Expanding India's Sphere of Influence* (New Delhi: HarperCollins, 2015).

2. It needs to be clarified that this argument differs from those who contend that the preoccupation with independence has been a constant in India's foreign policy since independence. For an alternative formulation, see Vipin Narang and Paul Staniland, "Institutions and Worldviews in Indian Foreign Security Policy," *India Review* 11, no. 2 (2012): 76–94.

3. Seema Sirohi, "India-US: Alignment and Autonomy," *Times of India*, June 18, 2012, at http://articles.timesofindia.indiatimes.com/2012-06-18/edit-page/32282584_1_india-and-obama-autonomy-partner.

4. Sumit Ganguly, "A New Era in India's Foreign Policy?" *Mint*, August 4, 2015.

5. For a preliminary assessment, see Sumit Ganguly, *Hindu Nationalism and the Foreign Policy of India's Bharatiya Janata Party* (Washington, DC: German Marshall Fund/TransAtlantic Academy, 2015).

6. Madhushree Mukherjee, *Churchill's Secret War: The Ravaging of India During World War Two* (New York: Basic Books, 2010).

7. Lorne J. Kavic, *India's Quest for Security, 1947–1965* (Berkeley: University of California Press, 1967).

8. The classic statement, of course, remains; Kenneth Waltz, *Theory of International Politics* (New York: McGraw Hill, 1979).

9. T. A. Keenleyside, "Prelude to Power: The Meaning of Non-Alignment Before Indian Independence," *Pacific Affairs* 53, no. 3 (1980): 461–483.

10. See, for example, Jawaharlal Nehru, *China, Spain and the War* (Allahabad, India: Kitabistan, 1940).

11. For an argument that suggests that Nehru also faced ideational opposition, see Rahul Sagar and Ankit Panda, "Pledges and Pious Wishes: The Constituent Assembly Debates and the Myth of a "Nehruvian Consensus," *India Review* 14, no. 2 (April–June 2015): 203–220.

12. For a discussion, see Baldev Raj Nayar, *The Modernization Imperative and Indian Planning* (Delhi: Vikas, 1972).

13. For an early and thoughtful critique of the strategy and its results, see Jagdish Bhagwati and Padma Desai, *India: Planning for Industrialization: Industrialization and Trade Policies since 1951* (Oxford: Oxford University Press, 1970).

14. V. P. Menon, *The Story of the Integration of the Indian States* (New Delhi: Orient Blackswan, 2014).

15. Selig Harrison, *India: The Most Dangerous Decades* (Princeton, NJ: Princeton University Press, 1960).

16. Much of this vision was spelled out in a speech that he delivered at a convocation at Columbia University. See Jawaharlal Nehru, "The Pursuit of Peace: Armaments Will Not Solve Basic Problem," Columbia University, New York, October 17, 1949.

17. Stephen P. Cohen, *The Indian Army* (New York: Oxford University Press, 2001).

18. On Nehru's concerns about foreign domination, see Jawaharlal Nehru, "Emergence of India in World Affairs," in Jawaharlal Nehru, *Independence and After: A Collection of Speeches, 1946–1949* (New York: John Day, 1950), 229–244.

19. The so-called princely states had been nominally independent as long as they recognized the British as the paramount power in South Asia. When independence and partition arrived, the British Crown gave them one of two choices: they could join either India or Pakistan on the basis of their demographic composition and geographic location. The option of independence was ruled out. Kashmir posed a unique problem, as it shared boundaries with India and Pakistan and had a Muslim-majority population with a Hindu monarch. On the princely states at the end of empire, see Ian Copland, *The Princes of India in the Endgame of Empire, 1917–1947* (Cambridge: Cambridge University Press, 1997).

20. The accession of Kashmir to India is nevertheless the subject of much contention. For an excellent discussion of the dispute over accession, see Shereen Ilahi, "The

Radcliffe Boundary Commission and the Fate of Kashmir," *India Review* 2, no. 1 (2003): 77–102.

21. On the UN's early role in seeking a resolution to this dispute, see Josef Korbel, *Danger in Kashmir* (Princeton, NJ: Princeton University Press, 1951); for evidence of British partisanship, see Chandrasekhar Dasgupta, *War and Diplomacy in Kashmir, 1947–1948* (New Delhi: Sage, 2002).

22. Report of a study group set up by the Indian Council of World Affairs, *India and the United Nations* (New York: Manhattan Publishing, 1957).

23. On India's role in the Congo crisis, see Rajeshwar Dayal, *Mission for Hammarskjold* (Princeton, NJ: Princeton University Press, 1975); on India's participation in the International Control Commission, see D. R. Sardesai, *Indian Foreign Policy in Cambodia, Laos, and Vietnam* (Berkeley: University of California Press, 1968); and for India's role in the Korean War, see Kim Chan Wahn, "The Role of India in the Korean War," *International Area Studies Review* 13, no. 2 (2010): 21–37.

24. Sergio Duarte, "The Future of the Comprehensive Test Ban Treaty," *UN Chronicle* 46, nos. 1 and 2 (2009).

25. On the origins of this rivalry, see John Garver, *Protracted Contest: Sino-Indian Rivalry in the Twentieth Century* (Seattle: University of Washington Press, 2001).

26. For details, see R. K. Jain, ed. *China and South Asia Relations, 1947–1980*, vol. 1: India (Atlantic Highlands, NJ: Humanities Press, 1981), 64–67.

27. On the origins and suppression of the Khampa rebellion, see John Kenneth Knaus, *Orphans of the Cold War: America and the Tibetan Struggle for Survival* (New York: Public Affairs Press, 1999).

28. Personal interview with Sumit Ganguly, New Delhi, July 1988.

29. For a candid account, see Major-General D. K. Palit (retd.), *War in the High Himalaya: The Indian Army in Crisis, 1962* (London: Hurst, 1991).

30. For a discussion of the concept of compellence, see Thomas Schelling, *Arms and Influence* (New Haven, CT: Yale University Press, 1967).

31. Michael Brecher, "Nonalignment under Stress: The West and the India-China Border War," *Pacific Affairs* 52, no. 4 (1979–1980): 612–630.

32. John Kenneth Galbraith, *A Life in Our Times* (New York: Ballantine Books, 1982).

33. Kenneth J. Conboy and M. S. Kohli, *Spies in the Himalayas: Secret Missions and Perilous Climbs* (Manhattan, KS: University of Kansas Press, 2003).

34. B. R. Nanda, ed. *Indian Foreign Policy: The Nehru Years* (Honolulu: University of Hawaii Press, 1976).

35. Sumit Ganguly, personal interview with former Indian foreign secretary, New York, September 1988.

36. For the plans for modernization of the Indian armed forces, see Lorne J. Kavic, *India's Quest for Security*.

37. Raju G. C. Thomas, *The Defence of India: A Budgetary Perspective on Strategy and Politics* (New Delhi: Macmillan, 1978).

38. John P. Lewis and Xue Litai, *China Builds the Bomb* (Stanford, CA: Stanford University Press, 1991).

39. Ashok Kapur, *India's Nuclear Option: Atomic Diplomacy and Decision-Making* (New York: Praeger, 1976).

40. Russell Brines, *The Indo-Pakistani Conflict* (New York: Pall Mall, 1968).

41. These tensions are explored in A. G. Noorani, "India's Quest for Nuclear Guarantee, "*Asian Survey* 7, no. 7 (1967): 490–502.

42. On Indian fears of Chinese nuclear blackmail, see Sisir Gupta, "The Indian Dilemma," in *A World of Nuclear Powers?* ed. Alastair Buchan (Englewood Cliffs, NJ: Prentice Hall, 1966).

43. Hasan Zaheer, *The Separation of East Pakistan: The Rise and Realization of Bengali Muslim Nationalism* (Karachi, Pakistan: Oxford University Press, 1997).

44. Surinder Nihal Singh, *The Yogi and the Bear: The Story of Indo-Soviet Relations* (New Delhi: Allied, 1986).

45. For an argument that suggests that Indian and Soviet interests largely converged, see Robert Horn, *Soviet-Indian Relations: Issues and Influence* (New York: Praeger, 1981).

46. Partha S. Ghosh and Rajaram Panda, "Domestic Support for Mrs. Gandhi's Afghan Policy: The Soviet Factor in Indian Politics," *Asian Survey* 23, no. 3 (1983): 261–279.

47. Zaheer, *The Separation of East Pakistan.*

48. Robert Jackson, *South Asian Crisis: India, Pakistan, and Bangla Desh* (New York: Praeger, 1975); Richard Sisson and Leo E. Rose, *War and Secession: Pakistan, India, and the Creation of Bangladesh* (Berkeley: University of California Press, 1991); Gary J. Bass, *The Blood Telegram: Nixon, Kissinger, and a Forgotten Genocide* (New York: Alfred A. Knopf, 2013).

49. Lieutenant-General J. F. R. Jacob (retd.), *Surrender at Dhaka: Birth of a Nation* (New Delhi: Manohar, 1997).

50. For details see Major-General D. K. Palit (retd.), *The Lightning Campaign: Indo-Pakistan War 1971* (London: Compton Press, 1971); also see Pran Chopra, *India's Second Liberation* (New Delhi: Vikas, 1973); and Srinath Raghavan, *India 1971: A Global History of the Creation of Bangladesh* (Cambridge, MA: Harvard University Press, 2013).

51. Christopher van Hollen, "The Tilt Policy Revisited: Nixon-Kissinger Geopolitics and South Asia," *Asian Survey* 20, no. 4 (1980): 339–361.

52. Steven Hoffman, "Anticipation, Disaster and Victory: India, 1962–71," *Asian Survey* 12, no. 11 (1972): 960–979.

53. For a discussion, see Devin T. Hagerty, "India's Regional Security Doctrine," *Asian Survey* 31, no. 4 (1991): 351–363.

54. For an alternative formulation, see M. S. Rajan, "The Indo-Soviet Treaty and Indian Nonalignment Policy," *Australian Outlook*, 26, no. 2 (1972): 204–215.

55. Rikhi Jaipal, "The Indian Nuclear Explosion," *International Security* 1, no. 4 (1977): 44–51.

56. On Ramanna's admission, see "India's Nuclear Weapons Program: Smiling Buddha: 1974," Nuclear Weapon Archive, at http://nuclearweaponarchive.org/India/IndiaSmiling.html.

57. Raj Changappa, *Weapons of Peace: Secret Story of India's Quest to be a Nuclear Power* (New Delhi: HarperCollins, 2000).

58. K. B. Lall, "India and the New International Economic Order," *International Studies* 17, nos. 3–4 (1978): 435–461.

59. See the Group of 77 at the United Nations, at http://www.g77.org/doc/.

60. Harsh Sethi, "The Problem," *Seminar* 516 (2002), at http://www.india-seminar.com/2002/516/516%20the%20problem.htm.

61. Fouad Ajami, "The Third World Challenge: The Fate of Nonalignment," *Foreign Affairs* 59, no. 2 (1980–1981), at http://www.foreignaffairs.com/articles/34586/fouad-ajami/the-third-world-challenge-the-fate-of-nonalignment.

62. On the subject of balancing against threats, see the standard statement in Stephen M. Walt, *The Origins of Alliances* (Ithaca: Cornell University Press, 1987).

63. Surinder Nihal Singh, "Why India Goes to Moscow for Arms," *Asian Survey* 24, no. 7 (1984): 707–720.

64. Robert J. Lieber, Kenneth A. Oye, and Donald Rothchild, eds. *Eagle Defiant: United States Foreign Policy in the 1980s* (New York: Little, Brown, 1983).

65. Sumit Ganguly and Andrew Scobell, "India and the United States: Forging a Security Partnership?" *World Policy Journal* 22, no. 2 (2005): 37–43.

66. This is a conscious inversion of Robert Axelrod's proposition about the possibilities of cooperation in an anarchic international environment. We argue that the "shadow of the past"—memories of past interactions—can profoundly affect the possibilities of cooperation. See Robert Axelrod, *The Evolution of Cooperation* (New York: Basic Books, 1984).

67. Thom Shanker, "Old India Mood, New Ideas Await Gorbachev Visit," *Los Angeles Times*, November 23, 1986, at http://articles.latimes.com/1986-11-23/news/mn-12608_1_soviet-union.

68. On this point, see the discussion in Kanti Bajpai, "India: Modified Structuralism," in *Asian Security Practice: Material and Ideational Influences*, ed. Muthiah Alagappa (Stanford, CA: Stanford University Press, 1998).

69. Rahul Mukherji, "India's Aborted Liberalization—1966," *Pacific Affairs* 7, no. 3 (2000): 375–392.

70. On ideational changes and their impact on policy-making, see Mark Blyth, *Great Transformations: Economic Ideas and Institutional Change in the Twentieth Century* (Cambridge: Cambridge University Press, 2002).

71. Sumit Ganguly, personal interview with senior Indian diplomat, Washington, DC, July, 1992.

72. S. D. Muni, "India and the Post–Cold War World: Opportunities and Challenges," *Asian Survey* 31, no. 9 (1991): 862–874.

73. For prior attempts at economic liberalization and their consequences, see Mukherji, "India's Aborted Liberalization."

74. T. N. Srinivasan and Suresh D. Tendulkar, *Reintegrating India with the World Economy* (Washington, DC: Peterson Institute, 2003).

75. Vijay Joshi, "India and the Impossible Trinity," *World Economy* 26, no. 4 (2003): 555–583.

76. Ramesh Thakur, "India After Nonalignment," *Foreign Affairs* 71, no. 2 (1992): 165–182.

77. C. Raja Mohan, *Managing Multipolarity: India's Security Strategy in a Changing World, Special Report #39* (Seattle: National Bureau of Asian Research, 2012).

78. On the issue of nuclear ambiguity, see Rajesh M. Basrur, "Two Decades of Minimum Deterrence in South Asia: A Comparative Perspective," in *The Politics of Nuclear Weapons in South Asia*, ed. Bhumitra Chakma (Farnham, UK: Ashgate, 2011), 11–28.

79. For a detailed discussion of the forces that led to the Indian nuclear tests, see Sumit Ganguly, "India's Pathway to Pokhran II: The Prospects and Sources of New Delhi's Nuclear Weapons Program," *International Security* 23, no. 4 (1999): 148–177.

80. Much of this can be gleaned from Strobe Talbott, *Engaging India: Diplomacy, Democracy, and the Bomb* (Washington, DC: Brookings Institution, 2006).

81. Manmohan Singh, as quoted in Sumit Ganguly, "Explaining Realignment," *ISAS Insights*, no. 115, Institute of South Asian Studies, National University of Singapore, 2010.

82. Ashish Kumar Sen, "U.S., India Discuss Ways to Enhance Economic Relationship," *Washington Times*, June 13, 2012, at http://www.washingtontimes.com/news/2012/jun/13/officials-open-us-indian-strategic-dialogue/.

83. Shashank Joshi, "China, India, and the 'Whole Set-Up and Balance of the World,'" *St Antony's International Review* 6, no. 2 (2011): 83–111.

84. James R. Holmes, Andrew C. Winner, and Toshi Yoshihara, *Indian Naval Strategy in the Twenty-First Century* (London: Routledge, 2009); also see the discussion in David Brewster, "Indian Strategic Thinking About the Indian Ocean: Striving Towards Strategic Leadership," *India Review* 14, no. 3 (April–June 2015): 221–237.

85. On this issue, see Sunil Khilnani, Rajiv Kumar, Pratap Bhanu Mehta, Lt. Gen. Prakash Menon (retd.), Nandan Nilekani, Srinath Raghavan, Shyam Saran, and Siddharth Varadarajan, *Nonalignment 2.0: A Foreign and Strategic Policy for India in the Twenty First Century* (New Delhi: Centre for Policy Research, 2012).

86. Rommel Rodrigues, "India Is No Rising Power, It Has Already Risen," *Indian Express*, November 8, 2010, at http://www.newindianexpress.com/nation/article278868.ece.

87. See for example, Stephen P. Cohen, *India: Emerging Power* (Washington, DC: Brookings Institution, 2002); also see William H. Avery, *China's Nightmare, America's Dream: India as the Next Global Power* (New Delhi: Amaryllis, 2012); and for the views of a prominent economist, see Arvind Panagariya, *India: The Emerging Giant* (New York: Oxford University Press, 2008).

88. Sumit Ganguly, "Delhi's Strategy Deficit," *National Interest*, March 20, 2012, at http://nationalinterest.org/commentary/delhis-strategy-deficit-6663?page=1; also see

Sumit Ganguly, 'Think Again: India's Rise," *Foreign Policy*, July 5, 2012, at http://www.foreignpolicy.com/articles/2012/07/05/think_again_indias_rise.

89. See the discussion in Rahul Sagar, "Grand Ideology, Bland Strategy," in *Grand Strategy for India: 2020 and Beyond*, ed. Krishnappa Venkatshamy and Princy George (New Delhi: Pentagon Press, 2012).

90. For a trenchant discussion of the ideological roots of the Bharatiya Janata Party and its implications for foreign policy, see Rahul Sagar, "Jiski Lathi, Uski Bhains: The Hindu Nationalist View of International Politics," in *India's Grand Strategy: History, Theory, Cases*, ed. Kanti Bajpai, Saira Basit and V. Krishnappa (New Delhi: Routledge, 2014); for a wider discussion, see Chris Ogden, *Hindu Nationalism and the Evolution of Contemporary Indian Security: Portents of Power* (New Delhi: Oxford University Press, 2014).

91. Ganguly, "Think Again: India's Rise."

ELEVEN Defense and Security Policies

1. For an excellent discussion, see Lorne J. Kavic, *India's Quest for Security: Defense Policies 1947–1965* (Berkeley: University of California Press, 1967).

2. For a candid account, see Major-General D. K. Palit (retd.), *War in the High Himalaya: The Indian Army in Crisis, 1962* (London: Hurst, 1992).

3. John W. Garver. *Protracted Contest: Sino-Indian Rivalry in the Twentieth Century* (Seattle: University of Washington Press, 2001).

4. Raju G. C. Thomas, *The Defense of India: A Budgetary Perspective on Strategy and Politics* (Bombay: Macmillan, 1978).

5. Steven A. Hoffman, "Anticipation, Disaster, and Victory," *Asian Survey* 12, no. 11 (1972): 960–979.

6. Sumit Ganguly, "India's Pathway to Pokhran II: The Prospects and Sources of India's Nuclear Weapons Program," *International Security* 23, no. 4 (1999): 149–177.

7. Verghese Koithara, *Managing India's Nuclear Forces* (Washington, DC: Brookings Institution, 2012).

8. For a rather critical appraisal, which attributes India's failure to realize its full military potential to the absence of a strategic culture, see "Can India Become a Great Power?" *The Economist*, March 30, 2013, at http://www.economist.com/news/leaders/21574511-indias-lack-strategic-culture-hobbles-its-ambition-be-force-world-can-india; for a thoughtful rejoinder, see Dhruva Jaishankar, "Gentle Giant," *Foreign Policy*, March 6, 2013, at http://www.foreignpolicy.com/articles/2013/03/06/gentle_giant_india_military.

9. Sumit Ganguly and David P. Fidler, eds., *India and Counterinsurgency: Lessons Learned* (London: Routledge, 2009).

10. PTI, "Naxalism Biggest Threat to Internal Security: Manmohan," *The Hindu*, May 24, 2010, at http://www.thehindu.com/news/national/article436781.ece.

11. See South Asia Terrorism Portal, at http:///www.satp.org/satporgtp/countries/india/maoist/data_sheets/2008–2011.pdf.

12. Bharti Jain, "Andhra Greyhound Model for Other Maoist-Hit States on Anvil," *Times of India*, February 17, 2013, at http://articles.timesofindia.indiatimes.com/2013-02-17/india/37144475_1_home-ministry-naxal-review-special-forces.

13. Sumit Ganguly, *The Crisis in Kashmir: Portents of War, Hopes of Peace* (New York: Cambridge University Press, 1997).

14. Praveen Swami, *India, Pakistan and the Secret Jihad: The Covert War in Kashmir, 1947–2004* (London: Routledge, 2007); Peter Chalk, "Pakistan's Role in the Kashmir Insurgency," *Jane's Intelligence Review*, September 1, 2001.

15. On national disapprobation, see Tapan Bose, Dinesh Mohan, Gautam Navlakha, and Sumanta Banerjee, "India's Kashmir War," *Economic and Political Weekly* 25, no. 13 (1990): 650–662; on international criticism, see Vincent Iacopino and Patricia Grossman, *A Pattern of Impunity: The Human Rights Crisis in Kashmir* (New York: Human Rights Watch, 1993).

16. Hamish Telford, "Counter-Insurgency in India: Observations from Punjab and Kashmir," *Journal of Conflict Studies* 21, no. 1 (2001): 73–100, at http://journals.hil.unb.ca/index.php/JCS/article/view/4293/4888; for an attempt to assess the costs, see Gautam Navlakha, "Internal Security: Cost of Repression," *Economic and Political Weekly* 34, no. 20 (1999): 1171–1174.

17. Randeep Singh Nandal, "State Data Refutes Claim of 1 Lakh Killed in Kashmir," *Times of India*, June 20, 2011, at http://articles.timesofindia.indiatimes.com/2011-06-20/india/29679480_1_militants-security-forces-sopore.

18. Abhishek Bhalla, "Maoists Kill One Soldier Every Three Days: Naxal Corridor Is Three Times Deadlier than Terror-Hit States," *Daily Mail India*, February 16, 2014, at http://www.dailymail.co.uk/indiahome/indianews/article-2560761/Maoists-kill-one-soldier-three-days-Naxal-corridor-three-times-deadlier-terror-hit-states.html.

19. Prime Minister's High Level Committee, Cabinet Secretariat, Government of India, *Social, Economic and Educational Status of the Muslim Community of India* (New Delhi: Department of Minority Affairs, Government of India, 2006).

20. For an excellent, data-based discussion, see Katherine Hoffman, Jiro Kodera, Peter LeFrancois, Charles Nicas, and Jackson Reed, *Sunni Militancy in India: An Analytical Atlas*, Stanford IPS/MPP Practicum Project for Joint Intelligence Task Force–Combating Terrorism, Defense Intelligence Agency, March 18, 2011, at http://publicpolicy.stanford.edu/system/files/SunniMilitancyIndia_DIA.pdf.

21. Anwar Husain Syed, *China and Pakistan: The Diplomacy of an Entente Cordiale* (London: Oxford University Press, 1975).

22. Isaac B. Kardon, *China and Pakistan: Emerging Strains in the Entente Cordiale* (Arlington: Project 2049 Institute, 2011).

23. For an alternative argument that highlights India's continued ability to shape the security environment in the Indian Ocean littoral, see Nilanthi Samaranayake, "India: Still at the Center of the Indian Ocean," *YaleGlobal Online*, February 22, 2013, at http://yaleglobal.yale.edu/print/8427.

24. On the role of the LeT in the Bombay/Mumbai attacks, see Stephen Tankel, *Storming the World Stage: The Story of Lashkar-e-Taiba* (New York: Columbia University

Press, 2011); also see Cathy Scott-Clark and Adrian Levy, *The Siege: 68 Hours Inside the Taj Hotel* (New York: Penguin Random House, 2014).

25. Pakistan's claim to the state is irredentist, as it is India's only Muslim-majority state and abuts Pakistan. On the issue of irredentism, see Myron Weiner, "The Macedonian Syndrome: An Historical Model of International Relations and Political Development," *World Politics* 23, no. 4 (1971): 665–683.

26. On this subject, see chapter 6 in Karen Rasler, William R. Thompson, and Sumit Ganguly, *How Rivalries End* (Philadelphia: University of Pennsylvania Press, 2013).

27. For a discussion, see Sumit Ganguly, *Conflict Unending: Indo-Pakistani Tensions Since 1947* (New York: Columbia University Press, 2001).

28. See "Catching the Dragon," *The Economist*, February 9, 2015, at http://www.economist.com/news/business-and-finance/21642656-indias-economy-grew-faster-chinas-end-2014-catching-dragon.

29. Sumit Ganguly and S. Paul Kapur, "The Transformation of U.S.-India Relations," *Asian Survey* 47, no. 4 (2007), 642–656.

30. Sumit Ganguly, Andrew Scobell, and Brian Shoup, *More Than Words: Indo-US Strategic Cooperation Into the 21st Century* (London: Routledge, 2007).

31. Rajat Pandit, "India to Rush Troops to Ladakh If No De-escalation on Face-Off with China," *Times of India*, April 24, 2013, at http://articles.timesofindia.indiatimes.com/2013-04-24/india/38789622_1_indian-army-flag-meeting-chinese-troops.

32. Mya Muang, "On the Road to Mandalay: A Case Study of the Sinonization of Upper Burma," *Asian Survey* 34, no. 5 (1994): 446–459.

33. Thant Myint-U, *Where China Meets India: Burma and the New Crossroads* (New York: Farrar, Straus and Giroux, 2012).

34. Renaud Egreteau, "A Passage to Burma? India, Development, and Democratization in Myanmar," *Contemporary Politics* 17, no. 4 (2011): 467–486.

35. Ramtanu Maitra, "India Bids to Rule the Waves," *Asia Times Online*, October 19, 2005, at http://www.atimes.com/atimes/South_Asia/GJ19Df03.html.

36. For a detailed discussion, see David Scott, "India's 'Extended Neighborhood' Concept: Power Projection for a Rising Power," *India Review* 8, no. 2 (2009): 107–143.

37. Mark Mazzetti and Somini Sengupta, "Defense Secretary Gates Visits India to Strengthen Security Ties," *New York Times*, February 27, 2008, at http://www.nytimes.com/2008/02/27/world/asia/27iht-gates.3.10480817.html; also see Rahul Bedi and Richard Spencer, "US-India Defence Deal 'to Counter China'," *The Daily Telegraph*, February 26, 2008, at http://www.telegraph.co.uk/news/worldnews/1579938/US-India-defence-deal-to-counter-China.html.

38. For a critical discussion of the strategy, see "Pivotal Concerns," *The Economist*, May 11, 2013, at http://www.economist.com/news/asia/21577369-call-it-pivot-or-rebalancing-americas-pacific-policy-looks-little-wobbly-pivotal-concerns.

39. Francine R. Frankel, "The Breakout of China-India Strategic Rivalry in Asia and the Indian Ocean," *Journal of International Affairs* 64, no. 2 (2011): 1–17.

40. Rajat Pandit, "India Readies Hi-tech Naval Base to Keep Eye on China," *Times of India*, March 26, 2013, at http://articles.timesofindia.indiatimes.com/2013-03-26/india/38039841_1_akula-ii-ins-chakra-underground-nuclear-submarine-base.

41. For an argument that suggests that the U.S.-Pakistan strategic nexus should be reconfigured, see C. Christine Fair and Sumit Ganguly, "The Unworthy Ally," *Foreign Affairs* 4, no. 5 (September/October 2015): 160–171.

42. Ravi Sharma, "Failing to Deliver," *Frontline*, April 17, 2013, at http://www.frontline.in/the-nation/failing-to-deliver/article4613900.ece.

43. Stephen P. Cohen and Sunil Dasgupta, *Arming without Aiming: India's Military Modernization* (Washington, DC: Brookings Institution, 2010).

44. Douglas Barrie, "Desires and Devices," *Aviation Week and Space Technology*, June 14, 2010.

45. Asia-Pacific Staff, "Indian Light Combat Aircraft to Fly in Exercise," *Aviation Week*, February 21, 2013.

46. PTI, "Dream of Fitting Indigenous Kaveri Engine into LCA-Tejas Over," *Economic Times*, January 25, 2013, at http://articles.economictimes.indiatimes.com/2013-01-25/news/36548063_1_kaveri-engine-gas-turbine-research-establishment-lca-mark.

47. Neelam Mathews, "India's LCA Limited Series to Fly with F404-GE-IN20," *Aerospace Daily and Defense Report*, February 1, 2008.

48. TNN, "CCS Asks DRDO to Expedite Military Projects," *Times of India*, April 5, 2013, at http://articles.timesofindia.indiatimes.com/2013-04-05/india/38305573_1_drdo-long-range-surface-to-air-missile-kaveri.

49. Yaakov Katz, "Israel Outstrips Russia as India's Main Defense Supplier," *Jerusalem Post*, February 15, 2009.

50. S. Nihal Singh, "Why India Goes to Moscow for Arms," *Asian Survey* 24, no. 7 (1984): 707–720.

51. P. Jayaram, "India-Russia Defence Ties Back on Track; Two PMs Reach Compromise on Dispute Over Aircraft Carrier," *Straits Times*, February 13, 2008.

52. Randeep Ramesh, "US Rushes to Get Slice of $45 Billion Indian Arms Pie," *The Guardian*, February 22, 2008, at http://www.theguardian.com/world/2008/feb/22/armstrade.india.

53. Neelam Mathews, "India Orders Eight Boeing P-8Is," *Aerospace and Daily Defense Report*, January 6, 2009.

54. Neelam Mathews, "Harpoon Sale to Boost Indian AF Air-to-Surface Warfare Ability," *Aerospace Daily and Defense Report*, September 16, 2008.

55. Neelam Mathews, "India Orders Eight Boeing P-8Is."

56. Jay Menon, "Pratt Gets Engine Order For Indian C-17s," *Aerospace Daily and Defense Report*, December 20, 2011.

57. Jen DiMascio, "Indian Air Force To Buy 22 Apache Helos," *Aerospace Daily & Defense Report*, September 24, 2012.

58. K. V. Prasad, "Rafale Edges out Eurofighter," *The Hindu*, January 31, 2012, at http://www.thehindu.com/news/national/rafale-edges-out-eurofighter/article2847987

.ece; also see Jay Menon, "India Shifts Allegiance from Russian Arms Suppliers," *Aerospace Daily and Defense Report*, May 10, 2011.

59. Ashley J. Tellis, *Dogfight: India's Medium Multi-Role Combat Aircraft Decision* (Washington, DC: Carnegie Endowment for International Peace, 2011).

60. Sumit Ganguly, personal interview with senior, retired American policymaker, Bloomington, Indiana, April 2012.

61. HT correspondent, "Parrikar Says India Will Buy 36 Rafale Jets From France Instead of 126," *Hindustan Times*, June 1, 2014.

62. Ashley J. Tellis, *India's Emerging Nuclear Posture: Between Recessed Deterrent and Ready Arsenal* (Santa Monica, CA: RAND Corporation, 2001).

63. For a trenchant, if overly theoretical discussion of the concept, see Rajesh Manohar Basrur, *Minimum Deterrence and India's Nuclear Security* (Palo Alto, CA: Stanford University Press, 2006).

64. For an excellent account of some of the key institutional factors that have hobbled India's nuclear forces, see Gaurav Kampani, "New Delhi's Long Nuclear Journey: How Secrecy and Institutional Roadblocks Delayed India's Weaponization," *International Security* 38, no. 4 (Spring 2014): 79–114.

65. Ravi Veloor, "India Extends Reach with N-sub Launch: Able to Stay Underwater for Months, It Gives New Delhi a Critical Edge," *Straits Times*, July 29, 2009; also see Ashok Sharma, "India Joins Nuclear Sub Club," *Toronto Star*, July 27, 2009, at http://www.thestar.com/news/world/2009/07/27/india_joins_nuclear_sub_club.html.

66. Samuel Osborne, "INS Arihant: India Nears Completion of Nuclear Submarine, 'Slayer of Enemies,' So What Does It Mean for the World?" *The Independent*, February 27, 2016.

67. T. S. Subramanian, "Agni-VI All Set to Take Shape," *The Hindu*, February 4, 2013, at http://www.thehindu.com/news/national/agnivi-all-set-to-take-shape/article4379416.ece; for a critique, on military and strategic grounds, of the DRDO's quest for the Agni VI, see Frank O'Donnell, "Managing India's Missile Aspirations," *IDSA Comments*, February 10, 2013, at http://idsa.inidsacomments/managingIndiasMissileAspirations_fodonnell_100213.

68. Eric Auner, "Indian Missile Defense Program Advances," *Arms Control Today*, January/February 2013, at http://www.armscontrol.org/act/2013_01–02/Indian-Missile-Defense-Program-Advances ; also see Y. Mallikarjun and T. S. Subramanian, "India Proves Capability of Missile Defence System," *The Hindu*, November 23, 2012, at http://www.thehindu.com/news/national/india-proves-capability-of-missile-defence-system/article4126430.ece.

69. PTI, "Strategic Command to Acquire 40 Nuclear-Capable Aircraft," *Hindustan Times*, September 12, 2010, at http://www.hindustantimes.com/india-news/newdelhi/strategic-command-to-acquire-40-nuclear-capable-fighters/article1–599141.aspx.

70. For a critique, see R. Ramachandran, "Unclear Nuclear Identity," *Frontline* 16, no. 18 _August 28–September 10, 1999), at http://www.frontline.in/static/html/fl1618/16180160.htm.

71. Agencies, "No-First-Use Nuclear Doctrine to Stay: SM Krishna to Lok Sabha," *Indian Express*, March 16, 2011, at http://indianexpress.com/article/india/latest-news/nofirstuse-nuclear-doctrine-to-stay-sm-krishna-to-lok-sabha/.

TWELVE Ascending India—Its State-Capacity Problems and Prospects

1. For a useful assessment, see Ashutosh Varshney, "How Has Indian Federalism Done?" *Studies in Indian Politics* 1, no. 1 (2013): 43–63.

2. Nehru was even opposed to the linguistic reorganization of India's states because he feared that the creation of states on a linguistic basis could lead to the disintegration of the country. For a thoughtful discussion, see Jyotirindra Da Gupta, *Language Conflict and National Development: Group Politics and National Language Policy in India* (Berkeley: University of California Press, 1970); for a more recent discussion, see Louise Tillin, *Remapping India: New States and Their Political Origins* (Oxford: Oxford University Press, 2013).

3. For a discussion of these issues, see Francine Frankel, *India's Political Economy: The Gradual Revolution, 1947–2004* (New Delhi: Oxford University Press, 2006).

4. For details, see Inder Malhotra, "India's Trial Run in Kerala," *Indian Express*, February 3, 2014.

5. Paul R. Brass, *The Politics of India Since Independence* (Cambridge: Cambridge University Press, 1994).

6. This, of course, does not hold true for those states that are economic laggards, as they remain heavily dependent of the central government for economic assistance. For a discussion of fiscal federalism after India's turn toward the market, see Baldev Raj Nayar, *Globalization and India's Economic Integration* (Washington, DC: Georgetown University Press, 2014).

7. On the creation of the National Investigation Agency, see Rama Lakshmi, "Lower House of Indian Parliament Passes Tough Anti-Terrorism Legislation," *Washington Post*, December 18, 2008; on the goods and services bill, see "Congress Warns of House Impasse over GST Bill," *Times of India*, June 10, 2015, at http://timesofindia.indiatimes.com/business/india-business/Congress-warns-of-House-impasse-over-GST-bill/articleshow/47608146.cms,

accessed February 17, 2016.

8. K. J. Holsti, *The State, War, and the State of War* (Cambridge: Cambridge Studies in International Relations, 1996).

9. Steven Levitsky and Lucan A. Way, *Competitive Authoritarianism: Hybrid Regimes After the Cold War* (Cambridge: Cambridge University Press, 2010).

10. Available at World Bank, Worldwide Governance Indicators, at http://info.worldbank.org/governance/wgi/index.aspx#faq.

11. See, for instance, Ranjit Goswami, "India's Population in 2050: Extreme Projections Demand Extreme Actions," *East Asia Forum*, April 5, 2013, at www.eastasiaforum.org/2013/04/05/indias-population-in-2050-extreme-projections-demand-extreme

-action/; also see BBC News, "UN: India to be World's Most Populous Country by 2028," June 14, 2013, at www.bbc.com/news/world-asia-22907307.

12. The Asian Development Bank rank orders forty-nine Asian states on water security issues *in Asian Water Development Outlook 2013: Measuring Water Security in Asian and the Pacific* (Manila: Asian Development Bank, 2013), at www.adb.org/sites/default/files/publication/30190/asia-water-developmment-outlook-2013.pdf.

13. See Geoff Hiscock, "Securing India's Energy a Major Challenge for New PM Modi," May 26, 2014, at www.cnn.com/2014/05/26/business/india-energy-modi/index.html.

14. Vidya Nadkarni, "India—An Aspiring Global Power," in *Emerging Powers in a Comparative Perspective: The Political and Economic Rise of the BRIC*, ed. Vidya Nadkarni and Norma C. Noonan (New York: Bloomsbury, 2013), 151.

15. Japan could be substituted easily for South Korea without distorting India's low position on the infrastructural hierarchy.

16. Homi Kharas, "India's Promise: An Affluent Society in One Generation," in *India 2039: An Affluent Society in One Generation*, ed. Harinder S. Kohli and Anil Sood (New Delhi: Sage, 2010), 23–24.

17. Baldev Raj Nayer aptly calls India a "lagging" state in *The Myth of the Shrinking State: Globalization and the State in India* (New Delhi: Oxford University Press, 2009), 173. Prichett's reference to India as a "flailing state" is a kindred notion. See Lant Pritchett. "Is India a Flailing State? Detours on the Four Lane Highway to Modernization" (Harvard Kennedy School Faculty Research Working Paper Series RWP09–013, May, 2009), at https://research.hks.harvard.edu/publications/workingpapers/citation.aspx?PubId=6599.

Index

Afghanistan, 9, 15, 71, 170, 241, 243, 244, 277, 282
Africa, 36, 78–79
agriculture: in China, 132, 142, 145; in India, 9, 130, 132, 143, 144–145, 152–153, 155, 186–187, 193–194, 195; waste from, 168; water needs of, 170
airborne warning and control systems (AWACS), 265
air conditioning, 165, 166
aircraft carriers, 8, 229
Air India, 11
airports, 158, 161, 163–164
All India Dravida Munnetra Kazhagam, 203
Andaman Islands, 260
Andhra Pradesh, 114, 254, 261
Antony, A. K., 262
Arcelor, 9
Argentina, 86
Armed Forces Special Powers Act (Jammu and Kashmir) (1990), 218
Assam, 110, 112, 217
Australia, 86, 231, 248
Austria, 26, 32, 35, 36, 86
Austria-Hungary, 29, 39, 96, 129

Austro-Prussian War (1866), 96
authoritarianism, 71, 216
automobiles, 164

BAE Systems, 3
Bajrang Dal, 223
Baldwin, Katherine, 152–153
ballistic missile defense (BMD), 267, 268
Baluchistan, 261
Banerjee, Mamata, 203
Bangalore, 154
Bangladesh, 71, 110, 112, 113, 169, 170, 222, 257, 259, 277
Baru, Sanjaya, 131
Belgian Congo, 237
Belgium, 86
Bengal, 232
Bhagwati, Jagdish, 183–184, 196, 198
Bhagwati, P. N., 210
Bharatiya Jana Sangh, 222
Bharatiya Janata Party (BJP), 222, 225, 256, 261; election law violations by, 206; electoral defeat of, 15, 223, 247; government led by, 11, 223–224; great power status pledged by, 8; ideology of, 203; secularists attacked by, 16, 223, 224

Bhutan, 113
Bihar, 203, 214, 217
biomass, 164, 166
Bismarck, Otto von, 36
blackouts, 165–166
Blake, William, 185–186, 214
Bonarriva, Joanna, 152–153
Brazil, 5, 21, 42, 133, 146, 275; coercive capacity in, 67–68; competitiveness of, 149; energy consumption in, 164, 165; extractive capability in, 66; hospital capacity in, 177; legitimacy in, 86, 277; middle-income trap in, 45, 46; stalled economy in, 147; state capacity in, 71; violence monopoly in, 69, 276
bribery, 219
Burma, 113, 257, 259, 260

Calcutta, 154, 226
Canada, 86, 136
caste system, 98, 116, 185–186, 195, 272
Catholics, 98
cell phones, 159, 170
Central Bureau of Investigation (CBI), 207, 208
central planning, 140, 160, 280
Central Vigilance Commission (CVC), 208
Chadda, Maya, 98, 104
Chauhan, Gajendra, 224
Chennai, 154
Chhattisgarh, 15, 114
child labor, 211
China, 5, 19, 21, 42, 113, 226, 230, 277, 279; assertiveness of, 248; authoritarianism in, 71; central planning in, 140; civil war in, 97; coercive capacity in, 67, 68; communist revolution in, 97; competitiveness of, 149; as economic power, 43, 45, 46, 132, 133–134, 136, 145; education in, 4, 142; energy consumption in, 28–29, 164, 165, 234; foreign direct investment in, 148, 149, 246; Great Leap Forward in, 225; as great power, 16, 26, 47, 128, 129, 181, 275; hospital capacity in, 177; India contrasted with, 132, 138–145, 152, 153, 164, 165, 181, 284–285; Indian border disputes with, 127–128, 231, 237–238, 241, 251–252, 255, 256–257; Indian Ocean ambitions of, 229, 260, 280; Indian rapprochement with, 246; Indian threats to, 267; India threatened by, 258, 259–260, 261; Japan vs., 17, 29, 39, 84; low-income economy of, 24; manufacturing in, 142; as naval power, 14, 256, 260; nuclear arsenal of, 240, 249; Pakistan allied with, 257; population of, 27; Soviet rapprochement with, 244–245; state capacity in, 71; taxation in, 66; urbanization in, 142, 143; U.S. rapprochement with, 241; violence monopoly in, 69, 276
Choucri, Nazli, 30–31, 33, 274
circular causation, 179
climate change, 7, 153, 168, 170, 281
Clinton, Hillary, 7
coal, 12, 32, 129, 164, 165, 167, 208
Coca-Cola, 9
Cohen, Stephen P., 20
Commonwealth Games, 207
communists: in China, 97; in India, 102, 103, 113–114, 203, 272
Comprehensive Test Ban Treaty (CTBT), 247
Comptroller and Account-General of India (CAG), 207–209
Congress Party, 100, 193, 213, 223, 224, 225, 239; decline of, 187–188, 202–203, 216, 272; land reform and, 186; in opposition, 212
Connable, Ben, 114–115
containment, 244
cooking, 159, 166, 180
Corbridge, Stuart, 143
Cossacks, 98
Cuba, 39

Dalai Lama, 237
dams, 113, 168
Defense Research and Development Organization (DRDO), 262, 267
deficit spending, 11, 130, 149
deforestation, 113
democracy, 200–228, 279–280; support for, 93–94
Denyer, Simon, 20
Dravidians, 118
Dreze, Jean, 183–184, 194–195
drinking water, 157, 159
drought, 168

East Pakistan, 240, 241–242
Eberstadt, Nicholas, 154
education, 33, 46, 48, 149, 158; in China, 4, 142; in India, 4, 143, 173–176, 186; inefficacy of, 148; primary vs. tertiary, 4
Egypt, 71, 277
Eighteen Nation Disarmament Conference (ENDC), 239
Election Commission of India (EC), 206
electricity, 11, 35, 153, 158, 159, 165–166, 180. *See also* energy consumption
energy consumption, 26, 28–29, 31, 164–167, 234, 282. *See also* biomass; coal; electricity; natural gas; nuclear energy; oil; renewable energy; solar energy; wind energy
Enforcement Directorate (ED), 208
England, 25, 26, 97
entrepreneurship, 11
Ethiopia, 36, 39
European Aeronautic Defence and Space Company (EADS), 3
exports, 47, 132, 142
extractive capability, 2, 6, 23, 41, 49, 57, 75–78, 273, 276; in Brazil, 66; defined, 54–55; economic growth linked to, 81, 84–85, 123; in India, 5, 18, 40, 73, 85–86, 277; in Italy, 82–84, 95; measures of, 60, 66, 71; military crises linked to,

80–81, 84; in southern hemisphere, 79; in United States, 82

Far Eastern Naval Command (FENC), 260
fascism, 36, 84
fertility, 154
fertilizer, 153, 168, 187
Film and Television Institute of India (FTII), 224
Finmeccanica, 3
First Gulf War, 130, 246
flooding, 282
Ford Motor Company, 9
foreign investment, 9, 12, 48–49, 145, 148, 149, 246
France, 26, 32, 35, 39, 66, 67, 97, 98, 129, 133
Franco-Prussian War (1870–71), 96
Frankel, Francine, 187

Gandhi, Indira: accession of, 240; assassination of, 116, 272; authoritarianism of, 216, 272–273; Congress Party undermined by, 203; institutions undermined by, 187–188, 198, 202; Parliament disdained by, 204; populism of, 187, 189; separatists suppressed by, 110, 113; Sikh extremists cultivated by, 116–17; Soviet Union cultivated by, 240–242, 243–244
Gandhi, Mohandas K., 213
Gandhi, Rajiv, 116–117, 189, 204, 244
Gandhi, Sanjay, 202
Ganges, 210, 211
Ganguly, Sumit, 116
gasoline prices, 11
Germany, 5, 16, 17, 26–27, 35; constraints on, 36–37; as economic power, 48, 128, 133; government revenues in, 83; industrialization in, 129; legitimacy in, 86; military capability of, 28, 29, 39; technological capability of, 275; war economy in, 80–81, 82, 85
Gilley, Bruce, 89–92, 93–94

Giridharadas, Anand, 19–20
Global Trends 2020 (National Intelligence Council), 7
Gorbachev, Mikhail, 244
Goswami, Ranjit, 176
Great Britain. *See* United Kingdom
Green Revolution, 132, 155, 186–187
Group of 77, 243
Gujarat, 118, 223
Gulf of Oman, 261

Harriss, John, 143
Hazare, Anna, 209, 219
Hendrix, Cullen, 56–57
Hindu Mahasabha, 222
Hindus, 109, 185, 216; fundamentalist, 110; migration of, 100, 111, 122; Muslim frictions with, 16, 111, 115, 116–118; political rise of, 222–223; poverty among, 190; rightist, 15–16
Hindustan Aeronautics Limited (HAL), 262
Holsti, K. J., 2, 5, 23, 49, 54, 57, 273, 276
Huguenots, 98
Hundred Years' War, 97
Huntington, Samuel, 188, 200–201
Hyderabad, 102

Ikea, 9
import-substituting industrialization (ISI), 246
India: affirmative action in, 214; agriculture in, 9, 130, 132, 143, 144–145, 152–153, 155, 186–187, 193–194, 195; bureaucracy in, 10, 11, 148, 160, 271; caste system in, 98, 116, 185–186, 195, 272; central planning in, 140, 160, 280; challenges facing, 11, 18; China contrasted with, 132, 138–145, 152, 153, 164, 165, 181, 284–285; Chinese border disputes with, 127–128, 231, 237–238, 241, 251–252, 255, 256–257; climate in, 153, 161–162, 165, 168, 281; coalition politics in, 10, 189, 223, 250, 272, 273; coercive capacity in, 67–68; competitiveness of, 5, 44–45, 148–152; corruption in, 11–12, 14, 73, 89, 104, 149, 160, 178–179, 195, 196, 201, 205, 209–210, 212, 219–222, 277, 278, 279; divisions within, 3; earlier works on, 18–23; economic welfare in, 93; economy of, 1, 2, 8–11, 18, 21, 45, 127–156, 275–276; education in, 4, 143, 173–176, 186; elections in, 88–89, 206, 211, 214, 216, 217, 225, 279; energy consumption in, 164–167, 234, 282; ethnic and religious strife in, 15–16; extractive capability in, 5, 18, 40, 73, 85–86, 277; federalism in, 272–273; financial crisis in, 246; food supply in, 130, 152, 281–282; foreign direct investment in, 148, 149; governing principles in, 98–99, 117; government revenues in, 85; growth potential of, 258, 285–286; hospital capacity in, 177; human rights in, 115–122, 215, 217–218, 279; as "in-between" state, 2–3, 5, 40, 54, 95, 148–149, 230, 271, 286; independence of, 3, 42, 99, 122, 232–235; inequality in, 6, 113, 123, 182–199; information technology in, 132, 142, 144, 146, 155; infrastructure in, 5, 18, 132–133, 149, 153, 157–181, 249, 278, 285; institutional innovation in, 209–212; institutional renewal in, 206–209; insurgencies in, 103–108, 114–115; internal warfare in, 102–114; judiciary in, 178–179, 202, 204, 211, 214, 279; land reform in, 186; legal system in, 178–179; legitimacy in, 6, 18, 67–68, 73, 86–89, 92–93, 95, 228, 277; manufacturing in, 143, 155; middle-income trap in, 145–148, 155, 276; military capability of, 1, 2, 6, 8, 12, 13–14, 232, 234, 238–239, 242, 247, 251–252, 256, 260–264, 266–268, 280, 281; naval capability of, 229, 239, 242; as nonaligned state, 13, 230, 236, 238, 240,

242, 243, 249, 251, 260; nuclear weapons program of, 8, 13, 21, 42, 78, 238, 240, 242, 244, 267; Pakistan vs., 14–15, 78, 109–110, 127–128, 230, 231, 236, 240, 246–247, 251, 252, 254–255, 261, 267, 280; parliamentary dysfunction in, 204–205; population growth in, 1, 3, 18, 153–154, 281; poverty in, 8–9, 13, 18, 22, 95, 128, 153, 155, 183–185, 187–191, 199, 212–213, 214, 235, 243, 249, 279; press freedom in, 214, 217; riots in, 15, 95, 97, 111, 115–116, 117–118; rise of, 1, 7–8, 17, 18, 271; secularism in, 16, 101–102, 109, 116, 118, 216, 217, 222–224, 225–226, 280; social services in, 172–179; South Korea contrasted with, 283–285; Soviet rapprochement with, 240–245, 249, 265; state capacity in, 2–4, 5, 7, 71; taxation in, 66, 73, 185, 273, 276; transportation in, 132, 149, 161–164; violence in, 97, 99–101, 115–122; violence monopoly in, 69, 73, 95, 276, 277; at war, 85, 95
India, Brazil and South Africa (IBSA), 248
India Calling (Giridharadas), 19–20
India: Emergent Power (Cohen), 20
Indian Administrative Service (IAS), 205
Indian Air Force (IAF), 3, 14, 262, 266
Indian Civil Service (ICS), 205
Indian Council for Historical Research (ICHR), 224
Indian National Congress (INC). *See* Congress Party
Indian National Sample Survey, 9
India: The Emerging Giant (Panagariya), 21
India: The Rise of an Asian Giant (Rothermund), 20–21
Indonesia, 136, 152
industrialization, 34, 73–74, 80, 81, 92, 128, 129, 235, 246
inflation, 130, 149
information technology (IT), 132, 142, 144, 146, 155
In Spite of the Gods (Luce), 19

Integrated Guided Missile Development Programme, 267
International Control Commission (ICC), 237
International Monetary Fund (IMF), 9, 130
International Security Assistance Force, 15
Internet access, 170, 172
Iran, 110, 136
Iran-Iraq war, 78
Iraq, 32
irrigation, 153, 165, 168
Islamism, 15–16
Italy: as colonial power, 39; divisions within, 16–17, 35–36, 37, 96, 98–99; economy of, 133; extractive capability in, 85; government revenues in, 83; as great power, 5, 16–17, 26–27, 35, 81, 128; industrialization in, 129; military capability of, 27–28, 29; at war, 81; war economy in, 80–81, 82, 84
Iyer, Krishna, 210

Jaguar, 9
Jaishankar, Subrahmanyam, 8
Jammu and Kashmir, 14, 15, 111, 118, 122, 180, 236, 240, 257; Muslims in, 102, 109, 110, 218; separatism in, 102–103, 211, 217–218, 225, 246, 253, 254, 255, 278
Japan: civil war in, 97; as colonial power, 17, 39; as economic power, 48, 128, 133, 147; energy consumption in, 28, 29, 234; government revenues in, 84; as great power, 5, 16, 17, 26, 28, 35, 128; Indian ties with, 231, 248, 261; industrialization in, 129; military capability of, 28, 29, 30, 38, 234; population changes in, 27, 154; technological capability of, 275; trial and error in, 38; at war, 29; war economy in, 80–81, 84, 85
Jarkhand, 114
Jayaram, Jayalalitha, 203
Jeffrey, Craig, 143

Jews, 98
Jharkhand, 15, 214
Johnson, Lyndon, 186
judiciary, 178–179

Kalmadi, Suresh, 207
Kargil War (1999), 207
Kashmir. *See* Jammu and Kashmir
Kerala, 194, 272
Khampa rebellion (1959), 237
Kharas, Homi, 46, 138–139, 285
Kishtwar, 15
Kissinger, Henry, 241
Kohli, Atul, 183, 184–185, 188
Kolkata, 154, 226
Korea, 17, 39, 47, 146–147, 154, 237, 261; India contrasted with, 283–285
Krishna, Raj, 10
Kuwait, 32

labor unions, 10, 11, 37
land reform, 186
Land Rover, 9
language policy, 107, 112, 214
Laos, 237
Lashkar-e-Taiba (LeT), 257
lateral pressure theory, 31, 274
Latin America, 77–79; middle-income trap in, 147
legitimacy, 2, 5, 23, 41, 49, 54, 57, 74, 273, 276; in Asia, 93–95; defined, 89–90; economic growth linked to, 277–278; extraction contrasted with, 75; in India, 6, 18, 67–68, 73, 86–89, 92–93, 95, 228, 277; internal security linked to, 55; measures of, 60–61, 66, 69, 71, 89–92
Levitsky, Steven, 60, 62–63, 68, 276
Levy, Jack S., 25, 26
Libicki, Martin, 114–115
Libya, 36, 39
Light Combat Aircraft (LCA), 262
limited war, 17
literacy, 18, 93, 143, 173, 182, 185, 214

Lockwood, William, 38
Luce, Edward, 19

Maharashtra, 194, 219
Mahatma Gandhi National Rural Employment Guarantee Scheme (NREGA), 193–194, 198
Malaysia, 169
Manchuria, 38, 39
Manipur, 112
Maoists, 15, 102, 103, 113–114, 122, 226–227, 249–250, 253
medium multi-role combat aircraft (MMCA), 3
Meiji Restoration, 97
Menon, V. P. Krishna, 235, 238
Mexico, 136
middle class, 20
Middle East, 8, 15–16, 78–79, 280
middle-income trap, 44, 45, 46, 47, 132; in India, 145–148, 155, 276
migration, 27, 100, 111, 122
MiG-21 fighter jet, 14
military spending, 8, 13–15, 234, 263–264
Ministry of Defense (MoD), 3
Mittal, Lakshmi, 9
Mizoram, 112
Modi, Narendra, 8, 12, 15, 206, 212, 223, 230, 232, 250
monsoons, 153, 161–162, 165, 168
Mughal Empire, 111, 112
Mukherjee, Shyama Prasad, 222
Mukherji, Rahul, 116
Mumbai, 154, 257
Muslim League, 100
Muslims, 98, 190, 222; Chinese, 257; extremist, 15–16, 226; Hindu frictions with, 16, 111, 115, 116–118; in Kashmir, 102, 109, 110, 218; migration of, 100, 122; state-sanctioned violence against, 223, 256
Myanmar, 113, 257, 259, 260
Myrdal, Gunnar, 19, 179

Nagaland, 112, 113
Napoleon I, emperor of the French, 98
Narlikar, Amrita, 21–22
Nasser, Gamal Abdel, 236
National Campaign for (the) People's Right to Information (NCPRI), 209
National Democratic Alliance (NDA), 8, 247
National Food for Work Programme (NFFWP), 193
National Food Security Act, 196
National Human Rights Commission (NHRC), 211
National Intelligence Council, 7
National Progressive Alliance (NPA), 193
Native Americans, 98
natural gas, 164
Naxalites, 102, 103, 113–114, 122, 215, 226, 253, 254, 278
Nayar, Balder, 40, 130, 274
Nehru, Jawaharlal: death of, 231, 239; as democratic nationalist, 213; governing principles of, 98; ideational foreign policy of, 232, 235, 237, 238, 243, 280; institution building favored by, 201–202, 272; as internationalist, 236, 251; Parliament respected by, 204; pluralism favored by, 113, 118
Nepal, 113, 169, 257, 259
Netherlands, 25, 26, 33, 43, 97
New Delhi, 210
New International Economic Order (NIEO), 242–243
Nigeria, 136
North, Robert, 30–31, 33, 274
North Atlantic Treaty Organization (NATO), 15
Nossiter, Bernard, 19
nuclear energy, 164
Nuclear Nonproliferation Treaty (NPT), 242, 247
nutrition, 11

Obama, Barack, 7, 260
oil: Indian imports of, 162, 164; price of, 11, 130, 243; supplies of, 32, 128, 280
O'Neill, Jim, 133
Organization of the Petroleum Exporting Countries (OPEC), 243
Ottoman Empire, 25

Pakistan, 42, 71, 100, 113, 122, 214, 277; China allied with, 257; corruption in, 222; India vs., 14–15, 78, 109–110, 127–128, 230, 231, 236, 240, 246–247, 251, 252, 254–255, 261, 267, 280; problems confronting, 258; U.S. allied with, 238, 243, 244, 262; water access in, 170
Panagariya, Arvind, 21, 183–184, 196, 198
Panetta, Leon, 7
Partial Test Ban Treaty (PTBT), 237
Paul, T. V., 40, 274
People's Liberation Army Navy (PLAN), 252, 260
Philippines, 39, 136, 170
Piedmont, 35–36
police states, 55–56
Political Order in Changing Societies (Huntington), 200
pollution, 168, 210
population growth, 1, 3, 18, 31–32, 33, 41, 153–154, 281
populism, 10, 11, 12
ports, 132, 158, 161, 162–163, 179
Portugal, 95, 97
Prevention of Terrorism Activities Act (POTA; 2002), 218
Privy Purses, 189
productivity, 12, 132, 158, 278
property rights, 47
Protestants, 98
Prussia, 26, 27, 32, 36, 96
public health, 33, 132, 149, 158, 168–170, 176–178, 179
Public Interest Litigation (PIL), 208, 210–211

Punjab, 101, 102, 111, 118, 187, 192, 217, 225, 254
Putin, Vladimir, 67

Rafale fighter jet, 3, 266
railroads, 132, 158, 161, 162, 167, 179
rainfall, 153, 161–162, 168
Rajasthan, 194
Rao, P. V. Narasimha, 189, 211, 246
Rao, Yellapragada Sudershan, 224
Rashtriya Janata Dal, 203
Rashtriya Swayamsevak Sangh, 223
Reagan, Ronald, 243, 244
Red Corridor, 114, 118
refugees, 282
renewable energy, 164
rent seeking, 10
rice, 152
Right of Children to Free and Compulsory Education (RTE), 196–197, 198
Right to Information Act (RTIA; 2005), 209–210
roads, 132, 157, 158, 159, 161–162, 179
Rogue Elephant (Denyer), 20
Rose, Charlie, 8
Rothermund, Dietmar, 20–21
Russia, 5, 42, 45, 133, 241, 277; civil war in, 97; coercive capacity in, 67, 68; competitiveness of, 149; energy consumption in, 164, 165; as great power, 26, 47, 275; industrialization in, 129; Japan vs., 17, 29; military aid to India from, 265; military capability of, 33, 46; state capacity in, 71, 72–73; taxation in, 66; violence monopoly in, 69, 276

Saarland, 32
Samporrna Grameen Rozgar Yojana (SGRY; Universal Rural Earning Scheme), 193
Sangh Parivar, 223
sanitation, 33, 157, 159
Schleswig-Holstein Wars, 96

sea-launched ballistic missiles (SLBM), 8
Security Advisory Board, 267
Sen, Amartya, 183–184, 225
separatism, 3, 97, 101, 112, 114; Dravidian, 118; in Kashmir, 102–103, 211, 217–218, 225, 246, 253, 254, 255, 278; prevalence of, 5, 95, 122; Punjabi, 111, 187; secularism as deterrent to, 222, 225–226; suppression of, 99, 113, 214, 217–218, 227, 279
Seshan, T. N., 206
sewage, 168
Shani, Ornit, 116
Shastri, Lal Bahadur, 204, 239, 240
Sikhs, 112, 115, 116; fundamentalist, 110; in Kashmir, 103, 109; migrations of, 100; in Punjab, 100–101, 102, 111
Silesia, 32
Singapore, 147
Singh, Gurharpal, 99, 100
Singh, Manmohan, 8, 9, 176, 226, 246, 253
Sinha, Yashwant, 8
Skowronek, Stephen, 37–38, 79, 84
solar energy, 164
Somalia, 71, 72
South Africa, 248
Southeast Asia, 8, 13, 38, 246, 248, 260, 261, 280
South Korea, 17, 39, 47, 146–147, 154, 237, 261; India contrasted with, 283–285
Soviet Union, 26, 97, 140, 231; collapse of, 13, 245, 280; Indian rapprochement with, 240–245, 249, 265; nuclear umbrella of, 247
space program, 8, 9
Spain, 29, 30, 35, 39, 86
Sri Lanka, 71, 214, 222, 257, 259, 277
standard of living, 92, 93
state capacity: in Brazil, 71; in China, 71; contrasting views of, 2, 16, 17, 22–23, 41; GDP and, 74; in India, 2–4, 5, 7, 71; links to, 6, 274–275; measures of,

40, 57–59, 62–66, 70, 276; obstacles to, 5–6, 49; in Russia, 71, 72–73; types of, 56–57
Stockholm Conference on the Human Environment (1972), 243
Strait of Hormuz, 261
Strategic Forces Command (SFC), 267
submarines, 8, 14, 261, 266–267
Subterranean Nuclear Explosions Project (SNEP), 239
Sukarno, 236
supply chains, 9
Sweden, 25, 26

Taiwan, 17, 147, 154
Taj Mahal, 210
Talbot, Ian, 99, 100
Taliban, 15
Tamil Nadu, 195, 203, 217
Tata Motors, 9
taxation, 55, 60, 65, 67, 71, 182; in China, 66; in India, 66, 73, 185, 273, 276; in Russia, 66; in United States, 66, 85, 276
Taylor, Brian, 55–56
telecommunications, 11–12, 157, 170–172
terrorism, 61, 97, 99, 104, 119–120, 122
Thailand, 170
Thakur, Ramesh, 13
Tibet, 168, 169, 237
Tilly, Charles, 76
Tito, Marshall, 236
total war, 17, 79, 81
Trinamool Congress, 203
Tripura, 112
Tunisia, 39
Turkey, 71, 277

unemployment, 107, 110
unions, 10, 11, 37
United Kingdom: as colonial power, 3, 17, 98, 99, 100, 109, 111, 112, 185, 207, 212, 213, 232, 235–236; competitiveness of, 36, 43; economy of, 133; extractive capability in, 66; as great power, 26; Indian dependence on, 130; industrialization in, 129; Japan vs., 17; legitimacy in, 68; nuclear umbrella of, 231, 240; small government philosophy in, 81; violence monopoly in, 69
United Nations, 7, 8, 25, 42, 236, 237, 241, 248–249, 281
United Nations Conference on Trade and Development (UNCTAD), 243
United Progressive Alliance (UPA), 193, 196, 207, 218, 247, 266
United States, 5, 19, 231; in Afghan war, 15; China vs., 47, 238; Chinese rapprochement with, 241; Civil War in, 37, 81, 96, 103; coercive capacity in, 68; as colonial power, 39; divisions within, 37–38; as economic power, 42, 43, 133; energy consumption in, 28, 29, 234; as great power, 13, 16, 26, 30, 35, 128; immigration to, 27; Indian military backed by, 238; Indian mistrust of, 247, 258–259, 260–261, 265–266; Indian rapprochement with, 249, 258; industrialization in, 129; Japan vs., 17; legitimacy in, 86; military capability of, 28, 29, 30, 234; nuclear umbrella of, 240; Pakistan backed by, 238, 243, 244, 262; taxation in, 66, 85, 276; violence monopoly in, 69; war economy in, 80–82, 85
Universal Rural Earning Scheme, 193
untouchability, 186, 272
urbanization, 80, 142, 143

Vashney, Ahutosh, 116
Vietnam, 17, 136, 152, 169, 237, 261, 284
violence monopoly, 2, 5, 18, 23, 40, 41, 49, 55, 96–126, 273; in BRIC states, 69; in China, 71; conceptual problems of, 57; defined, 75; in India, 69, 73, 95, 276, 277; measures of, 61–64, 66
Vishwa Hindu Parishad, 223

Walton, Michael, 147
water, 128, 153, 157, 159, 167–172, 179, 282, 285
Way, Lucan, 60, 62–63, 68, 276
West Bengal, 194, 203, 226
wheat, 152
Wilkinson, Steven, 115–116

wind energy, 164
World Bank, 60

Xinjiang, 257

Yadav, Laloo Prasad, 203–204

Zakaria, Fareed, 30